I0902290

KNOTS

KNOTS

or the Violence of Desire in Renaissance Florence

EMANUELE LUGLI

The University of Chicago Press • Chicago and London

The University of Chicago Press, Chicago 60637
The University of Chicago Press, Ltd., London
© 2023 by The University of Chicago
All rights reserved. No part of this book may be used or reproduced in any manner whatsoever without written permission, except in the case of brief quotations in critical articles and reviews. For more information, contact the University of Chicago Press, 1427 East 60th Street, Chicago, IL 60637.
Published 2023
Printed in the United States of America

31 30 29 28 27 26 25 24 23 22   1 2 3 4 5

ISBN-13: 978-0-226-82251-8 (cloth)
ISBN-13: 978-0-226-82252-5 (e-book)
DOI: https://doi.org/10.7208/chicago/9780226822518.001.0001

Library of Congress Cataloging-in-Publication Data

Names: Lugli, Emanuele, author.
Title: Knots, or the violence of desire in Renaissance Florence / Emanuele Lugli.
Description: Chicago : The University of Chicago Press, 2023. | Includes bibliographical references and index.
Identifiers: LCCN 2022034313 | ISBN 9780226822518 (cloth) | ISBN 9780226822525 (ebook)
Subjects: LCSH: Hair in art. | Art, Renaissance—Italy—Florence. | Hair—Religious aspects. | Hair—Social aspects. | Florence (Italy)—History—1421–1737. | BISAC: ART / European | HISTORY / Europe / Italy
Classification: LCC N8217.H27 L84 2023 | DDC 704.9/49646724—dc23/eng/20220724
LC record available at https://lccn.loc.gov/2022034313

The University of Chicago Press gratefully acknowledges the generous support of Stanford University.

♾ This paper meets the requirements of ANSI/NISO Z39.48–1992 (Permanence of Paper).

Written during the pandemic of summer 2020,
for my own pleasure

CONTENTS

ONE *Prologue: Hair Care*

This book is about hair. It is about the ways hair ignited the minds of Sandro Botticelli, young Leonardo da Vinci, and the artists of fifteenth-century Florence who turned hairstyles into venues of discovery. In the nature of spires, shadows, or haloes, the hair in their paintings is there not simply to adorn, but to shape your thinking. Braids coil around a woman's head as a snake spirals up onto a rock, so as to cast the silhouette of something sinful. Curls fold over like leaves, to make a human appear like a tree. You can pore through experiments in representing coiffures in museums and art books, and you will find an uneven landscape in which only a handful of works elevate themselves to levels of sophistication comparable to those of Botticelli and Leonardo. This book wonders what those heads found in hair. It also asks why so few people have taken notice, finding the reasons for such silence not in oversight but in the deliberate marginalization of hair. If you frowned upon the subject of this book when you first opened it—and if you still do not feel it may add anything to your life—it is also because at some point you may have been told that hair is a thing of no importance, something only silly girls care about.[1] But here is the wild idea that animates this book: Hair's apparent insignificance matters, since hair offers a cursive, unostentatious way to make powerful ideas about gender, morals, and the laws of nature take root in people's brains.

So this is really a book about power: the systemic creative power that relied on something as unsuspected as hair to coerce people into thinking and behaving according to a code of conduct from which power profited.[2] Its violence was subtle.[3] There is no indication that when people heard that women were inferior to men because they had long hair, their necks tightened. I found no record of any distress from the boy who was warned that contemplating the hair of a girl was not just a waste of time but a way to lose himself. I can locate some resistance to this violence in a few stories and objects. But I must say right away that those creations were dismissed as fantasies. Abandoned as quickly as they were started, they offered only momentary breaks from the opinion that hair was a worthless thing—not just an opinion, but public knowledge, since hair participated in many aspects of everyday doing. Kids were reminded that combing their heads was a way to not just clean themselves but purge their brains of strange ideas. Girls were scolded if they appeared at windows looking disheveled. The pervasiveness of those references (often found in private letters that repeat the self-assured ring of official regulations, as if hair provided a direct channel by which the public entered the private) did not exist purely in the mind, and in only one mind. They were social facts that circulated both as ideas and as embodied reality, which Florentines never questioned, and with which they lived more easily than I imagine, as if they were nothing more than disagreeable relatives you cannot kick out of your house.

I speak of power in general because an examination of the historical documents shows a muddled story.[4] It wasn't just apprehensive politicians, sly confessors, or pedantic doctors who leveraged hair to foster specific ideas about governance, religion, or well-being. It was all of those people and many more: a chorus of voices that were most effective as they were diffused—so widespread, in fact, that it is often difficult to trace the source of any single belief. Such convergence, but also such ordinariness, made Florentines place those recommendations under the rubric of care, because caring is the advice whispered by loving maids and the measure that city patriots invoke as necessary.

Care and violence are strictly connected here, because caring often means caring in one specific way. Care follows the assertive logic of the gift: *I am giving you a piece of advice from which you will benefit.* Yet it considers the gift not as part of an exchange or a dialogue, but as an utter surprise: *I am giving you a piece of advice that you cannot refute.* And since I give it for free and put all of myself in it, as I really believe in it, you cannot be offended. On the contrary, you must accept it and be pleased, and even excuse me if there is so much thoughtlessness in such advice, because it is less a gift than violence: a way to shape your life according to my needs.

So one way of thinking about this book is to take it as a study of the care which Florentines violently enveloped in hair to shape each others' lives. It is also about the help that men of letters and, above all, artists offered in cementing such a hegemonic culture at the time Lorenzo de' Medici became lord of Florence.[5]

Since Florence was a republic, Lorenzo wasn't exactly its lord. But then, as many historians have stressed, to call Florence a republic is somewhat delusional, since its institutions were filled with members of the city's wealthiest families, who took up governmental offices in rotation. Many of those families were related, either by marriage or trade, and the Medici paterfamilias leveraged on those ties to raise himself over all others as the city's mastermind.[6] This prominence had been reached by Lorenzo's grandfather, Cosimo, who increased the family's political influence while expanding its resources and international repute, which Lorenzo consolidated.[7]

Period sources patently show that Lorenzo's Florence was filled with hair talk. Medical treatises discussed the characteristics of hair to explain all sorts of behaviors. Poems and epics focused on stolen locks and wisps caught in branches. Paintings and sculptures capitalized on the blatant appeal of an expensive coiffure. My interest in hair, however, is not simply to revisit an overlooked aspect of fifteenth-century culture. I contend that examining the descriptions and representations of hair improves our understanding of something specific: namely, how Florentines thought of themselves as humans. Nineteenth-century scholars coined the term "humanism" to capture the density of those reflections, but over time the word has flattened into a label stuck on a rather limited group of concerns, ranging from men's recognition of their privileged place in the cosmos to the revaluation of everything that was secular and man-made—in particular, classical literature and architecture.[8] As these debates were intellectual, hair has never been discussed as having been among their concerns. In this book, however, I maintain that recuperating hair, or the concern for hair, offers rewarding insights into what it meant to live and be human at a time when the very definition of human life was being rewritten.

Growing out of the body's surface, hair marked the beginning and end of human life. It identified the point at which biological life stopped, as hair was, as it still is, thought of as dead matter emerging from a living body.[9] This is why fifteenth-century doctors started their anatomical treatises with hair, and this is why the hairline was taken as the point from which artists like Leonardo measured bodily proportions. Aristotle, one of the humanists' most revered authorities, explained hair as something paradoxically lifeless and yet sprouting, much as grass germinates from the earth—a simile that excited fifteenth-century poets, who saw great creative possibilities in a bodily appendage that shared more with vegetation than with humanity.[10]

But in Medicean Florence, hair contributed to define not only human life but what it meant to lead a worthy one. Bad girls were those who spent inordinate energies styling their hair. Men who let their hair grow down to their shoulders were mocked as effeminate and weak, unfit for fighting and ruling. Proudly sporting their shaven napes, friars scolded parents for letting their daughters' hair grow, telling them that they were raising animals.[11] I find it surprising that hair served to affirm biological classifications (humans/animals) and reinforce gender dualism (men/women), when in fact it could have offered a most powerful critique of those distinctions. For hair is more than short or long, soft or stiff. Hair does not know gender. But then it is because of its indifference to these and other categories that hair posed a singularly potent threat to what Florentines called "order." To put hair in order meant to keep the whole world organized: it set educational standards, and served to form good citizens and good Christians. It also meant to dispel the world's fears, since hair was singled out as the trigger of erotic desire, the appetite by which the devil turned humans into demons obsessed with what they saw.

Rather than following all these discourses separately, this book braids them together to emphasize points of convergence: the repetitions and thought patterns, as well as the ways they supported one another. Hence the title: *Knots*. A religious preacher relied on medical terminology to push governors to force women to wear veils. A woman washed her head with land fertilizer since she was told by a farmer, and also heard in a popular song, that there was no difference between scalp and ground. To build an awareness of this cultural entanglement, which I see as a privileged way of understanding the blind spots and patterns that sustained Florentine life, I have organized this book around four main thematic threads which, like strands of hair, reemerge after momentarily disappearing under each other: art (chapters 2 and 6), natural philosophy (3 and 8), poetry (4 and 7), and politics (5 and 9). Taken altogether, this material shows what hair was thought to be in Renaissance Florence: what aspects were teased out of it, and what was expected from it. Yet, it also shows how hair, despite its elusiveness, was regularly presented as an ephemeral and uncomplicated thing, reactive in nature and regular in appearance. Such unmarkedness, which was often taken for granted, was fundamental in turning hair into a sort of cultural baseline to which Florentines returned to assess what was true.[12]

Truth, now as then, can be seen as a way to express the epistemological success of content.[13] This is why Florentines searched for validation of their social politics and cultural beliefs in a given and spontaneous element like hair. Were women really inferior to men? Their naturally long hair, which grew faster than men's, pointed at their colder, wetter nature. So yes, most people thought that women were inferior to men: less energetic, less resolute—that is, less alive. Little did it matter that nature was not the self-evident source intellectuals would like it to be. Rather, it was heavily shaped by cultural filters, among which a most potent one was the Bible, whose reading offered a rather specific condemnation of hair.

The attempt to understand the extent to which cultural diktats shaped perceptions of and expectations about nature changed the mission of this study. In the beginning—more than a decade ago—I set myself to search for the tales, objects, and practices that constructed notions of hair; and once they revealed themselves to be more homogeneous than I had expected, I elaborated on them and sometimes broke them open to denaturalize hair and expose it not as the natural matter it was thought to be, but as a politically charged material. That is, I tried to reveal the fiction of Renaissance assumptions about hair, and yet continued to articulate them as powerfully as the Florentines did—devils dragging sinners by their hair, heads going up in flames—so as to understand the effects those fantasies had on their lives. At the same time, exploring this material in depth gave me the chance to sketch a history of issues that not even the Florentines themselves had yet identified as issues.

Many of those issues had roots that reached back to centuries before Lorenzo de' Medici was born, so deep in time that I started questioning the autonomy of the so-called Renaissance. If Florentines continued engaging with earlier notions about hair, it was because they did not consider them arcane but saw them as valid. They printed new editions of centuries-old texts and abridged them in new manuals to shape the present. Dividing the material into before and after, as I was doing at the start of my research, continued the illusion that history is split into distinct periods. What I thought more beneficial was to preserve the chronological blur that Florentines productively accepted.[14] So I decided to turn my focus away from stories of inceptions, as well as from chronology. After this introduction I will mention only three dates, and will do so at specific points in the book: at the beginning, at the end, and in the middle, which marks a new start, as you will see. Those readers who find value in hanging events on the clothesline of time will find plenty of indications in the endnotes, where they can also expect to find the nitty-gritty of historical research. Yet when writing this book, I tried to shake off my chronological anxieties.

Being light on temporal markers proved to be exhilarating, especially in discussion of poems and paintings, whose meaning continues to be seen at its highest at the time of their completion. Besides freeing their understanding from the moments in which they were made, this approach also opens up premodern artworks, especially those of Botticelli, whose chronology remains largely hypothetical despite art historians' reordering efforts.[15] Many scholars take those paintings as the results of specific events and, thus, as occupying distinct points in Botticelli's developmental arc. But artists may not think of their own works as being temporally determined.[16] Botticelli revisited themes and compositions throughout his life. Leonardo's reflections on the structures of nature, including the nature of hair, seem to exist outside of time. Writing a history short on dates avoids the construction of a false sense of progress.[17] It facilitates the recuperation of a more diffused outlook that is attentive to what does not conform to a narrative of success. And once you question what constitutes a historical event that deserves to be remembered, you may start seeing the conventions that regulate the story of the past and what has been routinely left out of it.

If this experiment in chronological loosening carries some value, it may be because this book focuses on a concise period, Botticelli's most productive, which roughly corresponds to the years between Lorenzo de' Medici's rise to power (1469) and his death (1492). Within these two decades, however, I concentrate on what happened between the publication of two texts by Giovanni Boccaccio. The dates to remember are 1478, the year of the first edition of his *Comedy of the Florentine Nymphs*, and 1487, when *The Labyrinth of Love* was published. These two books, written more than a century before Lorenzo was born but printed only during his life, offer opposite but equally poignant visions of hair. In the *Comedy*, hairstyles are pleasurable sights, whereas the *Labyrinth* presents them as time-wasting pursuits. Years ago, when I wrote about them in an article, I thought that each publication exemplified a specific moment in the Florentines' relationship to hair, as if each responded to a shift in the pulse of a fast-beating culture.[18] But that reading was too facile. Those two publications are not the oppositional bookends of a library of shifting hearts, but the poles of an electromagnetic tension that not only captured what stood in between but also resonated with what happened before and after. In other words, they exemplify two ongoing, codependent, indeed entangled attitudes toward hair, even if their publication dates make them appear as separate. In a way, those dates do not matter.

By maintaining a chronological blur, this book privileges repetition over change. Historians usually focus on change, as it is change—the tremendous, unmistakable change of bone-breaking crises—that is exciting and worth documenting.[19] Such life-and-death events are thought to bring freedom, and much history is written as an accompaniment, if not a means, to it. In a way this book is also about freedom, the hope that some artists found in liberating hair from the prescriptions of moralizers and the abandonments of sensualists. Yet my documents register variations of intensity rather than drastic reversals. The painters, politicians, and poets whose actions I discuss expressed principles that had been set and attitudes that had been displayed long before they were born, and which hardly faded after their death. In the conclusion, we will see how powerful many of those beliefs still are today. But before we do, I find it useful to finesse our understanding of how hair has been endowed with pervasive social agency.[20]

The historical material on Florentine hair is extensive. Botticelli painted many portraits and Madonnas in which hair takes center stage. Differently from other historians who have delved into them, I chose to focus on a few case studies and reject the pretense that sheer accumulation of information is enough to understand the past.[21] What is the goal of scholars, if not to develop an assessment of what deserves to be recorded, and to present it with clarity and humility to benefit others? But restraint is not enough to avoid the propulsive force of an ego, especially as history is in some important sense a bourgeois enterprise, a gathering of substance from the world in order to turn it into one own's profit. It is also a process of ineradicable biases presented as evidence. *See it my way*, the art historian whispers. *Look at this, not that. Trust these people, not those. And, above all, trust me.*

So in researching this book, I read the accounts of other historians less as unbiased interpretations than as attempts to carry specific values of the past into the present. This is particularly insidious in the study of Florentine artworks, since from the outset they have been accompanied by prescriptions of how to see them. Historians of fifteenth-century Florence can count on a remarkable outpouring of contracts, descriptions, and panegyrics—a wealth of textual information that is largely responsible for making this Renaissance city such a rewarding object of study. Yet it often goes unmentioned that the documents that provide so much information were produced within the milieu of the powerful families and corporations that commissioned the artworks in the first place. Sticking to them for interpretative clues then often amounts to little more than reading over the art patrons' shoulders.[22] Which means that staying close to the sources—the historians' mantra—risks divesting those historians of their critical mission. Relying on chronology is particularly problematic in this respect, as it often highlights a distance that is merely performative when historical writing contributes to revive the power imbalances of the past. But this book is interested in remembering the past without validating its acts of violence. How to construct a memory that will let us undo the past so that when we talk about it, it has nothing to do with us because we are no longer produced by it? How to write a history that throws us into the thick of Florentine culture but without falling for the sexist condescension that pervades so many of the voices I am about to broadcast?[23] This is where flimsy hair develops an unlikely grip.[24] Its history produces a different picture of Renaissance Florence, one that exposes the perversion of its life more forcefully than do most history books. It is also a picture that may destabilize some of our long-held ideas about what mattered.

I have started speaking in the plural, but I would like to stress that I direct these questions first and foremost to myself. How to make sure that my biases and preferences do not take over? How to produce an interpretation that, in seeking a balance between proximity to the sources and distance from them, does not merely assure me that I am unlike them?[25] How can I develop a voice that discloses the artificiality of its own timbre rather than passing as neutral? Throughout the book, I have tried to remain open about the hesitations I have developed over time. But to avoid distracting too much from the main argument—readability is a primary concern of mine—I discuss most of my doubts in the endnotes. My intention is to present you with an engaging text and a record of its making, so that you can develop your own understanding of the unevenness of this historical narrative. Sometimes the evidence is staggeringly loud and compact. Sometimes we listen to just one whisper.

I must admit I am not sure I have succeeded at keeping all these elements in balance. Absorbed as I was, reality started twisting to inform and reflect what I was thinking about in my work. This is how my mind seems to work: it organizes details of life into a narrative that orients itself to the content of the book. My eyes were sticky with the words I was reading, my thoughts interlaced with what I thought I was seeing. And so I should not have been surprised, as I often was, to encounter arresting hairstyles everywhere I traveled. At an airport in Modlin, Poland, I saw French braids contouring a passenger's ears in a way I had previously found only on a Florentine Madonna. In a Japanese supermarket in London, England, a blond customer had such long hair—it almost touched the floor—that I wondered how ordinary the mane of Botticelli's Venus must have been (see plate 1). At Stanford, California, a student waiting to collect books in front of me had branches laden with flowers and berries around her chignon, which made me think of the allure of Renaissance garlands. Each time, I called these encounters what they were—perceptual traps—and moved on. But I caught myself returning to them often as residues of old forms lingering in the present, wondering if their resilience had something to do with the fact that their old motives may have not vanished completely.[26]

TWO *Learning To See Thinness*

When young and inexperienced, Leonardo da Vinci learned a lesson he never forgot: If he wanted to succeed as an artist, he had to master the drawing and painting of hair. The advice came from his teacher Andrea del Verrocchio, who gave him a drawing of a beautifully coiffed girl with instructions to examine it carefully (see plate 3). Leonardo took the task to heart.

Some hairs, Leonardo noticed, were so light and meandering that Verrocchio's charcoal must have hardly touched the page. For other strands, Verrocchio had applied more pressure, lifting the charcoal as he went, so as to render the thinning of a hair from root to floaty end. By going over strokes again and again, he had made the hairs appear closer to the viewer, as if laboring over them pulled them out of the face. Stroke after stroke—that is, hair after hair, —Leonardo came to understand that a full head of hair was not the result of the clustering of locks together—that is, mere addition. Rather, it started with a plan. Short tufts made room for flowing braids, which cut through a drawing like staircases piercing the floors of a castle. These conduits were lianas for the eyes, swinging them from one corner of the paper to another. Experienced painters mapped out such channels and stops in advance, thinking across different scales at once. They needed to come up with a whole composition before drawing the very first line and making accommodations along the way. A hairstyle, in other words, forced artists to think in terms of intersections and opportunities. It was not the mere crowning of a head, but a creative field with its own logic.

I do not know what Verrocchio said when he handed his drawing to Leonardo; and I cannot tell you whether Leonardo discovered all this by himself or was guided step by step, like a student taught by a teacher who still remembers what it was like to be a student. And yet it must have happened. It may have occurred during Leonardo's training, even if this is just a guess, as the early years of Leonardo's career are hazy—the documents' lips are sealed. We are not even sure how long he trained; we know only that by 1472 Leonardo was no longer an apprentice, even if he worked occasionally for Verrocchio after that date.[1] Nonetheless, he must have taken his master's drawing in hand, since he faithfully copied its spiraling coils in two other Madonnas, known to specialists as the *Benois Madonna* and the *Madonna of the Carnation* (figure 2.1).[2] We also know that Leonardo's attention to hair did not emerge all of a sudden. It is something in which Verrocchio invested time.

In Florence, assistants contributed to their masters' commissions as part of their training. Leonardo was no exception, and art historians have detected his hand in some of Verrocchio's altarpieces. The Bolognese terrier strolling at the bottom of Verrocchio's Raphael and Tobias is Leonardo's: a mass of dangling fur without much of a skeletal structure (figure 2.2). Leonardo is said to have painted Tobias's curls and bangs, but only those, as Tobias's face is instead rendered in the heavy-handed modeling of Verrocchio.[3] Leonardo's soft touch has also been spotted in the angel of Verrocchio's *Baptism of Christ*, the one shown from the back to reveal his shining mane: a waterfall of rumbling waves of gold.[4] Leonardo cared for every strand, dipping his brush into lighter and lighter pools of paint to create what looks like filigree.

Many of Leonardo's earliest pictorial interventions dealt with hair, and this is because Verrocchio turned the drawing of hair into an essential component of his students' training.[5] Such practice made Leonardo become aware of the possibilities of art. An artist, he wrote in his most precious notebook—the one in which he kept scribbling for decades—needs to approach hair the same way he approaches drapery and the

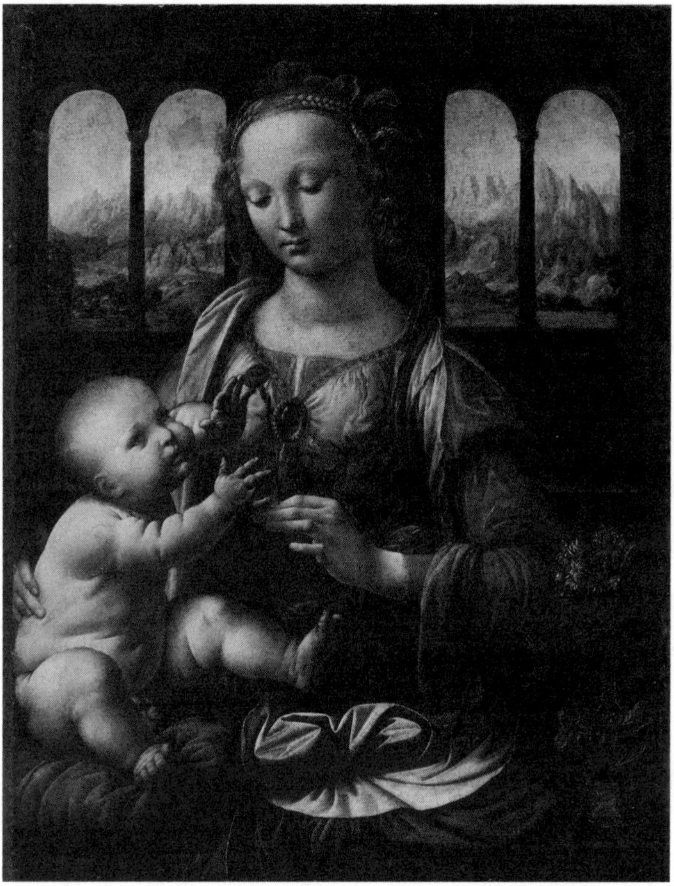

Figure 2.1. Leonardo da Vinci, *Madonna of the Carnation*. Alte Pinakothek, Munich.

landscape, since all three of those things change in relation to the viewer's assumed location. If the painter imagines viewers to be standing close to the things he paints, the surfaces of those things break down into crisscrosses of varying degrees of brightness: a hill becomes a patch of grass, clothes break up into threads, and a head dissolves into strands of hair. But if the painter envisages the viewers to be far away, that patch of grass grows back into a uniformly green mound, threads thicken into fabric, and blades of hair merge into a patch of paint.[6] By putting hair on

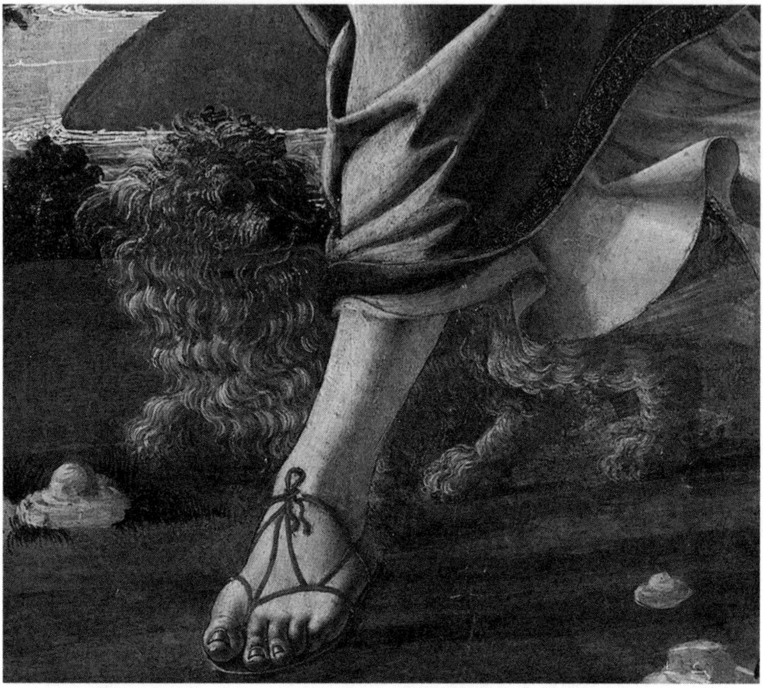

Figure 2.2. Andrea del Verrocchio with assistants, *Tobias and the Angel*. National Gallery, London.

the same plane with clothes and foliage, Leonardo articulates a theory of painting in which style expresses vision anchored in space.[7]

Leonardo jotted down this reflection after spending some twenty years in Milan, the city in which he found fame and perfected a new approach to painting. There, he came up with the idea of inserting figures into cavernous spaces and paying attention to the ways in which light enters the space and suffuses a face.[8] Still, even as he dedicated himself to optics and the study of anatomy, he hardly stopped reflecting on the creative possibilities of hair. He brought with him some of the arresting hairstyles he had sketched when he was in Florence, and created a few more while away (see figure 10.4).[9] This is not simply because his teacher's voice continued echoing in his mind, as hair was not the preoccupation of Verrocchio's workshop only. Rather, hair was the very field in which many Florentine artists found a direct expression of what constituted art.

When young and inexperienced, Verrocchio must have heard that paintings ought to be finished off with extremely fine brushes.[10] After shaping them into tiny pointed ends, artists used these tools to outline figures and add shimmering trimmings to clothes, sparkles to jewels, and twinkles to pupils. Such finishing touches comforted clients and viewers that a painting had been completed at a time when there was no clear sense of when the process of painting ended. Thanks to them, artworks were also recognized as things of beauty. In a manual transcribed in Florence's Le Stinche prison around the time Verrocchio was born, its author, the painter Cennino Cennini, recommended never overloading small brushes, "so that your handiwork will come out like fine hairs, which is the most beautiful work."[11]

The comment is a rare admission of quality for a period in which it is so difficult to associate artists with intentions. Most of the opinions on the pictorial process that have survived come from contracts, with their focus on costs and logistics, which casts painting as a trade in the hands of moneyed patrons.[12] Other information—on what elements people paid attention to, on what words they used to describe paintings—is extracted from panegyrics with their rhetorical parallels between living artists and the great masters of the past, even if those tributes are not always clear about what made them both so great.[13] In contrast, Cennini explicitly says what makes a painting worthwhile. He states that pictorial beauty lies in finesse, and that hair represents the touchstone of finesse. And while Cennini is often taken as articulating a medieval approach to painting—in his manual he boasts that his artistic grandfather was Giotto—his definition of quality was still valued in Verrocchio's lifetime.[14] Indeed, Verrocchio's paintings carry out Cennini's advice. In a *Madonna* (figure 2.3), thin wisps flame out from the top of an angel's brow. They are painted more delicately than the golden threads of the Virgin's sleeve.[15] Like the angel's eyelashes, carefully brushed over the eyelids, they were added last.

So when Verrocchio told Leonardo to pay attention to hair, he was

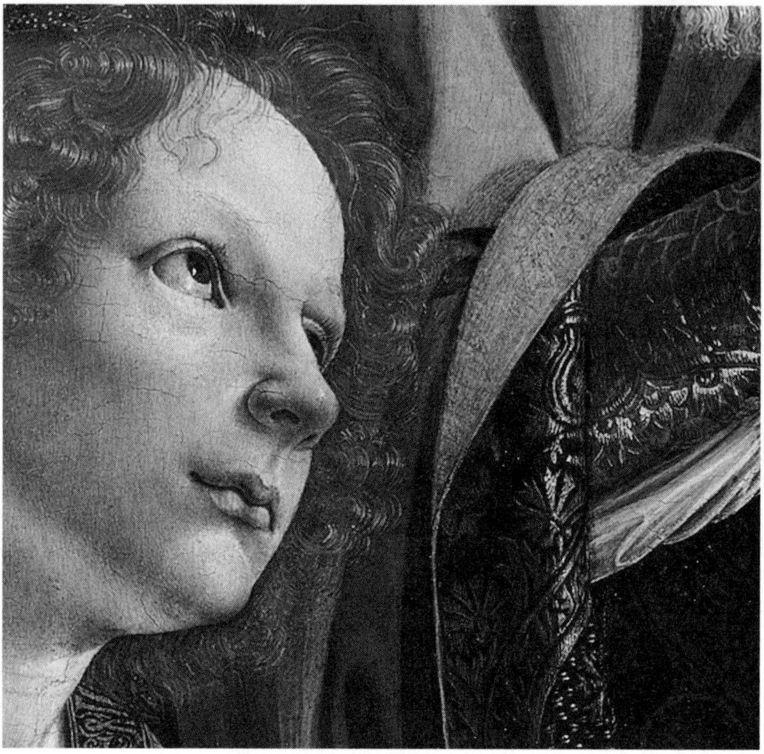

Figure 2.3. Andrea del Verrocchio with assistants, *Madonna and Child with Two Angels.* National Gallery, London.

teaching him how to find an end in painting, in the sense of when to consider a work concluded and complete. His advice responded to two overlapping pressures. The first, a demand for precision, was recent. A sensational book called *The Book of Why*—sensational because it was the first printed text in the vernacular to provide straightforward answers to questions about how the body worked—encouraged people to observe the smallest things, arguing that familiarity with visual extremes would improve sight.[16] The second pressure came from classical writers such as Pliny, whose *Natural History*—one of the first books Leonardo ever purchased—argued that many ancient artists achieved greatness by representing hair.[17] Pliny criticized the Greek sculptor Myron of Eleutherae (the author of the *Discobolus*) because, despite having come up with more diverse poses than any other artist, Myron rendered the hair and the pubes of his figures less scrupulously. And Pliny praised Lysippos, Pythagoras of Rhegium, and Parrhasius of Ephesus because they increased the detail they brought to the representation of hair.[18] Parrhasius, in particular, mastered hair because he mastered contouring, which "in painting," Pliny concluded, "represents the highest level of skill."[19]

By considering hair a subcategory of outlines, Pliny turned it into a test for the firmness of an artist's grip. And it is not surprising that Cennini nested his comment on the artistic value of hair amid instructions on how to make the most precise brushes. In Verrocchio's and Leonardo's times, painters constructed their own tools as they took care of any material aspect of their work: they selected the wooden planks that formed their panels, and whisked pigments with egg yolks to make paints. Similarly, Cennini explains, painters needed to learn what pelt to choose for their brushes. The coarse bristles of hogs, for instance, made the thick brushes that were used to cover large surfaces. If you wanted finer tools, you needed to get your hands on squirrels. He advised artists to pluck the best hairs and gather them together, push them inside wooden handles or quills, tighten the junctions with waxed thread, and glue them with resin. If the new paintbrushes were not needed right away, it was recommended to dip them in clay to protect them from moths.[20]

Because the thickness of bristles determined the width of the lines that a painter traced, the Florentine artist Piero Pollaiuolo identified brushstrokes with strands of hair. In finishing the portrait of a girl (see plate 7), he loaded his tools with thick paint and hit the panel, taking the traces that the brush left as equivalent to the directions that hair naturally took (plate 8). The process lent particular veracity to his representation. Pollaiuolo thought that real hair transferred some of its characteristics—width, softness, flexibility—to its pictorial rendering. But in doing so, he also showed how hair occupied a liminal place in artistic practice, one in which painting dissolved into a form of stamping, and where the semblance of a painted thing came very close to the shadow of its real self.

Cennini did not recommend Pollaiuolo's approach. He only insisted that to achieve the finesse that would win praise, painters should reach for the smallest brush. Painters should make "it really stiff and pointed so that the tip protrudes just a tiny bit from the shaft. Then dip a small part of it in the mordant and work up your decorations and the outlines" so that they look—we have seen it already—like hair.[21] Which shows, as Pollaiuolo must have also believed, that nothing thinner than hair could be depicted.

While not as extreme as Pollaiuolo's approach, Cennini's pairing of hair with outlines did bring hair to occupy a place at the limit of representation, where painting and drawing seemed to exhaust their capacity to stand for anything else. This mode of thinking is also evident in the drawing of a woman's face that Verrocchio gave to Leonardo (plate 3), in which her hair is rendered quite differently from the rest of the face. Verrocchio modeled her eye sockets and the dimples in her cheeks and chin with hatching, which he smudged with his fingers to create the sense of a shadow. He sometimes then deepened the shadow with another bout of hatching.[22] Yet, after tracing hair strands, he did not touch any. To do so would give their lines the thickness of ugliness. It would also amalgamate the hair with the rest of the body, which casts shadows whereas the finest hair does not, since hair is a figurative alternative to it: figments that spring from the body but belong to a different register of scale, and life. That Verrocchio wanted to visualize such distinctness is made clear by the way he related hair to the drawing's support. Unique in the drawing, hair only exists within the borders of the sheet. Look at the braid on the left side of the girl's head, which, after a double torsion, latches onto the jewel atop her head like a boat moored to a pier. The upper hoop pulls toward the top right corner of the sheet, and the space between the hoop and the corner is filled by the fluttering end, which rises like a tuft of smoke. Similarly, the locks falling on either side of her neck become progressively shorter the closer they reach the bottom edge of the picture. But the drawing of the girl's body does not follow this logic. It instead decomposes into feeble vectors that suggest the roundness of a disappearing shoulder or the widening of the neck. In other words, you are supposed to imagine a bust that continues past the bottom edge of the picture. The way the body is drawn tells you that the fiction of representation is independent of its material support.

Hair and body were rendered differently because they were drawn at different times. Turn the sheet over (plate 4) and you discover a sketch of the same head, probably drawn from life. (Those fugitive strokes on the left may record the hand holding the model's head still during the long drawing session.) There is no coiffure; the hair is slicked back as if held by gum or a net. And if this is the case, it is because Verrocchio planned to add her hairstyle at a later moment, when speed and veracity would no longer be concerns and he could release his imagination from what he saw: the only limits would be the borders of the sheet.

In a way, these two drawings do not represent the same head. Something shifts when the page is flipped. I am not even sure that the two heads belong to the same gender, as the hairless face could be that of a boy. (Artists often used their pupils as models, and historians have speculated much on whether young Leonardo posed for Verrocchio.)[23] It is only when the hair is added, propped like a wig, that the face reads as that of a girl. The drawing and painting of hair, in other words, had the power to transform a body. It offered a guide not only to looking, but also to nature.

By examining other artists' works, Leonardo quickly learned that just a few ringlets could convey identity. Yet he also reached the same conclusion by reading a book he had purchased, the popular epic *Morgante*.[24] One of its episodes starts with a crowd of Christian knights lasciviously viewing the body of the sultan's daughter Antea, starting from "her golden curls, which seemed to be those of Daphne."[25] Antea's hair is all the horsemen need to see to imagine her as a defenseless nymph, only good for being looked at. Little do they know that she is a master fighter who would defeat all of her male opponents, breaking their spears and their hearts along the way.[26] The ironic twist works only because Florentines instinctively took hair as a transparent indication of character. They were socially trained to read the head to infer status and identity, and were told that it was safe to do so.[27]

Verrocchio knew his patrons would expect hair to be legible, and he spent much time devising precisely eloquent hairstyles. Not only did his assistants copy them: they retraced them, line by line. In fifteenth-century Florence, many paintings started as drawings on paper, whose outlines were then transferred to walls or wooden panels. Assistants, often in charge of the transferral, pricked the outlines of the drawings with needles and pounced chalk through the holes onto the intended painting surface. The settled dust provided the guiding dots to recreate the drawing on the new support. Technical analysis of Verrocchio's Madonna (figure 2.3) has revealed that it was made this way.[28] And many perforated drawings from his workshop—a woman's bust in Oxford, a boy in Berlin, an angel in Florence—tell us that this was common practice.[29] Art historians have written about the technique extensively, as they have encouraged their readers to search for dots along the silhouettes of noses, ears, and chins, since they often assume that a drawing coincides with a face. Yet holes are also found around the puffs of hair dissolving into air, and along the parting line above the forehead.[30] A hairstyle was reproduced with the same precision of a profile. The very possibility of recognizing a figure's identity depended on it.[31]

Leonardo taught painting the way he learned it. Infrared reflectography has revealed dotting all along the hair paths of his Ginevra de' Benci, the first portrait he finished (plate 5).[32] And pricking returns in many of his other works—for example, all around the complex coiffure of one of his last drawings, the so-called "naked Mona Lisa" (figure 2.4).[33] Leonardo's pupils reproduced the knots of her hair as diligently as her facial proportions, since they were in no way secondary elements. Quite the opposite: they were among the features that made a figure's identity legible and distinctive.

This attention to the form of hair reflects a wide interest in personal appearance in an age of newly found economic affluence: something painters had to engage with as part of their patrons' lifestyle.[34] Some historians trace the origin of such unprecedented investment in luxury back to the Treaty of Lodi, signed when Leonardo was one year old—a pact that put an end to the wars that had torn apart the Italian peninsula for half a century and depleted the finances of many of its cit-

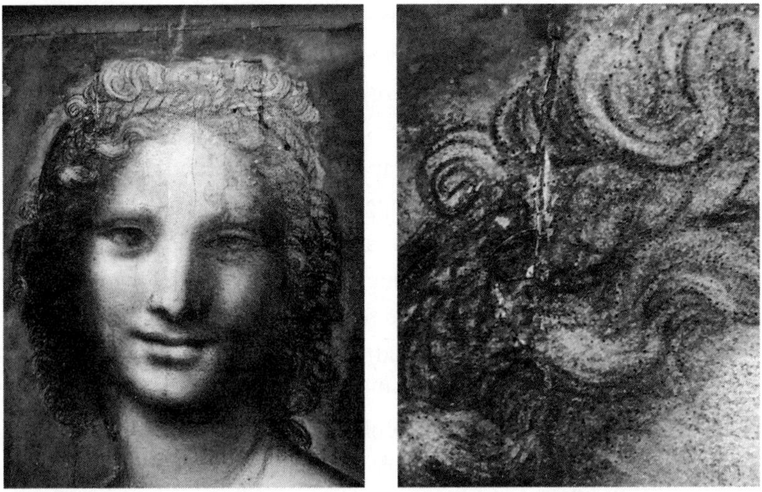

Figure 2.4. Leonardo da Vinci, *Naked Mona Lisa*. Musée Condé, Chantilly.

ies.[35] In particular, the peace put a stop to the extraordinary sums paid to the mercenaries who fought for the Florentine government, which could then slash taxation to less than one-fourth its previous amount.[36] Suddenly capable of retaining more of their capital, Florentine families could afford the luxury headgear once reserved to the very few, and came to not only justify it but revel in its elaborateness, wishing to preserve it through pictorial records.[37] The portrait by Pollaiuolo we have already encountered (plate 7) captures the fabulous coiffures that well-off girls proudly sported on special occasions such as feast days.[38] Families spent small fortunes on styling their unmarried daughters to display, through them, their refinement and economic might. As eyewitnesses observed, parents went as far as to parade their daughters on horseback along Florence's main streets, paying for trumpeters to announce their entrance to the city's squares, so as to draw a crowd that would add to their sense of success.[39] Women's hairdos were the bodily equivalent of clarion calls, pulling people's gaze as iron attracts magnetic needles.[40]

These arrangements became all-important for weddings, which marked the moment when a daughter left her father's household to become economically dependent on her husband.[41] Dowries—that is, capital accumulated by families over decades to lure suitors and forge alliances with other families—were discussed in detail before arranging any marriage.[42] A bride's parents invested money in protecting her virginity: girls were locked up in apartments, guarded day and night, and tutored by priests who massaged into their brains values such as honorability and reverence.[43] This is how a sense of class and respectability was maintained. At the same time, the groom's parents bet on their daughter-in-law's fertility and her ability to increase their family's assets by giving birth to many children. The foundational logic of capital emerged most forcefully at wedding ceremonies, during which the confined bride stepped into the public eye and paraded her ancestors' brooches and the jewels that she would take to her new family (or, for those less affluent, gems sourced from friends and professional lenders).[44] Her goal was to look like a splendid possession. Clothes embroidered with a family's coat of arms and shimmering brocades certainly helped in this regard.[45] Yet it was her hair, and her hair only, that revealed how the event represented, above all, an investment in her body.

In Florence, virgins sported the loose tresses of childhood while married women braided them and tucked them in updos, which they hid under veils.[46] Many paintings emphasize this difference when showing the few times a girl could step out of her father's house surrounded by older women, encircling her as guards protect a strongbox (figure 2.5). Those relatives did not simply shield her from the male gaze.[47] With their veiled heads, they were signposts of the girl's future. They reminded everyone that marriage marked the moment in which a woman's hair—that is, the very possibility of her desirability—would cease to exist in public.[48] The change in headgear signified a bride's submission to her husband's lead; and that was not just a symbol, since hair was the prime catalyst of erotic desire. It was the very element that drew the eyes of a man to a woman and made his blood boil. In this respect, the veiling of hair was an effective means to prevent adultery.[49] To hide a woman's hair under a curtain—to replace the natural covering of her head with its controllable and artificial substitute, a veil—was to point to a transformation in that woman's visibility.[50] A veil made a woman inconspicu-

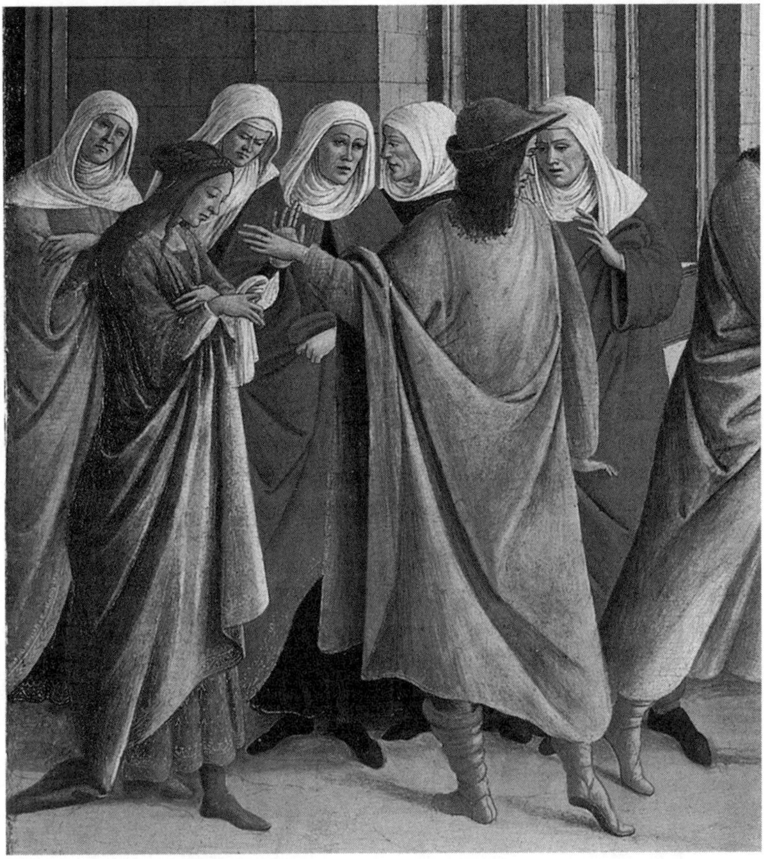

Figure 2.5. Sandro Botticelli, scene from the life of Saint Zenobius. National Gallery, London.

ous. Wives withdrew from erotic life by covering their heads: not doing so came with dramatic consequences. Florentine school masters taught their students that a husband could even repudiate his consort if she went out without covering her head.[51]

And yet, a bride's veiling was preceded by a moment of plastic spasm, when her hair, among the most sexually charged part of her little-exposed body, bloomed (figure 2.6). Bundled-up hairstyles, held together by strings and crowned by brooches and pendants (figure 2.7),

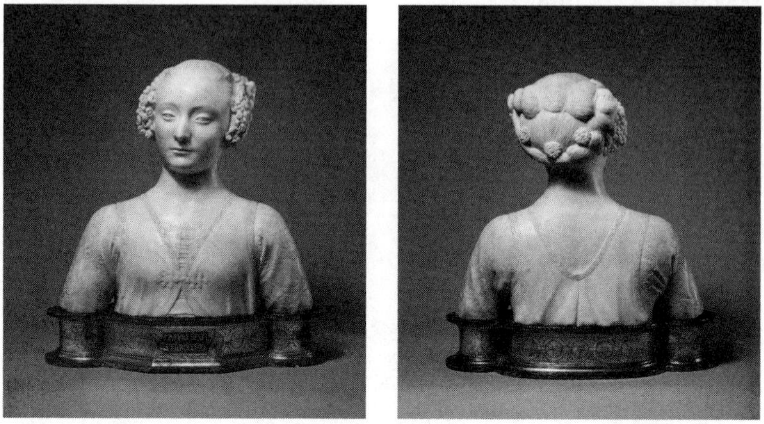

Figure 2.6. Andrea del Verrocchio, *Bust of a Woman*. Frick Collection, New York.

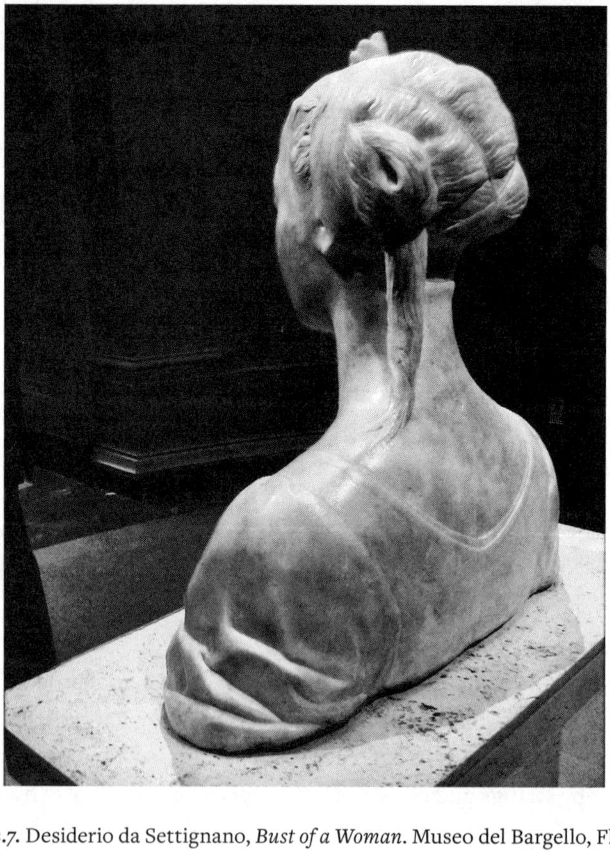

Figure 2.7. Desiderio da Settignano, *Bust of a Woman*. Museo del Bargello, Florence.

visualized the faith that Florentine families placed in both money and fertility to construct the future. Those two goals found a point of union in hair. It was hair that came to symbolize the economic dimension of marriage through laborious styling and expensive accessorizing. And it was also hair that, by its sheer length and suppleness, spoke about a woman's reproductive effortlessness, as the next chapter will clarify.

THREE *Desiccated Smoke*

Even when still, the body is on fire. Its heat comes from the pounding heart, pumping blood through the arteries that hover around the lungs and make their condensed air evaporate. Waves of warmth also spread from below as the stomach parches food long past its ingestion, laboring through it as if it were populated by an army of miniature smiths pounding fava beans and morsels of pork. Digestion, however, is less a forge than a stove: it breaks down chewed-up food until it turns into thin blood. It could be even compared to a rubbish dump in which bites of food exhale fumes, like putrefying corpses. And those fumes rise past the heart and the lungs, further up, carried by the veins that stem from the liver—yes, the liver—and take those fumes to every inch of skin. So even when motionless, the body is a chimney: erect, filled with smoke soaring to the top—that is, the brain, the body's radiator, which dissipates the ascending gas with its gelatinous coldness, insulated by the skull as a giant oyster is protected by its shell.[1]

But when the chimney is full, as after a rich meal of beans and pork fat, even the brain may fail at fanning away that smoke which gathers in the head, forming a greasy cloud that keeps expanding, denser and denser, pressing against the upper layers of skin in which the brain is pouched. And eventually that viscous steam oozes out, from one stratum to the next layer, until it reaches the thicker outer scalp whose pores it slowly fills, like water rising in a well.

And that is when things drastically change. After making their way out, those streaks of vapor hit a wall of fresh air which hammers them back in. But once it gushes out, vapor stops being vapor: that which is wet and hot geysers away, and the little dry matter that remains is curled back, scraping skin particles with which it mixes under the cold air's unremitting pressure. Those desiccated churns are thus squashed between two opposing forces, with the bursts coming from the head only slightly stronger than the load of external air; and that is why matter piles up slowly, like thick dough pressed out of tiny spaghetti dies, almost imperceptibly.

Suddenly-desiccated smoke: this is how fifteenth-century physicians thought of hair. They learned to see it that way after memorizing university treatises which insisted that arteries and veins belonged to separate networks centered on different organs. One such manual was by the doctor Mondino de' Liuzzi, but the picture of the body it painted was confirmed by many others, such as the abridgments attributed to the Persian polymath whom Italians knew as Avicenna.[2]

As Avicenna explained, hair was digestive surfeit, and thus excrement. After ingesting food, the body found ways to get rid of what was not necessary for its maintenance.[3] It expelled it first as feces, then as urine. What remained was refined by the liver and the spleen, which disposed of the excess as bile, mucus, or ear wax. Finally, if it did not coagulate in inflammations, the remnant was disposed of internally as vapor, which, besides condensing in sweat and tears, generated hair all over the body.[4]

Hair was the ultimate "superfluity"—that is, the residue of the very last phase of digestion. And even if classical authors such as Aristotle and Galen did not agree on what digestion amounted to—how many organs played a role in it?—they conceded that hair generated out of its dregs.[5] It wasn't just highly specialized medical manuals that repeated this point. Even a popular book written by an astronomer, *The Book of Why*, found the space to speak of hair as bodily excess despite providing a most succinct, indeed laconic, description of the digestive process.[6]

In the fifteenth century, speaking of digestion often meant speaking of complexion: that is, the combination of the two natural qualities—hotness/coldness and humidity/dryness—that were thought to regulate the body's organs and their fluids.[7] I read in the *Pantegni*, also a university textbook, that the hair growing out of a hot, dry body is black and curly, whereas that of a cold, humid person (I imagine sticky fingertips) is blond and smooth.[8] Aristotle wrote that an overheated, constantly parched body grows a short, rigid crest resembling porcupine spines.[9] And I learn from Avicenna to pay attention to the speed of hair's growth: a slow increase denotes a humid temperament, a fast increment dryness.[10] *The Secrets of Women*, a treatise on female anatomy, explains that women's naturally cold complexion could only produce thin hair.[11]

These texts, and I could cite more, give the impression that hair grew out of any combination of natural qualities. But, as Galen explains—and Galen's importance grew toward the end of the fifteenth century, when his opinions were no longer known only through fragments, but also through new transcriptions of his treatises—hair could not grow out of a completely cold and humid body.[12] "All kinds of cold mixture are lacking in hair, whether the degree of wetness is moderate or immoderate," he wrote, "but the mixture that is cold and wet is hairless to an extreme degree."[13] To stress this point, he noted that fish, the coldest of creatures, have no hair. But that is just an example, Galen fretfully stressed, as human bodies never reach such extremes. Quite the opposite: they are always animated by some sort of humid heat, and this is why their skin is always covered by some hair.[14]

So hair was thought to be a product of warm humidity: even very little of it could produce a stubble. This mixture did not necessarily need to come from within the body, which was porous and thus reacted to its climate.[15] Ethnography hammered away at the identity of hair and latitude.[16] Strabo: "Germans' hair is yellower than that of the Celts." Tacitus: "The Silures of eastern Wales have curly hair." Isidore of Seville (and also Pliny): "The Albanians shine with their white hair."[17] No surprise if this chorus of authorities shaped people's mental voices. *Guerino the Wicked*, an entertaining Florentine epic about a knight's journey across the Mediterranean (Verrocchio owned a copy), is full of stereotypical descriptions of people based only on hair.[18] Physicians were quick to point at environment to explain how foreigners looked (that is, how the physicians thought they looked). The origin of a thick head of hair, they reasoned, was to be found in the sultry air of summer, which entered the lungs and warmed the body. Hardly any discussion of hair omitted the Ethiopians, whose curls were thought to depend on the speed at which their inner fluids rushed to their heads, drilling through their scalp in winding ducts that shaped their curls.[19] Africans, this racist cliché continued, never experienced the coldness that prevented the inner vapors to reach the head.[20] Too little humidity, and hair would also fail to emerge from the scalp, as its vapor would not be viscous enough to retain any particle.[21]

Given the pages dedicated to its prevention, baldness must have been an obsession for Florence's aging population.[22] Stories dramatize old men's anger when the young mocked them.[23] When rereading these stories, I must say I am not always sure whether I am dealing with reports of something that happened, or literary riffs on the biblical story of Elisha, the prophet who was ridiculed by children for his hairless head, but who was much revered in Florence.[24] And I wonder what role these incidents may have played in making Florentines discount any praise of baldness (I found only one text that speaks in favor of baldness, and in Latin, a language that few could read).[25] Medical treatises offered some remedies to what was identified as the cause of hair loss: the dampening of the heat that doctors associated with vigor and life itself. And yet baldness figures extensively in medical discussions of hair, since any study of extremes served to define the middle ground of health.[26]

Hairlessness, after all, was not just a condition of the old. Why do newborns come to light with a head of hair and then completely lose it shortly afterward? Why do Africans never shed their curls? And why do women seem to be immune to baldness, regardless of their complexion? The answers to those questions all relied on an understanding of heat as a complex factor, something that did not depend on just one source. Infants were born with hair because they developed it inside their mother's sweltering wombs. Africans did not suffer from baldness because they offset the torrid heat of their climate, which would easily dry up a Florentine's body, by an exceptional production of humidity. And women never lost their hair because they did not have testicles.[27]

The heart was not the body's only major source of heat. Aristotle argued that especially during coitus, the testicles desiccated so much of the body's fluids that sex addicts were at risk of even losing their eyelashes.[28] Orgasms detonated like heat bombs, scorching the body and depleting its moisture as quickly as they exploded. It is at such sudden combustion that *The Book of Why* pointed to explain men's receding hairlines: "Sex cools and dries the head much; and by decreasing the humidity [especially] in the front of the head and thinning the viscousness which holds hair, it causes the hair to fall out."[29] Which explains why women were unlikely to ever lose hair. Like eunuchs, whose long beards were regularly mentioned as proof that testicles quenched hair vapors, women did not have genitals to offset their natural humidity.[30]

And yet sexual acts did turn the heat up in women too, providing them with the warmth that yielded strong, supple hair.[31] It is enough to think of this causal connection to see Sandro Botticelli's *Birth of Venus* in a new light (see plate 1). Venus's fabulously lavish mane advertises a woman ready for love. Her hair is not a mere reference to classical sources, and her figure does not beguile simply because it is frozen in a cheeky striptease.[32] There is nothing cold in her after all. The extraordinary suppleness of her long, lush, liberated hair, which elegantly links her head to her genitals as if to visualize the inner journey of hair vapor, is evidence of her physical warmth. Botticelli paints it in exquisite detail as a jellyfish-like organism animated from within. It must have aroused many men; and I mean that quite literally, since men were taught to look at hair for cues about a woman's readiness to love. When standing in front of Botticelli's Venus, a Florentine man saw a cloud of tepid moistness. What happens all around her is merely confirmative. She is warmed by Zephyr, the most temperate of breezes, and bathed in the Mediterranean sun, which makes the grass all around bloom. Botticelli even includes a nymph, seen moments before she clothes Venus in the mantle of spring, so as to emphasize that the goddess is in no need of warm clothing. Botticelli keeps the nymph at a distance to capture the extraordinary, indeed divine, moment in which all natural qualities are in balance. Anchored to an axis of symmetry, his composition is an attempt to produce utter stillness, a perfect equivalence of inside and outside, where time stops. This Venus who has just been born out of warm air and foamy water—the line at which the sky and the sea meet intersects her navel—is ready to give birth.

This was where hair stopped being the marginal element that medical manuals pretended it to be, and took up a foundational, affirmative role. The *Pantegni* states that the key distinction between men and women, namely that "men are hotter and drier while women colder and richer in moisture[,] is demonstrated by their hair."[33] The text does not ask whether women are different. It instead asks what makes them different, shoring up the custom of letting female hair grow by pretending that it is dictated by nature's eternal laws.[34]

Hair's capacity to naturalize ideas that had nothing natural about them was so pervasive as to seem irrefutable. The much-revered philosopher Albert the Great—whom Florentines read as if he were a contemporary and not a writer who had lived two centuries earlier—took hair as both a gender differential and an indicator of sexual appetite. He believed that because women were naturally moist, those among them whose manes were more luxuriant than average must have had an inordinate amount of sex. On the other hand, men with beards appeared to enjoy lovemaking in moderation. They must have been restraining themselves, Albert reasoned, since the heat produced during intercourse was so strong that it could have extinguished any bodily vapors, as was proved by erotomaniacs' bald heads. Sex was painted in such violent tones that a contemporary of Botticelli, the philosopher Marsilio Ficino, stated that the sperm released during coitus amounted to losing forty times the same amount of blood.[35] Beards—we are back to Albert—were caused by a drop in the body's temperature, which meant that the body's inner vapors could not make it to the scalp but fell in the dip of the jaw, where they collected like rain in a pool and, while lagging there, percolated into facial hair. "And this is why the hairs of the beard multiply among old people, whereas in youths [who are full of heat] they multiply on the head, and the reason is evident."[36]

One of Albert's disciples, an English friar known as Bartholomew, registered these distinctions as a fait accompli in an encyclopedia that became a staple of conventual libraries. Right from the index (figure 3.1), he distinguished between the hair propelled to the head by the stron-

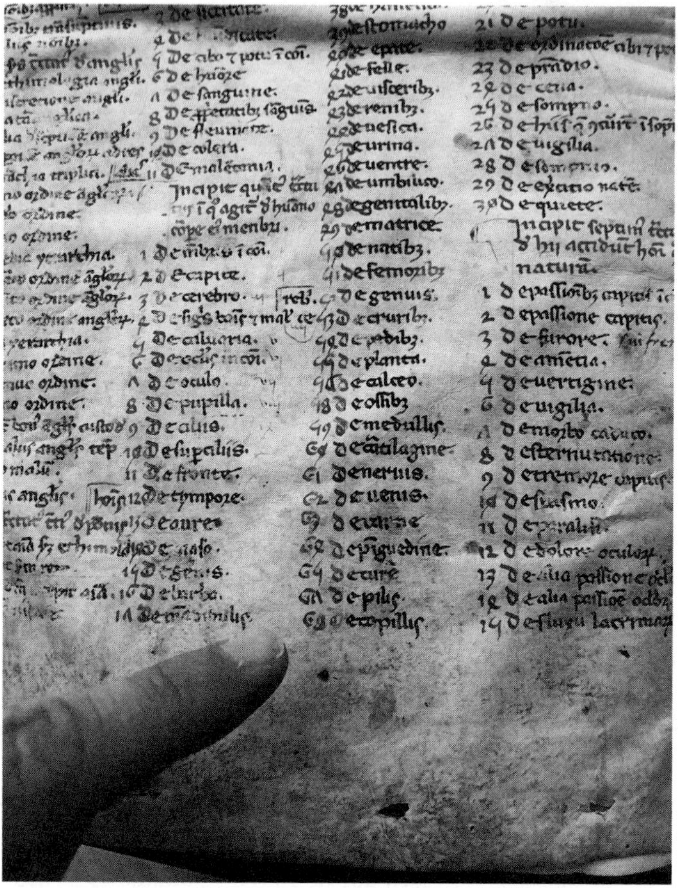

Figure 3.1. Index of Bartholomeus Anglicus, *De proprietatibus rerum*. Ms. Conv. Soppr. 462. Biblioteca Medicea Laurenziana, Florence.

gest force, which he called "capilli," and the thinner hair produced by a decline in the trajectory of inner vapor, which he named "pili"—that is, body hair. He also emphasized how hair revealed the separation between genders so clearly that language had naturally developed alternate terms for it. Women's long hair was called "crines"—a term also employed for horsetails and animal manes (parallels that do not go unnoticed here). Men's hair was denoted by the neutral word "capilli."[37] Bartholomew took the dual terminology to validate a shift in essence and even justify a difference in treatment. *Capilli* were regularly cut; they ought to be, as men's bodies were full of vigor and regenerated quickly. Women's much more slowly-growing hair, on the other hand, did not require such attention, and a papal decree cemented this misbelief when it leveraged it to forbid women from clipping their *crines* above their shoulders.[38]

In Botticelli's Florence, Bartholomew's encyclopedia could be found in the monastery of Santa Maria Novella, whose library, with more than seven hundred books, was one of the largest in Italy.[39] The index seen in figure 3.1 is the one that opens its copy of Bartholomew's work. The book is an imposing volume—two spans in height—which is particularly interesting, as Bartholomew not only provides more information about hair than was found in most books of the time, but encourages his readers to check his sources. And if friars followed his advice—if they went to consult the *Pantegni* (on the same shelf as Bartholomew's tome) or Isidore of Seville's etymological manual (nine shelves away)—they would have found passages that validated his presentation of human physiology.[40]

Bartholomew's referencing is less a matter of intellectual honesty than a strategy for gaining the reader's respect for a field that was mired with controversy.[41] Every authority who wrote about hair agreed that it was desiccated steam produced by food excess. What differed was the ways in which they put this belief to work with others.

A first point of discrepancy revolved around the origin of hair: how it changed from smoke into dried matter.[42] Those who followed Plato considered it a process of felting, the pressing of folds of gelatinous cells on others to produce filaments as wide as the pores through which the bodily vapor emerged.[43] Very few, however, could access Plato's treatises in their entirety.[44] Leonardo, for instance, was not among those who could. Nonetheless, he assembled information from other books and came up with an alternative explanation of the formation of hair.

In a drawing that today is in the collection at Windsor Castle (figure 3.2), Leonardo shows hair as the fraying of the outermost layer of the head. He read in medical treatises that the head was made of ten layers.[45] "If you'll cut an onion through the middle," he says in a note that

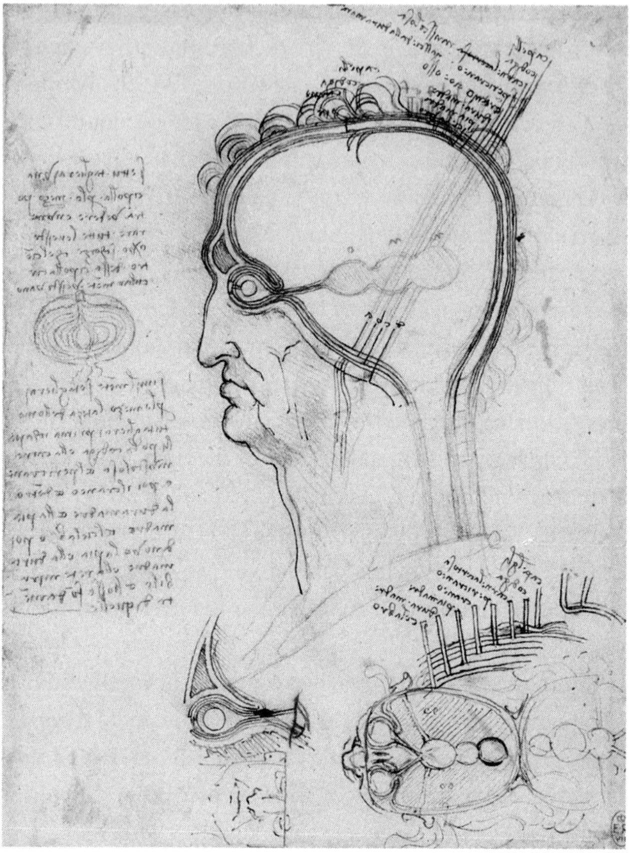

Figure 3.2. Leonardo da Vinci, the layers of the scalp and the cerebral ventricles. Windsor Castle, Windsor.

accompanies the sketch, "you'll be able to see and enumerate the coats or rinds which circularly clothe the center of this onion."[46] He does not add anything more, perhaps because the drawing provides all the remaining information. It is there that Leonardo identifies each layer, one by one, labeling the most external—that paper-thin film that cracks into waves—as "capelli."

It is not surprising that Leonardo thought of an onion to represent the brain, given that he believed nature's most arcane mysteries could be accessed by finding their analogies in more mundane objects.[47] And, despite the uniformity of the definitions of hair in the specialized literature, its physiology remained very much a mystery. How could hair be a product of a living body, and yet dead? And how could hair fall, change color, or even be cut without anyone noticing? Only nails enjoyed similar properties. Indeed, Leonardo read that, as both bodily surfeits and dead matter, nails were physiologically one with hair.[48] So this may be why he drew hair not as fluid oozing out of the scalp, but as the curling peel of an onion separating from the skin, not unlike a long, thin nail jutting out of a cuticle. The sameness of hair and nails was asserted by a treatise that became particularly famous in Milan, where Leonardo made the sketch, and which insisted that hair and nails were "not like the other members of the body, for those have natural virtues by which they are controlled. Hair and nails instead have nothing: they merely grow. Indeed, they are propelled into existence bit by bit. And even if cut while being secreted, they grow back."[49] And it is from this paradox—of being denied any substance, and yet seen as tapping into the body's constant regrowth—that hair was taken as a most reliable indicator of people's inclinations. Another book on physiognomy to which Leonardo often returned during his lifetime stated that straight, thin, and soft hair was typical of cowards, whereas thick, bristly hair indicated a brave heart.[50]

Notice the directionality of these descriptions: first comes a person's hair, and then her character. At the beginning of this chapter I presented the opposite: hair as an effect of complexion. But that causality was very much a theoretical reconstruction. It is not what you find in most medical treatises of the fifteenth century. A doctor's goal, after all, was to identify a patient's state of being, and a reliable way to make an accurate diagnosis was to examine the patient's hair. The backward description of most books, from effect to cause, reflects medical practice, which took hair as the litmus test for a condition about which doctors tried to know something.[51] But because it was unclear what aspects of a person's life (digestion? sex life? general heat production?) were revealed by their hair, doctors' conclusions were disparate.

The *Pantegni*, for instance, taught university students that hair revealed the condition of the organs nearest to it. Chest hair, for instance, spoke about the state of the heart: "If the hair is dense and dark, the heart is hot."[52] Abdominal hair, meanwhile, disclosed the liver's health. Still, not every reader was convinced by this circumscription. The famous physician Michele Savonarola—famous because he was the private doctor of the Lord of Ferrara—took a less exacting, more holistic stance.[53] A warrior with a heart on fire, he asserted, could well have a hairless chest if his liver was just as active (to make sense of this point, you need to know that the liver was believed to cool down the heart's heat waves).[54] Hair, continued Savonarola, communicated not a localized production of heat, but a person's overall complexion. For this reason, the most eloquent feature of hair was its color, which did not change from one part of the body to another. A redhead, he insisted, would sleep a lot, whereas people inclined to melancholic thoughts were likely to have black hair.[55]

Examining hair gave people much more than just a sense of what their bodies could and could not do; it paved the way for an assessment of their character. Rooted in the body and dependent on the very organs that made a man a man, hair signaled what remained out of sight. And it did so more readily and more surely than any other part of the body. Such a preeminence was stated in treatises on pathology, many of which discussed conditions of hair from the very start. The *Thesaurus pauperum*, a medieval text associated with numerous authors including the physician who became known as Pope John XXI, listed its prescriptions in a sequence running from the hair to the feet, as did the even more famous *Viaticum* and the third book of Avicenna's *Canon*, the one that discussed diseases.[56] Savonarola's own *Manual of Diseases, from the Head to the Feet* also followed this scheme, stated in its title.[57] We do not know the reason for this ordering, and there may be no reason; after all, some texts do not follow it. But those that do—and they were many, and very influential—cemented the notion of hair as not just a way to access the human body, but its main threshold. The recognition of a person's identity depended on it.

Preeminence mattered, but hair ultimately derived its power from being routinely valued as nothing. Hair had no agency; it barely had any substance. It was dead and, more than that, it was easily disposable since, even as something lifeless, it kept growing, and thus actively worked toward its own replacement. Its physical fleetingness and derivative physiology gave the impression that it was something uncomplicated that registered reality rather than intervening on it. But this passivity strengthened its role as offering a privileged mechanical way into a persons's interiority. It thus attracted the interest of those who did not simply care about anatomy and well-being but were preoccupied with the control of human passions—that is confessors, politicians, and artists, as well as the poets who sought to explore life's most inscrutable pull: erotic desire.

FOUR *Tie Me Down, Burn Me Up*

When Lorenzo de' Medici writes, "At the first sign of love, I saw her hair," I have difficulties understanding what is happening.[1] Does he mean that after he confessed his love to a woman, she took off her veil and showed her head, a gesture of availability, even intimacy? In other words, could he see her hair because first he had made his love recognizable? Or is the opposite the case: he fell in love because he saw her hair, as if seeing a woman's hair were a precondition for it, even a requirement? There is also a third option, which I would paraphrase as "The moment I fell in love, I could only see her hair"—as if Lorenzo's love implied a rewiring of his eyes, so that whatever had kept her hair out of sight no longer mattered, and he could bask in the vision of her locks? Any of the three options is possible—the verse is slippery—but what I detect nonetheless is the coincidence of love and hair: love emerged the moment a woman's hair entered Lorenzo's visual consciousness.

Lorenzo wasn't just the political mastermind of Florence. He was an accomplished poet, as famous in his day as he is celebrated today, when we take his lyrical flair as an important addition to his political profile: a depth of commitment that characterizes those who practice the arts rather than the rulers who merely surround themselves with artists.[2] Lorenzo could count on an impressive literary education, the pride of the many intellectuals his family assisted.[3] Not only that; he put it to use. Probably encouraged by one of his teachers, Cristoforo Landino, Lorenzo first modeled his own voice after Petrarch's fourteenth-century love poems.[4] (A professor at the University of Florence, Landino was the first to dedicate a course to vernacular poetry instead of Latin treatises and epics.)[5] And Petrarch's poems spoke of female hair as the loops that imprison a woman's lovers and squeeze their hearts.[6]

If readers did not meet these metaphors with disbelief, it is because Petrarch taught them to think of love less as a piercing arrow than as an ensnaring force. Lorenzo articulated this shift in one of his poems, in which he sings of how a woman's tresses trap Cupid and rob him of his bow and arrows, described as ineffective weapons against her hair.[7] Both Petrarch and Lorenzo defined love (*amor*) as a hook (*hamo*). This was a reference to the go-to treatise on erotic desire in their times: "For whoever loves (*amat*) is caught in the bonds of desire and yearns to catch another by his hook (*hamo*)."[8]

In Petrarch's most famous work during Lorenzo's youth, *The Triumph of Love*, love is also described as a form of entrapment.[9] Petrarch dreams of attending a procession in which Cupid stands on a horse-drawn chariot, like a victorious general parading before the Roman populace. All around are the victims of his arrows, but Petrarch does not focus on them—too many are the casualties—and instead zooms in on a series of couples who march before the float: Caesar handcuffed by Cleopatra, Mars choked by Venus's chain, and Jupiter tied by the "countless snares" of his many lovers.[10]

Poetry offered a space for Florentine men to present themselves as victims of women even if women's lives were largely in men's hands. Locked up in houses and convents, women mostly existed as busts leaning over windows for most of the populace.[11] (And even the window was often seen as too much of a concession. A preacher had no qualms in suggesting that husbands and brothers should hit their wives and sisters if they were found laughing and chatting at windows.)[12] Prohibited from inhabiting the public space, as they were banned from drawing up any legal document without the consent of a male relative, women, if they had means, could enjoy some freedom only in reclusive activities and in special circumstances, such as widowhood.[13] In Florence's pathologically sexist society, men saw women's grievances—a domestic complaint or a financial worry—as oppressive, and turned their violence on them as exhibitions of might.[14] It is thus hardly surprising that men saw the one thing they could not control in women's bodies, hair, as menacing. By insisting that hair grew regardless of any circumstances, doctors presented it as something that did not belong to you even if it came out of you. Escaping everyone's will, and especially that of women, hair helped men to buttress fantasies of their own submissiveness.

So if you were a Florentine man interested in expressing love's hold over you, poetry offered a number of appealing, ready-to-use metaphors centered on hair. You could compare a woman's long ponytail to a leash that controlled you.[15] You could describe a woman's coiffure styled with flowers and pearls as a bait.[16] Or you could draw on both metaphors to conclude that "love is killing me by her beautiful hair alone."[17] Out of context—that is, without the emotional charge and social pressure that lend weight to these statements—it all sounds so ridiculous. But it only appears that way from a distance.

Step closer to the paintings of the time, and everything makes sense. In his portrait of Simonetta Vespucci, a woman celebrated for her soul-lifting beauty, Botticelli gave her two long, tight braids, which meet and swell at her heart, where they have led your eyes (plate 10).[18] The painting is a fitting illustration of one of Lorenzo's poems about the braids that frame a woman's white neck and which he interprets as the "hard chain of passionate lovers and the strong snare that never unties."[19] The portrait also resonates with a poem known as *The Beautiful Hand*, which praises "the loose tresses around her throat, from which her slow and kind words come out, so that, by listening, they steal my heart and my soul."[20] I sometimes wonder if a Florentine who heard those verses interpreted the slight opening of Simonetta's perfectly aligned lips, like the two bumps of a heart cracked at its center, as a hint that she is about to speak.

Lorenzo knew *The Beautiful Hand*, as he knew the other metaphors I have cited; the writers employed by his family included them in a manuscript he gave as a gift to the son of the king of Naples, part of his attempt to popularize Tuscan poetry. It is in that collection that some of these compositions have come down to us.[21] But Lorenzo did not just imitate this tradition: he added to it, writing about hair regularly and imaginatively. When singing the love of a farmer for a shepherd, he compared her curls to a thousand rings fastened to her head, so as to cast her as a most precious thing.[22] And in another of his famous poems, about the river god Ombrone's obsession for the nymph Ambra, Lorenzo turned hair into a narrative key. After seeing her bathing in the river over which he presides, Ombrone tries to seize Ambra, but she quickly escapes, leaving him with a lock of her hair. He holds the hair in his fist while chasing her across rocky ground. Frustrated, he asks for the help of Arno, the king of Tuscan rivers, who increases the flow of his waters, creating a wall that corners the nymph. Seeing no escape, Ambra begs Diana for help and the goddess turns her into a stone, which the river Ombrone eventually covers in tears. The focus on Ombrone's sorrow, as well as the poetical invention that a river is nothing else than a god's tears, obscures Ambra's annihilation. Naked, defenseless, basically voiceless, the nymph is a ghost long before she is swallowed by a rock. And yet the poem regularly reminds the reader of her alleged power as Ombrone returns to the lock of hair in his fist, which reignites his desire and stands as a memento of his failed abduction.[23] In a way, all of Ambra's might radiates from that lock of hair, and the power dynamic of the poem can be summed up by the image of a male hand clutching it.

Scholars have spoken of Lorenzo's verses as a pastime. But his poetry was not just a hobby; it helped him raise the cultural status of Florence across Italy, an investment in what today we would call "soft power." When Lorenzo reaches out to other rulers to praise Dante as Italy's greatest poet, when he argues in favor of why the Tuscan language should be elevated above all other Italian idioms, he is being political. This agenda puts his selection of poems, authors, and themes under scrutiny. Writing about local nymphs and rivers was a way to justify Medicean control over the Florentine territory, as well as to elevate it culturally, bringing it to a status equal to that of the ancient Roman countryside, the campfire of classical gods. But if Lorenzo's poetry is streaked with political undertones, what would his insistence on hair serve to do? After all, hair had not been a major theme in Tuscan poetry.

Dante, for instance, spent very little time on it, and the references to the verses by Petrarch that I have made at the beginning of this chapter occupy mere minutes in a lifetime of writing. If Lorenzo elevates hair to an unprecedented level of scrutiny, it is because being attentive to hair has helped him achieve something. But what is this something?

A good way to approach this question is to return to the way hair enabled poets to articulate powerlessness—their own, and that of their alter egos. It is hard to believe that Lorenzo, who like most Italian lords welcomed remarks that compared him to idols and the son of a god, ever felt inadequate in front of women.[24] His poems must then be performative: attempts to feign normality in line with the program of his family, who insisted on being regular, law-obeying citizens to maintain control of Florentine politics. Yet pretending to be a prisoner of love also enabled Lorenzo to riff on a mode of experience that he considered vital, as poets considered vital the troubles, the sighs, even the heartaches caused by love. Which is everything that implies adventure and promises joy and growth, and whose achievements feel all the more exciting if under the constant threat of destruction.[25] So contemplating hair's hold allowed him to enter a new space in which he could indulge in one of the main pulls of desire and give himself to someone who did not exist but was created in his imagination.[26] In a way, it was a space in which he could reach a richer life.

Botticelli's portrait of Simonetta also responds to such a space (plate 10). Perhaps painted after the premature death of the sitter, whose beauty was said to surpass that of any Florentine alive, the woman in the painting is a creature of dreams.[27] She wears a light shirt, with lace stitching throughout, conjuring up a level of sartorial extravagance that goes beyond the evocation of prohibited bedroom fantasies to hint at the fineries of nymphs, dancing barefoot in mid-spring air.[28] Most Florentine women would not have dared to wear such lingerie in public.[29] They emerged from their houses in armors of thick wool, skirts, and overskirts that dragged on the ground—deliberately so, as even the peep of a toe was a betrayal of honesty.[30] Pending from Simonetta's necklace is a gem that refers to a fabulously expensive jewel engraved with an image of subjugation that had fueled the imagination of Florentine artists for decades.[31] Her other accessories point to the highest class. Aristocratic ladies sported plumes on their heads, like the four ostrich feathers crowning Simonetta.[32] And the number of 212 pearls that I count in her coiffure was rare. While pearls were prohibited by law, wealthy families dodged the ban by pleading with influential politicians.[33] We know, for instance, that Lucrezia Tornabuoni, Lorenzo's mother, received at least one such request.[34] And I imagine that she took it sympathetically, given that she owned a hairband sewn with 224 pearls.[35] Such lavish accessories were flaunted during exceptional events, like weddings.[36] (At the wedding of the Duke of Milan, the bride showed off a hairstyle encrusted with 544 pearls.)[37] Other occasions for such ostentation were jousts, like the one organized to celebrate the alliance between Florence, Venice, and Milan, during which Lorenzo's younger brother sported a magnificent shield studded with pearls.[38] When the shield was hit by a spear, a chronicler writes, the pearls burst off and were up for grabs.[39]

Simonetta's appearance is in line with these displays of agonizing wealth. Yet the painting's search for the highest distinction comes not from her outfit and accessories, but from her hair and her hair alone. Twisted and scalded and puffed out so to produce a hilly landscape of braids and tails, Simonetta's head is a showoff of craft: those side braids and tufts of hair imply a search for the fine calibration of distances and pull, the labor of a hand that did and undid knots until their placements and tensions were just right. It must have felt extraordinary to whoever made the drawing that is today in Oxford (figure 4.1).[40] Art historians do not quite know whether it was a preparatory sketch by Botticelli (but how different from his other sketches, full of second thoughts and hesitation!) or a record of the finished painting, perhaps by a pupil (but then why omit the shirt and famous necklace?).[41] Either way, the drawing transcribes Simonetta's coiffure with the same diligence that is reserved for her face, thus revealing that Botticelli's portrait was seen first and foremost as a painting of hair. And as a painting of hair, it had a distinct sense of purpose. All elaborate coiffures, after all, did as Giovanni Boccaccio argued in his *Comedy of the Florentine Nymphs* (figure 4.2).

Largely ignored today, Boccaccio's *Comedy* was a success in Lorenzo's Florence. Its scenes appeared on the furniture of wealthy families.[42]

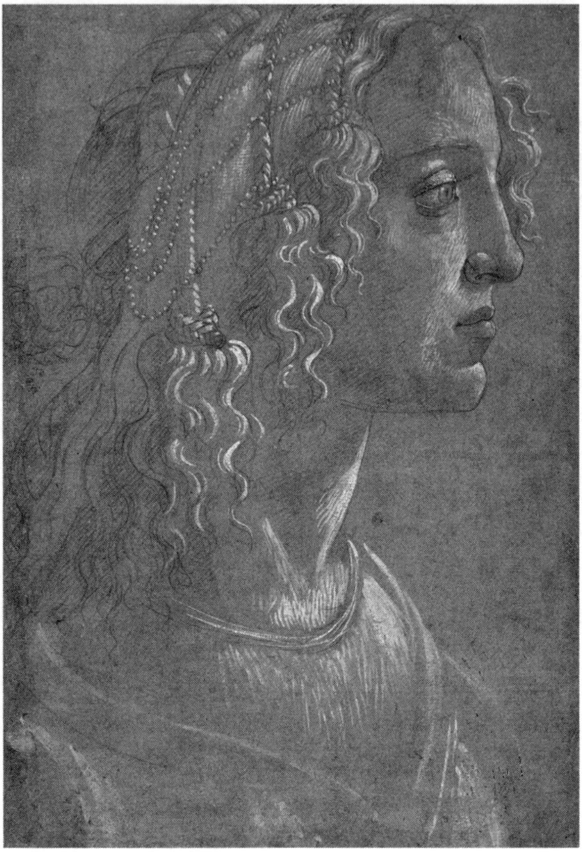

Figure 4.1. Sandro Botticelli or follower, copy of or preparatory drawing for portrait of Simonetta Vespucci (plate 5.1). Ashmolean Museum, Oxford.

Manuscripts were exchanged by merchants, who feared they would not be returned.[43] The number of them available was not enough, and many Florentines took on the task of reproducing them themselves.[44] Girolamo Morelli, who served as Lorenzo de' Medici's correspondent in Milan, reproduced the *Comedy* on some twenty-five sheets while quarantining at home during one of the plague waves that hit Florence.[45] Hand-copied manuscripts did not stop circulating even after the *Comedy* was printed, amusing readers with what was a fable of transformation.[46]

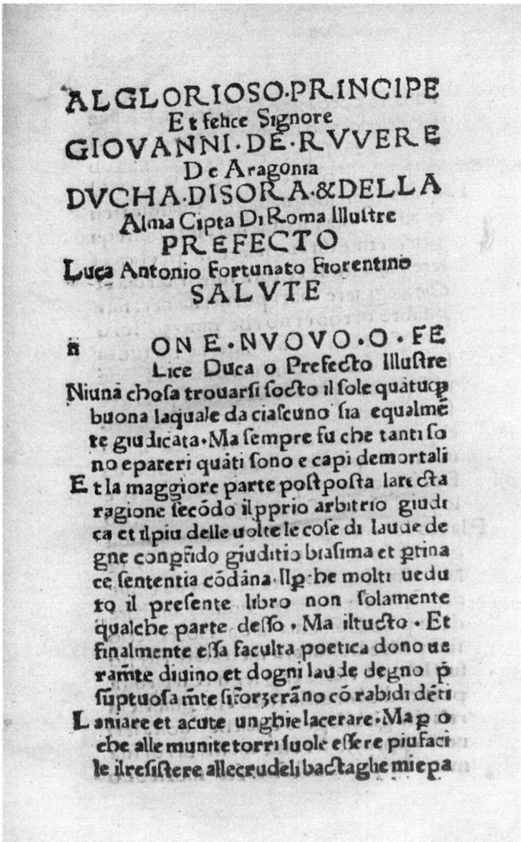
AL GLORIOSO·PRINCIPE
Et felice Signore
GIOVANNI·DE·RVVERE
De Aragonia
DVCHA·DISORA·&DELLA
Alma Cipta Di Roma Illustre
PREFECTO
Luca Antonio Fortunato Fiorentino
SALVTE

ON E·NVOVO·O·FE
Lice Duca o Prefecto Illustre
Niuna chosa trouarsi socto il sole quātunq
buona laquale da ciascuno sia equalmē
te giudicata·Ma sempre fu che tanti so
no e pareri quāti sono e capi de mortali
E t la maggiore parte postposta la recta
ragione secōdo il pprio arbitrio giudi
ca et il piu delle uolte le cose di laude de
gne conp[illegible]do giuditio biasima et ptina
ce sententia cōdāna·Il p̄che molti uedu
to il presente libro non solamente
qualche parte desso·Ma il tucto·Et
finalmente essa faculta poetica dono ue
ramte diuino et dogni laude degno p̄
suptuosamte si sforzerāno cō rabidi dēti
L aniare et acute unghie lacerare·Ma p o
che alle munite torri suole essere piu faci
le il resistere alle crudeli bactaglie mie pa

Figure 4.2. Front page of the first edition of Giovanni Boccaccio's *Comedy of the Florentine Nymphs* (also known as *Ameto*). Bayerische Staatsbibliothek, Munich.

Boccaccio's *Comedy* tells the story of the hunter Ameto: how he goes from savage to suave thanks to the help of seven nymphs. Not unlike in today's television shows about makeovers and the judges who influence them, each nymph contributes to Ameto's transformation by sharing her story, centered on a specific virtue. One nymph teaches him to look at his future through his past (what Botticelli called prudence), another to control his own impulses (temperance), a third to be hopeful. Ameto listens to every one of them to earn his access to Lia, the advocate for faith and the leader of the pack. Lia has struck Ameto from the very start, when he encounters the nymphs bathing in a river and is captured by her "blond hair flung over her ivory shoulders with graceful locks and gathered in a garland of oak, laden with acorns. And admiring all of her with an attentive eye, he praised every part of her to himself."[47] The *Comedy* starts as an exploration of daydreaming. Ameto listens to every nymph because each allows him to get lost in what he has seen.[48] And to get lost, Ameto has started from their hair.

Take Emilia, who gives a speech about the importance of being just. At first, Ameto can barely understand her words, as he is so amazed by "her very long blond hair, worthy of comparison to any splendor, which was gathered in part on top of her head without any artifice, and bound with a lovely knot of her same hair; and other locks, either shorter or not bound in the knot, were still more beautifully dispersed and twisted in a laurel wreath, while still others were blown by the wind around her temples and around her delicate neck, marking her even more graceful."[49]

It wasn't particularly original of Boccaccio to introduce a woman by describing her hair. In keeping with the medical textbooks we examined in the previous chapter, writing manuals recommended describing bodies from head to toe, which is what epics also did.[50] In the *Roman de la Rose*, just to mention a story that was ubiquitous in both Boccaccio's and Botticelli's times, the first female character is introduced by her "blonde hair."[51] So there is nothing particularly striking in Boccaccio's starting point. What makes his writing unusual, however, is his level of detail.

Boccaccio does not simply describe hair: he drowns his readers in it. He spins long, winding sentences that split a mass of hair into braids, locks, and strands—a way to convey Ameto's visual immersion, on which Boccaccio regularly comments.[52] Take another nymph, Fiammetta. Boccaccio reports:

> Carefully scrutinizing her, Ameto noted her hair, to which he could find no comparison in its blondness; and he observed a mass of her hair twisted by a masterly hand in a long shape over each ear; and for the rest, he noticed full braids that fell over the top of her neck and, crossing there, returned, one toward the right and the other

> toward the left, up to the top of the blond head; and there the remaining lengths returned downward, and their ends were hidden in the same manner under the first climbing piece; and the braids stayed in their place adorned with shining gold and pearls braided together; nor did he notice a single hair that escaped from the imposed order.[53]

Boccaccio shifts qualifiers from action to effect, merging Ameto's seeing and the seen thing—that is, subject and world—to convey a sense of labyrinthine dizziness.

For Boccaccio, a labyrinth is the condition of whoever "does not know how to get out without effort." He gave this definition when lecturing on Dante's *Divine Comedy*, and compared his idea of the underworld to a mountainous palace full of square rooms, each with four doors that lead to other identical square rooms, forcing whomever entered it into a journey that felt not like a journey, but like pointless labor.[54] And in another work, known to Botticelli as *The Labyrinth of Love*, Boccaccio explained its title as both an "enchanted valley" and a "muddy pigsty" in which love prisoners deplore their entrapment but do nothing about it.[55] Such a viscous state eventually leads Ameto to a realization: the labyrinth is man-made, as the hair that ensnares him is an effect of his desire to keep on looking.[56]

Botticelli's portrait of Simonetta (plate 10) is also constructed to be visually sticky. Her arrestingly intricate coiffure is a network of ropes, levers, and cantilevers that pull your attention in and hold you there. There are direct, precise connections between Botticelli's paintings and Boccaccio's descriptions in his *Comedy*. In both, hair is both shapeless matter and disciplinary knot.[57] In both, hair's tortuous paths defy any explanation.[58] By constructing mazes of hair in which eyes get lost, Botticelli produced tools for visual vagary. Boccaccio describes Ameto's unremitting stare with a beautiful expression: "continuous eye" (*occhio continuo*).[59] Ameto keeps looking and looking. Even when he manages to look away, his desire pulls him back in. And to pull stares back, Botticelli spreads Simonetta's hair across the picture plane, often shaping it in U-formations. Locks flutter against the background and braids merge with the costume so that any departure from them is only temporary. By wandering through the coils and wondering about where they start and end, Botticelli turns his spectators into lovers. For what are lovers, if not those who are enslaved by their own looking, both a source of delight and the cause of perdition?[60]

Those interested in the history of costume may be quick at pointing out that Botticelli's intertwining of braids and pearly strings is called *vespaio*.[61] A vespaio is a bejeweled ribbon or net by which Florentine women held their braids in place (see plate 7) and by presenting a version of it, art historians point out, Botticelli may have been alluding to the family name of Simonetta's husband, Marco Vespucci.[62] Yet I think that labeling this net of hair misses the point, as it minimizes its threatening viscousness, reducing the pictorial invention to a conventional accessory. This is particularly important, because what you see here is not a regular vespaio. Botticelli plays on the hairband by making it out of hair, but the result is unique because it is supported by a different mode of looking. This is another instance in which hair is suspended in a mode of being that is hard to grasp. I started this chapter commenting on a verse that I defined as slippery, but perhaps Lorenzo's words were not ambiguous: it is hair that operates in a way that can hardly be pinned down verbally.

With the unfolding of his *Comedy*, Boccaccio moves away from indulging in physical delight to seek spiritual self-awareness. Hair then reveals itself to be but a stage in a process of knowledge. Whereas it is Ameto's eyes that first jump from one side of a nymph's head to the other, it is then his intellect that leaps ("salta con lo 'ntelletto"), and which he trusts more than his eyes ("più lo 'ntelletto che l'occhio dispone"), in his yearning for a virtuous life.[63] Boccaccio states the shift quite plainly: "Whereas [first] the nymphs had pleased more his eye than his intellect, now they delighted his intellect more than his eye."[64] Such newfound pleasure in philosophical reasoning eventually neutralizes the erotic charge of the story. If Boccaccio has initially emphasized the nymphs' hair, it is to prepare for its dissolution. Boccaccio's readers took notice of this shift. After finishing the book, one of them penned in a margin of the last page: "This book by sir Giovanni Boccaccio is about not nymphs, as the title says, but virtue."[65] And I wonder if such a sentence was jotted with disappointment, or the complacency of those who commit a sin knowing that it will eventually be forgiven.

So the hair of nymphs—that is, the hair of desirable women—was rejected twice. After being described as a delightful trap, it was dismissed as a mere vanity. It was not Boccaccio who came up with this snub. He read about it in the Latin novel *The Golden Ass*, a tremendous editorial success that chronicled the adventures of Lucius, a man obsessed with female hair, his first and ultimate delight.[66] "As to the rest of her [body], I've nothing to say," Lucius confesses; "it's only a woman's head and her hair that I'm really interested in. It's what I like to feast my eyes on first in the street, and then enjoy in private indoors. There are good and positive reasons for this preference. The hair is the dominant part of the body: it's placed in the most obvious and conspicuous position and is the first thing we notice." He concludes on the point that, when "women want to show off their personal attractions, they discard their clothes" and let their hair do the talking. Lucius goes on and on, insisting on the preeminence of hair over all other features. "If you were to despoil the head of even the most beautiful of women of its hair—though it's blasphemy even to mention it, and I devoutly hope that such a thing will never happen to make the point—though she had come down from heaven, though she had been born from the sea and reared among the waves, I say though she were Venus herself . . . , if she were bald, not even her Vulcan [that is, the most desperately devoted of husbands] would love her."[67]

Boccaccio revered *The Golden Ass*.[68] He transcribed it in his own hand and must have flipped through its pages regularly when composing his *Comedy*, given the density of the borrowings.[69] He carefully paraphrased Lucius's rapturous account of Photis's hair, the one cited above, in his description of Emilia:

> Ameto recognized that the long abundant blond hair was the special beauty of this maiden; and if Venus, born and nourished in the waves and loved in heaven, were to find herself divested of such hair, though perfect in all other graces, she would scarcely appeal

> to her Mars. Therefore he deems the beauty of her hair so important for a woman that anyone, whoever she may be, though she go covered in precious garments, in rich stones, in glimmering gems and bright gold, without her hair tressed in due order, cannot seem properly adorned; yet in this maiden the disorder thereof renders her still more charming to Ameto's eyes.[70]

It is not just the image of the bald Venus that comes from *The Golden Ass*. Boccaccio takes from it both the comparison of hair to gems and jewels and his play on *ornato/disordinato*, a calque of "inordinatus ornatus."[71] Emilia's fetchingly casual hairstyle is modeled after that of Photis. "As for my dear Photis," *The Golden Ass* reads, "it wasn't that she had taken great pains with her hairstyle—it was its casualness that was so fetching."[72]

So Boccaccio's feasting on hair was inspired by a classical text. And *The Golden Ass* is also the model for Ameto's final renunciation of hair, as Lucius ends his day as a monk, explaining—in the last sentence—how proudly he has shaved his head as an act of worldly renunciation.[73] Boccaccio even radicalized this stance in successive works. In *The Labyrinth of Love*, he minutely describes a session of hairstyling in great detail, only to parody the vanity of a woman "who highly desires to be seen."[74] And his moralizing even pervades his mythological encyclopedia, the *Genealogy of the Pagan Gods*, wherein he talks of Medusa's beautiful hair as a pointless vanity.[75] Medusa, Boccaccio recalls, was one of the children of Phorkys, the god of oceanic abysses. She was the daughter with such an arresting golden mane that Neptune fell in love with her only because of it. The two had sex in the temple of Minerva, who, offended, turned Medusa's most alluring feature into a mane of snakes.[76]

The very first time I read the tale, I could not believe that it was Medusa who got punished. It took me a few moments to realize how intensely naive I was. Boccaccio was writing at a time when women's beauty was considered aggressive, something from which a man should defend himself.[77] It was also a time in which a monster could only have been a monster, even before committing any crime. An author like Isidore of Seville, in his much-read *History of the World*, had no qualms about defining Medusa as "the whorish Gorgon who had serpents for hair."[78] Misogyny ran so deep in fifteenth-century Florence; it affected the structure of its society in such a profound way that it predetermined what people could imagine.[79] It is hard to keep sexism consistently in mind if you want to keep reading the literary products of that time. But in this case it is particularly hard, since Boccaccio's sexism is not overt but procedural.[80] Trying to decode a myth through what he knew—that is, reading Medusa's story alongside love poems, classical texts, and encyclopedic definitions—created a kind of optical illusion in which everything made sense. So he took Medusa's beautiful hair—and by beautiful, he confesses, he meant irresistible to men's eyes—as indicative of her vanity. By presenting the visibility of her hair as intentional, the myth not only explained how Neptune and other men were Medusa's victims and not the other way around, but also signaled her deceiving toxicity, which Minerva exposed when she turned her hair into snakes.[81]

It is all perfectly circular, and indeed, no other writer of the time thought of an alternative. When Landino recounted the story of Medusa in his popular commentary of Dante's *Divine Comedy*, he followed Boccaccio. "[Neptune] loves above all her hair, that is, the superfluities," he wrote; "and Minerva turned her beautiful hair into snakes because wisdom eventually unveils trickeries and reveals their poison."[82] And when the eminent chancellor of Florence, Coluccio Salutati, who in his youth had met Boccaccio, spoke of Medusa as the embodiment of deception, he also pointed to her hair, which he defined as women's main and ultimate attraction.[83] It may come as little surprise that Salutati had read *The Golden Ass*.[84]

Once again, women's poetical hair had little to do with reality. Men indulged in it to revel in erotic fantasies, and then rejected it as vanity to reinforce a newly found sense of their virtuous self. Female hair inspired desires—desires that many Florentine men, but also women, took as valid because they saw them articulated by authors who did not even try to hide the masturbatory nature of their protagonists' delusions. When closing in on Lucius's fascination for Photis's hair, *The Golden Ass* describes its "color and sheen: now vivid enough to outshine the rays of the sun, now gently reflecting them; [. . .] sometimes perfumed with

Arabian essences and delicately parted, it is gathered behind to give back to the lover's gaze a more flattering reflection."[85] The woman's eyes have fallen off her face, since she has no face but is just a head of hair, which shines so bright that it turns into a mirror for the lover. Familiar with *The Golden Ass*, Lorenzo de' Medici must have found this idea exhilarating, and he played on it in his eulogy for Simonetta, whom he describes as "so sweet and charming that all the people who either knew her or knew of her firmly believed that she was in love with them."[86] It does not matter whether Simonetta was in love with anyone. The only thing that mattered is that her "insurmountable kindness" (his words) gave men the possibility of believing that she was in love with them.[87]

It is only after reading such distortions that Botticelli's portrait transformed before my eyes. In her expansive mane I no longer saw sticky tentacles, but the flames that consume a lover's heart. Look at the three tufts on the side (plate 10). Voluminous and wavy, they are shaped like reversed flames, similar to the speckles of fire that rain on Mercury's mantle in Botticelli's *Primavera* (plate 11). Dante wrote that love behaves like a blaze, which starts as a spark but soon burns everything down, leaving no place to hide.[88] Lorenzo also thought that a lover was like a burning man. He wrote that his heart was "surrounded by so many flames that it seemed to him impossible to tolerate the breathlessness caused by his blazing desire."[89]

What if Simonetta's head is on fire because it is not the portrait of a woman, but a reflection of blazing desire? Botticelli included flames on Mercury's tunic precisely to visualize this feeling. They reveal that he is being desired by Chastity, the grace behind him who unfastens her tunic to expose her heart to him.[90] (She has no choice but to fall for him, since she has been targeted by Cupid's fiery arrow, as shown in plate 12).[91] Similarly, Botticelli worked downward-pointing flames into Simonetta's coiffure to visualize what an observer must have felt when looking at her. Not only did her hair bind men with its snares, as Petrarch believed, but it triggered the flame of desire that combusted their hearts.[92]

In his *Triumph of Love*, Petrarch describes the ardor of passion in great detail. He writes that Cupid's arrows pierce through the flesh and hit people's bones, which, because of their dryness, catch fire instantly.[93]

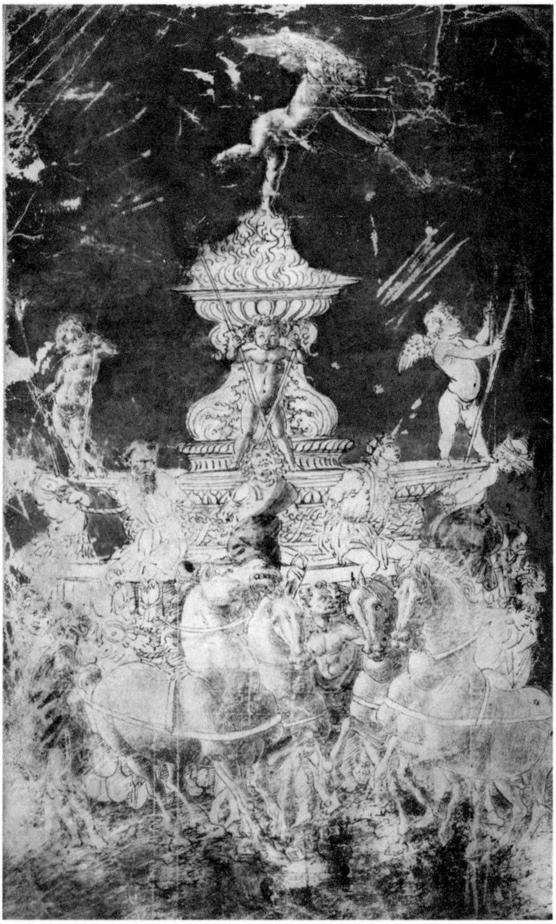

Figure 4.3. Sandro Botticelli, *Triumph of Love.* Ms. 143, f. 141v. Istituzione Biblioteca Classense, Ravenna.

On fire is also the chariot on which Cupid stands, and which Botticelli illustrated on a manuscript (figure 4.3).[94] He imagined it as a blazing fountain, pulled by beasts out of control and running like mad. Ricciardo di Nanni, one of Florence's most in-demand illuminators, painted it but emphasized its fiery dimension, as he placed Cupid amid bowmen ready to release arrows whose tips burn with enormous flame (plate 13).[95] They

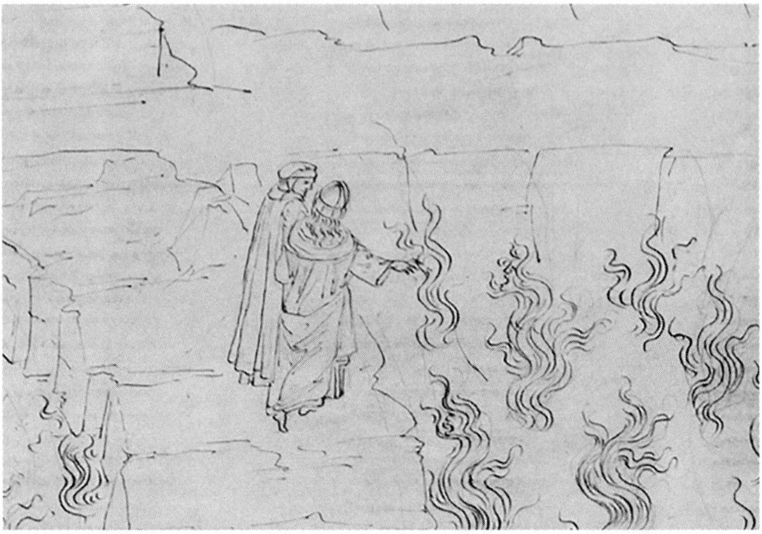

Figure 4.4. Sandro Botticelli, illustration to Inferno 27 in Dante's *Divine Comedy* (detail). Kupferstichkabinett, Berlin.

sit around two female busts whose back braids curl up and intertwine, forming two torches which serve as the platform for the god of love. Above and below, puttis' heads are literally on fire. The idea must have struck Botticelli, since he used it for one of his illustrations for the *Divine Comedy*, in which the profiles of the damned merge with the flames that surround them (figure 4.4).[96]

But even if Botticelli did not know Ricciardo di Nanni's illumination—we are not sure that he did—he had been encouraged to believe there was a natural convergence between hair and flames. Hair, we saw earlier, was thought of as the smoke released by a burning stomach. The convergence was engraved in the Italian vocabulary. Florentines called solar rays—any ray, in fact—*crini*, the same word used for hair. They also called a comet *cometa* because it spread out its light like a mane (*coma*).[97] In *Morgante*, the farcical epic we have already encountered—and which, it now seems pertinent to add, was much enjoyed by the Medici—the sun dips his golden hair in the ocean at dusk.[98] The poem also describes lighting bolts as the shedding of Apollo, whose face corresponds to the

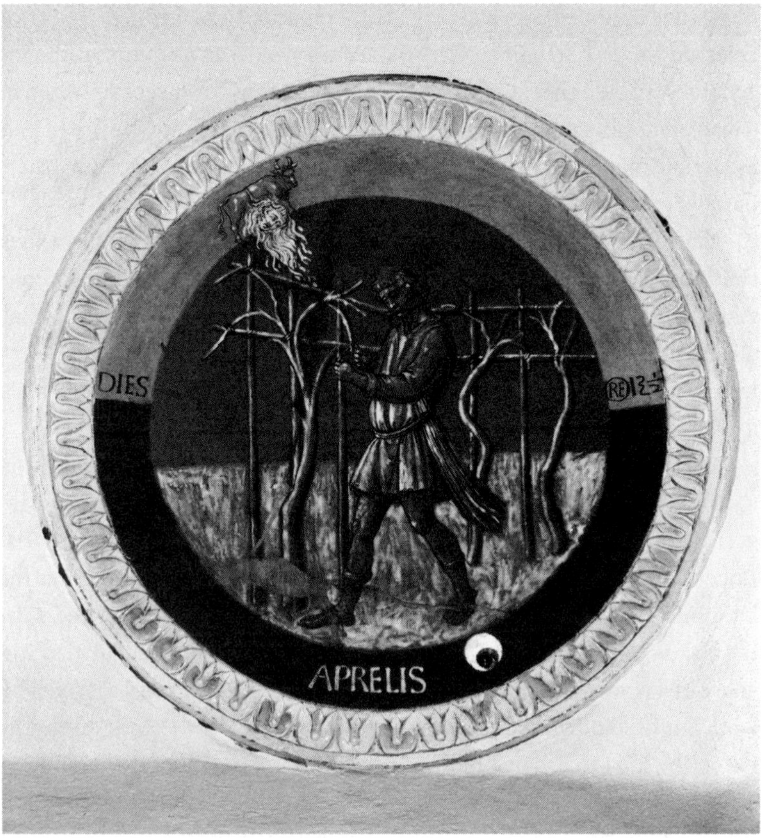

Figure 4.5. Luca della Robbia, *The Month of April*. Victoria and Albert Museum, London.

disc of the sun.[99] These metaphors facilitate seeing hair as flame, and once one is made aware of the convergence, it becomes difficult to undo. The office of Lorenzo's father, for example, was decorated with a coffer vault with roundels depicting the monthly activities energized by the sun, represented as a face with flowing hair that turns into drops of light (figure 4.5).[100] The decoration of the ceiling was so arresting that a Neapolitan friend of the Medici asked them to send him a drawing of it.[101]

Botticelli leveraged the idea of divine hair as descending flames to construct Simonetta as a supernatural creature who brought a sort of celestial warmth to earth. Yet Simonetta's side tufts also hint at the incendiary passion that, as *The Golden Ass* states, any lover sees reflected in a woman's shiny mane. Or—to follow preachers who saw the fire of lust as the ultimate goal of hairdressing—by caring for and adorning their hair, women "wish to inflame men and have sex with them."[102]

Those are blunt words. The literature of the time chose softer tones that however hardly tempered such an antifeminist view. Angelo Poliziano, the tutor of Lorenzo's son, describes Cupid hiding inside a woman's pupil and pulling the ocular nerve, as if it were a bowstring, to release a fiery arrow into the eye of the man watching her, so that he feels a fire igniting his heart.[103]

What is enlightening in this image—and I could mention others—is the orientation of the action.[104] The poem presents the woman as triggering something that lingers in the viewer. Simonetta, Medusa, Photis, Boccaccio's and Lorenzo's nymphs: they are just pegs.[105] The matter hanging is the viewer, presented as oscillating between victim and willing risk taker. The poem *The Beautiful Hand* even adds that the flaming snare of a woman's hair caused its author to set the intensity at which he would himself burn, thus sparing himself from death.[106] While strengthening the idea that hair kindles a sort of erotic burning, this emphasis on control—as it is the poet who decides to have his heart on fire, and sets the temperature of his desire—further identifies the pleasure that paintings such as Botticelli's elicited as masochistic. Botticelli's painting of Simonetta, then, is not just a portrait. The flames and enticing knots of her hair make us reconsider its genre, whose goal is not to record the likeness of a woman but to shape, and indeed precipitate, the viewer's emotions. We should rename the painting to accommodate this other function: "Simonetta Vespucci; or, a Mirror for Those Who Want to See the Fire."[107]

FIVE *Superfluities*

Those turnabouts are telling. If Giovanni Boccaccio indulged in looking at labyrinthine hair only to present it as a frivolous activity, if Sandro Botticelli reworked the hairstyle in a portrait so that it responded more to the viewer's desire than to the sitter's appearance, it is because they both felt uneasy about the idea that hair could be presented as it was. It is almost as if it were not enough for hair to reveal a woman's natural disposition; hair also had to consider and adapt to the emotional weakness of whoever took an interest in her. Thus it is not difficult to imagine how Florentines may have grown circumspect about anything related to hair, especially if they believed what the moral authorities said about it. Those patronizing voices did not go for soft tones. For them, hair was shit.

I take the definition from a sermon by the preacher Giordano da Pisa, who thundered from a pulpit:

> One woman will put one hundred florins' worth of gold on her head for decoration's sake. What is this! And the poor do not even have clothes to cover themselves, nor anything to eat while that sack of dung holds one hundred or two hundred gold florins on her head in accessories, and the unlucky husbands consent to it, and they lose their souls together with their wives. They should make laws and proclamations about such vanities if they were the sort of

> men they ought to be. Do not marvel if the superfluities in which women are engaging are the reasons for the destruction of this city, because God abominates and holds contemptible excesses and superfluities."[1]

There is a lot to unpack in this tirade: the portrayal of husbands as victims, and the hard-to-believe costs of fifteenth-century headgear, which, Giordano insists, could cause the bankruptcy of not only a family but an entire city.[2] We have encountered aspects of these alarms. What is new is the juxtaposition of coils of hair with the feces that Florentines tried to avoid in the streets. And yet, Giordano was not trying to be provocative; he was being orthodox.[3]

The definition of hair as excrement comes straight from Thomas Aquinas, the greatest theologian and intellectual guide of the Dominicans, the religious order famous for the learnedness of its preachers, who included Giordano. In studying medical books, Aquinas learned that hair was a residue of the body's regenerative process, whose technical term was "superfluity."[4] Yet, theologians provided their own definition of the term: superfluities were all the things that would be left behind on Judgment Day. "You see?" Aquinas wrote in his *Summa theologica* (his much-memorized *vademecum*, the one to which preachers turned for all sorts of difficult questions, such as what the afterlife would be like). "Like urine and sweat and feces and other superfluities, hair and nails are generated by an excess of food, and as those do not resurrect, so neither should hair and nails."[5]

Now, this is an exaggeration. When Aquinas imagined that no one in the afterlife would have hair, he was deliberately exaggerating. According to his way of reasoning, a method known as scholasticism, he ought to analyze any hypothesis, no matter how far-fetched, by checking what borderline conditions made it true.[6] And scholastic thinking could validate something as long as it was consistent with the sacred scriptures. Aquinas knew, however, that the Bible provided no support for a hairless hereafter. Of the afterlife, the Gospel of Luke said, ". . . but not a hair of your head will perish."[7] And a Deuteronomic verse added that it would not perish because "all works of God are perfect."[8] Augustine, whose treatises were thought to contain universal truths even if they were not part of the sacred scriptures, interpreted these two passages as proof that hair ought to have something valuable in it.[9] So Aquinas, who could not invalidate any reasoning by a Church authority like Augustine, concluded that "hair is an ornament of humans, and thus needs to resurrect as the body of men resurrects in its entirety."[10] With one clarification: since the human body was not homogeneous—some of its parts had noble, vital functions while others were dispensable—hair belonged to a lesser degree of perfection. After all, it served not to maintain life but only to protect the organs that did.[11] And yet, he wrote, "it will nonetheless resurrect with the body as humans resurrect in the entirety of their perfection."[12] But granting hair some utility did not mean accepting it in toto. I have been through Aquinas's procedure of creating a straw man because it shows the range of negative opinions that hair attracted: from tepid tolerance (*Hair must be somewhat useful*) to rejection (*Hair is utterly superfluous*).

The dismissive attitudes of theologians had been shaped by Saint Paul, who told his readers to be suspicious of hair, since it gave way to vanity. In one of his letters, he wrote that women ought to "adorn themselves in modest apparel with shamefacedness and sobriety; not with braided hair, or gold, or pearls, or costly array."[13] Paul's letters were considered worthy of memorization and unworthy of critique: they formed one of the three books that Dominican novices studied during their training.[14] So it is not surprising that Tommaso da Lentini, the prior of the monastery in Naples where Aquinas took his habit, invoked hair when discussing vanity in his sermons.[15] He insisted that Mary Magdalene's sin resided in the excessive care that, as a prostitute, she bestowed on her hair. (The evidence for this claim was that she dyed it.)[16] And Augustine added that by cleaning Christ's feet with her hair, she understood it as the superfluity it was—the first step of her conversion.[17]

Botticelli was aware of those correspondences when working on an altarpiece for the so-called *convertite*, Florence's convent for prostitutes and destitute women.[18] Painting for an audience who took the Magdalene as the example for the transformation they set for themselves, Botticelli turned her into a creature of hair (plate 15). While it was common to represent the saint covered by loose tresses—an indication of the years she spent in the desert and her total renunciation of worldly goods, clothes included—no other painter made her arms disappear under them, as Botticelli did.[19]

Botticelli preceded this episode with another in which the Magdalene listens to Christ preaching (plate 14). This event is nowhere to be found in the saint's biographies, and must have been requested by Botticelli's patrons. The scene he sets is stupendously moving. Mary Magdalene listens to Christ from far away, hiding behind a pillar and hunching under a heavy cloak, separated from the rest of the crowd by an empty doorframe that opens onto darkness and stands for the insurmountable abyss between her and them. Three, four times removed from Christ, her sense of shame is palpable: she knows she does not belong there. Anyone who saw the altarpiece needed first to experience this severance in order to appreciate the miracle represented in the following episode, in which the Magdalene assumes the host (plate 15). There, she has covered the gulf between her and the church. She has stepped forward, working through her shame, to reunite with Christ—here replaced by a bishop, Christ's vicar on earth. It is through hair, however, that Botticelli signals the Magdalene's conversion more potently.

Preachers like Giordano told women that to transform their souls, they needed to get rid of any vanity, and that the best way to do so was to strip their hair of any jewel or sign of care.[20] This is how the Magdalene presents herself to the priest after having internalized Christ's words: as a creature of loose, unadorned hair. (Botticelli makes a tight connection to the sermons of his time by showing Christ speaking from a platform, not unlike the pulpits from which preachers delivered their orations.) In the very moment that the Magdalene receives the eucharist—which, as food, provides the matter of hair but, as Christ's body, precipitates the prodigy of her conversion—her appearance signals the moral shape of her new existence. She has become a mass of hair because hair is the only part of her body that can single-handedly express her transformation from vain woman to humble drier of God's feet.

But Botticelli's Mary Magdalene responded to the widespread belief that hair was not only the most eloquent expression of a soul, but the very site at which to change it. To curb women's vanity—that is, to convert their hearts—preachers told them to stop dyeing their hair. This is what Bernardino da Siena said in Florence in front of a crowd that was likely to include Botticelli's relatives as well as his teacher Filippo Lippi, then a nineteen-year-old Carmelite friar.[21] During another sermon, which he gave in Siena, Bernardino told mothers they were cheating their daughters of salvation if they continued to care for their hairstyles.[22] His attacks were amplified by the many preachers who aspired to be like him.[23] Citing Bernardino, Giovanni da Capistrano affirmed that the mother who allowed her daughter to dye her hair was the worse of the two.[24] And Girolamo Savonarola, the leading preacher of Florence during the last years of Lorenzo de' Medici, reproached mothers for adorning their daughters "with many superfluous hairstyles."[25] We are at the close of the fifteenth century, and Aquinas's vocabulary of two hundred years earlier was still current.[26]

Every time I read a few of those sermons in quick succession, I feel that my vision becomes blurred and the words merge into one sequence, no matter that they were composed centuries apart: the same caustic tones and over-the-top expressions, the same demands to refocus one's attention. It is not just that preachers cited their predecessors and learned from them which biblical passages to reference. (In his travels, Bernardino carried a pocket-size book packed with theological commentaries, which he drew upon for his sermons).[27] They employ the very same words, because only those conveyed orthodoxy with potent accuracy.[28] Their repetitions made sure that the Church—that is, they themselves—continued acting as people's conscience. The majority of Florentines, after all, did not read the Bible or Saint Paul's letters.[29] They certainly did not lift the covers of Aquinas's heavy volumes. Even those very few who could understand Latin would not have dared do so.[30] It wasn't just that those manuscripts were hard to get, chained as they were to the pews of conventual libraries. The people were told that they could not access God's powerful truths by themselves. And they felt no need to do so, since preachers did the job for them, selecting relevant passages and shaping them around their audience's needs. Hence the constant need for new sermons.

But adapting and translating the scriptures wasn't the sole mode for making sure that their lessons never fell out of people's minds. Church officials also tried to influence lawmakers. Already in the thirteenth century, Cardinal Latino Malabranca Orsini obliged married women to hide their hair under veils.[31] To ensure that the norm did not remain a moot point, he instructed preachers to publicize it from the pulpit, all around Tuscany.[32] It caused an outcry, if we are to believe a chronicler who wrote that it "was more bitter to women than death itself."[33]

I am not sure how accurate this record is, since we do not know how many women complied. We do know, though, that a few dodged the norm by substituting veils with other signs of distinction, and that subterfuges like this eventually led to new bans. By the time Lorenzo de' Medici came to power, the list of prohibited items in Florence included silk braids and feather garlands.[34] Married women knew they could not replace veils with hoods, caps, or hats of any shape.[35] They were also banned from wearing expensive metal crowns, and this time the law targeted the goldsmiths' guild, whose members included Verrocchio and Botticelli's brother, Antonio.[36]

While in other Italian cities those prohibitions were enforced by the very church authorities that devised them, this was not the case in Florence, where they fell under the city's jurisdiction.[37] The Florentine government, however, does not seem to have been very committed: it established norms only in response to specific events, and formulated them loosely so as to condone and condemn case by case.[38] The fines were so low that wealthy families had no problem in paying them to continue wearing outlawed fashions.[39] Moreover, the responsibility of their enforcement kept changing office.[40] Only under Lorenzo de' Medici did their administration firmly pass into the hands of the law keepers (*conservatori delle leggi*), who also judged the misconduct of public officials.[41]

And yet, even if hardly effective, bans on head accessories existed. Lorenzo prohibited women from wearing all sorts of pearls and metal bands. He only tolerated seeing one pendant dangling from a woman's head.[42] I wonder if such strictness was responsible for unleashing the years of beguiling coiffures I am describing, as women conjured up a sense of luxury not through jewelry, but through the styling of hair in arresting configurations.[43] What is certain is that those norms fulfilled what preachers had requested for decades, showing that the concerns of the church and the state aligned.

In fifteenth-century Florence, after all, church and state were not hard-edged rivals but interlocking networks of people and interests.[44] Florentine magistrates collected money from church property while the clergy heavily relied on donations from laymen—who were often their relatives, as Florence's ruling families had members in both church and state. When pledging to implement fashion bans, the Law Keepers swore on the Bible and promised to expect God's punishment if they were negligent.[45] Notaries justified Lorenzo's sumptuary laws by arguing that they not only helped citizens save their hard-earned money but also discouraged accusations of infamy, a crime that fell under the moral jurisdiction of a bishop, not a city.[46] And notaries did so because the most decisive attacks against hair accouterment, a sort of blueprint for the bans Lorenzo implemented, had been laid down not by the government but by a bishop of Florence, Antonino Pierozzi.

When Lorenzo was a child, Pierozzi had been held in great esteem throughout Italy.[47] He had become popular for writing a manual for confessors on how to interrogate penitents.[48] Today it reads like a cluster of ridiculous tautologies, but back then it provided a new level of detail to the mechanics of sin. For instance, Pierozzi explained that women's attraction for hair products and accessories derived from their small-mindedness, which prevented them from trading or teaching. Only in matters of beauty could women find success.[49] Pierozzi felt compelled to explain that understanding women's limitations did not mean condoning everything they did. Their care for their appearance, "and especially hair," was repulsive since it aroused men's lust.[50] Pierozzi went so far as to tell women that showing their curls was like flashing their breasts.[51] Which was why, he concluded, even a countess who gave to charity would go to hell if she spent an inordinate amount of time doing her hair. And in hell, he felt the need to add, her head would be covered in snakes biting the very pores from which her hair had once grown.[52]

Pierozzi's convoluted reasoning—which aimed at distinguishing between natural instincts, intentions, actions, and even social standing—

presented hair care as an activity with no possibility of redemption. Caring for hair, he repeated, was motivated by pride, which he defined as externalized delusion.[53] In his opinion, the woman who curled her hair, wore wigs, or bought horn-shaped hats did not just express vanity, as previous Dominicans had stated, but committed a more dangerous transgression: she questioned God's creation.[54] And it is because of this doubt that Pierozzi demonized any form of attention to hair in more violent terms than Aquinas, who had taken it as a mere sign of luxury. (Aquinas had condoned hair care as long as it truthfully communicated a woman's status and pleased her husband——that is, as long as it did not serve her own vainglory.)[55]

Pierozzi differed from Aquinas not only in emphasis but also in focus. Aquinas never wrote about hairstyling explicitly. He limited his attack to the jewels that a woman put on her head. But in his treatise on female adornment, Pierozzi lists treatments such as crimping and bleaching on the same plane as fabulous accessories.[56] The items with which he takes issue are many, but a way to visualize them all is to look again at Simonetta's profile (plate 10), which, through Pierozzi's words, finally emerges as a brave visual archive of immoral things.

In his writings, Pierozzi shows himself to have direct knowledge of hairstyling. He was informed not only about its regulations—he participated in a papal commission that deliberated on fashion bans—but also about its processes.[57] He knew, for instance, that hair was easier to bleach if slimed with mud, a delicate operation that was not without complications.[58] He had learned about it during his many conversations with his female patrons.[59] Among them was Lucrezia Tornabuoni, Lorenzo's mother, to whom he sent a reflection on how to lead a worthy life. He exhorted her to avoid losing time in trivial things such as hairstyling, which was likely to inflate her pride, a deadly sin. And to make her remember this point, he recalled the tragic fate of Absalom, "who, because of his hair, which was long, got hung on an oak tree and was killed by his enemies."[60]

Absalom may be a fairly obscure figure today, but that was not the case in the city that worshipped his father, King David, as the embodiment of good government.[61] Absalom was David's third son. He was also the most handsome man to have ever existed. The famous writer of Arthurian romances Chrétien de Troyes compared one of his own characters, the king of Escavalon, to Absalom to make his readers immediately appreciate the former's supernatural beauty.[62] The poet Cecco Nuccoli took Absalom as so irresistible that even men could not help falling in love with him.[63] And a second poet, Dino Compagni, made fun of a third, Guido Cavalcanti, for believing that his own attractiveness not only surpassed Absalom's but was so potent that it pulled women to their windows, and even risked making them fall due to their leaning too far forward.[64]

The Bible has a wonderful way of conveying Absalom's allure: "In all Israel, there was not a man so highly praised for his handsome appearance as Absalom. From the top of his head to the sole of his foot [note the conventional form of top-down description we have discussed in the previous chapter] there was no blemish in him. Whenever he cut the hair of his head—he used to cut his hair once a year because it became too heavy for him—its weight was two hundred shekels by the royal standard."[65] The reference to weighing when speaking of weightless hair (two hundred shekels roughly correspond to five pounds) brings the description to the hyperbolic levels of ancient poetry while placing beauty on the scale of quantifiable commodities.[66] But the reference to exceptional volume is also a way to prepare the readers for Absalom's infamous death. How else could his head have been caught by a tree?

If you walk into the cathedral of Siena, you will find him there, his body suspended in midair, like a hanged man, the central locks of his enormous mane wrapped around a branch (figure 5.1a).[67] "Suspended" is how Absalom is routinely described by Tuscan preachers, even when they spend only a few words on him. Here's a most concise example, by the Dominican Ugo from Prato: "Absalom, suspended by his hair, was killed."[68] But "suspendere" also initiated a comparison with Christ, since the verb was usually reserved to describe him on the cross. *The Mirror of Human Salvation*, a popular preaching manual, made the parallel explicit right from its prologue: "Even a wicked man like Absalom may sometimes prefigure Christ. Absalom was very beautiful and hung [*suspensus*] on a tree: Christ was the fairest of the children of men and

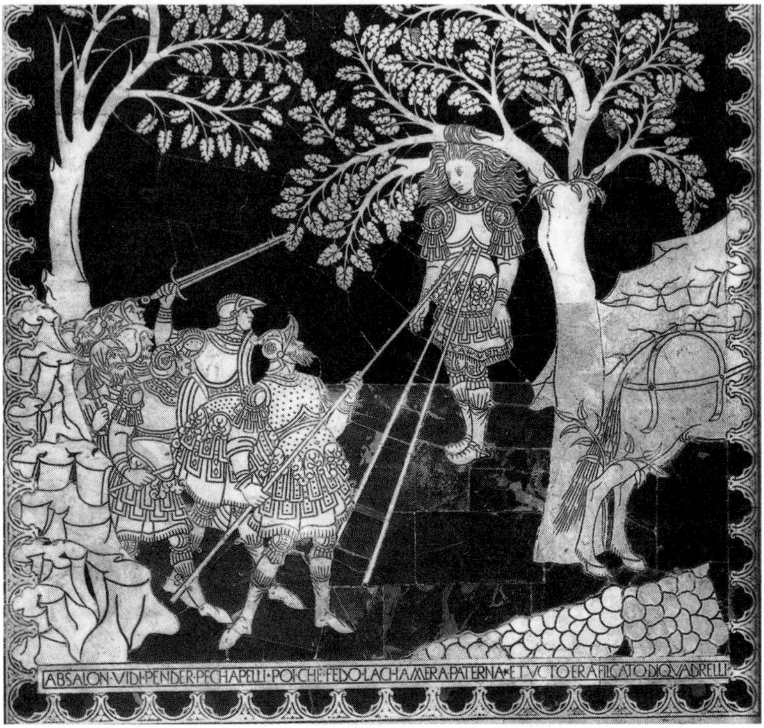

Figure 5.1a. *Death of Absalom,* after a drawing by Piero del Minella. Duomo di Siena.

died on the tree of the cross."[69] A Florentine manuscript copy of the text comes with a drawing of Absalom shown from behind, run through by a lance (figure 5.1b), which is how Florentine crucifixions also represented Christ on the cross (figure 5.1c).[70]

Church decorations and doctrinal manuscripts presented Absalom as a negative of Christ, the man who created the existential void that Christ came to fill. Absalom, however, also offered a body and a face to much more mundane warnings. So when the painter Pesellino was commissioned to illustrate his death, he relaxed any Christological association in order to depict him like a stupid kid, caught by surprise (plate 16).[71]

Here, Absalom's horse has not yet exited the frame. The knight be-

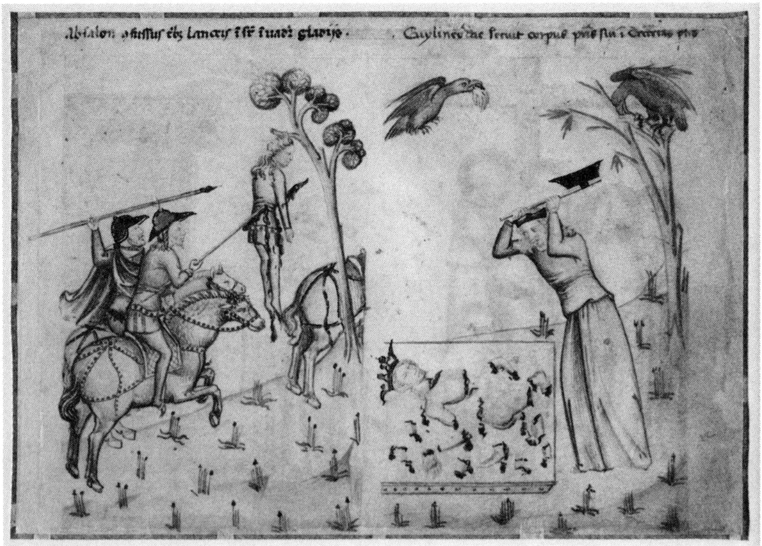

Figure 5.1b. Death of Absalom, from *Speculum Humanae Salvationis*. Fitzwilliam Museum, Cambridge. Ms. 43-1950, f. 10r.

hind him is drawing near. With his arms bent, head tilted, and legs flexed, Absalom is suspended in a pose of instability, which at the time also denoted mental sickness, as evinced by the allegory of foolishness (*stultitia*) as a king whose crown is falling from his head. This is seen in an illumination from the breviary for the French king Charles V, in which foolishness is paralleled to Absalom, the prince who did not look ahead while riding (figure 5.2).[72] The parallel was known to Pierozzi, who mentioned Absalom when mocking arrogant women for wearing crowns at public dances even if they struggled to keep them on their heads while pirouetting.[73] Some Florentines took his words to action, and scratched depictions of Absalom's face with the same twigs and knives by which they attacked any representation of the devil or Judas (plate 17).[74]

Their anger must have met Pesellino's approval, since he underscored Absalom's obtuseness by including an approaching knight in the painting. The knight's presence is less a menace than a standard against

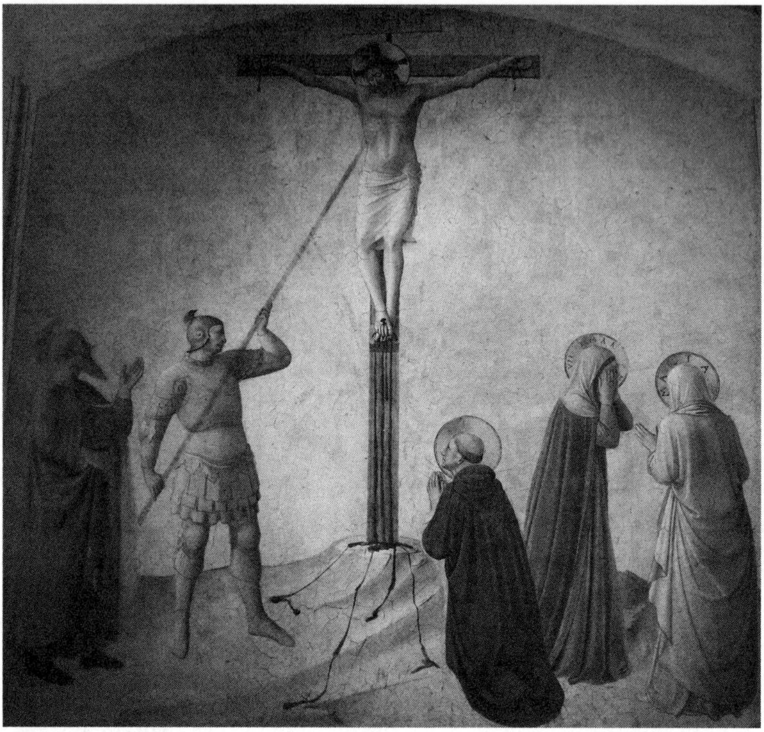

Figure 5.1c. Fra Angelico and workshop, *Crucifixion*. Cell 42, Museo di San Marco, Florence.

which to judge the prince. He is clad in armor, while Absalom is decked in fashionable velvets that speak of how he cared more about impressing people than about safety. The knight wears a helmet, while Absalom has deliberately left his at home because it would have hidden the mane from which his allure derived. And the tail of Absalom's charger hangs loosely to emphasize the forgetfulness of his master, who, unlike the knight, did not tuck the tail in a loop to keep his horse from getting caught in random branches.[75]

Pesellino's criticism becomes particularly clear when we read his painting through an episode of Pulci's *Morgante* in which the protagonist comforts a woman chained to a rock. After killing the lion who had held her prisoner, the giant Morgante asks her about her past. It turns

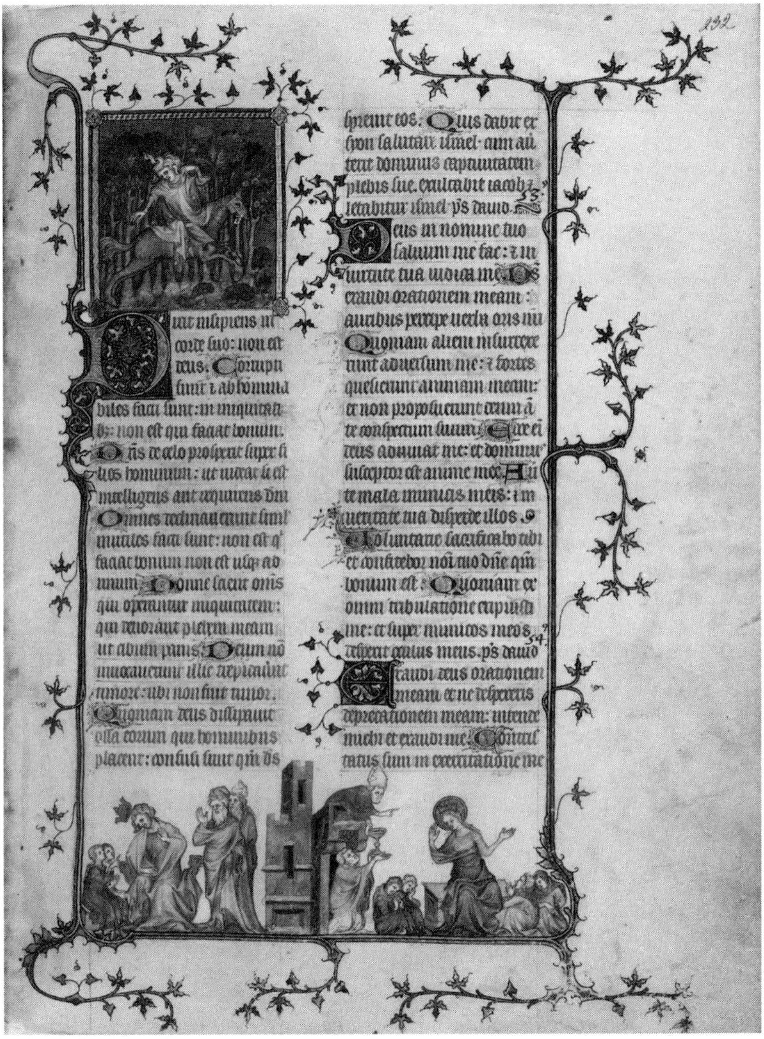

Figure 5.2. Jean Pucelle, *Absalom* in breviary of King Charles V. Ms. Latin 1052, f. 232r. Bibliothèque nationale de France, Paris.

out that Florinetta—that's her name—is a Disney princess who, on a sunny day, left her parental castle to chase the sweet song of a nightingale flying into the forest. The image, then even more than today, was one of excruciating naïveté: she followed the stream of a river, picking up flowers along the way, oblivious of leaving footprints behind as "her hair fluttered in the wind."[76]

After reading those words for the first time, I paused. I thought that the reference to hair was a nod to the traditional description of a carefree nymph about to be chased by a monster, running at full speed—which proved to be the case, by the way. Yet the detail carried another order of meaning. The princess explains, "I would have been able to escape it [the lion] if, while running, a branch didn't catch my beautiful braid, and he found me all tied up."[77] The episode is a remake of Absalom's story for a fifteenth-century audience in love with medieval romances. Pulci even cites his reference when he makes his princess admit: "My beautiful hair got caught in a thousand branches and you must imagine it all ragged after being dragged across woods and ravines and wolves and snakes. Like Absalom's, it [my hair] was unlucky."[78]

Pulci dramatizes hair's intrinsic danger. It does not matter what preacher he and his circle of friends listened to; they all were likely to have run into descriptions that reduced hair to a hazard.[79] And it does not even matter if they did not take those warnings seriously, because all around Florence, stories and images presented hair as the site at which to exert one's dominance. On an altarpiece, a headsman turned the hair of Saint John the Baptist into a shackle to keep his neck down (plate 18).[80] In many other paintings, soldiers violently pulled women by their hair (plate 19). On the baptistery could be found sculptures of boys engaged in games of domination, tugging each other's locks (plate 20).[81] Botticelli painted a version of the gesture in his *Pallas and the Centaur* (figure 5.3), an allegory on how wisdom can control libido by holding the one bodily appendage that characterizes those who fall prey to their instincts.

Hair-pulling is a fixture of classical imagery—many sarcophagi show Roman soldiers holding prisoners by their hair, and coins make use of the gesture to identify the powerful—but I do not want to focus on Flo-

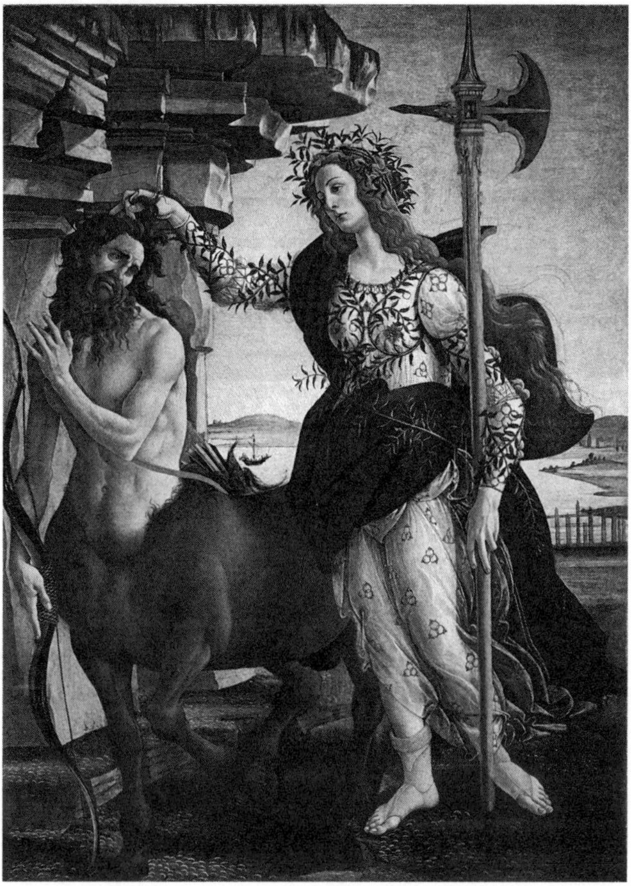

Figure 5.3. Sandro Botticelli, *Pallas and the Centaur.* Gallerie degli Uffizi, Florence.

rentines' adaptation of models from the past. What matters to me is that those gestures made sense in their present, as many voices gave them currency and laws made them real.[82] The statutes of Florence prohibited anyone from pulling a citizen's hair, since the offense was considered equivalent to a punch on the nose or a kick in the teeth, both of which attracted fines of up to fifty lire if they caused a wound, or twenty-five if the violence was bloodless.[83]

Hair, especially loose and voluminous hair, was taken to be a site of violence: the visual trap that women set for defenseless passersby, the grip that could seize anyone's hair at any time.[84] This is why nuns had it cropped. Its cutting was part of a ritual of humility and submissiveness that marked a novice's acceptance of the withdrawal of conventual life.[85] Even more than the profession of solemn vows, the clipping of her hair stood for a woman's entering a convent, as it clearly communicated her renunciation of the very possibility of sensuality.[86] It stood for a rejection of procreation too, since, as we have seen, families advertised their daughters' fecundity through their blooming hair, which attracted the male gaze like bees. In stark opposition, nuns covered their heads with veils that made fluttering eyes fly past. The decorous and controllable mane of fabric served not just as symbolic dispossession of female treachery, but as its prevention.[87]

Friars and priests trimmed their heads too. A haircut called a "tonsure," with a shaven patch at the top of the head, acted as a remedy to the risk that religious authorities saw in hair.[88] Pope Gregory the Great wrote that "the shaving of the head . . . is the cutting of all superfluous thoughts from the mind"—thus equalling tonsure to humility and self-restraint.[89] While tonsure had been a clerical requirement since medieval times, its implementation had been fairly inconsistent.[90] In the fifteenth century, the Florentine papal secretary Poggio Bracciolini saw it as a ritual emptied of any meaning. While decrying priesthood as exploitation of privileges rather than abandonment to a life of faith, he wrote that "the priestly tonsure cuts away not only hair but conscience and virtue."[91] Priests thought that by receiving a tonsure they were gaining virtue, whereas Bracciolini showed that the opposite was often the case, and that once that mark of distinction was in place, it served as a smokescreen for all sorts of wrongdoing.

It is in response to such criticism that Pierozzi made tonsure compulsory for every cleric of his bishopric:[92] "Since it is proper that clerics differ from secular people both in the tonsure and in their habit, and as they need to flee any vanity (which we would like to eradicate given that some bad practices happened in that direction), we order that no cleric can wear his hair to his shoulders [that is, a hairstyle known as *zazzera*], but needs to cut his hair in a bowl, even between his ears. And above, he cut an inner circle, not so small that it cannot be seen, but not too large,

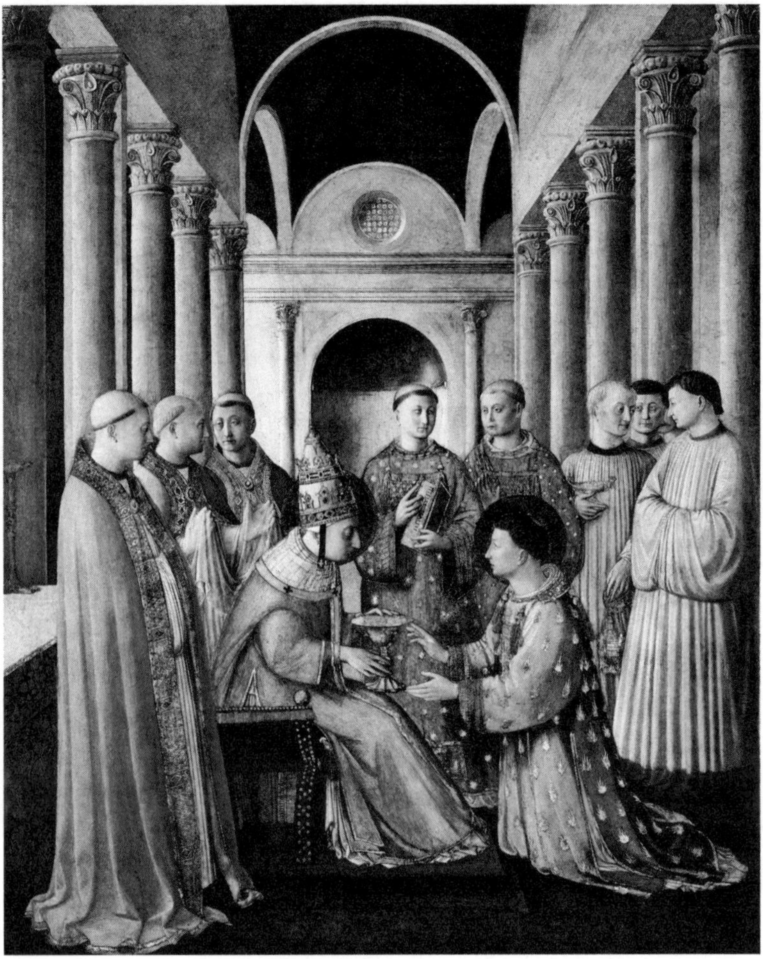

Figure 5.4. Fra Angelico, *Ordination of Saint Lawrence.* Capella Niccolina, Vatican City.

so that he is not mistaken for a monk."[93] I read this deliberation from a set of constitutions that Pierozzi had nailed to the doors of Florence's cathedral, the city's moral billboard.[94]

Today we may be indifferent to the size of tonsures that Pierozzi mentioned, but to get a sense of their diversity, it suffices to consider Fra Angelico's *Ordination of Saint Lawrence*, a fresco he painted in the Vatican palace (figure 5.4). In it, Saint Lawrence's small patch reminded on-

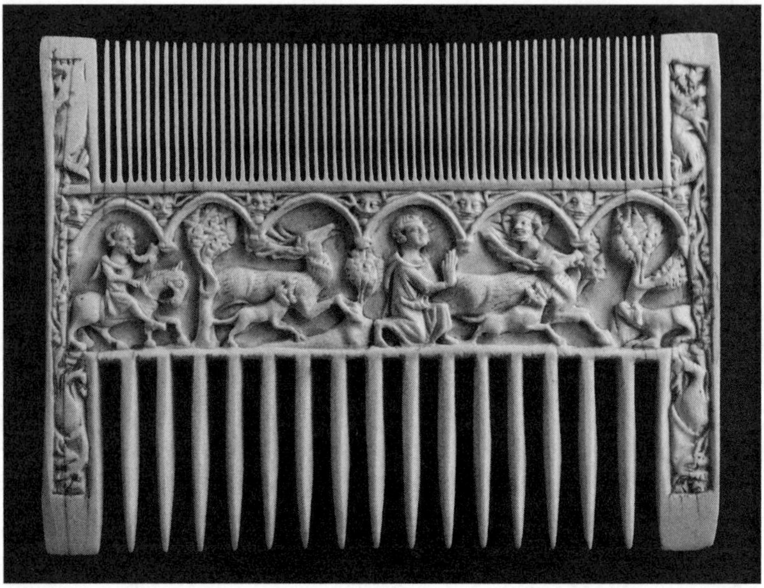

Figure 5.5. Comb with depiction of the legend of Saint Eustache. Museo Civico d'Arte Antica, Palazzo Madama, Turin.

lookers, among whom we can probably count both Poggio and Pierozzi, that he was a young and inexperienced deacon, not one of the venerable advisers to the pope, who stand tall all around with their basically shaved heads edged by thin ribbons of hair.[95]

By redefining tonsure as an antidote to pride, Pierozzi confirmed hair as a prime site for the construction of morality. As a bishop, he knew he had to comb his head before celebrating the mass, collecting loose hair with a comb and separating every strand. The liturgical manual of the time considered the activity necessary for predisposing the bishop's mind to the celebration, freeing it of the superfluous thoughts of which hair was the direct offshoot.[96] A comb bearing a depiction of the story of Saint Eustache (figure 5.5) may have well served this purpose, as the saint, a valiant knight with unshakeable faith, was taken as an inspiration for priests, who by celebrating the mass contributed to fighting the spiritual war on behalf of the Church.[97] But a liturgical comb was one of the many objects that identified hair as the very space for the suppression of impulses. The cautionary tales of Absalom, the story of the Magdalene, and the countless sermons of preachers like Giordano from Pisa made it clear to the Florentines that hair was the filthy ground of vices. They had to act on it resolutely because, as Pierozzi stressed, hair developed social agency and could initiate things independently of its owners.[98] It assailed people, it poisoned their brains, it could even bring wealthy cities to the brink of collapse. And it was precisely in such a wealthy city that Botticelli began his career by painting hair with a level of care, and a carelessness for what moralists said, that had never been encountered before.

SIX Achonciare

Here we are: in the middle of the book. And now that I have laid down some of the most widespread ideas about hair in the two decades this volume covers, I would like to return to their start, 1469. This is the year in which a twenty-year-old Lorenzo de' Medici got married. It is also the year of his rise to power following his father's death. And this sea change may be the reason why the six councillors presiding over the Mercanzia, the commercial court of Florence, found themselves unsure about what to do regarding an artistic commission that, surprisingly, launched the career of Sandro Botticelli.[1]

Everything had been decided: the contract signed, a payment already made. The councillors just had to wait for the panels to be delivered.[2] The previous summer, they had recruited another painter, Piero Pollaiuolo, to paint the seven virtues, each as large as an altarpiece, for the meeting hall of their headquarters, a palace overlooking Florence's main square.[3] Hanging over their heads, those crowned allegories would inspire noble values in the six deliberating on mercantile litigations, frauds, and bankruptcies. With their countenance, they would also placate the anger, resentment, and pettiness—in other words, the vices—that clung to business disputes as dirt stuck to money.

After the presentation of the first, central panel—a queen seated on a throne, holding a baby suckling at her breast and the forever-burning heart of charity (figure 6.1)—the six could not agree on whether to stick

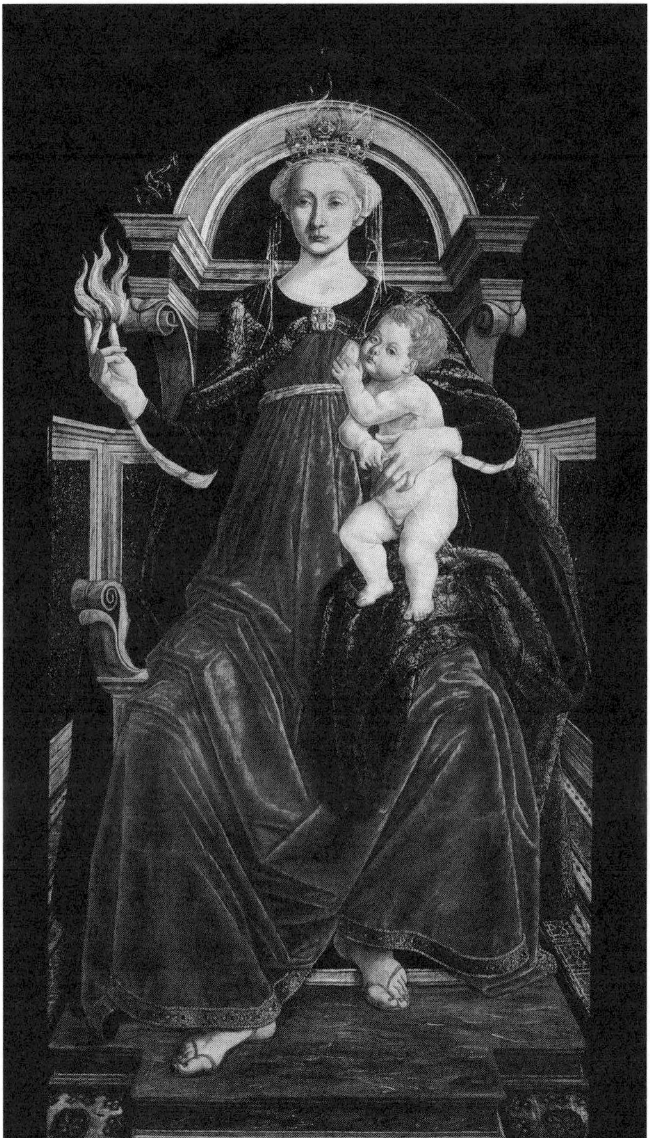

Figure 6.1. Piero del Pollaiuolo, *Charity*. Gallerie degli Uffizi, Florence.

with Piero or involve other artists. Many painters had set their eyes on the commission. Verrocchio, then on the Mercanzia's roster for an expensive bronze sculpture to be installed somewhere else, submitted a drawing.[4] But after examining his sketch and hearing the case of Piero and his older brother Antonio, who acted as his underwriter, the six renewed the contract for the full series to its original appointee. They expected Piero to deliver the remaining panels every three months, two at a time.

Writing down those arrangements, however, did not seem to have dispelled a certain uneasiness—which must have precipitated something, even if it is difficult to know what that was, since Botticelli received payment four months later for an allegory of Fortitude (plate 22). Did Piero miss a deadline and the six did not concede him an extension for fear that it would lose them the community's respect? Did any of the conditions change, given that new councillors were elected to the Mercanzia every three months, as was customary in Florentine magistracies? Did the recent loss of Lorenzo de' Medici's father cause a destabilization of political balance that was also felt in the artistic arena?[5] In other words, was there a breach of contract? Did Piero fail to protect himself adequately in a city where competition was fierce? It is hard to say. We only know that Piero hurried to supply two more virtues (Temperance and Faith) before Botticelli was paid in full. I also deduce that Piero must have raised his voice, as did his brother and the people who sided with them, since shortly after, the painters' guild amended its statutes to protect its members from future violations.[6]

While the scar of the scandal has faded today, its memory still shapes the way visitors encounter Botticelli's *Fortitude* in the Uffizi, where it hangs next to Pollaiuolo's virtues like a celebrity visiting her common relatives. And yet, what is said about the painting is little more than a retelling of the competition. Perhaps this is so because the documents mentioning the painting say nothing else, and Botticelli's panel has become beautiful in the somewhat generic manner that most of the Italian Madonnas of the fifteenth century have become beautiful: works in which the figure of the Virgin hardly varies, since it serves to illustrate the same theological points about advocacy and majesty—which may be why art historians therefore focus on craft. In *Fortitude*, his first public work, Botticelli records the variations of the paneled throne, the sunken folds, and the many lighting effects (the striped gloss of the scaled forearm guards, the pupil-like shine of the pearls). That level of detail presented him as a hand capable of deceiving the eye into thinking it was looking not at brushwork but at a blushing cheek or a gilded armrest. And yet, by comparing this painting to the virtues that followed, the ones into which Piero threw all of himself to retain the commission, it is clear that what stood out in Botticelli's *Fortitude* was not its illusionistic quality or the opulence of its details, but its coiffure. Fortitude's hair represented the true element of change.

Contrary to Piero's first virtues (Charity, Temperance, and Faith, all modestly veiled), Fortitude sports a head in which every inch offers a surprise. Its elaborate styling must have been all the more striking given that Fortitude had been traditionally shown as a severe, stout woman, clad in a Herculean lion skin or carrying a column. (One example, a relief by Giovanni Fetti, is still just outside the Mercanzia, on the left, attached to the Loggia dei Priori, now known as the Loggia dei Lanzi.)[7] In contrast, Botticelli turned Fortitude into a princess. He placed on her a winged diadem which reminded coin collectors of the helmet worn by the personification of Rome on the back of Roman denarii.[8] Around Fortitude's forehead he nested three massive pearls that must have struck the affluent, law-abiding men who frequented the Mercanzia as fabulous, since the statutes of the time banned solitary gems and restricted their usage.[9] It was only by tucking her two braids into her belt that Botticelli alluded to the princess's martial training. Soldiers fastened anything loose, to avoid it getting caught while they were fighting. Absalom's end (plate 16) was in everyone's mind.

Reading meaning into hairstyles as I do may seem exaggerated to those who do not see hair as giving away a person's nature and character. Botticelli, they may point out, shows here that he cared about hair as he cared about the rest of the painting. And to those people I reply: *This is the point*. In Botticelli's hands, hair becomes a field which deserves the plastic inventiveness that until then had been reserved for thrones and armor. Nothing similar had been seen before in a painting, not even in the Madonnas by Filippo Lippi (figure 6.2), the person who taught Botticelli to approach heads as sites of artistic prowess. Botticelli turned Lippi's pleated, pearl-studded veils into swellings of hair. His Fortitude must have caused a strong impression—particularly in Piero, since all of Piero's later virtues have hair arrangements that match that of Botticelli.

Take Prudence, whose locks, centrally parted, become progressively longer and, after a tidal élan, gather in two braids that join in an ample fold behind her neck (figure 6.3). Their roots are fastened by a transparent veil which, draped over her head, hangs between two golden brooches. To make sure that no one overlooked her hairstyle, Piero reproduced it in the mirror, one of the traditional attributes of Prudence, since we are prudent when we evaluate our environs before taking any decision (plate 9).[10] Held like a lollipop, Prudence's mirror appears less like a tool for circumspection than like a device to reveal Botticelli's intention. By cropping the bust of Prudence and framing it in an inky blue sky, Pollaiuolo exposes the mundanity of Botticelli's operation, which reduced godlike virtue to the level of a bourgeois bride (plate 7).[11]

Prudence casts a suspicious, sideways glance at the mirror, initiating a loop of reflections in which hair is present regardless of where we look, as if Piero were here borrowing not from a painting but from a sculpture (such as those in figures 2.6 and 2.7), in which front and side are one.[12] This idea should probably be credited not to Piero but to his more experienced brother Antonio, who came to Piero's rescue after Botticelli's intrusion. Antonio is often said to have painted *Prudence* because of its graphic exactness, which he would have achieved by priming the panel in gesso, as Botticelli also did with his own panels, since a white base brings out every stroke laid on it. Look at the shimmering gauze of Prudence's tunic and those brackets, where the marble veins intersect with the sculpted ridges (figure 6.3). Or look at the dotted scales of the serpent, which create white geometrical patterns like those on the Anatolian carpet beneath. Twisted, down to the end of its tail, the snake mimics and foregrounds the contortions of Prudence's hairstyle. The parallel is not causal; it makes an observer reflect on braids as the hideout of demons. By veiling Prudence's head, Antonio marks Fortitude's

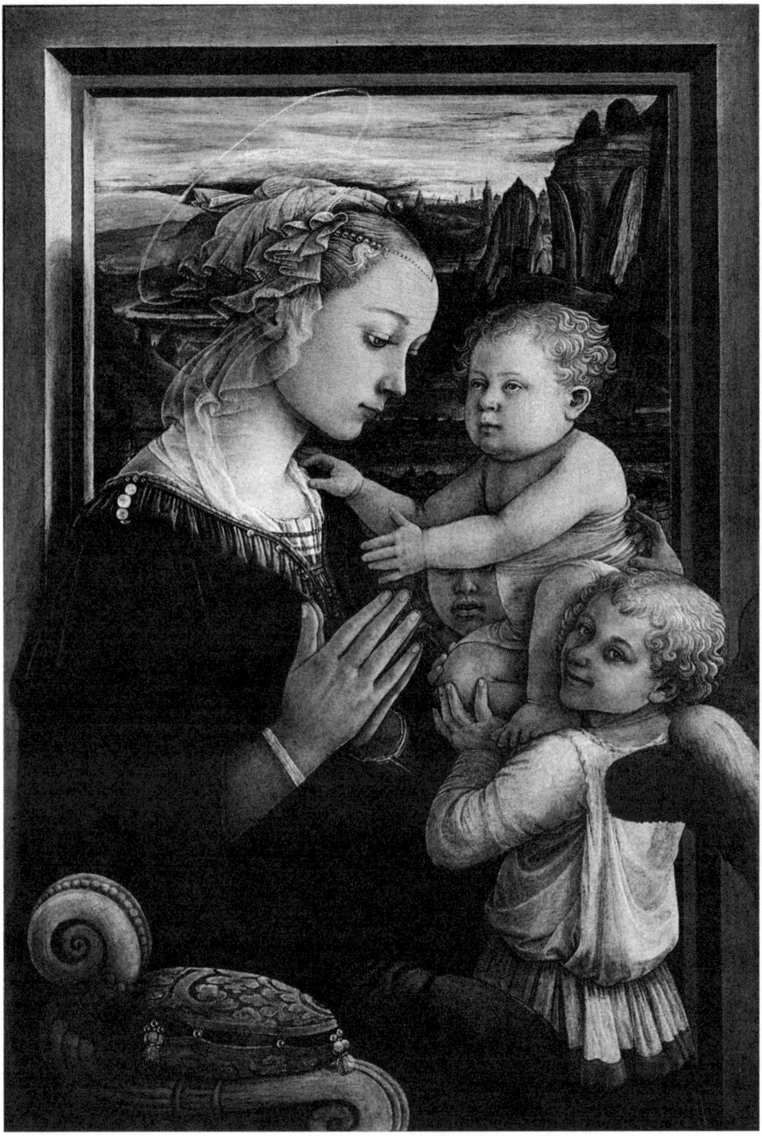

Figure 6.2. Filippo Lippi, *Madonna and Child with Two Angels*. Gallerie degli Uffizi, Florence.

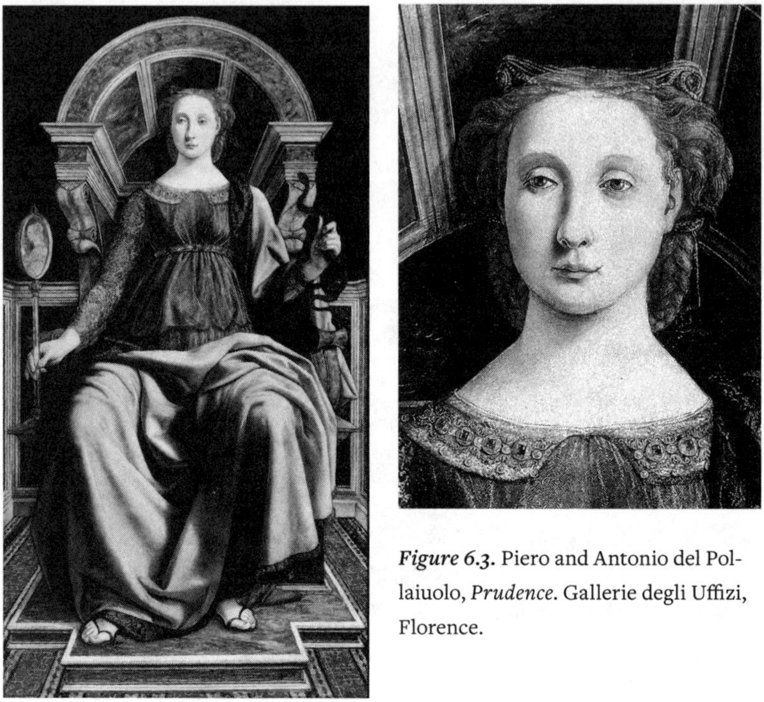

Figure 6.3. Piero and Antonio del Pollaiuolo, *Prudence*. Gallerie degli Uffizi, Florence.

bare hair like some sort of forbidden skin, casting doubts on Botticelli's care for respectability. In a way, the snake is also a mirror—or, better, both mirror and snake are prefigurations of possible future selves: the mirror visualizes a proper spouse worthy of memorialization, while the snake stands for a lethal end.[13] Prudence presents them both, as if the viewer were Hercules at the crossroads, choosing between virtue and Medusa.[14] By slightly turning her cheek toward her right, it is clear which path she encourages the viewer to take.

If the Pollaiuolo brothers and Botticelli turned headgear into a site of competition, it is because they lived in a city where people looked at each other's heads for clues about their identity. It wasn't just a matter of recognizing the pope by his tiara, doctors by tight-fitting caps, and knights, whose faces regularly disappeared under visors, by the crests on their helmets; headgear conveyed nuanced information about moral inclinations.[15] Such attention was thematized in Prudentius's *Psychomachia*, an allegorical poem on the battle between virtues and vices in which all the fighters are identified uniquely by their hairdos. Thrift covers her hair with a veil, Faith leaves it untrimmed, Discord puts olive branches on her head to pass as a virtue, and Pride coils her braids around a mold that she fixes to her head so that "there might be a lofty and more imposing peak above her haughty brows."[16] Short, adventurous, and edifying, Prudentius's poem was much read and discussed in Florence.[17] It could well have persuaded Botticelli and the Pollaiuolo brothers that virtues ought to be identified first and foremost through their hairstyles.

Botticelli hardly needed any encouragement, though, given the sense of identification that people developed with their headgear. The politician Franco Sacchetti ridiculed it in a story of a Florentine knight who is challenged in a duel by a German because they both have a relief of a rampant bear on the crests of their helmets.[18] The coincidence is not just a nuisance; the law in Florence required noblemen to carry devices, and disciplined their shapes and displays.[19] So Sacchetti's idea of a rivalry of the crests was a stab at the emptiness he saw in chivalric symbols, which only a few delusional aristocratic families were trying to keep alive in a world increasingly shaped by the standardizations and commodifications of mercantilism, insignia included.[20] Sacchetti's sarcasm is particularly biting when he describes the Florentine as a coward on the verge of a panic attack. The coward does all he can to avoid the fight, including having the bear on his helmet retouched to become a baboon. The animal transformation is a stroke of comedic genius, since monkeys were seen as the animals that failed to imitate humans.[21] To put a baboon on your helm—and, more importantly, to identify with it—was a way to present oneself as a semihuman. The act of self-sabotage speaks volumes not only about the Florentine's dullness, but also of the cunning of the artist who tweaks the crest.[22]

Botticelli and the Pollaiuolo brothers, as well as Leonardo and Verrocchio, all crafted devices and armor.[23] One of Piero's two documented commissions prior to the Mercanzia virtues was for the trappings of a knight and his pages for a joust in honor of Lorenzo de' Medici.[24] Much more expensive than paintings, such elaborate garb fulfilled fantasies of

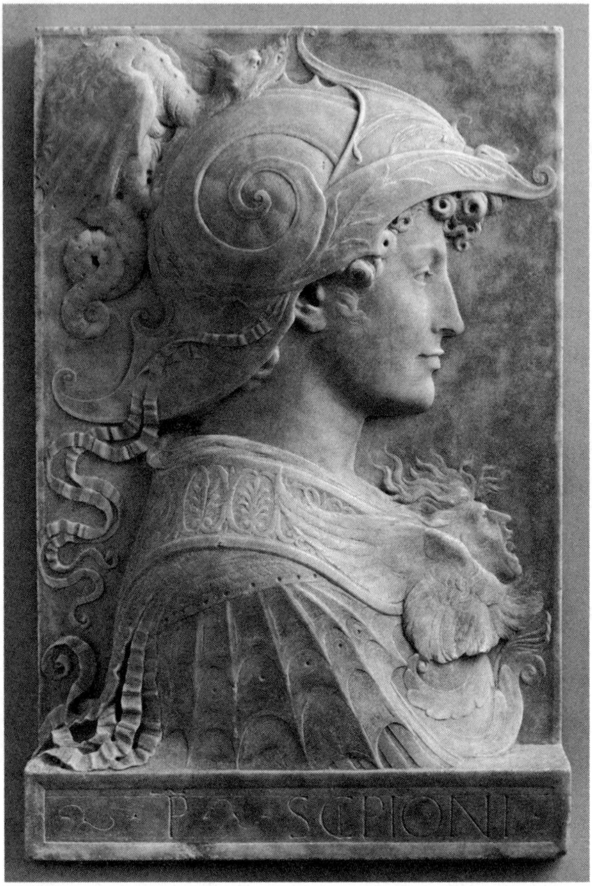

Figure 6.4. Andrea del Verrocchio(?), *Scipio*. Musée du Louvre, Paris.

aristocratic distinction while fueling ideas of military glamor that lured generations of men to take up arms, only to find that the cuirasses actually worn on the battlefield had little in common with the fancy arms and armor they had seen before leaving home.[25] So Florence was flooded by images of outlandish knights (figure 6.4), whose minutely chiseled sallets paired reptiles with birds, flowers, and shells, making full use of heraldic symbols.[26] The accumulation of insignia validates Sacchetti's doubt: what could possibly be the value of those symbols in an age of di-

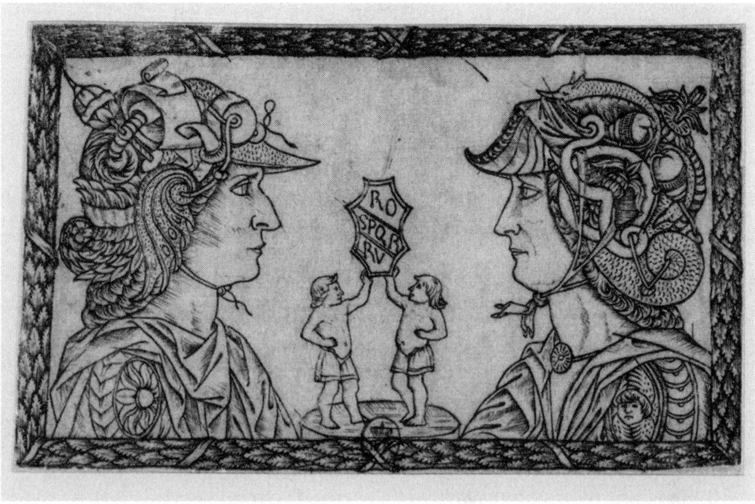

Figure 6.5. Print depicting the busts of two warriors. Bibliothèque nationale de France, Paris.

minished chivalric possibilities?[27] And so did their selection and shapes, which reveal how readily those helmets attended to the formal vocabulary of hairstyling. A print of two knights, perhaps Romulus and Remus (figure 6.5), displays dazzlingly complicated helms that, through torsions, rolls, and bundles, collapse the idea that these are protective hats into a collage of forms. Even the heraldic animals lose their facial features and stretch their anatomies to become little more than spirals, strings, and waves—that is, the forms we regularly encounter in the hairstyles of female portraits and Madonnas (see figure 6.2).[28] Their relatedness emerges particularly clearly in one of Matteo di Giovanni's depictions of the massacre of the innocents (plates 29 and 30).[29] There, the central crests of soldiers' helmets mimic the parting of women's hair; their wings and protruding shells resemble the tousled mops that escape the veils women wound around their heads and often pinned to their foreheads, so as to appear like the pointy vizors of their aggressors. Besides illustrating a biblical episode, this painting reflects on the connections between military prowess and urban refinement—perhaps because, far from being in opposition, they were both effects of a culture pivoted on violence.[30] The bishop of Florence, Antonino Pierozzi, stressed the similarity between male sallets and female hairstyles. He called the latter "the armors of the devil," thus imparting a specific order between the two, as if women got dolled up to bring conflict into the placid space of men's city.[31] But perhaps his remark does not attach so much importance to questions of origin—about which of the two came first—and should instead be read as a comment on the violence of artistry.[32] In other words, Pierozzi here may be speaking of how the visually arresting can control bodies, and of how any product of human labor—either helmets or hairstyles—should be recognized as a matter of politics, since only power develops the framework that not only regulates its existence but legitimizes it.

This is not to say that warfare is enough to explain the choices made by Botticelli and the Pollaiuolo brothers. Consider *Justice*, whose short turban presses against the top of her throne, chromatically engaging with its surroundings as the veins of the marbled panels return in the streaks of gold and blue of the fabric wrung around it (plate 23). In a way, her headgear searches for an integration with its surroundings rather than standing silhouetted against them. This sense of connection is confirmed by her turban, which is shaped like an architectural element. More precisely, it is painted to resemble an abacus, the slab that joins a capital to the architrave. Piero even went so far as using a type of brooch that women placed on top of their head (plates 3, 7, and 10) to simulate the *flos abaci*, the sculpted flower that marks the top of capitals.[33] Florentines were well familiar with these architectural decorations, since the pilasters of their much-admired baptistery, the building that acted as the fulcrum of civic life, had them at the top of their capitals (plate 24). Piero studied capitals attentively, and one of them is employed as a freestanding structure in a painting attributed to him which today is in the Jacquemart-André Museum in Paris (plate 25).[34]

The realization of a connection between Florentine architecture and hairstyles transforms one's experience of Pollaiuolo's hairstyles. Their depiction no longer seems to emanate from a desire to astound or visualize a person's identity. Rather, it points at a sort of hermeneutic—

that is to say, a mode of figuration that hurries its viewers to regard hairstyles as signs pointing elsewhere, so that they are not just bodily appendages but bridges that cross over streams of knowledge and lead to the unexpected.

This tension toward architecture would have been easily caught, since the human body, and in particular the head, was routinely mapped on columns. Vitruvius, author of the only treatise on architecture that has survived from ancient times, thought that the Greeks had shaped their capitals after their well-coiffed women. "On the right and on the left of the capital," he writes, "the Ionians placed volutes that looked like hanging hair curls. They also decorated the front with inward-looking volutes and festoons so as to simulate coiffures."[35] This passage made the painter and architect Francesco di Giorgio Martini reflect on how the two could possibly overlap. He tried to illustrate their relationship a few times (as in figure 6.6), taking architectural moldings as somewhat representative of facial features, and producing drawings that resonate with the solutions of the Pollaiuolo brothers.[36] And when the eldest brother, Antonio, draped over Prudence a veil whose spiraling around two golden brooches mimicked the saggy hammocklike band between the volutes of Ionic capitals, his choice may have been prompted by an engagement with Vitruvius.

Both Martini and Antonio Pollaiuolo were, after all, familiar with Leon Battista Alberti's *De re aedificatoria*, a treatise that also discussed architectural elements by way of hairdressing.[37] "In Tuscany," Alberti wrote, "we call *nastro* a tiny ribbon that young ladies wrap around their heads to fasten their hair. For this reason, let me call *nastro* the ring-shaped band which can be found at the end of the column."[38] In suggesting a term for what specialists today call "astragal," Alberti revealed his ambitious plan to produce a new, precise vocabulary for architecture.[39] This lexicon could not be extracted from Vitruvius's treatise, which was notoriously difficult to understand. Some of the Latin terms Vitruvius employed were, as they still are, unique—no other Latin text documents them. Also, the manuscripts of Vitruvius that Alberti accessed were so corrupted—parts were missing, words were unintelligible—that he had to admit that "it is almost as if he wrote nothing."[40] But even if he was

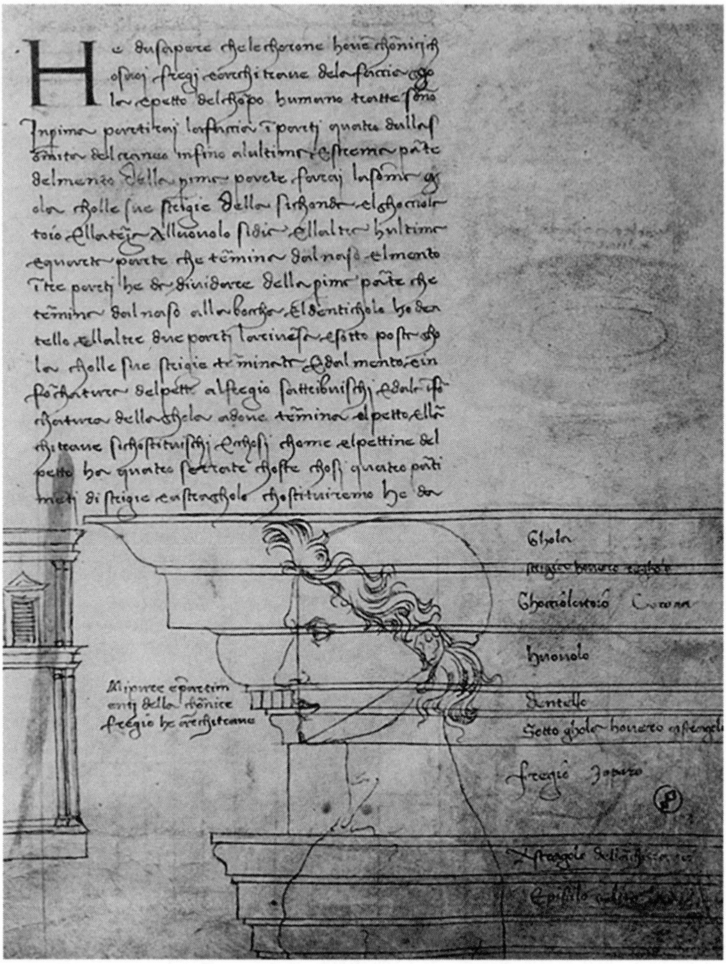

Figure 6.6. Francesco di Giorgio, *Entablature on the Human Form* (detail). Ms. Saluzzo 148, f. 21v. Biblioteca Reale, Turin.

struggling with Vitruvius's words, Alberti did not discount his association of building and hairstyles.

I sometimes wonder whether there were reasons beyond reverence that prevented Alberti from abandoning Vitruvius's coupling. The more I think about the ways in which Alberti and other Florentines might have approached it back then, the less I see any alternative, since in the vernacular that fifteenth-century Florentines spoke, both architecture and hair were heard of as effects of "*achonciare*."

Today the Italian verb *acconciare* denotes the styling of one's hair, but such a narrow meaning has taken over only in recent times. When Pollaiuolo painted his virtues, the semantic range of the term was as loose as its spelling, since it was used in contracts and entry books to speak of fitting an object to a site: for example, providing a crucifix with hooks so that it could be lifted by ropes and hung in a church.[41] The term also spoke of the need to improve the appearance of something, like retouching a coat of paint that was flaking, burnishing a metal cross that lacked luster, or removing the hair from animal skin to produce smooth leather goods.[42] The word "achonciare" was used to speak of anything in need of repair, from a wound in need of healing to handwriting in need of being kept legible. Yet, most commonly, the term denoted architectural work, such as the refitting of a room.

A note from Verrocchio's workshop written after the master's death complains to the Medici about their not having paid for the "achonciatura" of some busts over the doorframes in their palace.[43] The use of the term conveys the precision of a job done well. It may have implied the application of "pietre conce," blocks of polished stone that were reserved for the revetment of walls rather than the filling of them.[44] "Achonciare," in other words, did not simply imply the notion of bringing a room back to order after a state of disarray. It also connoted the improvement required to bring the reality of a building closer to its ideal state.

That such an ideal state was understood as a return rather than a step forward is why Boccaccio employed the verb "acionciare" when describing the styling of women's hair.[45] In his view, women's labors pulled them out of their "bestial confusion" and toward an original pleasantness that only the action of "acionciare" could restore.[46] And the verb returns in a manual about female manners by the Florentine Francesco da Barberino, who encouraged women to "acconciare" themselves despite their nature, as if the labor of being a woman was to maintain an appearance that would be inexorably dragged down by time and physiological failings.[47] So the term "achonciare," which was never employed for men's hair, placed women and buildings on the same plane. It contributed to defining them as natural prey to the destruction of time, from which they could be saved by iterative work that restored their ideal—that is, their usual—state.

And it is at this level of tight linkages—where the ideal is taken as a return, where construction is seen as restoration—that the term "achonciare" proves useful to interpret the decisions of both Botticelli and the Pollaiuolo brothers. They all registered its semantic slippages when envisioning their respective headgear. Botticelli gave his Fortitude (plate 22) the braids of a caryatid (figure 6.7), a fitting architectural reference to convey the unshakability of virtues.[48] And the Pollaiuolo brothers went a step further by shaping coiffures in response to their descriptions in renowned architectural treatises. We could take it even a step further, as the verb "achonciare" identifies the very goal of all three painters: what they ought to do to win the commission.

With *Fortitude*, Botticelli offered an improvement on Piero's *Charity*, which he took as a flawed model. In reflecting on how to correct it, Botticelli added lavish marble panels, decorative moldings, and an arresting hairstyle—all operations denoted by "achonciare"—to bring the virtues to a new standard of artistry, thus restoring the series to the Mercanzia councilors' expectations. But when the Pollaiuolo brothers tried to win the commission back, they also cast Botticelli's panel as inadequate, and presented restorative panels. They learned from Botticelli's styling of Fortitude's head—an achonciatura—that hair offered the opportunity to craft many correspondences, and they took advantage of this versatility to make references to orthodox concepts. Interestingly, by covering their female allegories' heads with veils and turbans, they presented all of their innovations as a return to how moral virtues ought to dress—that is, achonciare. And by engaging with treatises that found a shared origin of hairstyles and architecture, they presented their new paintings as if they had emerged from a foundational past that could offer no wrong.

The deep-seated connections between hair and stone stuck with Botticelli. Take another look at the Frankfurt portrait of Simonetta Vespucci (plate 10). The pearl-studded braids edging the plunging neckline

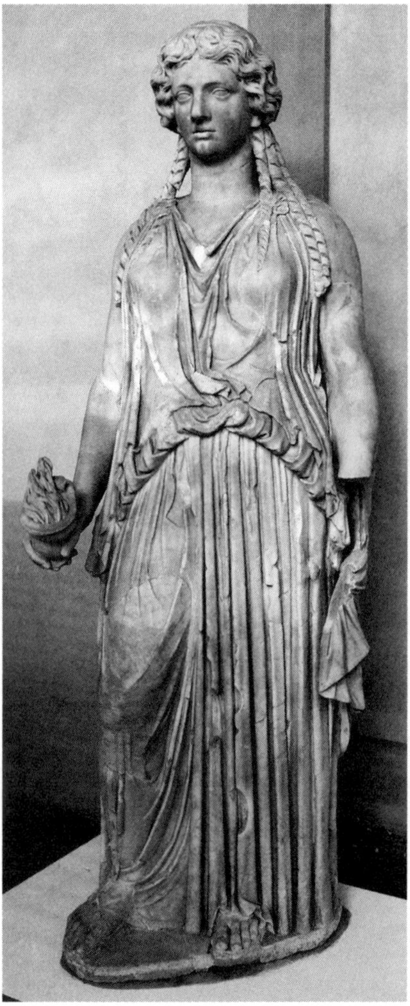

Figure 6.7. Roman caryatid, with integrations. Villa Corsini a Castello, Florence.

of her tunic resemble the moldings of the door frame that the architect Benedetto da Maiano designed for the Hall of the Lilies in Florence's governmental palace (figure 6.8a).[49] It was an important room used by top governmental officials as well as for diplomatic receptions.[50] Botticelli sketched the decoration—two parallel bands, twisted around

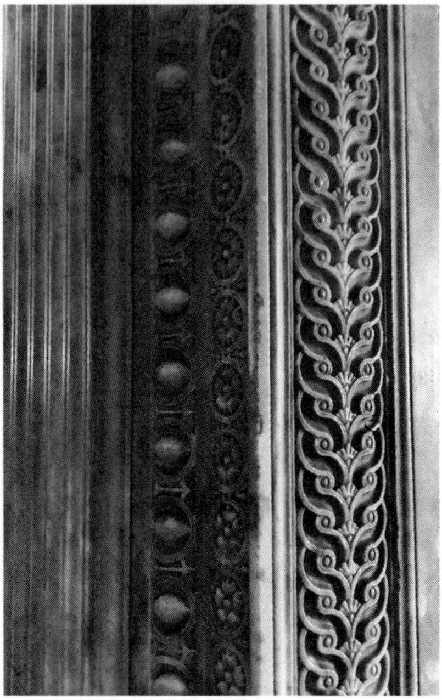

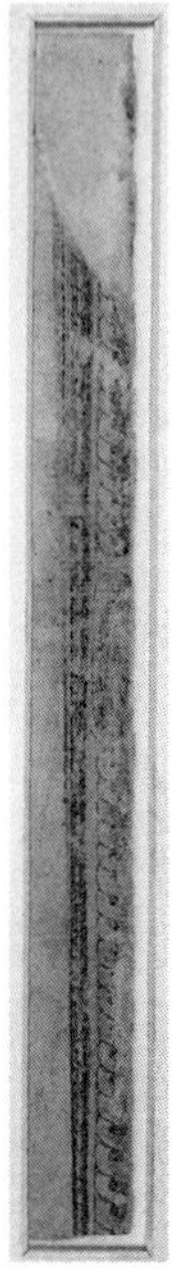

Figure 6.8a. Left, Benedetto da Maiano, portal of the Hall of Lilies. Palazzo Vecchio, Florence.

Figure 6.8b. Right, Sandro Botticelli, decorative border. British Museum, London.

eyelets—on a piece of paper (figure 6.8b). He was well aware of their architectural value, as he repeated them in framing the gallery of the popes that he frescoed in Rome's Sistine Chapel.[51]

Yet the question is no longer why Botticelli and the Pollaiuolo brothers felt the need to shape hairstyles after architectural elements, but what reasoning permitted such a possibility in the first place. I have suggested that fifteenth-century language enabled, even dictated, such a coupling. I have also proposed that these artists engaged with history—that is, they thought female hairstyling offered some answers to questions about the origins of architectural forms. But to believe the artists viewed hair in this way means to believe in the authoritative force of texts, as if the artists could do nothing other than illustrate passages from them; and I am not sure that hair metamorphosed into architecture simply because a few respected voices from the past coupled them. If artists saw a kernel of truth in the pairing, it is because it was sustained by another truth which they could see for themselves. And this truth encouraged the dissimulation and contamination of fields. It did not rest on the acceptance of a hierarchy among the arts—that architecture and armor making necessarily came before hairstyling, or vice versa. It shattered the belief in any dependence to make the point that the domestic, the feminine, and the supple were not necessarily following the public, the masculine, and the erect.[52] On the contrary, this truth, produced by metaphors, gave hairstyling an epistemological role, as the next chapter will show.

SEVEN *Never Just Itself*

"It behaves like hair." This is what hit Leonardo while observing a stream of water flowing around a pole. He had stuck the rod into the riverbed to see what type of waves its presence in the water would produce: what height their crests would reach, how deeply their troughs would sink.[1] He sketched what he saw, and scribbled his reflections next to a drawing (figure 7.1): "Consider the movement of the surface of water, which has two motions, like hair: one conforms to the weight of the mane, the others to the curvature of each strand. Likewise, water has its eddying movements, one part of which follows the principal current, the other the reflecting and reversing motions."[2]

I would like to know more about the origins of the simile; what made Leonardo think of hair in the first place? All I find in the literature are remarks on Leonardo's ongoing interest in water—an element on which he built a career, since he was regularly asked to plan dams, design canals, and express opinions about the management of rivers. This leaves his reference to hair in describing waves unexplained. Scholars present hair as an unexpected element in the equation, the one that attests to Leonardo's unparalleled creativity and changes the perception of water, as water is certainly what matters here. Even if you pick one of the Latin grammars that were available in Leonardo's time, such as Quintilian's dependable *Instituto Oratoria*, the word "vertex," the crown of

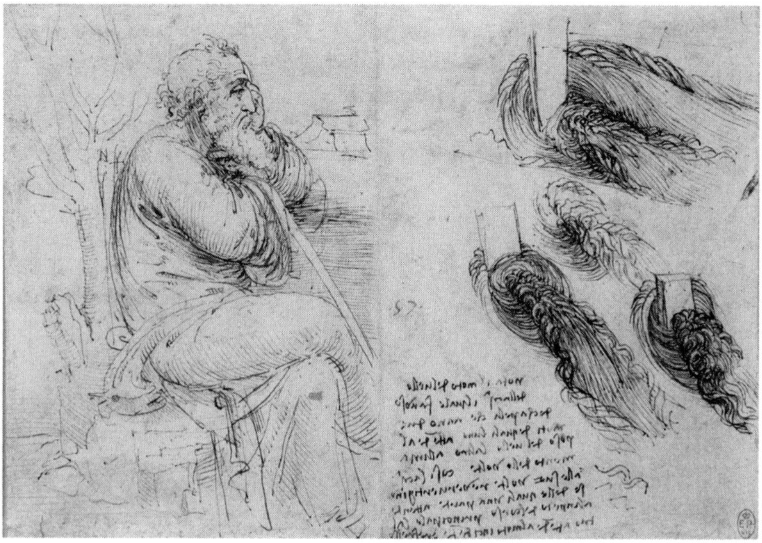

Figure 7.1. Leonardo da Vinci, studies of water. Windsor Castle, Windsor.

one's head, is said to originate from the word for whirlpool.[3] It is the element of water, once again, that offers a starting point. And even if you discover in Pliny and Albert the Great, as Leonardo did, that sea waves leave an impression on the hides of seals, water is again the only element that matters: hair is a mere record of its movements.[4]

But this is not what Leonardo writes. Leonardo, who had not studied Latin in his youth, deliberately went against the grammar books and zoological manuals to state that in thinking about the nature of water, it was hair that served as the prototype, and not the other way around.[5] I am then reminded of his artistic training with Verrocchio, and how drawing hair taught him something about complexity. In the case of his water experiments, which took place some thirty years after his apprenticeship, however, the reason may not be biographical.

If Leonardo saw a deep connection between hair and fluids, it is because he learned to approach the world imaginatively rather than verbally, letting his thoughts being driven by visual likenesses.[6] Or, to put it slightly differently, he tried to see the world metaphorically by linking

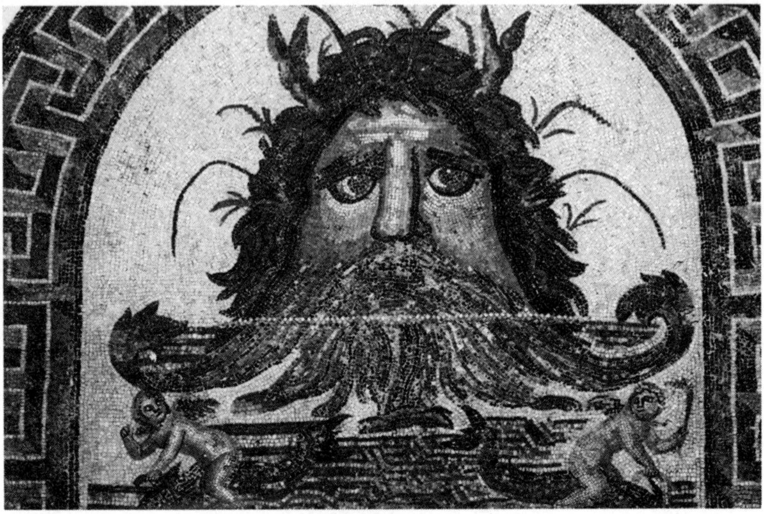

Figure 7.2. Head of Oceanus. Musée National du Bardo, Tunis.

aspects of the natural world that were regarded as distant from each other, and dared to wonder whether their appearances could have been produced by the same forces.[7]

And when I search for hair among metaphors, I find that its connection to water wasn't actually that daring. When Isidore of Seville explained what a metaphor was, he did so by offering this telling example: "You, Father Neptune, whose white temples, weathered with crashing brine, resound: to whom the great Ocean flows forth as your eternal beard, and in whose hair rivers wander."[8] Isidore, who was hostile to pagan poetry, borrowed the metaphor from Augustine.[9] And Augustine, like Isidore, encountered mosaics in which the god Ocean raises from the sea, lifting seaweed with his head, water dripping down his beard (figure 7.2).[10] Seeing hair waves as water must have been common, but Isidore nonetheless felt the need to spell out the rationale of their coupling: ". . . for beard, temples, and hair pertain not to the ocean but to men. In this way, some terms for things are transferred very elegantly from one kind to another for the sake of beauty, so that the speech may be greatly adorned."[11]

There is nothing particularly original in Isidore's notion of the metaphor as a transferral. Aristotle, Cicero, and Quintilian all stressed the motor power of the metaphor, which connects things that are unrelated.[12] What is worth stressing, though, is the boost that the metaphor received as an epistemological tool in fifteenth-century Italy. It was not just seen as a figure of speech, a technique to make a discourse compelling. It also came to be regarded as a fundamental operation of knowledge.[13]

The Florentine Coluccio Salutati defined the epistemological profile of metaphors in what became his most famous book, *The Labors of Hercules*. Hercules, a proxy for all men, asks the Muses about how he can know the truth, and the Muses, coaching him as Boccaccio's nymphs coached Ameto, explain that true knowledge lies past first impressions.[14] It can only emerge when one slashes one's way through those impressions to find similarities between things one would not normally relate.[15] The Muses stress that the question needs to be pursued rigorously—that is, judiciously and selectively. The findings also must be articulated with creative precision.[16] Only the poetical language of metaphor, explains Calliope, leader of the Muses and protectress of eloquence, would enable Hercules to grasp the complexity of the real. Writing was not a mere recording of knowledge—that is, a supplement to it—but the very site where it was produced.

Let's reflect for a minute on this way of defining knowledge. It was thought of not as the result of proofs and deductions, but as the product of a mind that pierces through the thick specificity of things, creating unexpected underground channels between them. And now let's consider the practical consequences of encouraging this type of education. What would happen if the pursuit of metaphors were not just part of the musings of a scholar at his desk, but the goal of an eminent politician, such as Salutati, who sat in Florence's executive meetings, drafting their proceedings and expressing opinions on what deserved to be funded, and more generally, shaped the ways the city saw itself and was seen from far away?[17] How would a community change? How would people speak, what would they see, and what would they dream if they were told that they should read fables rather than legal compilations and religious treatises?[18] This was not just a hypothesis, uttered with the casualness of something that might never happen, but a set belief that shaped thinking and seeing. In Salutati's time, and in the generations that separated his from Leonardo's, the pursuit of poetry reoriented the values of many who rewarded their children not for making profits, but for the care with which they described what could not be owned.[19] When I reflect upon this drive, it does not surprise me to hear Florentines speaking of rivers as having mouths and calling springs "nostrils," rivers "mustaches," and glaciers "the white hair of mountains."[20]

Metaphors were not just the stuff of poems. Even in a technical treatise by Filarete, an engineer employed by Lorenzo de' Medici's father, I run into the designation of the surface of rivers as "skin" (*pelle*), a metaphor that eventually led to the common expression "the down of water" (*il pelo dell'acqua*).[21] These phrases reoriented people's minds, as did the drawings that made water look like hair. Turn to another engineering treatise, by the Sienese Mariano Taccola.[22] There, a sketch (figure 7.3a) presents the stream erupting from a dam like the tuft of hair flaring up from Simonetta Vespucci's twisted braid (plate 10). As the stream widens, so it gains in complexity, producing the whirlpools that fascinated Leonardo. Leonardo also drew, amid heads with curly heads, a bridge whose pier separates the streams of water as a comb digs its teeth into hair (figure 7.3b).

It was only through drawing, or *disegno* in Italian, that intangible and ever-changing water turned into the filaments that made it resemble hair. A working concept for many fifteenth-century artists, *disegno* actually does not mean "drawing," even if it is often taken as its synonym. Rather, it is drawing sublimed to an abstract idea that exists beyond the physical trace that a charcoal or a pencil leaves on a sheet of paper.[23] Disegno is to drawing what the geometrical definition of a point is to its graphic rendering as a dot. It is a way of thinking about form that disconnects it from any physical rendering but projects it to a mental plane that facilitates the merging of objects regardless of their differences.[24]

Drawing dematerialized hair and turned its strands into a prime field for the construction of visual metaphors. The parallel did not depend on resemblance; hair did not simply look like lines and thus like anything else that could be drawn as an outline. If hair came uniquely close to

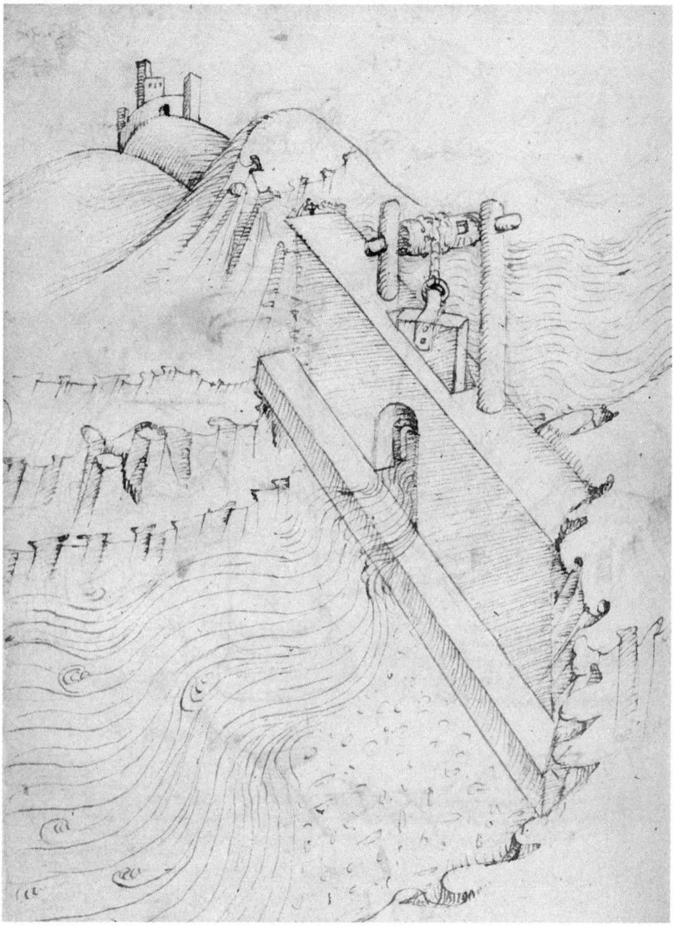

Figure 7.3a. Mariano Taccola, dam mechanism. Clm 197.II, f. 114v. Bayerische Staatsbibliothek, Munich.

disegno itself, it is because hair was thought of as pliable—as pliable as drawing, that is. Numerous voices identified flexibility and versatility as the prime features of hair, but no author was more insistent than Ovid. In his treatise *The Art of Love*, Ovid offered a catalog of hairstyles that quickly moved from curls hanging down the shoulders to ponytails, and from tight-drawn braids to locks sinuously folded "to resemble waves."

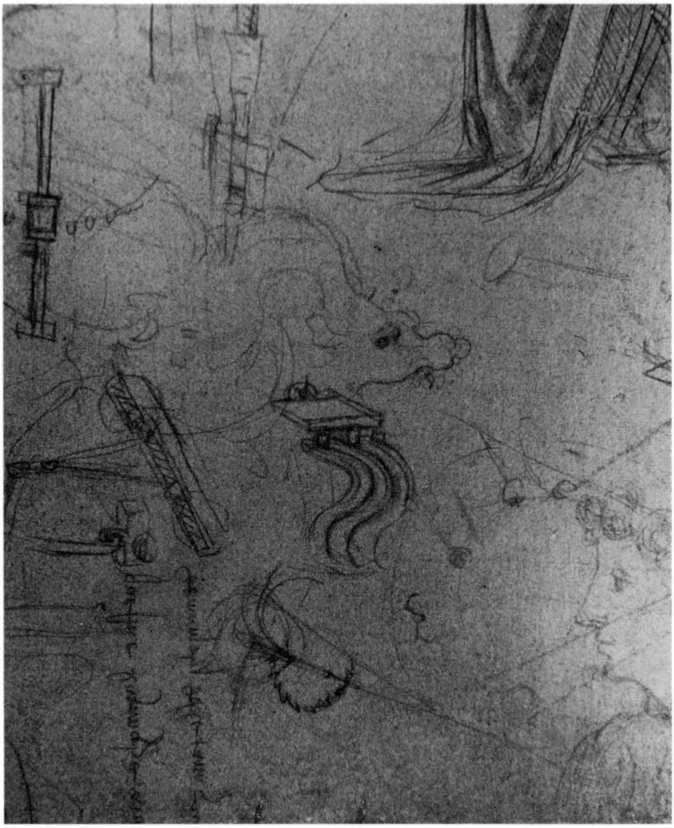

Figure 7.3b. Leonardo da Vinci, water flowing under a bridge. Florence: Gallerie degli Uffizi, Florence.

He concluded: "It would be sacrilegious for me to put a number to the many ways by which you can style hair."[25] In his descriptions, hair did not just take up different shapes; its many styles transformed its wearers into Ariadne, Diana, and Laodamia.[26]

In three paintings of goddesses, Botticelli's workshop tested Ovid's principle that hair is an endless source of forms. The bodies of the women hardly vary (the same tilted head, relaxed shoulders, and weight on the left leg), and the background is painted black so as not to distract from the true element of change: their hairstyle. In the painting today in Berlin (figure 7.4a), the hair is pleated tightly in the front and

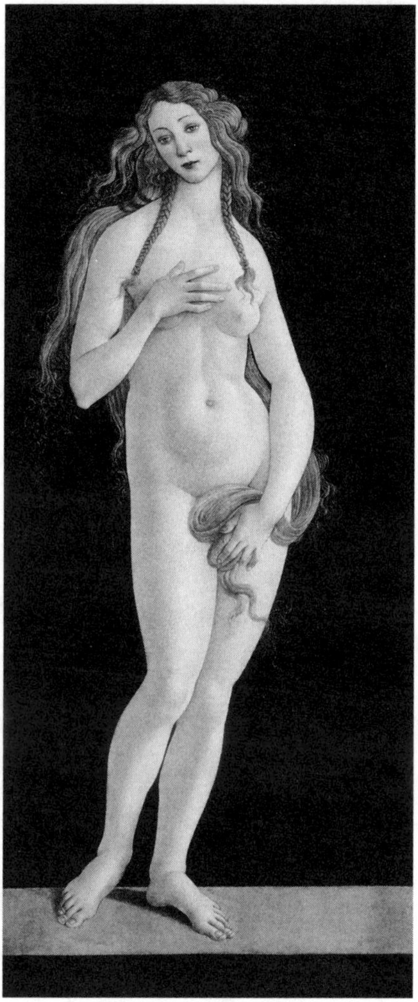

Figure 7.4a. Workshop of Sandro Botticelli, mythological figure. Gemäldegalerie, Berlin.

erupts in a frayed tail in the back. In Geneva (figure 7.4b) it is parted in the middle, crimped, and topped by a ropelike braid. And in Turin (figure 7.4c) it is decorated by a pearl on the top, with pigtails bouncing on each side. Art historians have treated these figures as the work of assistants or imitators.[27] They have cast their verdict with a focus on the

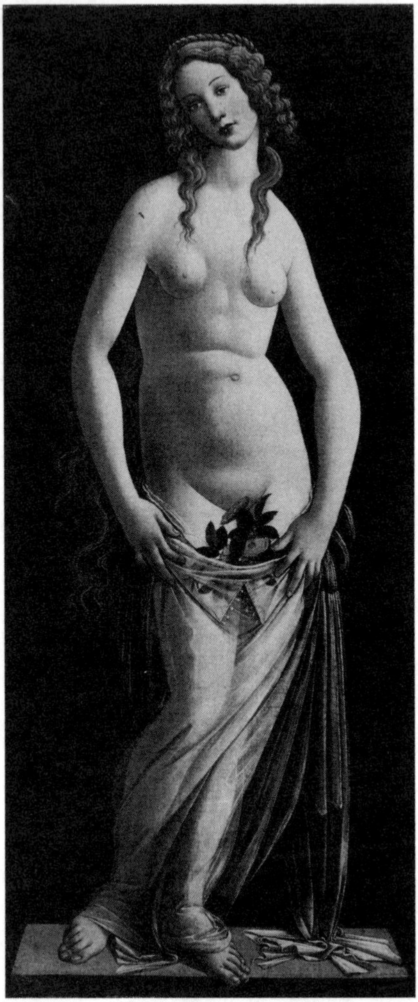

Figure 7.4b. Workshop of Sandro Botticelli, mythological figure. Private collection, Geneva.

bodies, and the bodies are repetitive. With overlong forearms and tiny oval heads, they feel disappointing when compared to Botticelli's famous Venus (plate 1). But to judge these panels solely in relation to anatomical proportions—to assume that those women are flawed attempts to replicate Botticelli's masterpiece—is to ignore the possibility that they may

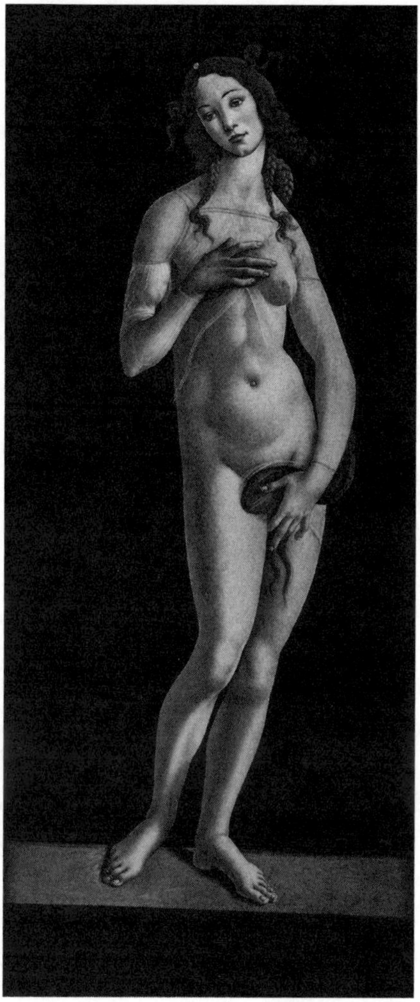

Figure 7.4c. Workshop of Sandro Botticelli, mythological figure. Galleria Sabauda, Turin.

represent three different mythological figures. (How many saints, and female saints in particular, were painted identically except for attributes that disclosed their identity?) After all, the bodies of this series may be lacking, but there is nothing sloppy about their hair—and hair alone, as Ovid insists, is the thing that distinguishes one goddess from another.

But "series" may not be the right word here. Despite their similarities, these goddesses feel less like the elements of a sequence than like an explosion of making. Each of them also challenges the private, sketchy nature of Leonardo's and Verrocchio's drawings of coiffures (see figure 2.4 and plate 3) by elevating hairstyles to the grand scale and high polish of finished public works. In doing so, they invite questions about the location of meaning in a picture. As pictorial fields, hairstyles somewhat softened the realistic uniformity that artists simulated in limbs and faces to display their formal artistry more directly, unrestrained by figuration. Hair, these paintings seem to imply, enabled artists to enter a space with its own rules. While the profile of a nose or a leg followed a set of conventions—the proportions of real noses and legs, or those of famous prototypes—such norms did not apply to hair.[28]

Those experiments found currency in Florence because Ovid was widely read there, especially in the last thirty years of the fifteenth century, when printed editions of his writings flooded the market, adding to the many manuscripts that already circulated.[29] And almost everything by Ovid—his collection of poems, *The Loves*, or his extremely popular *Metamorphoses*—exposed hairstyling not as a useless, depraved activity but as a source of aesthetic stupor.[30]

Ovid was not just read; he was imitated. Poliziano did so in an elegy for the funeral of the daughter of one of Florence's most respected families: "Whenever she let her hair tumble loose without restraint, she seemed a Diana, terror of the wild beasts. If she gathered her tresses again into tawny gold, she seemed a Venus, her hair dressed with the Cytherean comb"—a reference to the goddess's birthplace, the island of Kythira.[31] And even a populist preacher such as Bernardino da Siena exploited hair's tolerance for metaphors of all sorts when he laughed at women for looking as if they carried pancakes, funnel cakes, and tripe on their heads.[32] Even if Bernardino told his audience not to read the "poisonous" *Art of Love*, it is pretty clear that here Ovid served him as inspiration.[33]

So it is hardly surprising to notice that Leon Battista Alberti also explored the dynamic possibilities of hair when he was fighting the static medium of painting: "Let hair move in a circle, striving to form a knot, let it flow like waves, imitating flames, and let it sometimes creep like snakes under other strands of hair, raising itself now in this direction and now in that."[34] Art historians have relied on this passage more than any other for interpreting the hair of many fifteenth-century paintings, even if Alberti's passage did not have the reach, or the richness, of Ovid's.[35] Among its most famous applications is in Botticelli's *Venus* (plate 2). Her hair animates the picture: it is what makes the air visible, what gives the scene pathos.[36] Her fluttering tresses reveal that she is being fanned by the wind gods, that the picture is alive. Together with the waves, it is what gives the scene the sense of a landing.

But rather than a departure, it seems to me that Alberti's hair metaphors ought to be seen as a response to Salutati's invitation to revel in analogical thinking. Alberti, writing a generation after Salutati's death, offers a practical application of Salutati's appeal by foregrounding the ease with which painting makes flames, waves, and hair appear as one. In doing so, Alberti argues for the gnostic potential of the arts. I suggest this because, in writing about hair metaphors, Alberti thinks like a writer, not a painter. That is, he emphasizes the end of the metaphoric transfer as he presents hair as something that receives meaning from the element to which it is paired.[37] Hair resembles snakes, and not the other way around.

But this is not what Botticelli did, nor Leonardo in his drawings of water. For them, the transfer of the metaphor could never be fully achieved. For hair to remain legible, metaphoric painting had to stop short of making its features disappear into the referent. The portrait of Simonetta Vespucci (plate 10) is a wonderful exploration of this failure: her tufts resist being read just as fire. Their transfer is loose, like the concern some famous actors have for their acting, since they know that regardless of the role they may play, they will be seen as themselves. Botticelli's engagement with the metamorphism of hair made him aware of the ways artists engaged with the tension between interpreting the visual world as it was and moving away from it, constructing another world whose resemblance to it was up to them to decide.

We are in front of an awakening. But this realization may have been pressed on Botticelli not by the painting of hair, or at least not only by that, but by the study of a peculiar object. Known to specialists today as the Farnese Cup, that object was the most precious antiquity in Lorenzo de' Medici's collection (plates 26 and 27).[38] Lorenzo received it from the pope at his first embassy in Rome, and displayed it in his study room—the one built by his father, which had a dozen suns whose hair dribbled toward the earth (for one such sun, see figure 4.5).[39] The cup was and still is an extraordinary piece. Lorenzo showed it to only those "who were able to appreciate it"—that is, collectors of the stature of the king of Naples.[40] He also showed it to the artists he trusted, to collect their thoughts about the figures on both of its sides. They took it in their hands, as any cup would invite doing.

The exterior of the cup displays the magnetic face of Medusa against the goatskin of Athena's aegis, her hair frozen in mid-explosion (plate 26).[41] On the inside are a few figures, masterfully carved out of a thin white vein so that they stand out against the marbled ground (plate 27). I can hardly describe them since, despite their level of detail, these figures defy meaning today just as they did in the fifteenth century.[42] (Tellingly, Poliziano, who wrote a poem about the cup, did not say anything about the figures, limiting himself to praising the lucky kings and popes on whose dining tables the cup once stood.)[43] To remain on safe ground, I provide only some vague features: a stately bearded man steadies an empty cornucopia surrounded by an entourage that includes a woman lying on a sphinx, another offering a bowl, a third combing her hair with her fingers, and, in the center, a brawny crossbowman. Above them, two figures fly in the sky.

In a way, what is carved is not even a scene. Its elements hang loose, up for grabs. Some artists copied from it only what they understood. The celebrated illuminator Attavante degli Attavanti reproduced Medusa's face and the sphinx to decorate a manuscript (figure 7.5).[44] Others studied features that were independent of figuration. Bertoldo di Giovanni, the Medici's chief medallist, imitated the cup's shallow carving, around which he shaped his own style.[45] Verrocchio carefully studied the cup's agate variations to create a companion urn that Lorenzo showed to his guests together with the cup, probably to boast about the skillfulness of contemporary Florentine artisans.[46] No one, however, seems to have studied the Farnese Cup more carefully than Botticelli.

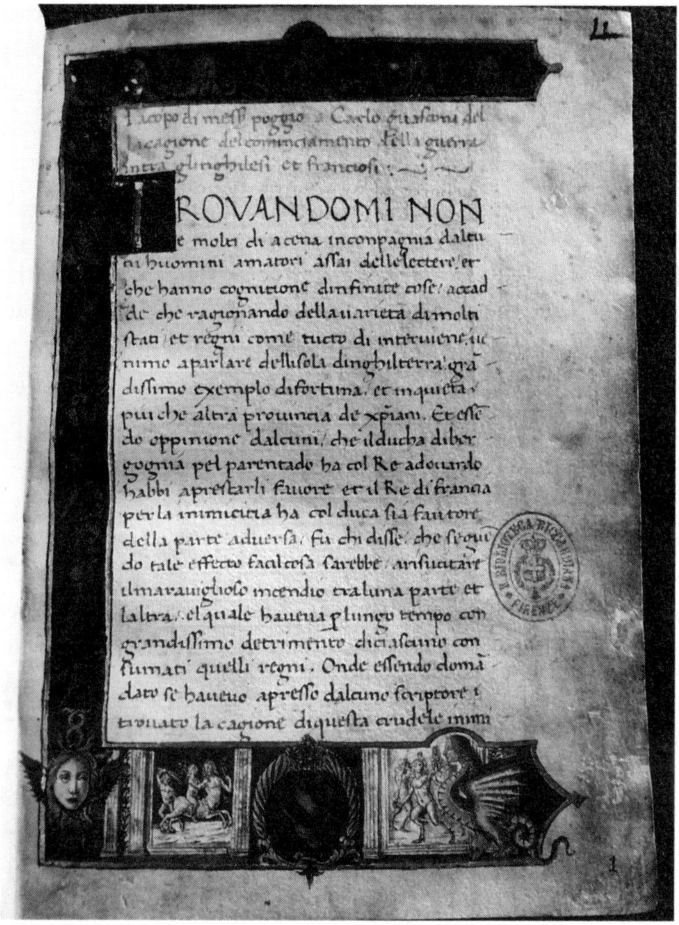

TROVANDOMI NON

Figure 7.5. Attavante degli Attavanti, manuscript illuminated with head of Medusa. Ms 2056, f. 1r. Biblioteca Riccardiana, Florence.

Art historians have long recognized that the cup's two flying figures served as the prototypes for the winds in Botticelli's Venus (plate 1).[47] Botticelli also reproduced the cornucopia in one of his studies for an allegory of Abundance.[48] But most of Botticelli's attention was on Medusa's hair (plate 26). He precisely translated her fluttering tresses to his Venus: he reproduced their waves and interlacing, exploiting their length to move them to the front and the back, like the lattice on a pie (plate 2).

The Farnese Cup offered lessons that Botticelli had not heard before. His teacher, Filippo Lippi, taught him how to bundle up hairdos and pleat veils, thinking of heads as fields of plastic inventiveness, loosely representative of the fashions of his times (see figure 6.2). But Lippi, too, did not treat hair differently from his predecessors. For him, one strand of hair corresponded to one line. The friar Giovanni da Fiesole, who began to be known as Fra Angelico around the years when Botticelli's career took off, popularized this approach.[49] In a *Lamentation of Christ* that he painted for the convent of San Marco (figure 7.6), he rendered the waves in Christ's hair and the strands of his beard with the thinnest brush, the one he reserved for the outlines of nails.[50] This approach had been described in Cennino Cennini's manual, which we encountered in chapter 2. The difference is that when Lippi studied Fra Angelico's works, it was no longer just Cennini's approach, nor Angelico's; it was everyone's. The bishop Antonino Pierozzi, a major supporter of Fra Angelico's painting, appreciated this style since it treated hair as the incidental element he considered it to be.[51] It was also because of this opinion, which was not confined to Florence's top moral authority, that Lippi covered the hair of his figures and spent time emphasizing the materiality of such headgear so that hair disappeared under it.

So when Botticelli started painting hair, he still relied on Fra Angelico's technical apparatus. Like Fra Angelico, he precisely went over hair strands with lighter shades of paint, so as to give the impression that hair moved in and out of sunbeams. However, while Fra Angelico's strands of hair are limp—a sign that he did not want to draw attention to them—Botticelli's are inspired, painted with the attention Fra Angelico reserved for halos and other devotional features, such as the blood that streaks Christ's temples and flows out of his chest wound.

Botticelli's revaluation of hair is patent in his *Madonna of the Magnificat* (figure 7.7), where the gold accents of the Virgin's locks are the same size as the halo rays. It was the Farnese Cup that must have taught Botticelli to give value to hair: to paint it confidently and give it room. The Madonna's tresses, which escape the hold of her veil to energize the visual encounter of mother and son, are directly borrowed from the cup's Medusa. (They come from the lower right sector, to be pre-

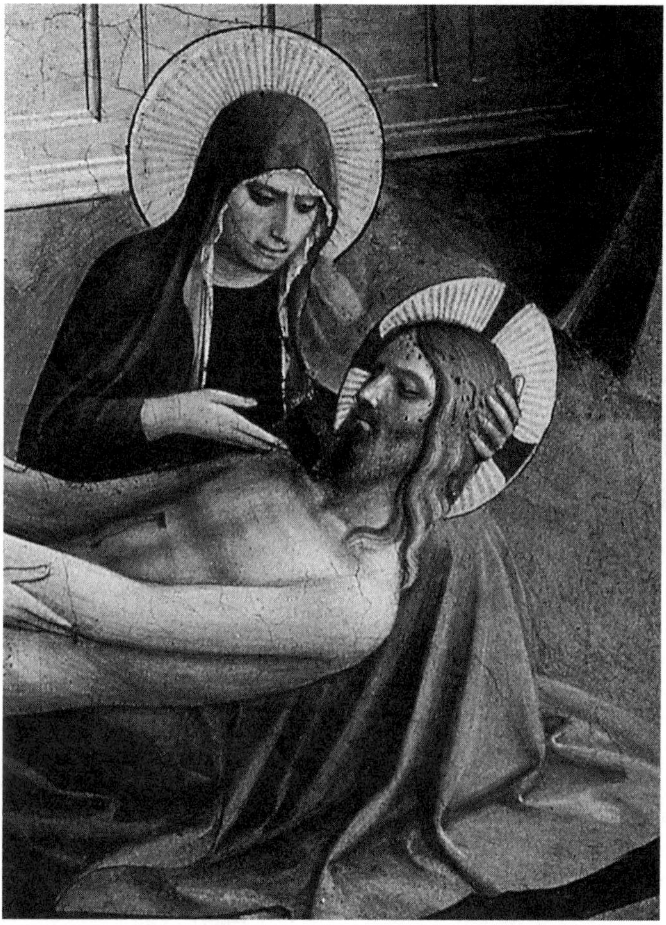

Figure 7.6. Fra Angelico, *Lamentation of Christ*. Cell 5, Museo di San Marco, Florence.

cise, in which the thickest lock of hair twists so that the tufts in the foreground disappear behind those emerging from the back. The angels around Botticelli's Mary also sport Medusa's facial features—plump lips, bumpy chins, conspicuous upper eyelids. Their faces almost register as blank spaces in comparison to their twirling locks. Look at the whirlpools over their foreheads: they are lifted from the cup, which ad-

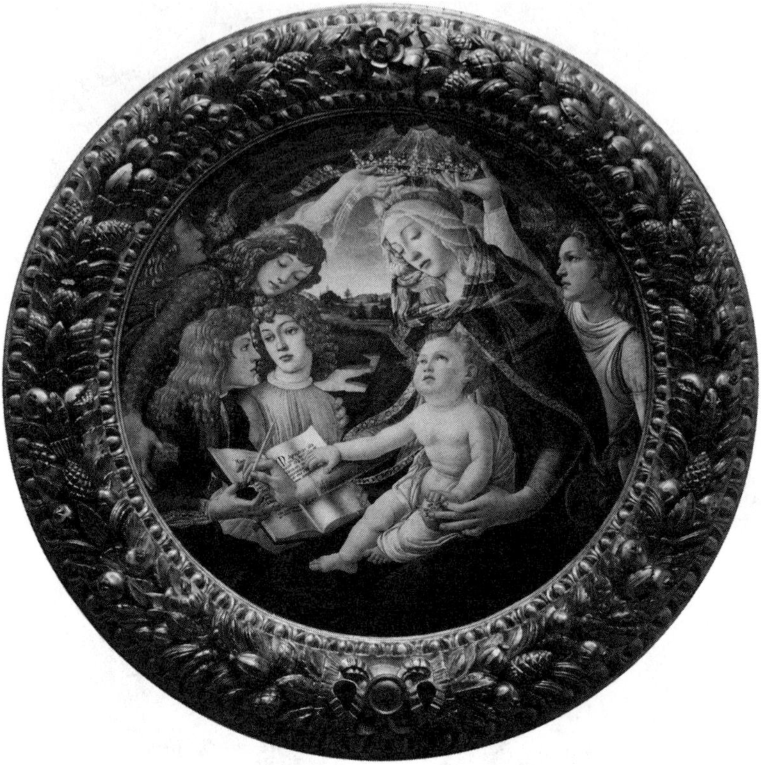

Figure 7.7. Sandro Botticelli, *Madonna of the Magnificat*. Gallerie degli Uffizi, Florence.

ditionally suggested to Botticelli that he mark the volumes of the angels' cheeks with pointy locks, as if they served as a form of shading.

So many are the borrowings that I wonder if one could catch Botticelli in the act of studying Lorenzo's prized possession. He must have held the Farnese Cup in his hands, but how did he scan its surface? Did his gaze claw at every curve the hair offered, making his ocular wanderings feel less free or personal to himself?[52] Did the sea of crescents teach him how hair could control the viewer's gaze, thus moving past the descriptive language of Ovid, who identified hair configurations with specific words (braids, tails, buns) to keep his readers engaged? The control of a viewer's eye is different from the control of a reader's mind. It does not rely on words to sequence the real. Nonfigurative, undulating lines could even be more powerful in holding one's gaze, as the meanings of figures fade over time—those of the Farnese Cup certainly did—whereas the meaning of lines does not require learnedness. The lines are in fact against erudition, as they find their power in their denial of representational preoccupations.

But I am talking in hypotheticals. I have taken the liberty of attributing these thoughts to Botticelli, but the truth is that I have no idea what words he told himself, or whether he even felt the need to articulate why and how the cup struck him. Maybe he just got it, as some artists do, without feeling any pressure to express it. Nor did he need to come up with any of this, since he was not the first Florentine artist to whom the cup had spoken. When Botticelli was five or six, Andrea del Castagno painted David with Medusa's hairstyle—same whirlpool of locks, same cheek-marking tuft (figure 7.8).[53] He painted him on a shield, also the support of Medusa's head on the Farnese cup. Castagno saw the classical vessel in the Florentine palace of Ludovico Trevisan, the wealthiest man in Italy when Lorenzo was a child, and another collector who was pleased to share his treasures with artists.[54]

I bring up Castagno's encounter to make the point that the cup was nothing new: it did not make waves in Florence's artistic world, like a meteorite that falls into the ocean from outer space. Instead, its presence resonated in town for decades. And it did so because it was an object that spoke more of the present than of the past (we still do not know when and where it was made). Or better, it was one of those rare objects that bridged between the past and present, folding past motifs into contemporary thinking. Take, for instance, those snakes swirling inconspicuously amid hair waves. You can sometimes spot them on the ancient coins that some Florentines collected.[55] They come and go: their appearance is unstable, loose reminders of the Gorgon's danger.[56] Yet, transported to Christian fifteenth-century Florence, they must have offered an unmistakable demonstration of the vices that hide amid superfluities, as Lorenzo's literary advisor Cristoforo Landino claimed. In writing about Medusa's beautiful hair, Landino interpreted her hair as representing "the superfluities . . . and Minerva turned it [Medusa's

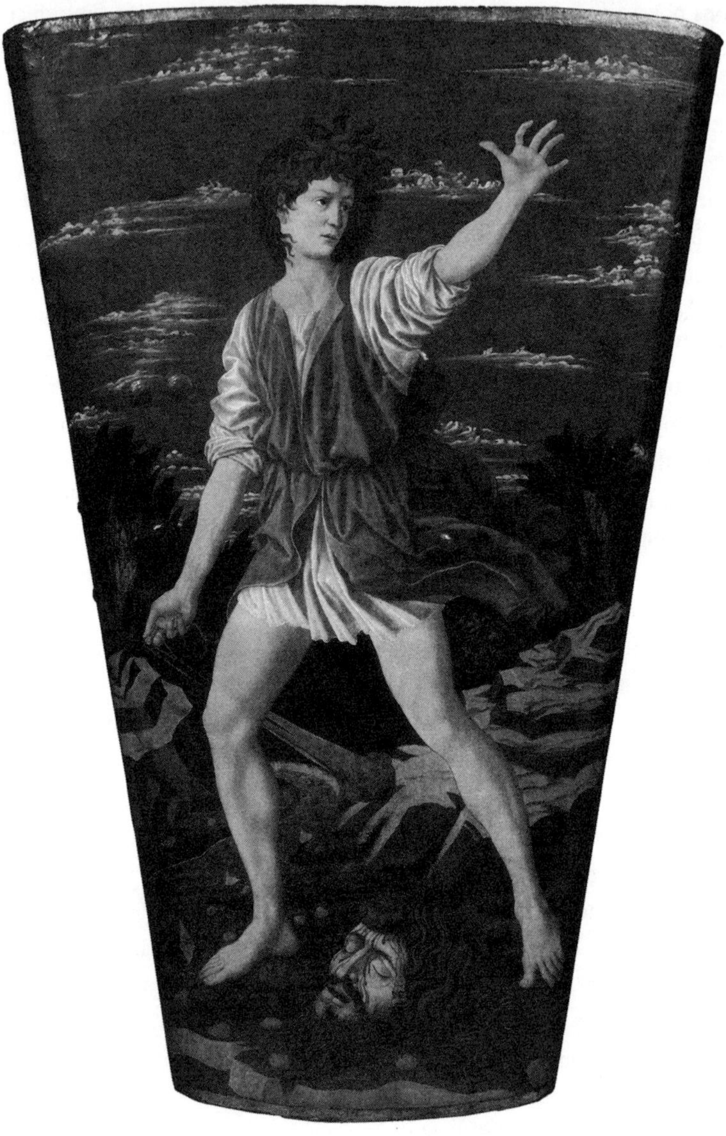

Figure 7.8. Andrea del Castagno, *David with the Head of Goliath*. National Gallery of Art, Washington.

hair] into snakes because wisdom eventually unveils trickeries and reveals their poison."[57]

Landino's words express a distinct moralizing ethos. They are in line with the diktats of Pierozzi and the attacks by preachers who, had they been invited into Lorenzo's office, would have taken the cup as confirming their beliefs. Yet Landino's reading of Medusa's myth also contributes to a different discourse about the ornamental value of metaphors, in which hair played a foundational role.

Hair became a prime field for the construction of metaphors because it was repeatedly equated to ornament, and, in the words of Isidore, metaphors existed "for the sake of beauty, so that the speech may be greatly adorned."[58] The medical authority Galen called hair the ornament of both men and women.[59] The leading theologian Thomas Aquinas insisted that hair, like nails, was the natural ornament of humans.[60] Boccaccio reasoned in his lectures on Dante that, because hair is an "ornament to the body, those who interpret hair as [symbolizing] secular riches are right: and the people who are thriftless will resurrect with cropped hair to demonstrate [in reverse] how stupidly they indulged in their temporal wealth."[61] I know the passage is complex; I still have to read it a few times to unpack the many points he compresses into one sentence. Its density stems from the fact that Boccaccio is not just reflecting here on Dante's portrayal of clerical greed by talking of hair cropped from priests' bodies; he is also referencing Geoffrey of Vinsauf's writing manual *New Poetry*. And Geoffrey's manual, a copy of which Boccaccio owned, compares beauty in writing to hairstyling.[62] Geoffrey was not the first one, nor the only one, to make such a comparison. Cicero described a plain essay as "disheveled."[63] And when the famed philosopher Pico della Mirandola criticized humanists for caring too much about elegance when writing, he leaned on hair as the stand-in for ornament.[64] Well-coiffed lectures are shameful, he insisted. People should grow suspicious of them and prefer speeches that are "bloated, clumsy, and with untidy hair."[65]

The pairing of hair with ornament makes sense only when considered in relation to Aristotle's dogma that everything in nature must have a function.[66] As a generative surplus, hair had no function. Yet, since the teleology of the time required any element of nature to have one—

otherwise people ought to conclude that God's creation was imperfect—hair was assigned far too many purposes, none of which was catalyzing. Boccaccio was aware of this fiasco: "Of what use is the hair on the head? None, as all agree. Yet many claim such value for it that, if Venus were without it, she could not please Mars, for all her attendant graces. . . . This is enough to show that a thing precious for no other reason may become so for ornament's sake."[67] You may have recognized Apuleius's bald Venus in these words.[68] Yet Boccaccio's reference is not merely erudite. He makes it to single out an Aristotelian fallacy, according to which something with no function is, by default, invested with a decorative one.

You can now see the extensive application of this reasoning in the terms that interest us. As a bodily leftover, hair was decorative. And because they resisted mere description, metaphors, which were defined through hairstyles, were also decorative. Boccaccio stated that his own writing, which included many descriptions of hairstyles, "is valuable merely on the score of ornament."[69] Given the force by which these ideas continued to be held in fifteenth-century Florence, I wonder if Boccaccio's reasoning could explain Botticelli's focus on hair. By painting bold, arresting hairstyles, did he dedicate his life to a form of visual poetry in spite of what moralizers said? Was his abandonment to hair a way to express his cultural faith in the power of metaphors?[70] Or was he showing that painting could reach into what poetry failed to grasp, and that an eye for things apprehends differently than a reading eye?

I am articulating all this as we draw toward the end of this book, but such cultural preoccupations were the preconditions for the interlocking of many of the events I have presented so far. This is also where the story gets more interesting, as even if metaphors attracted attention because of their coupling with ornament, they were not seen as inhabiting only the abstract world. Such was their force that some metaphors were seen as constitutive of physical life as well. After all, hair's bodily transformation from viscous smoke to dried matter provided the ultimate demonstration that metamorphoses existed in nature. In doing so, it legitimized everyone's search for the metaphoric relationships between seemingly distant states of being.

EIGHT *Raking the Skin*

I find it sometimes difficult to express how directly beauty was a product of class in the fifteenth century. But the task is made somewhat easier by pointing to a popular book on cosmetics.[1] In the beginning, it reads: "The first thing a woman should do to make herself pleasant, and smooth, and without unnecessary hair, from her head to her feet, is to go to the baths."[2] But for Florentines, going to the baths meant to leave their cities. The baths sprung up on the slopes of mountains, and clusters of buildings grew around them to service those who could afford traveling and staying there. Those wealthy people were few—so few, in fact, that when they stopped going to the baths, many of those villages fell into disarray, their dissolution quicker and more absolute than that of Greek settlements built on the Italian coasts two millennia earlier.

To look for Tuscan baths today is largely to explore a geography of rubble: forgotten piles of bricks devoured by vegetation, near indifferent highways that cut through what were once water basins and are now dried fields. Most historians have given up on searching for them. Even the few sites for which information is handed out through historical descriptions and architectural remains are so empty as to disorient the visitor. One needs quite some imagination to picture the blur of life. But I want to make the effort and try to populate with chatter the stone basin of Bagno Vignoni, near Siena, one of the best-preserved spas,

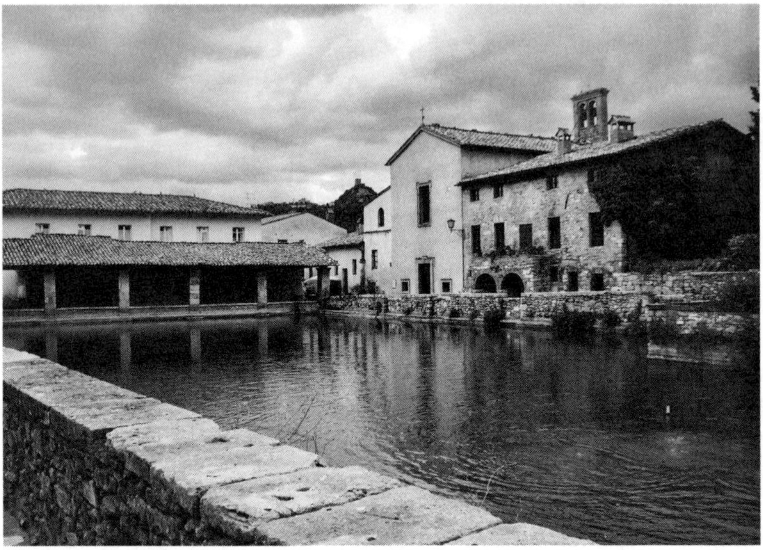

Figure 8.1. Thermal pool, Bagno Vignoni, Siena.

which attracted the likes of Lorenzo de' Medici (figure 8.1).[3] Even in his times, it was a modest urban agglomeration: a chapel, a hostel, a tavern, a few houses for workers that stood across from a palatial residence for the rich, all of them facing a hot pool as large as a small piazza.[4] Crowds of bathers entered the pool with garlands on their heads while visitors relaxed under a loggia, telling stories and drinking glasses of mineral water. They cast glances at naked bodies on the other side of the wooden bridge that divided the pool in two, and which was less a bridge than a covered corridor that separated the men from the women.[5] A lutenist probably played in the corner, to cheer the melancholics or calm their nerves.[6]

But not all baths were this well equipped or this accessible. Some were remote. They hid in woods, where murky pools of water stood between rocky slopes covered in musk. I imagine visitors removing their shoes and breeches and hesitantly treading on the pebbles, full of excitement for sites that were regularly described as wonders: cracks in the earth's crust from which nature's ebullient power flowed out.[7] I read of

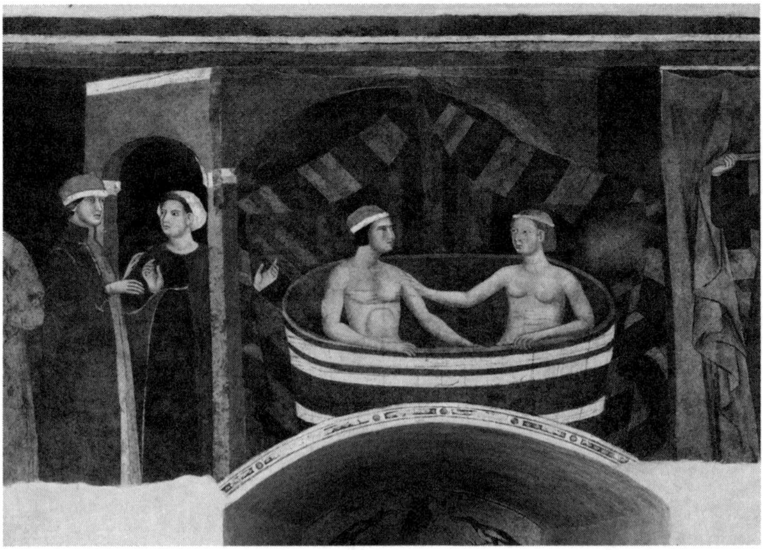

Figure 8.2. Memmo di Filippuccio, two people bathing. Camera del Podestà, Palazzo Comunale, San Gimignano.

women, but also men, making the most of this energy, digging holes and filling them with mud and the herbs that grew nearby, as they thought their roots were soaked with that magical water.[8] I imagine that some bathers recited prayers, hoping that nature's miraculous touch would grant them health.[9] But to speak just of nature, as if these hopefuls were wandering fauns and nymphs (about whom some of the bathers did write, in between immersions) would be misleading.[10] Lords tried to capitalize on these sites, rerouting rivers and building dams and cisterns to ensure that the healing hot water kept flowing, as well as the money that flowed with it.[11]

Occasionally I find some images that help my reconstructions, but they never are about what I am looking for. In the municipal palace of San Gimignano, I see a man and a woman sitting at the ends of a wooden tub, which allowed the very wealthy to enjoy a steam session in the comfort of their homes (figure 8.2).[12] "If the woman is not used to travel," the book on cosmetics says, "she can build a steamy room by heating some tiles and rocks in the fire so that she starts sweating."[13] The sauna in the fresco in front of me does not have this DIY feeling. Its gaudy pavilion must have been expensive, since multidye stripes were laborious to make and retained their vibrancy only if cared for by maids, who were quick at folding the fabric and putting it away from the sun after the structure was dismantled.[14] But this picture of privilege has difficulty in capturing the transformative power of bathing, and the hope for change that increased when the bathing took place at a celebrated site.[15] Brides hoped to be pregnant when they left the pools; bald men wished to leave with lush, shimmering manes.[16] Everyone knew their wishes required patience, as it was difficult to foresee how quickly a body would react and how long the benefits would last. Sometimes things did not work out. On one occasion, Lorenzo's mother Lucrezia had to postpone her journey back to Florence because "the effects of the baths," as she put it, had been debilitating.[17] The work to transform oneself was full of risks. It also started on day one, as doctors instructed patients to scrub their skin vigorously, alter their diets drastically, abstain from sex, and rest—rest all the time. The doctors' manuals often provide many details of heavy-handed treatments, as they were manuals for professional showoffs who aimed at grabbing the attention of the wealthy and convincing them that change was possible.[18] The doctors flaunted their expertise in numerous ways, listing the specific benefits of every spa in a territory.[19] I wonder if those catalogs were taken seriously by Florentines who went through them as carefully as tourists scroll through travel blogs today, ditching convenience and riding all the way down to Naples just to take a boat to Ischia and then make their way to the Sucellario baths, celebrated "for making hair abundant, and lighter."[20]

If I linger on manuals on spas and cosmetics, it is because they provided an approach to the human body that was different from anything that we have seen.[21] In opposition to university textbooks, they presented hair not as a product of digestion but as an offshoot of skin. The waters rich with the iron of Ischia, just to stick to the latest example, were praised for not only thickening hair but also removing scars—two benefits that should be seen as one, since hair was viewed as an extension of skin.[22] Books on cosmetics insisted that to improve the appearance of their hair, readers had to work on their skin by burning follicles and then anointing them, as if a person were a field fertilized by the ashes of its own vegetation. Perfumed waters and medical preparations were massaged into the scalp so that their benefits would shine through the hair. A case in point was depilatory creams: alkaline concoctions of arsenic and quicklime which blocked the pores and stopped the release of bodily fluids, turning the skin into a compact material like ivory, which many poets took as the paragon of a glossy complexion.[23] Far from being a solitary, intimate endeavor, depilation was an activity that took two people at the spas, where women could count on barbers—that is, second-rank physicians entitled to handle knives. Barbers were easy to find at spas, as they often managed them; they did not only shave people with shards of glass and hair-scorching lotions.[24]

Approaching hair through skin made its way through medical practices of the highest order. The physician Aldobrandino da Siena, a Tuscan doctor who made his career treating French aristocrats, embraced it. Of course he first told his readers that if they wanted to improve the appearance of their hair, they had to alter their diet (eat hot, wet dishes, he suggested, and do not exaggerate them with salt, since it dries up the digestive gas).[25] But he then conceded that bathing in hot waters could be just as effective, since hair depended on the quantity and openness of the skin pores.[26] He wrote this because to think of hair as a product of the skin was anything but a superficial popular belief, a simplification endorsed by those who could not stomach complex theories about digestion. Quite the opposite: it was vindicated in a series of texts attributed to Aristotle that gained much currency in the second half of the fifteenth century.

The most powerful definition of hair as a product of skin was found in the *Problemata*, a miscellany of explanations about why things are the way they are. Its chapter on hair made no reference to digestion, but stated that hair's thickness depended on the flesh from which it grew, since hair burst forth from subcutaneous glands. Since the brain was the body's largest gland, the *Problemata* reasoned, most of the body's hair had to grow out of one's head.[27]

Today we know that the *Problemata* is a collection of quotes from many philosophers, compiled in the sixth century.[28] In the fifteenth century, however, it was taken to be a genuine Aristotelian treatise, and thus received the attention of the best scholars.[29] The pope tasked Theodore of Gaza, a most in-demand teacher of Greek, with a new Latin translation.[30] Interested in making a book that would be liked by its contemporary readers, Gaza rearranged parts and manipulated words so as to improve the quality of the prose. And while he was criticized for making brazen choices, his translation did become a literary success.[31]

Gaza also translated Aristotle's three treatises on animals. Known under the collective term *On Animals* (*De animalibus*), they were the only works by Aristotle that were not available in Latin; their translation caused a sensation in literary circles.[32] Among their effects was that they reoriented perceptions about the physiology of hair from the stomach to the skin. Indeed, in one of the three books, Aristotle (the real one) writes that "hair differs in the way of thickness and fineness, and of length, according to the locality of the part in which it is found, and according to the quality of skin or hide on which it grows. For, as a general rule, the thicker the hide, the harder the hair."[33] He does not stop there, and clarifies the point in another of the books: "The hair or its analog is not formed out of the flesh but out of the skin. If then the skin is rarer and thicker, the hair is thick because of the quantity of earthy matter and the size of the pores, but if the skin is denser, the hair is thin because of the narrowness of the pores."[34]

Please notice Aristotle's choice of words. He distinguishes between the matter and the form of hair, but says nothing about the former, focusing instead on the latter by stressing that it is "the size of the pores" that defines the shape of hair.[35] He weighs the impact of digestive gas on hair as he weighs bronze as the explanatory factor for a sphere. Consider a sphere made of bronze, he says. What feature do you prioritize when thinking about it? You need to account for bronze at some point for your mental description to be adequate, but it is in no way as important a factor as the sphere's form.[36] After all, you are more likely to say "look at that sphere" than "look at that bronze." And so the word "hair," which identifies filaments rather than shapeless substance—for how could one think of hair, even in the abstract, as having no form?—substantiates

Aristotle's approach to making. It all makes sense, but only until you realize that Aristotle's definition of hair has little to do with physiology. Indeed, it is not based on how bodies work (even if he discusses it in a treatise on animal physiology), but is part of a general reflection on creation that finds its guiding principle in sculpting.

Artificial though it may sound now, Aristotle's explanation of hair as a product of molding was taken to be natural. And if it was so, that is because Aristotle enveloped his discourse in nature's swaddling. When writing about the skin, he called it of "earthly nature," thus presenting it as a ground for the growth of hair.[37] Besides repeating the point in other works, commented upon and thus amplified by Thomas Aquinas and Albert the Great, Aristotle's characterization also found validation in Hippocrates, who reasoned that the growth of both hair and grass depended on the moistness of their respective grounds.[38] Aristotle's coupling spread even further in the fifteenth century thanks to the Florentine physician Tommaso del Garbo, who wrote that plants were like hair, as demonstrated by the fact that they could be cut without causing pain.[39]

In the choir that insisted on the homologies of skin and ground and of hair and grass, there were some authoritative voices that advised caution. Plato pointed out that olive oil "is extremely bad for all plants and is the worst enemy of the hair of all animals except humans, for whose hair it is beneficial, as it is for the rest of their bodies."[40] Pliny noted that hair could not be entirely like plants since, "once cut, it does not grow back from where it has been cut, like in vegetation, but from the root."[41] And even Aristotle could be found saying that hair becomes white while grass withers.[42] None of these counterarguments seemed to have gained much traction, though. On the contrary, their very existence—that is, the fact that those authors felt the need to point out that there were differences between hair and plants—indicates that most people saw hair as a form of vegetation.

Galen tried to strike a balance. On the one hand, he stressed that grass and hair ought not to be compared because, while they shared many characteristics, their respective grounds were fundamentally different in the amount of heat that they tolerated: "Dry earth is called dry in relation to the earth, and dry skin in relation to the skin; what is dry in the former sense is totally devoid of moisture to an extreme degree, what is dry in the human body, and in those of animals similar to humans, is not devoid of moisture, and is in fact preeminently suited to the generation of hair."[43] On the other hand, he supported their coupling, even if with one caveat: that the hair on the head ought to be seen "not like grass, but like plants that have been fashioned by nature as part of the original plan, rather than being dependent upon the mixtures by necessity."[44] And it was such a clarification that stimulated many Florentine writers and artists, who could read that hair, shrubs, and trees were physiologically identical in Lucretius's *On the Nature of Things* and gardening treatises like *The Divine Villa* by Corniolo della Cornia.[45] Manuals about natural philosophy, like *The Book of Why*, described hair loss in old men as being like the shedding of leaves by trees in winter, thus building up the idea that hair was essentially vegetative and behaved like plants.[46] The author of *The Book of Why*, Girolamo Manfredi, took the analogy from Albert the Great, the distinguished thirteenth-century commentator of Aristotle, who also insisted on the insensitivity of both plants and hair.[47] And Leon Battista Alberti reported that astronomers suggested getting a haircut when it is time to cut trees down—that is, when the moon shines bright—as both hair and trees are reactive to the moon's influence. (Not to follow the lunar phases would lead to baldness, depression, and moldy wood.)[48]

For generation after generation, this process of mental welding resulted in words such as the Italian *chioma*, which like its Latin equivalent, *coma*, referred both to a person's hair and to a tree's foliage.[49] Angelo Poliziano poetically played upon the convergence by speaking of vegetation as "locks of the eternal garden."[50] He felt confident in doing so because Ovid had done the same in describing the tresses of the nymph Daphne, prefiguring her transformation into a laurel tree.[51] Many high-ranking artists painted her metamorphosis in Florence, and the illuminator Ricciardo di Nanni illustrated leaves sprouting from her hair and nails, the vegetative parts of a body (figure 8.3).[52]

The correspondence of hair and plants gave way to a tendency in painting to frame the sitter's head with foliage. In creating the rep-

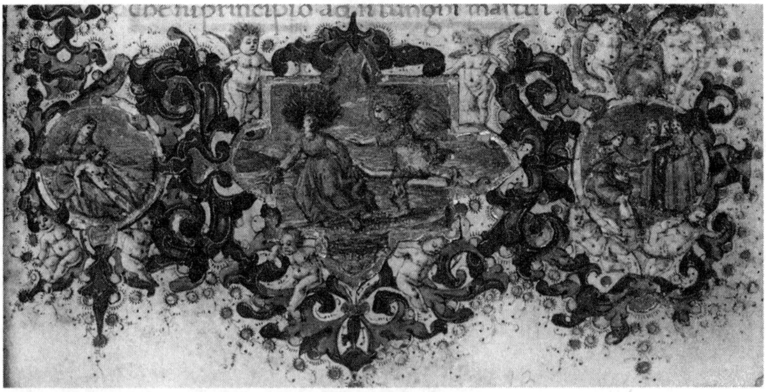

Figure 8.3. Ricciardo di Nanni, *Apollo and Daphne*, last quarter of the fifteenth century. Ms. VITR/22/4, f. 13r. Biblioteca Nacional de España, Madrid.

resentation of a prince to wow the visitors of the Medici's private chapel (figure 8.4), the painter Benozzo Gozzoli made his head overlap a laurel bush, the symbol of political and artistic eminence. Gozzoli knew that the garlands worn by brave rulers, immortal poets, and the truly great were made of laurel. He had seen them on ancient coins, and had read that writers aspired to them. By placing the prince in front of a laurel, Gozzoli provided a level of magnificence that not even the prince's finery conveyed. The prince's perfect framing pretends to be a fortunate stroke of serendipity: as he moves at the pace of the busy procession of which he is part, carried by a white horse rather than riding it, he is not in control of his own speed. Gozzoli gives the impression that the superimposition simply happens in the viewer's eyes for a moment. The prince's passage in front of the rather small, isolated laurel bush must be taking less time than the furtive glance he casts on his viewers, less time than the fugitive sunbeam that makes the laurel leaves come alive for a second, revealing the glory that the ancients saw in that evergreen plant and to which the prince is certainly destined.[53] This is what fifteenth-century images sometimes did: they offered accounts of future lives to make those accounts real in the present.

Leonardo da Vinci understood Gozzoli's intention. In portraying Ginevra de' Benci, he also inserted her curls into the dark mass of

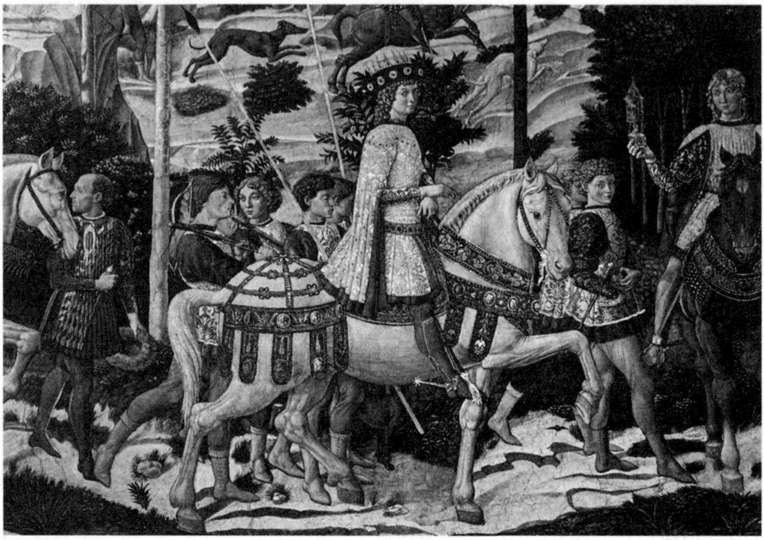

Figure 8.4. Benozzo Gozzoli, *Procession of the Magi.* Medici Chapel, Palazzo Medici Riccardi, Florence.

a juniper (plate 5).[54] The tree reminded viewers of her name and her chastity—of which juniper was a symbol, as art history books emphasize.[55] But I sense that those who stress this connection may be too quick in speaking of emblems, which seem moot if separated from the reasons that supported them. So instead of thinking that juniper evokes chastity because of conventions and literary tropes, I remind you that juniper was the go-to contraceptive in fifteenth-century Florence. Florentine boys and girls crushed juniper cones in mortars, and smeared the grainy, resinous juice on the tips of their penises and inside their vulvas before having sex.[56] Unmarried women and prostitutes took infusions of juniper as morning-after pills.[57] How does your perception of Leonardo's painting change once you know about those practices? Encircled by the starry spikes of juniper branches, Ginevra looks like a virgin protected by pharmaceutical barbed wire.

Let me insist on this point, as I find that the framing of Renaissance heads by leaves has often been dismissed as nothing more than a rhetorical strategy to display symbols, hint at morals, and preserve names—

that is, another way to place value in the abstract.[58] In a way, the metaphoric approach to hair is still within us. Renaissance accounts saturate the reasoning of today's interpretations, which not only draw from historical documents but continue their strategies to produce meaning. So we are told that Ginevra's arboreal halo must refer to her name, as the laurel in the Medici chapel must stand for Lorenzo, whom the family recognized as the only possible referent for that impeccable prince in their chapel. But speaking in this way is to say that in looking at these images, you are not supposed to take in the continuity between hair and leaves that language made plain. Instead, you are supposed to see higher values and hear nobler lessons—perhaps an echo of Petrarch's verses, which famously played on the allusion of his muse's name, Laura, to the laurel plant.[59] Petrarch wrote of how he dreamed of turning into the laurel tree with whose leaves he hoped to be crowned one day: how, in front of Laura, he lost reason and his sense of the self to become an unresponsive tree.[60]

Petrarch mattered, but I wonder if his poems ought to be taken less as the origin for these overlaps than as one of the many demonstrations of the vegetative potential of hair. Fifteenth-century takes on his metamorphosis varied, after all. The poet Antonio Grifo, whom Leonardo met in Milan, painted it on the margin of a copy of Petrarch, as tendrils springing from Petrarch's nails and head (figure 8.5).[61] He shaped the image after that of Daphne's transformation, to which Petrarch's verses explicitly nod.[62] Yet, by shaping Petrarch's growing hair as if it were a garland, Grifo's representation moves away from Petrarch's description to point to the material continuity between hair and leaves.[63]

Leonardo also framed Ginevra's head in such a way as to conjure the garlands Florentine adolescents sported that were considered too frivolous and tasteless to be included in portraits. Etiquette manuals, which warned against any outlandish gesture, recommended against making such garlands too big.[64] A law prohibited garlands of precious materials, since they could be mistaken for crowns.[65] The ban showed that garlands were scrutinized for the most minute addition. It also created new business opportunities. A Florentine came up with the idea of making garlands of ordinary materials: small feathers, enameled flowers, even

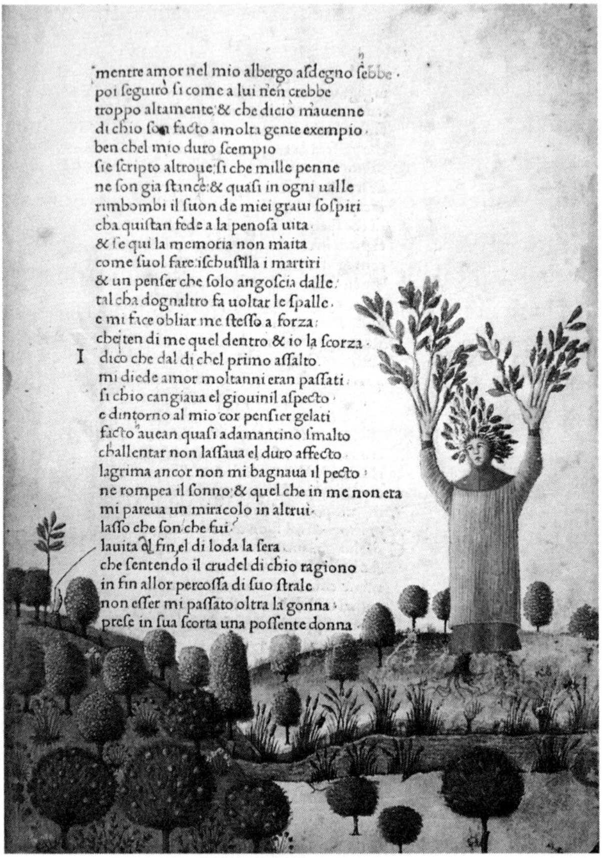

Figure 8.5. Antonio Grifo, Petrarch turning into a laurel. Illustration in a copy of Petrarch's *Canzoniere* and *Triumphs*. Inc. G.V.15, f. 7r. Biblioteca Queriniana, Brescia.

copper medals, dangling from what must have been strangely arresting accessories that simulated the wealth of the past by sheer variety. This Florentine was the father of Domenico Bigordi, a painter slightly older than Leonardo who became known as the son of the successful garland maker, *il ghirlandaio*.[66]

Such was the status of garlands in fifteenth-century Florence: they are regularly identified as an accessory of the young, who wore them to shield themselves from sunlight, as if they were an alternative to the straw hats worn by their parents, or the ancestors of our own sunglasses.[67] Florentines gave garlands as gifts, as tokens of affection. They wore them for fun and as a prerequisite for kisses.[68] This joy was only occasionally articulated verbally but it must have been potent, as people risked fines and the criticisms of moralists for wearing them.[69] I sometimes see garlands in the same category as drugs: things that intoxicated the senses and excited the hearts of the young, as their flowers and the glittering ribbons that held them together reminded them that sex belongs to spring, and that a life driven by excitement hangs on the ephemeral.[70] One way to appreciate garlands is to look at those painted by Botticelli. Resting on a goddess's shoulders (plate 6), cinching a nymph at the neckline and waist (plate 1), those braids of leaves and flowers express how bodies could fuse with nature.[71]

Far from being mere accessories, garlands foregrounded people's vegetative side, an aspect that found its most direct expression in hair. We have seen numerous ways in which hair's connection to vegetation was actualized—through words, arguments on physiology, pictorial representations, and now fashion. But perhaps the most basic association—and the one that reminds us that seeing heads as plants was not just a highbrow game reserved to those versed in classics—comes from hygienic practices, which treated hair with agricultural products.

Take the most common of all remedies, *ranno*: ash boiled in water for hours and then sieved, producing a clear liquid that was praised for its capacity to degrease hair.[72] Farmers employed *ranno* to fertilize the ground, and Pier de' Crescenzi, who recorded agricultural techniques employed in various Italian regions, recommends it for fruit trees.[73] *Ranno* could be made of many types of ash; but more often than not, experts recommended a fern known as *capelvenere*, whose English translation into "maidenhair" misses its grand mythological promise: to make a person's hair (*capel*) shine like that of Venus (*Venere*).[74] De' Crescenzi thought *ranno* useful also for fighting hair loss and dandruff.[75]

Ideas about a person's scalp also mixed with those about the ground because combing was presented as a form of raking. The close teeth of combs (plate 28) were used to remove all sorts of particles, from fleas to dust, so as to unclog the pores that could prevent hair growth.[76] Likewise, rakes were used to remove pebbles in the ground that occluded the furrows for seedlings. The Roman writer Columella underscored this parallel by calling raking a way of "combing the earth."[77] Other farming treatises recommended fertilizing the ground with urine and dung—materials which manuals on cosmetics also suggested as head tonics.[78]

I am moving between the fields and the washtub, noticing a belief that the application of the same process (combing or raking) to related substances (skin or ground) would yield equivalent effects (lush hair or happy trees).[79] The success of this transference lay in its ramifications: it wasn't just the take of a small circle of intellectuals, but a basic approach, as broad as it was deep, that could resurface at any moment. So when Leonardo wrote that hair, grass, and leaves were effects of the same "spirit of growth, and that its flesh is the soil," he was noting nothing new. He was riffing on a belief that was shared by many and was rich in gradations.[80]

Leonardo was interested in the physiology and care of hair. He transcribed recipes for hair dyes and, if his sixteenth-century biographer Giovanni Paolo Lomazzo is right, he even used hair products as paint.[81] Like any other registered Florentine painter, he was a member of the guild of the physicians and apothecaries. He went to mass with them; made pigments out of the minerals and ingredients they imported, and contributed to the cost of their funerals.[82] But besides enmeshing their practices and leading each other toward a common language, the members of that guild also combined their thoughts. Among them was the belief that hair and grass were united because of their capacity for never-ending renewal. The philosopher Marsilio Ficino, born into a family of doctors and apothecaries, stated it better than anyone else: "Life is infinite in all the world's things as it can be clearly seen in trees and grass, which are like the world's hair and body hair."[83]

NINE *On the Politics of a Comb*

I lifted the last words in the previous chapter from Marsilio Ficino's reflection on how to improve a scholar's output. It was eventually published under the title *The Healthy Life* (*De vita sana*), but its earliest versions circulated as *De cura valitudinis eorum qui incumbunt studio litterarum*, which I would translate as "How To Keep Those Who Study the Humanities Healthy."[1] The text has been heralded as the first set of instructions for helping scholars reach their potential intellectual might.[2] And while I find it excessive—how many medieval regulations aimed at keeping monks lucid?—this is a text that fully embraces the brain as both an intellectual and a physical organ.[3] It asks how intervening upon the body could improve mental labor.

Ficino answers like a doctor: To think better, monitor your humoral production.[4] He even recommends a formula: Scholars' bodies should run on a mixture of eight parts blood, two parts black bile, and two parts phlegm. More phlegm would dull the brain, while more bile would drive it out of control, leading to melancholic agitations, if not depression. A constant supply of light blood would keep the scholar's brain vivacious; a splash of bile would increase stamina.

Ficino suggests working on your body daily, starting from what I find to be an unexpected piece of advice. After waking up, he writes, "do not apply yourself wholly and suddenly to reading and meditation, but give over at least half an hour for expurgation. Comb your head carefully and moderately with an ivory comb, drawing it from the forehead to the neck and back about forty times. Run your neck with a rough cloth. Finally, devote at least one hour to studying."[5]

Why combing first? This is not what contemporary manuals on hygiene prescribed. If you take one of their prototypes, the *Regimen sanitatis Salernitanum,* you'll find that the morning should start by washing your face with cold water and brush your teeth, after which, yes, eventually you should also comb your hair but without the emphasis that Ficino places on it.[6]

One reason behind Ficino's prioritization of scrubbing lies in the limited water supply in fifteenth-century Italian cities, which ruled out the possibility that hygiene could ever be about washing and soaping.[7] When people spoke of cleaning, they meant friction: unclogging their pores to facilitate the release of superfluous humors. Pulling a comb through their hair removed extraneous elements. It wasn't just a domestic practice but a clinical one: doctors performed it too, as shown on the frontispiece of the famous treatise *Thesaurus pauperum*, in which a physician combs a patient's hair as a way to take care of his vital heat (figure 9.1). So there's nothing trivial in Ficino's attention to combing. He also insists on keeping one's head warm, clear of bugs, and anointed with marjoram or fennel: three instructions that all make use of the comb.[8] How to use the comb may be obvious for the first two recommendations. But it took me longer than I am willing to admit to realize that, after the head was rubbed and dirt was removed from the hair, combs were dipped in perfumed oil to distribute it evenly on the scalp.)

Ficino does not simply advocate combing. He prioritizes it and elevates it, providing uniquely detailed instructions. He specifies the direction of the comb and its material (ivory, a cold substance that, according to humoral logic, counters the noxious heat produced by scrubbing).[9] He goes so far as to recommend forty repetitions: the symbol of the perfection of life, according to Augustine—a goal that turns combing into a magical activity.[10]

It was not the first time that Ficino reflected on the benefits of brushing. In his previous book, *Advice Against the Plague*, he considered it a way

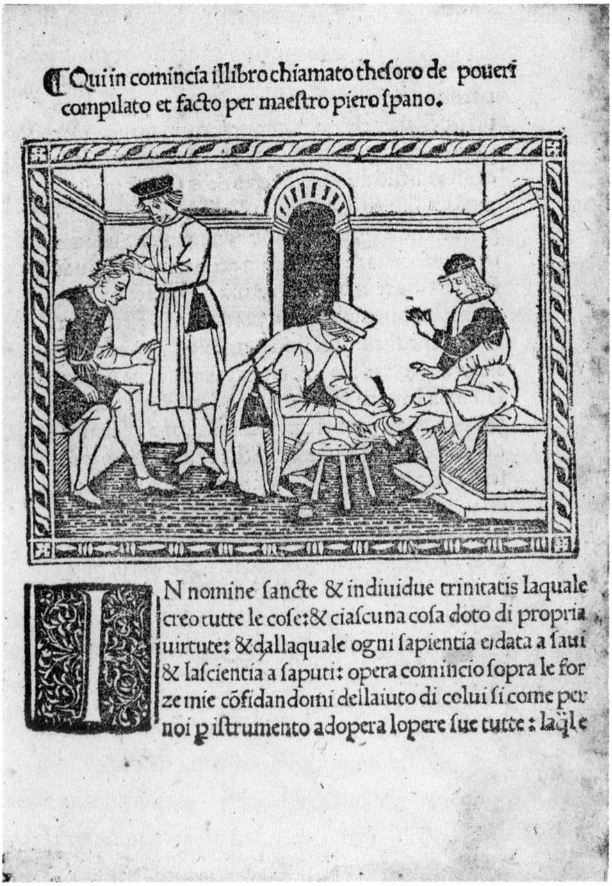

¶ Qui in comincia illibro chiamato theſoro de poueri compilato et facto per maeſtro piero ſpano.

IN nomine ſancte & indiuidue trinitatis laquale creo tutte le coſe:& ciaſcuna coſa doto di propria uirtute: & dallaquale ogni ſapientia e data a ſaui & laſcientia a ſaputi: opera comincio ſopra le forze mie cōfidandomi dellaiuto di colui ſi come per noi p iſtrumento adopera lopere ſue tutte: laq̈le

Figure 9.1. First page of the *Thesaurus pauperum*. Wellcome Collection, London.

to preserve the cleanliness of the world, to which hair was intimately tied.[11] Combing became essential during epidemics, since by keeping the pores tight and small, it made sure that toxic particles did not enter the body through the skin.[12] Doctors insisted that opening the mouth and breathing through the nose led to immediate poisoning, but a neglected break in the skin was just as dangerous, as were the swollen pores of angry people.[13] I wonder if the mechanical repetitiveness of combing helped to calm them down, too.

Ficino's reliance on combing as a measure to preserve the health of the world found its logic in the assumption that the body was somewhat separate from the soul: it was something that was given to people, but which did not coincide with them. So everyone needed to take care of their body as a way to encounter the world. In particular, for Ficino, to care for one's hair implied a will to find one's place in the world. It meant thinking of one's existence in relation to that of others, and thinking of how others could shape and limit one's existence. In other words, taking care of one's hair was political, in the sense of governing oneself and preparing one's body so that it could be used by others.[14]

This widening perspective on combs takes us past the notion that they are just expurgatory devices for cleansing. On the comb seen in plate 28, look at the other row, where the teeth are thicker and spaced more widely apart. These teeth were used to partition the wild mass of hair into regular, manageable strands that could then be braided, twisted, and tucked in.[15] That operation was not secondary. The design of the comb accords it the same importance as the cleaning that was accomplished with the row of more finely spaced teeth, and it is to this parity that I am drawn.

When dealing with loose, unruly hair, the first step was to compact it. After washing, dying, drying, and anointing her long hair, a woman combed it and pulled it to the back, where she gathered it in a long braid. She tightened it with a ribbon that spiraled all around it, and then coiled the resulting pleat around her head, fastening it with pins and tucking its end in the back (figure 9.2a). She may have pulled a ribbon across the whole bundle, pressing it as a string holds pastries in a loaded basket.[16] This compact hairstyle had been deemed practical for centuries. It was adopted by maids who feared that their hair, like that of Absalom, could be caught in something while they were working (plate 16). It was also recommended for virgins, who saw it on the Virgin Mary, God's humble servant (figure 9.2b).[17]

Leon Battista Alberti praised women for keeping their hair bundled up. He took it as a sign that a woman knew her place in the world: "What idiot would doubt that the woman who does not enjoy to be seen clean and in order, not only in her body and clothing but also in every one of

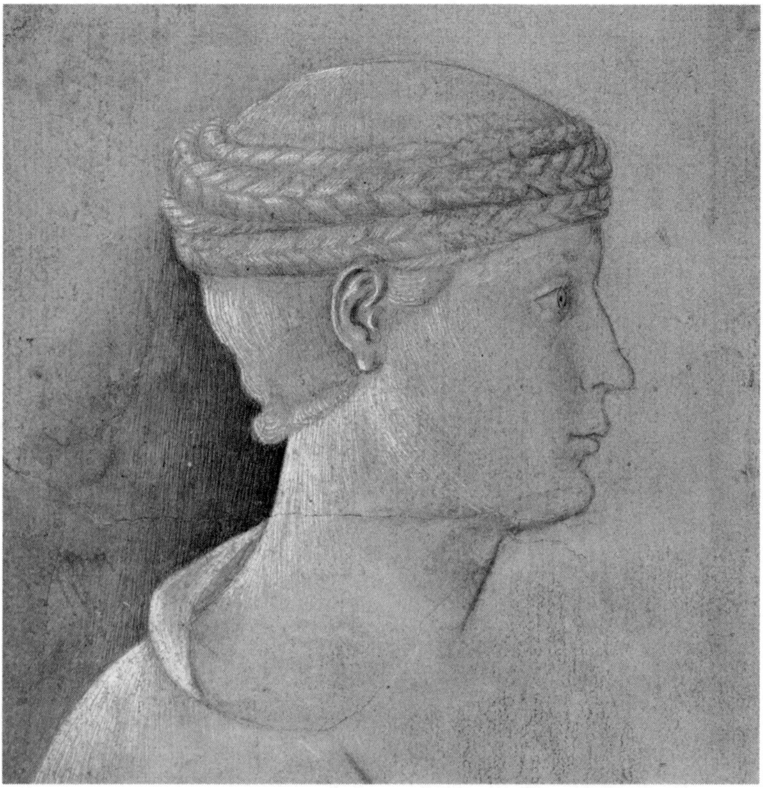

Figure 9.2a. Benozzo Gozzoli, *Bust of a Woman.* Cleveland Museum of Art.

her gestures and actions, would not be considered civil?"[18] His more lenient brother, Carlo, conceded an element of surprise. He appreciated "some small deliberate negligence when styling hair, so as to make your beauty more patent."[19] It is a nod to Apuleius, according to whom a touch of calculated casualness made a woman more fetching.[20] It was also an invitation into what I consider the second phase of fifteenth-century female hairstyling.

After compacting and securing their hair—the first step—Florentine women loosened it up and pulled locks out. They freed wisps from their nape, which bounced when they walked. They also unfastened fringes on each side of their face and crimped them. Especially for social events,

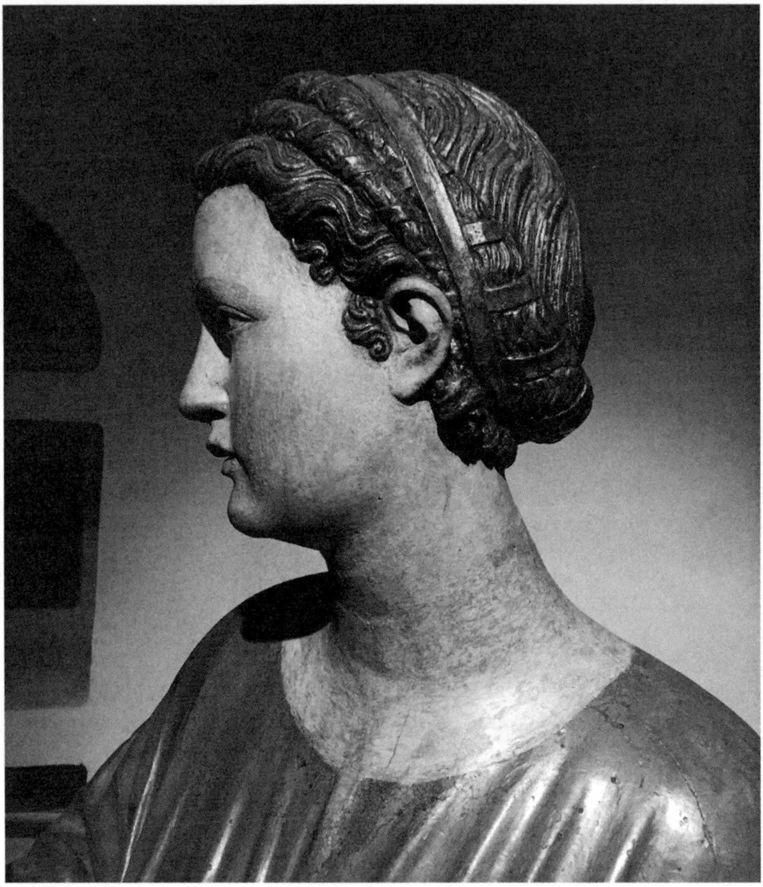

Figure 9.2b. Francesco di Valdambrino, *Annunciation*. Palazzo Corboli, Asciano.

women pushed the coil of their braid from the back of their head to the top, fixing its end to the side of their head and fanning it out in a giant tassel that they left hanging (see figure 2.7). They also took strings or gauze ribbons and draped them more elegantly—that is, more freely—over their hair, intertwining them with locks that sprouted at the top, creating a florescence that, particularly when mixed with brooches, pearl strings, and feathers, turned a woman's head into a plastic spectacle (plate 7; see also figure 2.6).[21]

Men's hair did not require nearly as much attention; but then, they were not told from a young age that hairstyling was essential to their nature.[22] In public they often wore hats that marked their profession or office.[23] When they took the hats off, their manes could reach their shoulders, indicating a measured humoral production. With longer-than-average hair and beard (see figure 7.6), Christ offered a look of philosophical dedication that put him on the same level as sages and emperors.[24] The physician Michele Savonarola, Girolamo's grandfather, considered Christ, with his moderately straight hair, the perfect example of a balanced complexion.[25] A salient feature of Christ's hairstyle, he heard preachers stressing, was its careful central parting, which they took to signify the control he offered to humankind.[26]

Only young, well-off socialites dared to wear their hair bigger, cropped above the eyes, and longer on the sides and especially the back, where it could reach the shoulders (plate 31). Some of them had it trimmed it all around in a continuous half-moon line that followed the imaginary visor edge of a helm, under which it would disappear (see figure 6.4). Even those who were not as fussy paid good money to have their hair straightened with hot tongs, insouciant toward those who mocked such a style as *zazzera*—a derogatory term that cast men who sported it as effeminate.[27]

The same insult was directed at women, but in their case it took the meaning of unkept and dirty hair. If women resisted social pressure and let their hair grow in a *zazzera* style, they were reproached for conceding to their raw, bestial self. They were also urged to comb, braid, and arrange their hair as part of a daily reaction to the natural disorder of the world in which hair, and female hair in particular, participated. By growing at night, during which bed bugs crept in and the dregs of brain humors accumulated, the hair showcased the danger of a world that constantly collapsed on itself, giving way to chaos. The facility by which hair slipped out of the grip of pins and ribbons offered a reminder of the necessity to keep a vigilant eye. Forgetting to fix things, like neglecting to shave one's body with glass shards or anything scorching, compromised the sociovisual order in which the Florentine community found its strength.[28] In fact, the set of wider teeth in a comb was an invitation not to styling, but to governing.[29] Even when it lay untouched in a box of cosmetic tools, a comb unleashed comforting fantasies of discipline: it promised that vermin-infested, superfluous—that is, shitty—hair could be untangled, straightened, and eventually repackaged into a compact, reassuring, and healthy bundle that reduced if not erased the dangers of the world.

The task of putting the world back in order could be successful only if embraced collectively. Wives scrubbed the heads of their husbands, searching for fleas (figure 9.3).[30] Barbers went to their homes and shaved their chins.[31] The task of styling the hair of a woman of means usually fell to her maid. *Pinzochere*—that is, women who renounced secular life to dedicate themselves to a religious confraternity—also came to women's rescue with tweezers, razoring tools, and ointments while offering themselves to men as procurers and intercessors.[32] Less privileged girls went to the street, where they found beauticians (*lisciatrici*) or hairdressers (*mazzocchiaie*). A popular carnival song reproduces the ways hairdressers advertised their services: "Who styles her own hair can only do a bad job, as styling needs two; lie down, gorgeous, and leave the braiding of your hair to us."[33] I hear the chuckles of the listeners: those verses have strong sexual connotations. By insisting that the client lie down, the *mazzocchiaie* showed that the hair they intended to braid was not that which grew on their clients' heads. Yet the vulgar joke would not have landed if it did not play on something obvious: that styling was something that, like sex, was done by two people.

The involvement of two people meant that every hairpin was a matter of negotiation. Women must have discussed the curling of a lock, the effectiveness of a hair parter, the explicitness of a braid, the audacity of a dye. Clients also questioned the morality of their helpers, in the street as well as at the baths, since they reminded themselves that "whoever is not proper cannot clean another."[34] Requests of decency and modesty did not only echo in the rooms inhabited by jealous husbands and overbearing parents, but anywhere a toilette took place, including the stool where a woman sat, holding a mirror with one hand and the comb with the other. For what are mirrors if not means to double oneself, so as to be both model and stylist? Far from being just visual aids, mirrors also carried the look of patriarchy within them.[35]

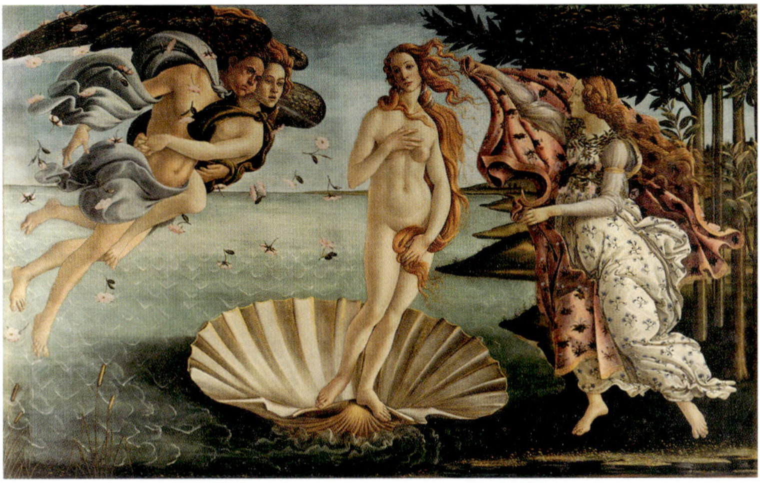

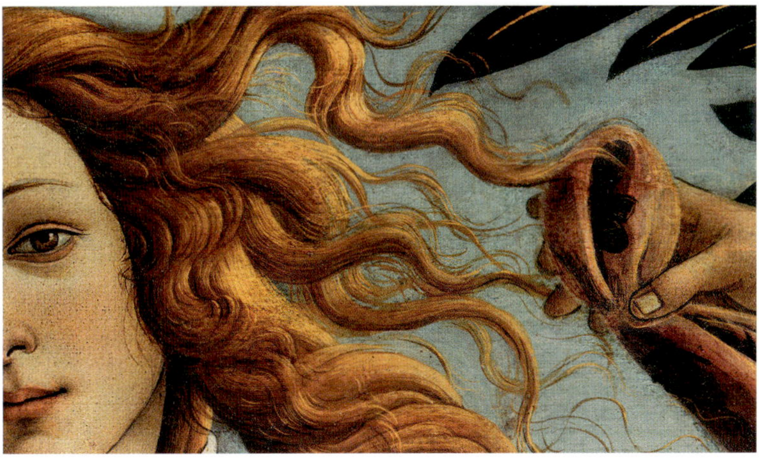

Plates 1 and 2. Sandro Botticelli, *The Birth of Venus*. Gallerie degli Uffizi, Florence.

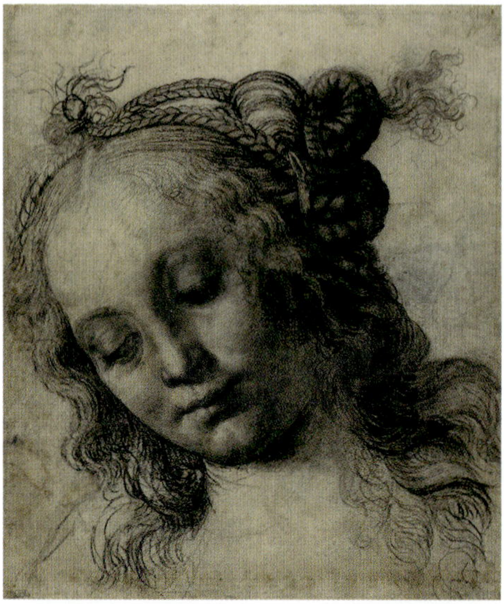

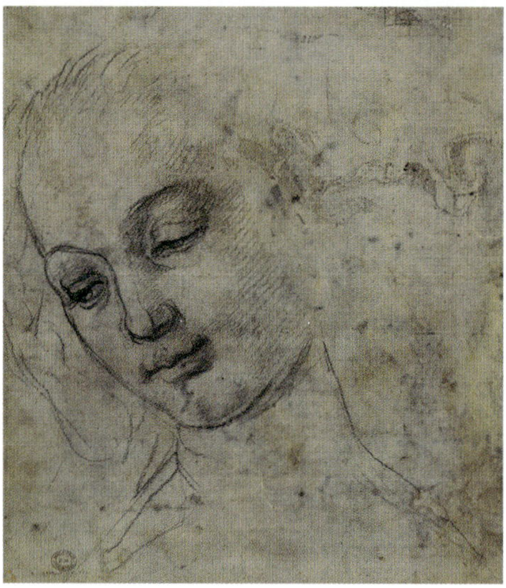

Plates 3 and 4. Andrea del Verrocchio, *Study for a Head*. British Museum, London.

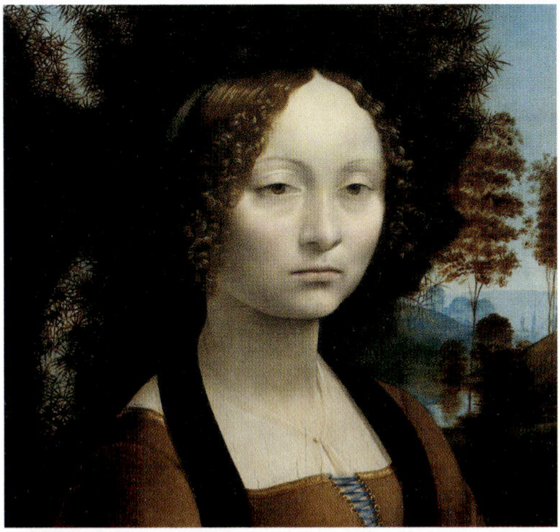

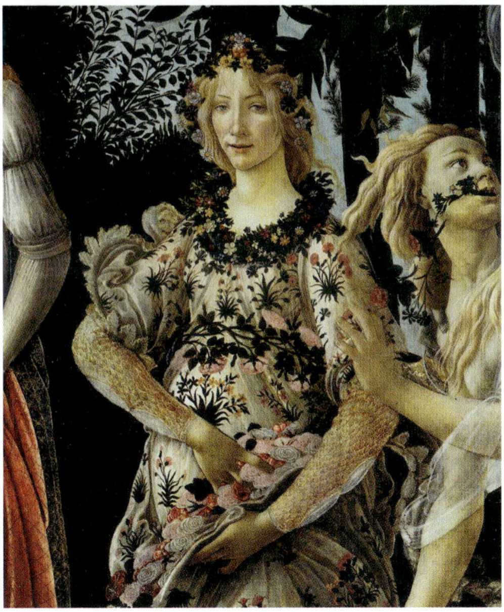

Plate 5. Leonardo da Vinci, *Portrait of Ginevra de' Benci.* National Gallery of Art, Washington.

Plate 6. Sandro Botticelli, *Primavera*. Gallerie degli Uffizi, Florence.

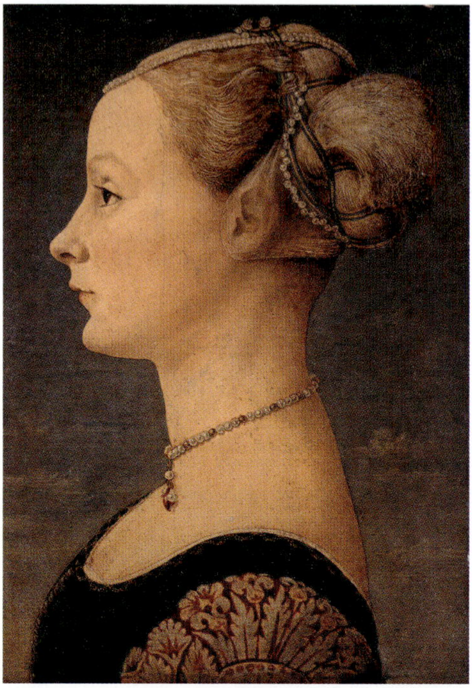

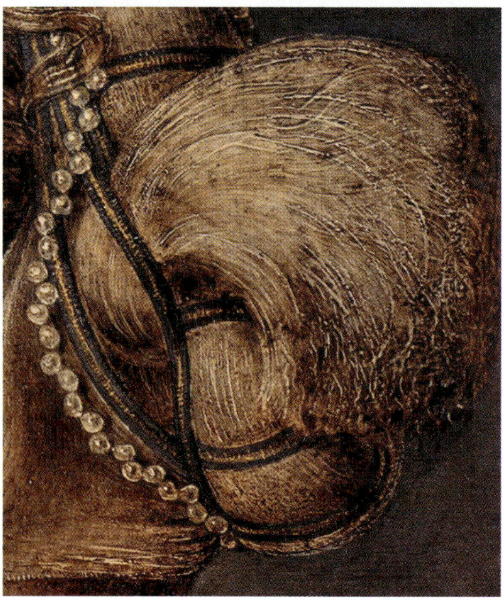

Plates 7 and 8. Piero Pollaiuolo, *Portrait of a Lady.* Museo Poldi Pezzoli, Milan.

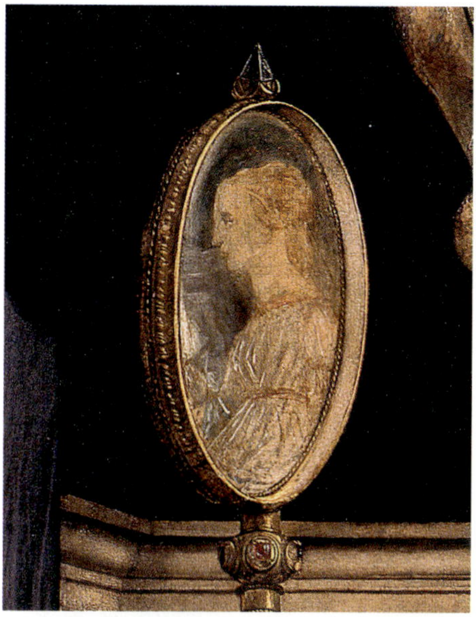

Plate 9. Piero and Antonio Pollaiuolo, *Prudence* (detail of figure 6.3). Gallerie degli Uffizi, Florence.

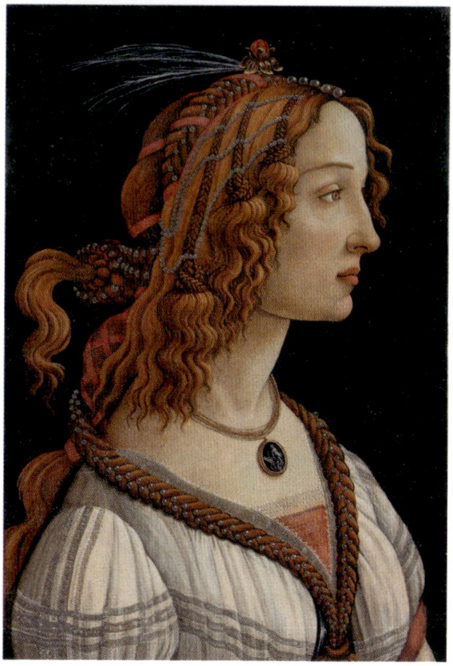

Plate 10. Sandro Botticelli, *Portrait of Simonetta Vespucci*. Städel Museum, Frankfurt.

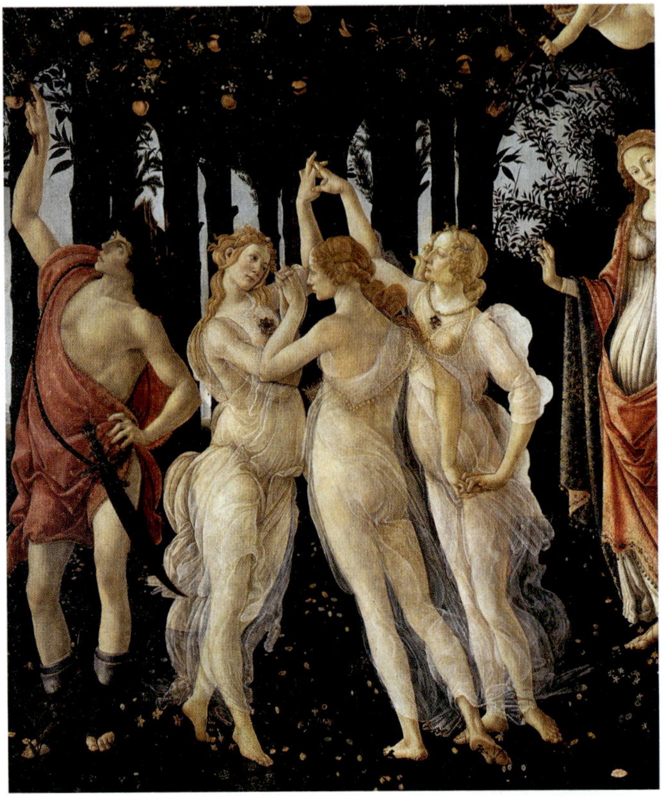

Plates 11 and 12. Sandro Botticelli, *Primavera*. Gallerie degli Uffizi, Florence.

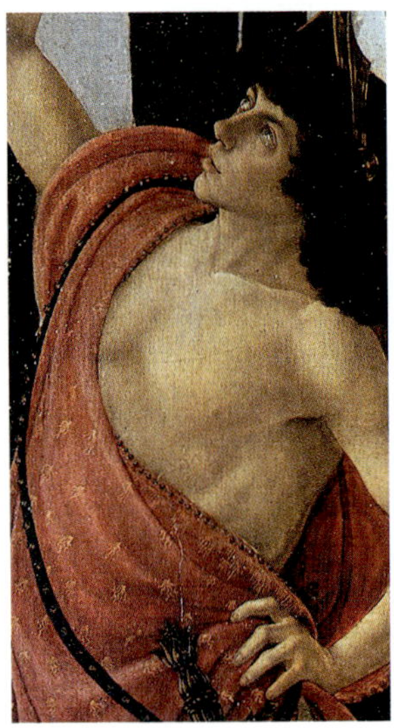

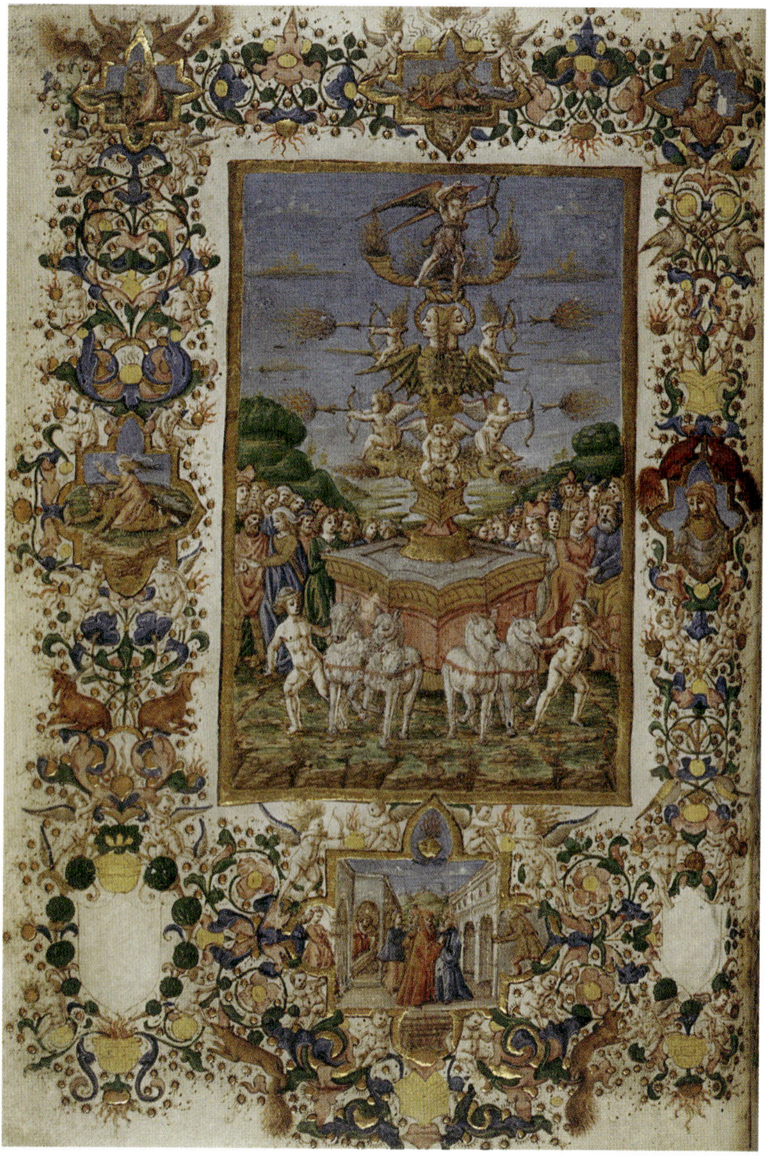

Plate 13. Ricciardo di Nanni, *Triumph of Love*, an illumination of Petrarch's *Triumphs*. Ms. Vitr. 22/4, f. 12v. Biblioteca Nacional de España, Madrid.

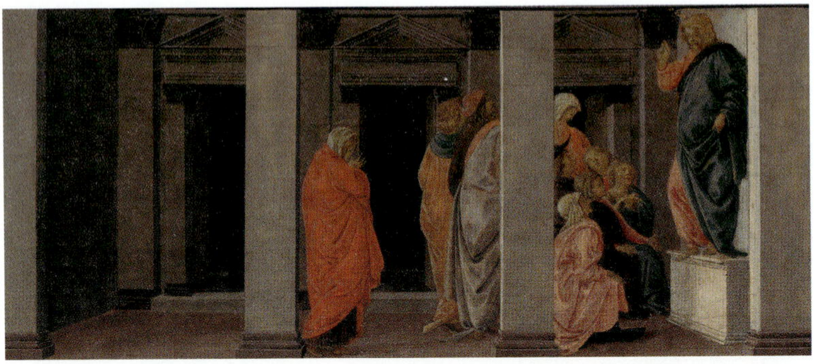

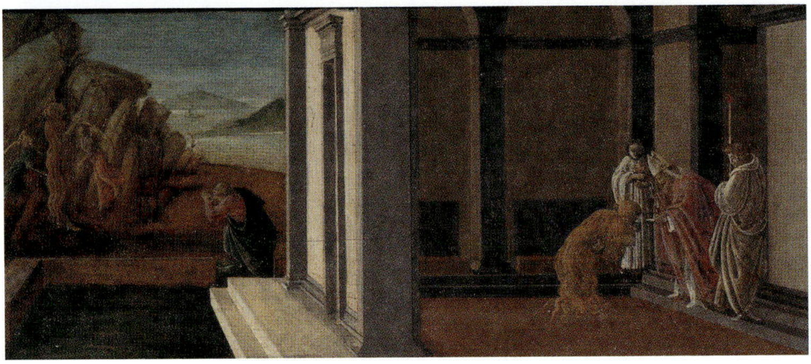

Plates 14 and 15. Sandro Botticelli and Filippino Lippi, *Mary Magdalene Listening to Christ Preach* and *Mary Magdalene Receives Last Communion from Saint Maximinus.* Philadelphia Museum of Art.

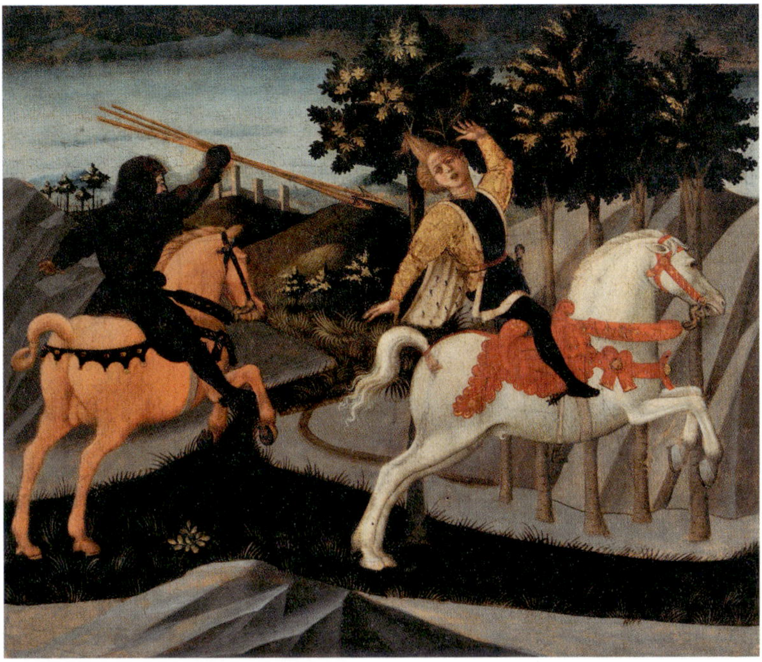

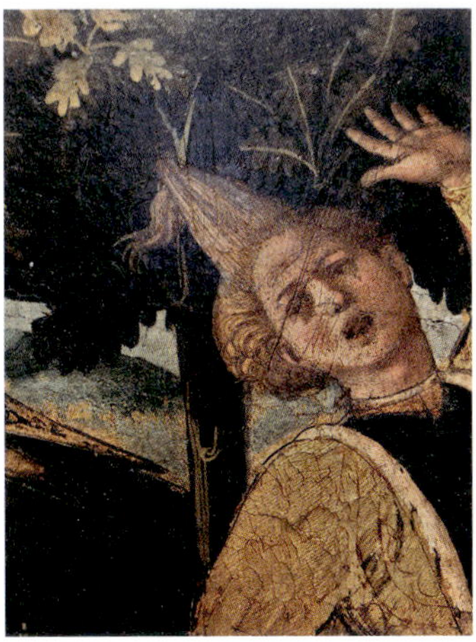

Plates 16 and 17. Francesco Pesellino, *The Death of Absalom*. Musée de Tessé, Le Mans.

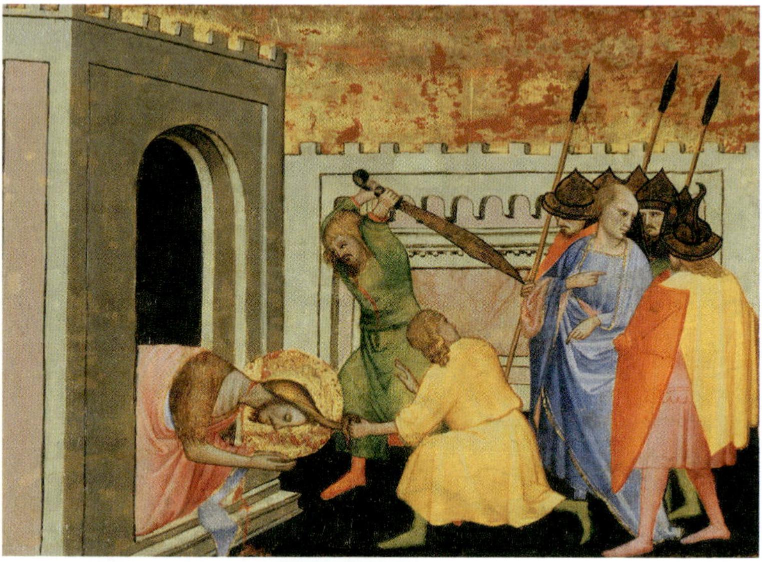

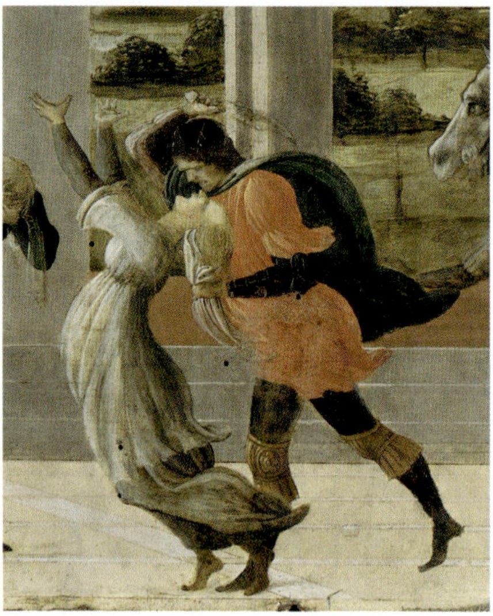

Plate 18. Cenni di Francesco, martyrdom of Saint John the Baptist. Philadelphia Museum of Art.

Plate 19. Filippino Lippi, *The Life of Virginia*. Musée du Louvre, Paris.

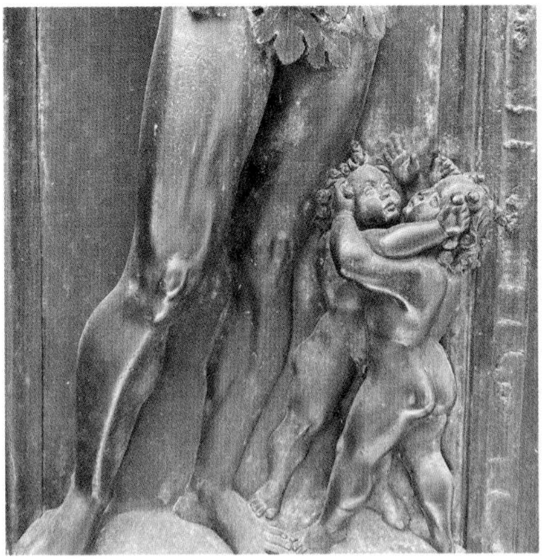

Plate 20. Vittore Ghiberti, frame of south door depicting two children fighting. Baptistery, Florence.

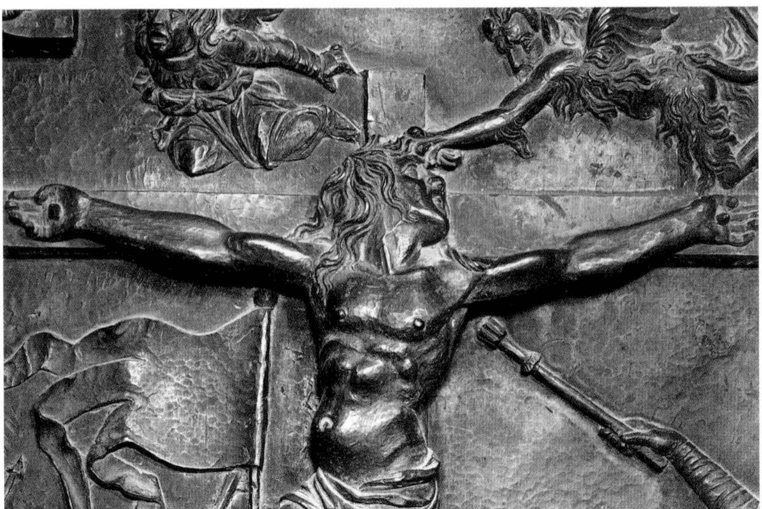

Plate 21. Donatello, crucifixion. in *Passion Pulpit*, Basilica di San Lorenzo, Florence.

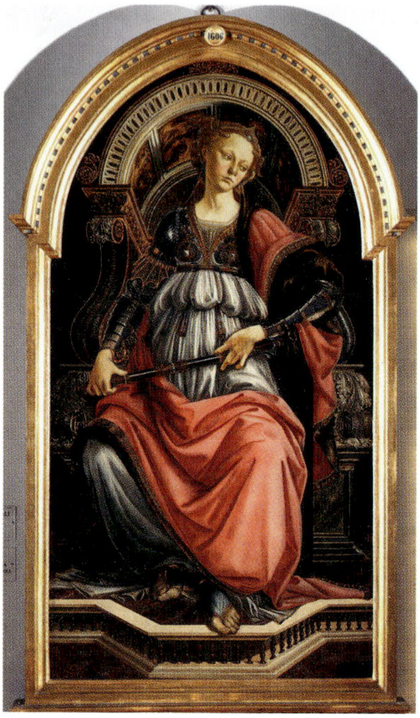 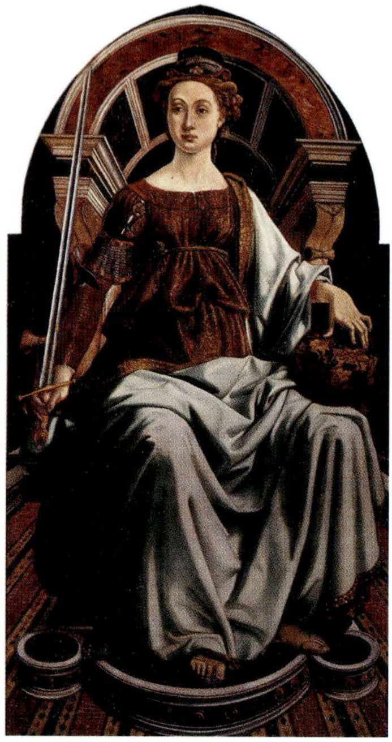

Plate 22. Sandro Botticelli, *Fortitude*. Gallerie degli Uffizi, Florence.

Plate 23. Piero del Pollaiolo, *Justice*. Gallerie degli Uffizi, Florence.

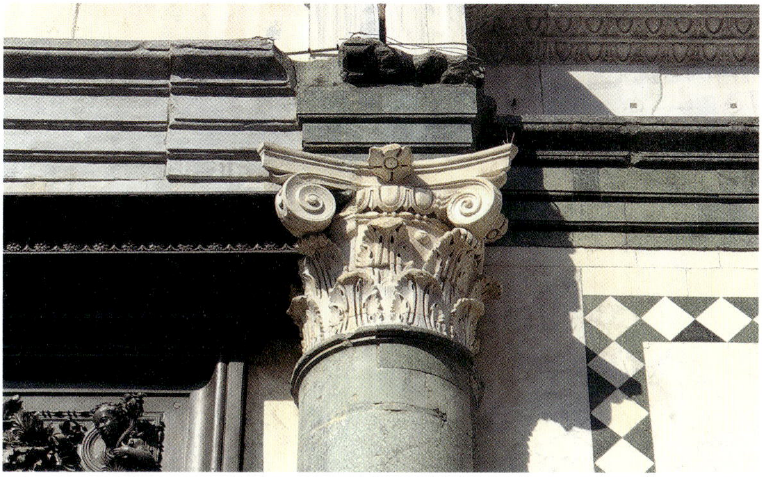

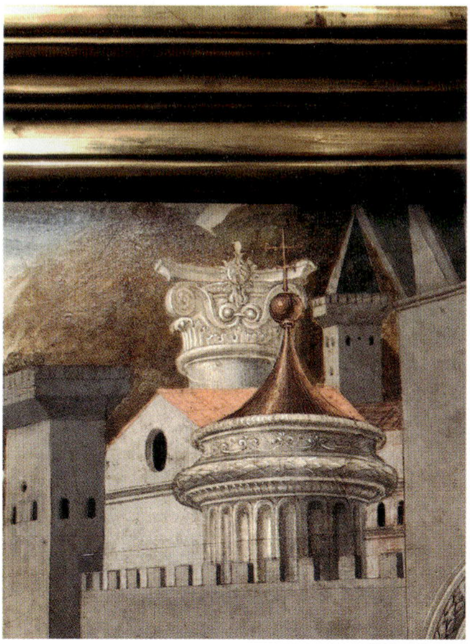

Plate 24. Capital on the south side of Florence's baptistery.

Plate 25. Workshop of Piero del Pollaiuolo, *The Triumph of Aemilius Paulus*. Musée Jacquemart-André, Paris.

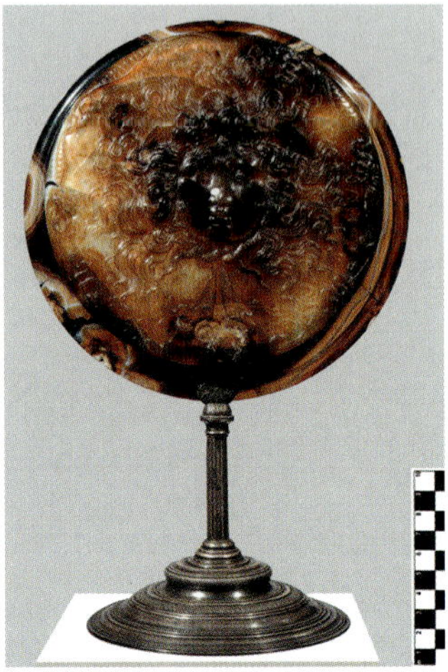

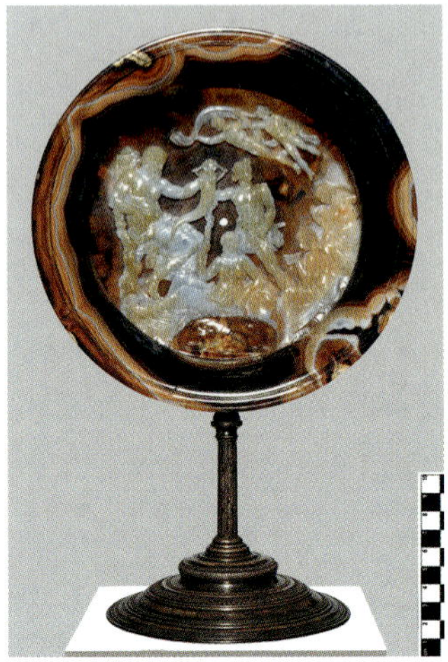

Plates 26 and 27. The so-called Farnese Cup. Museo Archeologico Nazionale, Naples.

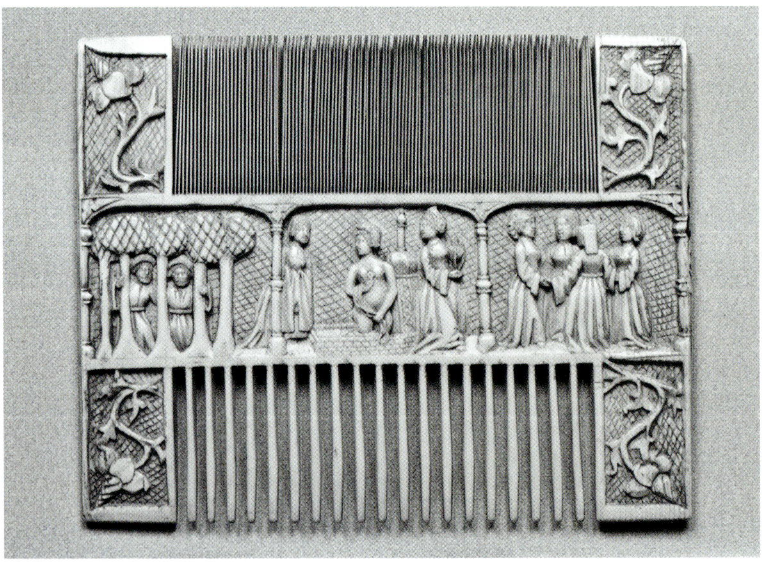

Plate 28. Comb with image of Susanne and the Elders. Museo Nazionale del Bargello, Naples.

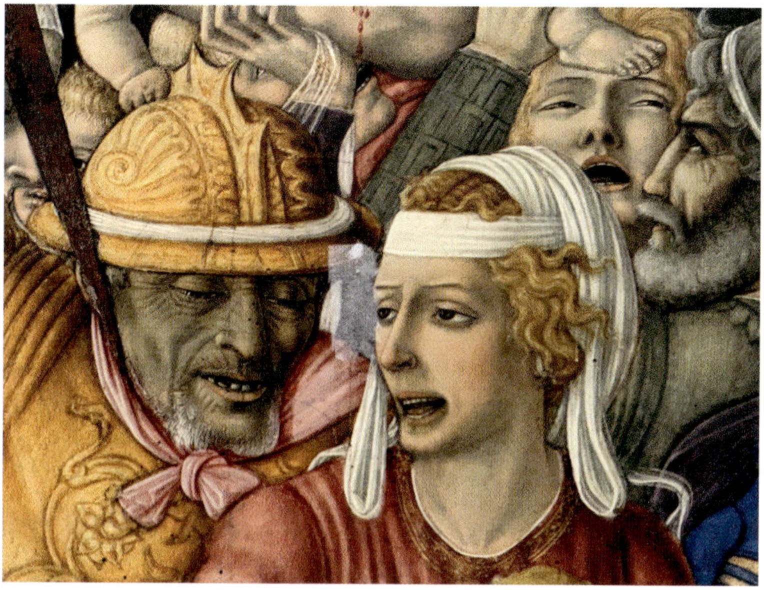

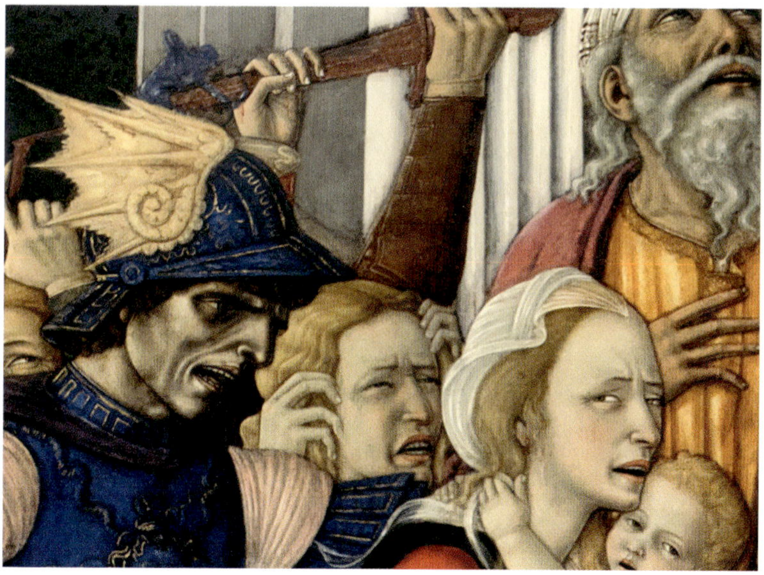

Plates 29 and 30. Matteo di Giovanni, *Massacre of the Innocents*. Museo di Capodimonte, Naples.

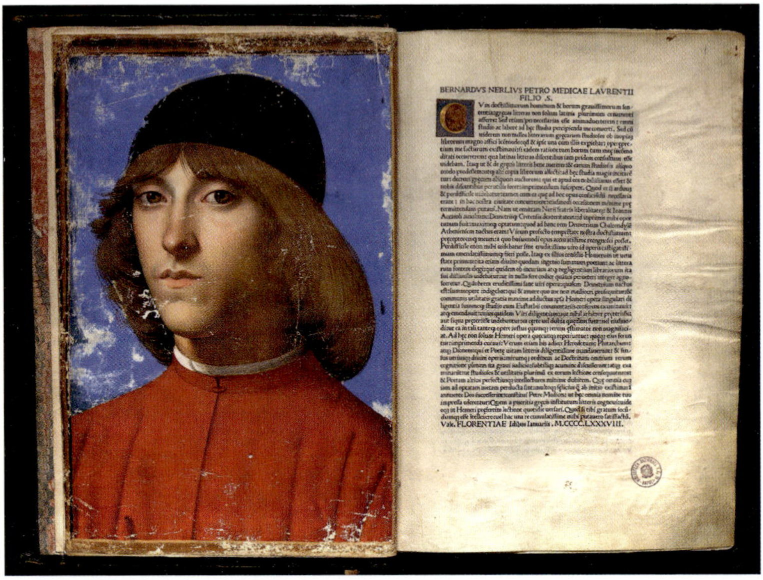

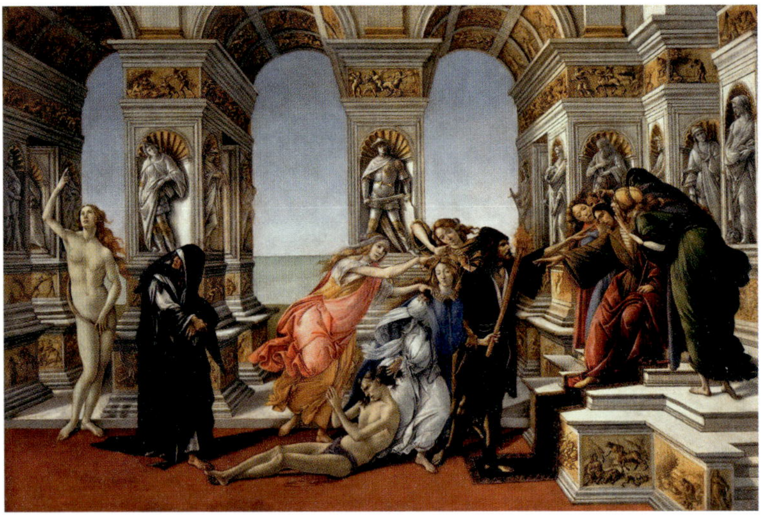

Plate 31. Gherardo di Giovanni del Fora, *Portrait of Piero de' Medici*. Ms SQ XXII K 22, f. 2v. Biblioteca Nazionale "Vittorio Emanuele III," Naples.

Plate 32. Sandro Botticelli, *Allegory of Calumny*. Gallerie degli Uffizi, Florence.

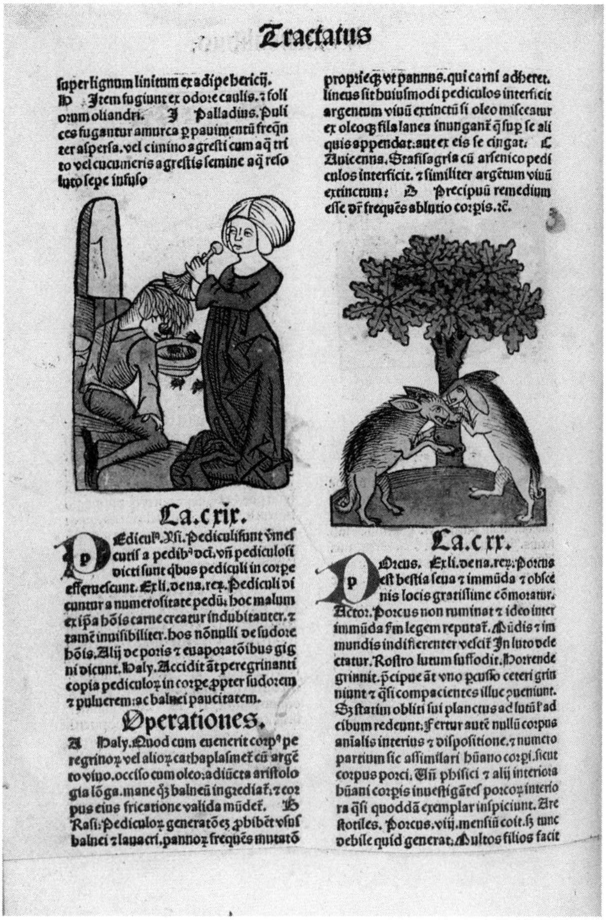

Figure 9.3. Woman delousing the head of a man. Illustration in the *Ortus Sanitatis*. Wellcome Collection, London.

The National Library of France, in Paris, keeps the large frame of a small, round mirror that represents the bust of a dolled-up woman (figure 9.4). Looking down at the viewer, the bust offers a model to copy: plucked, linear eyebrows, downcast eyes, two butterfly wings of curls framing the face—as if the mirror were to contain a reflection of its frame eventually.[36] The sculpted woman invited mirror-gazers to drape strings of pearls across their foreheads, a touch of luxury that may not

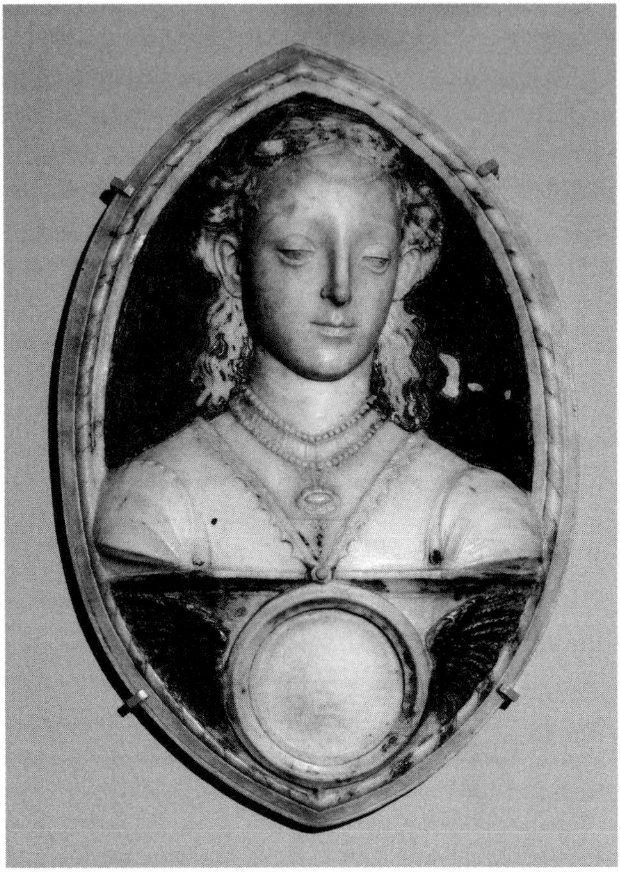

Figure 9.4. Workshop of Mino da Fiesole, bust of a young woman in mirror frame. Cabinet des médailles et antiques, Bibliothèque nationale de France, Paris.

have undermined the belief that propriety was achieved first and foremost by manipulating one's features. It may all sound slightly despotic, but we have encountered such logic before. The Parisian mirror, after all, finds its counterpart in the double drawing Verrocchio gave to Leonardo (plates 3 and 4). Constructed around a transformative act, the drawing reproduces the before-and-after process of any makeover. The model goes from unassuming presence, which Verrocchio quickly sketches, to ideal beauty, which he carefully draws and shades.[37] As we saw, it is her hair that reveals the extent of female manipulation. And now we can see that it was through hair that Florentine families came to appreciate beauty as a form of control.

But highlighting this control may give the impression that Florentine women were subject to a form of draconic authoritarianism, and that would be an exaggeration. As Carlo Alberti's recommendation of loosening up exemplifies, women were also invested in a quest for distinction. This tension was probably felt by all members of Florentine households as they found themselves caught in an oscillation between allegiance to civic regulations and competition. While combing their hair, men and especially women prepared themselves to abide by general norms: they reinscribed themselves into what Leon Battista Alberti defined as civility and Ficino considered a commitment to universal order. Yet with the very same comb, they also prepared themselves to break from those norms and participate in the different enterprise of familial prestige, shaped by relations that sometimes reached beyond the city's boundaries.

Forced to respond to two opposite pulls, how did women and their families compromise? Who set the sense of an acceptable middle point? A Florentine mother is recorded as advising her soon to be married daughter that her appearance should always meet her husband's taste. "If your husband saw you dishonestly embellish yourself beyond his pleasure, he would take you lightly and could even become suspicious. If you instead keep your appearance honest, he will love you and keep you dear to him."[38] Notice that the husband's reaction is never questioned; it is up to a woman to prove herself innocent. This disparity returns in sermons that insist that well-coiffed women should watch their every step and gesture, since everyone had the right to comment on them.[39] Preachers counted on a mass audience as indistinct as it was idealized: a community of faceless people who could recollect Saint Paul's commandment against hairstyles with implausible rapidity. But no matter how unlikely this scenario—the many portraits of men sporting *zazzere* demonstrate that moralistic commandments did not always hit the target—friars attacked women so often that many of their listeners must have followed suit.

To avoid criticism, a woman trod the middle ground of decency. In his popular treatise on women's manners, which men read as well, Francesco da Barberino insisted that in arranging female hair, one ought to follow "what Temperance teaches."[40] Francesco's instructions, built on negatives, cast hairstyling as a business on the constant brink of wrongness. Hair should not be washed too often, nor too seldom. It should not have too many artificial extensions attached. It should also not be constantly covered.[41] The search for the mean led to a moralizing equation, in keeping with the religious diktat that hairstyling was not dangerous by default, but could easily turn into a hazard. What was a venial sin—that is, adorning the hair out of silliness—could become an immoral act if prompted by other motives.[42]

Intentions mattered. Indeed, it was at the level of wishes, when intentions were reasoned into actions or reasoned away, that people searched for a limit in hairstyling. The didactic manual *The Flower of Virtue* reminded its readers—children and their schoolmasters—that to learn temperance, one ought to keep one's heart in check and stay away from hairstyling.[43] Pierozzi, the bishop of Florence who did so much to shape the city's moral life, identified three main emotions that turned hairstyling into a mortal sin: pride, vanity, and lust.[44] His advice was in line with Francesco da Barberino's lessons, which end in an unforgettable image: "A woman is to hairstyling what the deer is to the fountain."[45] This is a reference to a biblical psalm in which King David compares his ultimate wish to join God to the longing for water of a deer aching with thirst.[46] By invoking the dying deer, Barberino characterized women's drive for hairstyling as an instinct for survival. And not just an instinct, since the deer's desperate quest, Tuscan bestiaries taught, was caused by the ingestion of snakes, which were symbols of luxury.[47] These associations were leveraged by Pierozzi, who stated that hairstyling was deadly if triggered by lust.

These commands were not encountered occasionally: they crept onto toilette tools. A comb decorated with the story of Eustache, the saint who saw Christ in a deer he was hunting, may have resonated with Barberino's simile (see figure 5.5).[48] We encountered it in chapter 5, where I described it as a liturgical comb. Yet the identification is not certain, and it is possible that the comb was made for private use.[49] (Regardless of its initial function, I do not think we should diminish this carving, or any carving, to its hagiographic meaning. Combs shifted hands over time, and their decorations invited reflections of different magnitudes.)[50] Historians tend to read the decorations on combs in relation to the amorous game in which the tools participated, since the stories of the time often speak of lovers exchanging combs that bore mottos of loyalty, dancing scenes, and hearts pierced by arrows.[51] The recipients of these gifts must have looked at the carvings on them in anticipation of meeting with their suitors—even the imaginary ones described in romances.[52] Yet more often than not, combs bore illustrations of cautionary tales that warned against the perils of an unfettered life.[53] They recall the story of Susannah's reckless bathing, which led to two old voyeurs blackmailing her, and to an exhausting trial (plate 28). They focus on the libidinous Paris, who, by impulsively crowning Venus as the most beautiful goddess, triggered the bloody Trojan wars.[54] Many combs focus on Bathsheba's toilette, during which she neglected to shelter her body. Even just one episode—the moment King David, from his towering palace, saw her naked —must have been enough to evoke the rest of the story: how David's desire led to Bathsheba's adultery, the death of her husband in battle, and eventually the death of her illegitimate child.[55] Women must have thought about Bathsheba's fate when arranging their hair. The famous preacher Giovanni da Capistrano invited them to do so in a sermon in which he argued that lust was aroused out of lack of attention.[56] As one of the strictest moralists of his time, Capistrano insisted that women had to think about their hairstyles carefully. Hair care was acceptable only insofar as it revealed one's status. Yet even a noble woman ought to approach it reluctantly, as did the Jewish queen Esther, who professed: "I abhor the sign of glory and pride that has been placed on my head."[57]

The depth to which religious preaching tried to dominate the domestic space is revealed by another comb, today in Liverpool, which shows a friar lecturing a crowd of seated women (figure 9.5).[58] Of what sermons did this scene remind its owner? What warnings could she have heard in her head when holding this carving between her fingers? I can only guess

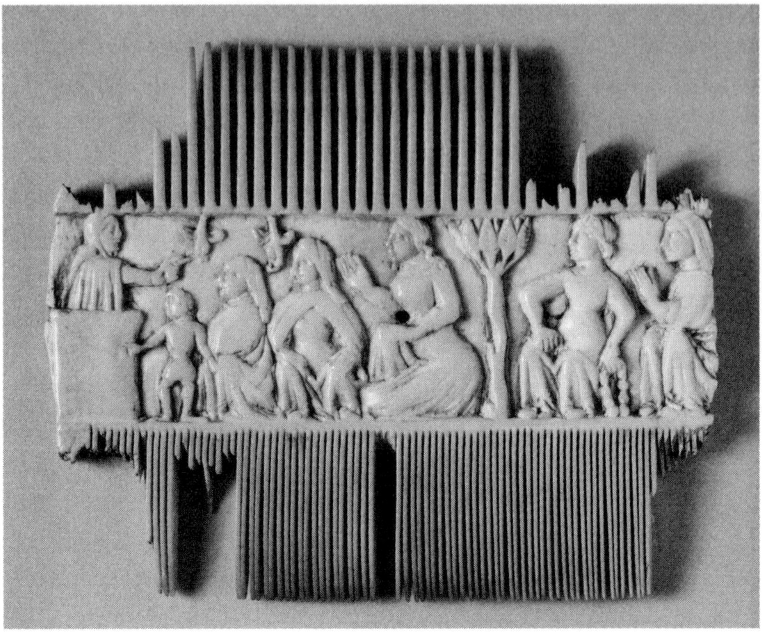

Figure 9.5. Comb. Walker Art Gallery, Liverpool.

at the wishes that may have accompanied the offer of another comb, one of the many that represent the Annunciation (figure 9.6). There, a well-built, indeed impenetrable, brick stand shields the Virgin's womb—an allusion to its inaccessibility. The message of this carving is the opposite of the cautionary tales we have seen so far, and thus is in continuity with them: If the exposure of a woman's body could ruin a family, its successful control would lead to the ultimate miracle of Christ's birth.

Reminders that the only will that mattered was God's were hardly subtle in fifteenth-century Florence. Return to Simonetta's portrait (plate 10) and look at her necklace. It shows Apollo defeating the satyr Marsyas, a myth that warned against the hubris of those who challenge God's design.[59] Here again, an accessory for women is turned into an invitation to caution. Not complying with the status quo would attract divine fury, upon oneself and one's city. This sense of danger returns in chronicles such as Giovanni Villani's history of Florence, which recalls

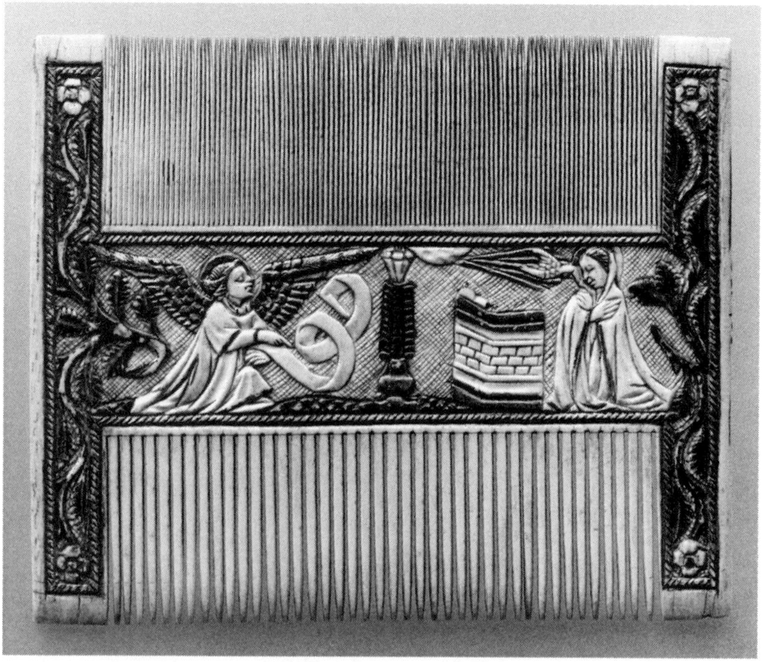

Figure 9.6. Comb bearing image of the Annunciation. Musée national du Moyen Age, Thermes de Cluny, Paris.

how fourteenth-century Florentine women started wearing braids made of yellow and blue silk, and how that was the beginning of the end.[60] Even if it now seems hard to believe, there was a time when unconventional hairstyling was a credible threat to a city's sense of identity, since it was taken as an affront to its traditions, a symptom of collective alienation.[61] Governments sought to watch out for any hesitation; even the substitution of a hairpin could set off an alarm. "Whoever neglects the little things will fall, little by little," insisted the preacher Giovanni da Capistrano, who served as a moral advisor to many administrative councils.[62]

It is to this need to preserve order even in seemingly unimportant things that Boccaccio clings when, in his book *The Labyrinth of Love*, he fulminates against hairstyling. Printed less than ten years after his

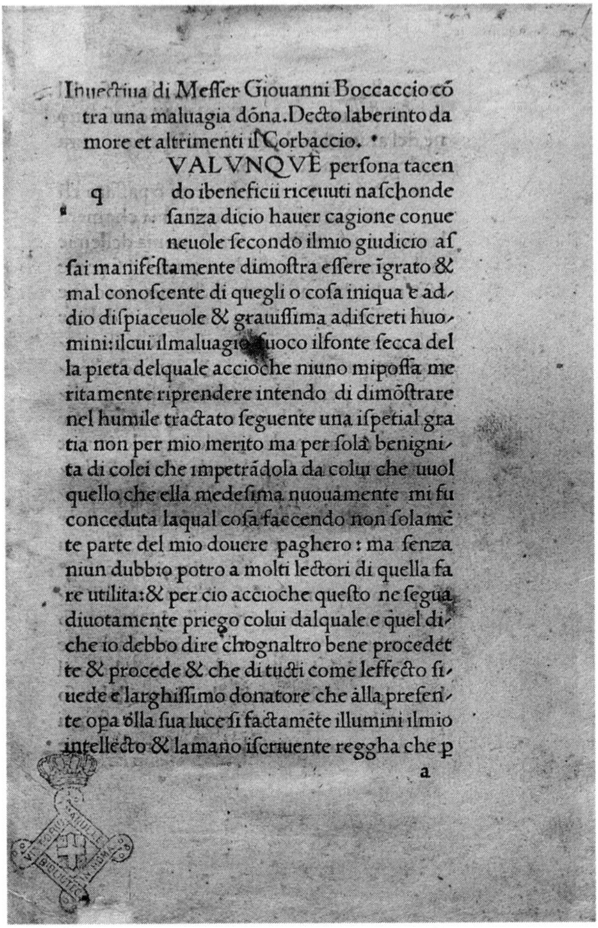
Inuectiua di Meſſer Giouanni Boccaccio cõ
tra una maluagia dõna. Decto laberinto da
more et altrimenti il Corbaccio.
q VALVNQVE perſona tacen
do ibeneficii riceuuti naſchonde
ſanza dicio hauer cagione conue
neuole ſecondo ilmio giudicio aſ
ſai manifeſtamente dimoſtra eſſere ĩgrato &
mal conoſcente di quegli o coſa iniqua e ad-
dio diſpiaceuole & grauiſſima adiſcreti huo-
mini: ilcui ilmaluagio fuoco ilfonte ſecca del
la pieta delquale acciochc niuno mipoſſa me
ritamente riprendere intendo di dimõſtrare
nel humile tractato ſeguente una iſpetial gra
tia non per mio merito ma per ſola benigni-
ta di colei che impetrãdola da colui che uuol
quello che ella medeſima nuouamente mi fu
conceduta laqual coſa faccendo non ſolamẽ
te parte del mio douere paghero: ma ſenza
niun dubbio potro a molti lectori di quella fa
re utilita: & per cio accioche queſto ne ſegua
diuotamente priego colui dalquale e quel di-
che io debbo dire chognaltro bene procedet
te & procede & che di tucti come leffecto ſi-
uede e larghiſſimo donatore che alla preſen-
te opa olla ſua luce ſi factamẽte illumini ilmio
intellecto & lamano iſcriuente reggha che p
a

Figure 9.7. First page of the first edition of Giovanni Boccaccio's *Labyrinth of Love* (also known as *Corbaccio*). Biblioteca Nazionale Centrale "Vittorio Emanuele II," Rome.

Comedy of the Florentine Nymphs (see figure 4.2), *The Labyrinth of Love* (figure 9.7) details a man's suffering for the unrequited love of an evil woman, about whom he complains to the ghost of her dead husband, who appears to him in a dream. While the *Comedy* indulges in the exuberance of hairstyles, *The Labyrinth of Love* exposes the pains in their making, stripping them of any pleasure: for how can you enjoy something that causes so much stress? Boccaccio chronicles the mad search for beauticians in the streets of Florence, the struggle of finding fresh flowers out of season. In Boccaccio's hands, hairstyling becomes clockwork. While art is pure freedom, hairstyling is a succession of boring habits: hours spent boiling ash while discussing the imperceptible differences between anointments. Boccaccio also presents hairstyling as fueled by an obsession for control: the fifty times it takes to decide the position of a lock, the delicate arranging and rearranging of veils, the comical preoccupation with white hairs (which cunning women plucked or concealed).[63] Even if hyperbolic in tone, Boccaccio's parody hints at the emotional drain caused by hairstyling: the mounting impatience with unruly hair, which breaks off into swearing. This is not to mention the delusional justifications women give to men (*All of this is for you*) and to themselves (*I must do this or he'll go with another woman*). Boccaccio states that an emptiness pervades a woman when no one takes notice of her efforts, and that such blankness, a sort of inner inertness, is what makes her rush to the window upon hearing approaching steps. As the astute writer he is, Boccaccio imagines that even after the woman realizes that the steps belong to a stranger who has lost his way, she cannot help but put all of her hopes in him; and that once those hopes are shattered and the man goes away, as she knew he would, they turn into a retch of dark hatred.[64]

Boccaccio's level of detail is so unique that, if he did not make his condemnations explicit, his description could be mistaken as an act of love.[65] "It was a laughable thing to have seen her when she adorned her head—with what art, diligence, and care it was done: on that verily hung the law and the prophets."[66] Throughout the book he describes women as insatiable, calculating beasts whose actions "aim at nothing else but to rob, lord over, and deceive men."[67] And he insists on this denigration, since this is not a book of help for young men, even if that is what Boccaccio claims, but a misogynist tirade whose mission can be summed up by its last line: "See that you do not come into the hands of evil women, especially into those of she who surpasses every demon in wickedness."[68]

Demonic: this was the attribute regularly thrown at women whose relationship with hair fell out of moderation. It was not an insult aimed only at the girl who spent too much time on her hair. It was directed also at those who failed to take care of their hair and were then flagged as threatening if not fiendish. Bernardino da Siena told the Florentines the story of an old woman from Lucca who found a lost purse full of gold, thanks to her skills at satanic enchantment. The way he characterized her? She had unkept hair.[69] Disheveled hair was also the defining characteristic of Matteuccia da Todi, who was caught charming an animal and was convicted for witchcraft in a case that became famous throughout Italy. It was so famous that it set a precedent for the case of Filippa da Città della Pieve, who, the official record specifies, was found naked, "undoing her hair to a state beyond any form of order," after which she gave herself to the devil.[70]

Undone, untidy hair became the salient trait of witches. This felt appropriate to anyone who read classical literature. In one of his satires, Horace feels threatened by "women who coil men's minds into knots with their enchantments and spells and poisons." He is particularly terrified of "Canidia, with her skimpy black skirt tucked up, barefoot, howling, her hair flying wild"—the prototype of the night-loving, beastly sorceress of the fifteenth century.[71] Preachers and humanists did not read Horace's text as a fantasy. They read it as a reality, and searched for the traits he listed—the unkept hair, the vampiric thirst for blood, the expertise with herbs—as evidence that a woman was flirting with the devil.[72] So when in *The Labyrinth of Love* Boccaccio describes the widow who did not reciprocate his love as wanting to make her skin more white and luminous by means of the "blood of various animals, and herbs," readers immediately got what type of woman he was talking about. I suppose that it came as no surprise that her house was "full of stoves and alembics and pans and cruets."[73]

Bernardino asked Florentines to refrain from reading *The Labyrinth of Love*. He took Boccaccio's descriptions of female fixations as so vivid as to whet the desires of the weak, no matter how strongly he denounced them.[74] And while Bernardino drew from *The Labyrinth of Love* for his homilies, he insisted that it was better if simple people did not deal with it themselves.[75] His warning was in line with those of priests who insisted on the need to supervise women all the time since, especially during their toilettes, they could hide things under their hair.[76] What things they hid are not to be known, but Dominicans grew so wary of female hair that they shaved the heads of those accused of witchcraft. Only when unshielded by their hair—the friars insisted—could witches be restored to their natural submissiveness. And this lunatic reasoning did not remain in the abstract: it is what happened to forty-one women, accused of eating children, who were burned alive in Wormserbad, today the Italian town of Bormio in the Alps.[77]

So try to imagine a chorus of voices—voices that apparently had nothing to do with one another—that described women's hair as a threat, and a particularly dangerous one since the devil was behind it. Think of overhearing on one occasion that hair was the gift of the devil to a woman, and on another that hair served as the weapon by which demons controlled human bodies.[78] Imagine hearing one song about an old hag who, while encircling her head with a long braid (see figure 9.2a), appears to be a pirouetting devil, and another that refers to women's hairy vagina as an "angry devil."[79] Imagine listening to a scholar instruct farmers to shoo snakes (the devil's pets) by burning women's hair.[80] Envision your confessor telling you that the hair growing on your body revealed your intention to sin.[81] You may have even believed him, since your wet nurse had warned you in your childhood that all demons, including the ogre who would come for you if you kept crying at night, were covered in hair.[82] After all, you could see such demons in churches, even on an altar in the venerable church of Santo Spirito: a demon with fangs, horns, and a beaded tail sticking out of a body of flaming red hair, holding the hook with which it kidnapped boys (figure 9.8).[83] The idea that hair belonged to the netherworld was confirmed by depictions of death as a female skeleton with long, flowing hair, waiting at the doorsteps of sick men.[84] So you may not have needed anything else—*case closed!*—to be convinced of the demonic nature of female hair, especially after someone added that women had long, strong manes so that the devil could easily drag them to hell.[85] But this was what happened to men too; the pulpit in the church of San Lorenzo showed a flying de-

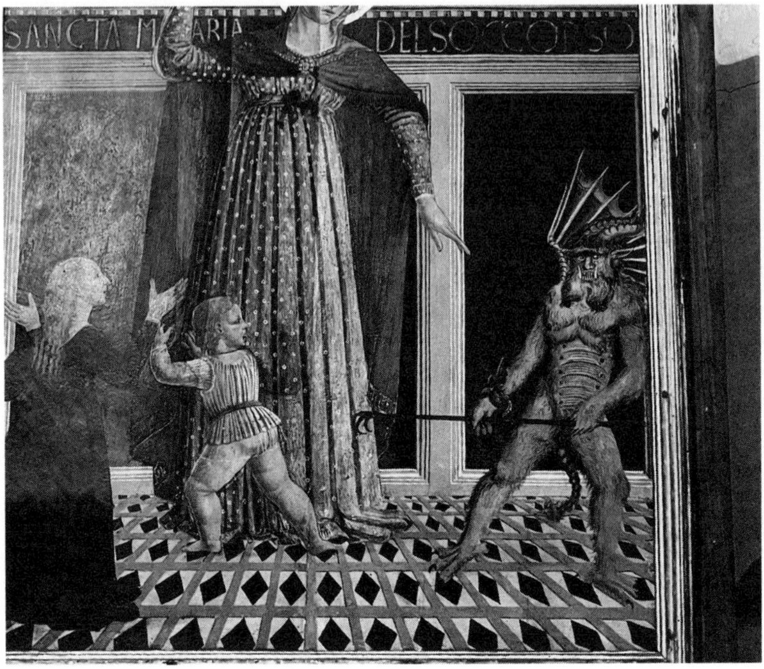

Figure 9.8. Domenico di Zanobi, *Madonna del Soccorso*. Velluti Chapel, Basilica di Santo Spirito, Florence.

mon reaching for the hair of the thief who was about to be thrown into the abyss (plate 21).

It all made sense. Demons were particularly effective at grabbing dead stuff, and hair was dead matter; this is why it was the only thing growing out of death's skull. Wigs must have been doubly dead, as they were made from the hair shorn off corpses.[86] After removing them before going to sleep, stupid women kept them in their bedrooms, unaware that they served as portals for dark forces.[87] "It is shocking that even very shy women do not shrink away from wearing the hair of the dead," Bishop Pierozzi warned. "But they should fear vanities, or rather the devil providing them, and even that because of them they are suspended over hell, as Absalom remained suspended on the tree because of his hair, to which he attended with great vanity" (plate 16).[88] This wasn't just local hearsay. Warnings against "dead hair" (*capillos mortuos*) came from Pope Sixtus IV in Rome. (And back then, "dead hair" meant wigs.)[89]

Francesco della Rovere had been a high-ranking Franciscan friar before becoming pope and changing his name to Sixtus IV. Thus he knew the sermons of the Franciscan Bernardino da Siena particularly well, including those in which Bernardino warned against "the hair of corpses."[90] If both Francesco and Bernardino were persuaded that the devil could grab the hair of corpses, it was because a branch of demonology insisted that, like angels, demons could operate on physical bodies. What angels and demons could not do was to change people's minds—that was God's prerogative. Yet demons could shape the external world by summoning images and implanting nightmares to sway people's hearts and influence their decisions.[91] And one of their privileged fields of operation—indeed, one of the few that served as a channel between the human world and the netherworld—was hair. Spirits could even lift people by their hair, transporting them across continents.[92] Demons, regularly identified as female, were particularly adept at manipulating hair, the fuse of lust. They could enter the invisible space between two lovers, playing with the hair of one to control the other's focus and occlude his mind.[93] This is why priests portrayed love as a seizure, a fettering of the brain.[94]

All of these convictions return in the *Hammer of Witches*, a summary of more than two centuries of treatises on witchcraft, commissioned by Sixtus IV's successor, Pope Innocent VIII.[95] The compilers were two Dominican friars, Jakob Sprenger and Heinrich Kramer. While it took decades for the treatise to impose itself as the leading manual for exorcists, I stress its publication date of 1486 as representative of a culture that encouraged to see the demonic in women.[96] Sixtus IV had endorsed this stereotype ten years earlier, when he announced that God's incarnation rested on the erasure of women's nature. As the female nature was the devil's domain, the son of God could in no way have been gestated in it. The papal declaration is best known as the Immaculate Conception, and, like witch hunting, was an extreme expression of centuries-old efforts to categorize women as beings in whom the sinfulness inherent to the whole human species revealed itself in more straightforward forms.[97] And one of those eloquent forms was hair, which, as the most expressive metonym for women's nature, ought to be turned against itself to become useful to men.[98] It is perhaps not surprising that the first edition of Boccaccio's misogynist *Labyrinth of Love* was printed the year after *The Hammer of Witches*.[99] And it is perhaps even less surprising that its publisher was Bartolomeo di Francesco, a Florentine cleric who produced moralizing pamphlets about episcopal and papal directives.[100]

Sixtus IV continued his campaign against women's nature in a bull in which he banned hairstyling. Titled *Etsi dominici gregis* and issued to reduce the remission of sins (since, as some theologians argued, the possibility of forgiveness made Christians more prone to vices), the bull listed all the transgressions that only the Holy See could absolve, such as heresy and the invasion of a state subject to the Church.[101] Yet what is interesting is that, nested amid bans against conspiracy and selling arms to the infidels, the papal chancery prohibited women from preaching, and from styling their hair. Sixtus IV spent no word on any other part of their bodies. He did not need to do so, because no other part of the female body lent itself to express the ambitions of politics as clearly. To comb and style a woman's hair was not just a means to tidy her appearance, to make it deferential and thus acceptable; it was a way to control her nature and defuse Satan's operations. Nothing else was so dangerous; nothing else reached into so many aspects of life. The political hold of hair may have been perceived as soft; pressing citizens to pay attention to it, as the Alberti brothers and Ficino did, was not like forcing them to pay taxes. But it nonetheless served to teach people to not just embrace order but yearn for it and delight in its benefits.[102]

But now is the time to leave the term "order" behind, since it is the word that those in power repeated to convince their subjects that their organization of the world was the only one possible. To continue speaking of "order," as some historians do, is a way to validate that world view and the violence that went with it. As usual, Ovid put it better than anyone else: "What attracts us is to see that a woman takes care of herself: the hair ought not to be without law."[103] Which is a way to say that a man is attracted not by the form a head of hair takes, but by discovering that a woman has labored to bring herself into his worldview.

And now that hair emerges as an ultimate repository of politics, I wonder if Sandro Botticelli's meticulous paintings of coiffures, to which we are about to return, showed Florentines the image of a society cleansed of chaos, which took care of itself. Fifteenth-century Florence may have been an ostentatious city, in love with the visually arresting and vulnerably attached to the precious. But Botticelli's confident linear style and elaborate coiffures, in which every strand seems to have a reason, also hint at a society that flaunted high faith in control. Control was the ultimate goal of combing, parting, and braiding—that is, the aspects of hairstyling that came close to painting in their capacity to communicate the ambitions of power without saying a word.

TEN *Split Ends: A Conclusion*

On Christmas Eve 1495, or maybe it was four days later, Donatello's sculpture of Judith slaying Holofernes was installed in front of the Palazzo della Signoria, Florence's city hall (figure 10.1a).[1] Governmental officials had taken the bronze from the Medici palace, where no one stopped them. Lorenzo had died more than three years earlier, and his son had recently fled; a hefty reward was on his head since he had ceded, unauthorized, many territories of the Florentine state to the king of France.[2] The Medici had become traitors, and the new government had seized their famous art collection, including Donatello's Judith, which was relocated to the main square. It was the first free-standing sculpture to be installed there.

Once in the square, that murder scene was reinterpreted as a conquest of civic liberties. And by reinterpretation I mean a violent one: they stripped the statue of its inscriptions and carved a new one around its marble base.[3] With its abbreviations stretched out, it reads: "The citizens installed it as a paragon of public salvation."[4] They even added the date of 1495, as if what people were seeing was a new sculpture, and not one that had been cast some fifty years earlier.[5] In line with such a rebirth, I ignore the statue's Medicean history, and imagine the sculpture as emerging from the chatter about hair that was breathed out in those winter days. And hair matters a great deal here, since it is by one of Holofernes's coils, looped between her fingers, that Judith holds his head. She pulls the hair ever so slightly, to draw attention to how long and supple it is (figure 10.1b), which was a way to express how vain and sex-driven he was.[6] Even today, it is still a touch of undimmed erotic force.

The tension between Judith and Holofernes is palpable because Donatello constructed them as opposites. She stands and stares bug-eyed; he sits, lifeless, like a twisted rug. Judith is clad in a tunic, brass bracers fastened around her arms. A breastplate presses the heavy fabric against her breast so that you cannot see anything of her body besides her hands, a few toes, and that mask of a face. Holofernes, on the other hand is basically naked. His loincloth is loose. Tasseled strings hang from his thighs and down his back, as if to show that this is a body from which clothes are falling off. And as they fall off, he is revealed to be a creature of hair. He sports decadent mustachios, a lustrous beard, and that wavy mane erupting in all directions, like an overflowing cup from which drink has pooled in the tablecloth folds underneath. Fringes of hair droop from Holofernes's armpits, and Donatello even slashed a few strokes in the middle of his chest (figure 10.1c), so as to expand the artistic existence of hair and make you notice it, regardless of whether you are looking for protuberances or for incisions. On the contrary, Judith's hair is invisible. Its mass is covered by a hood, befitting the proper orthodox woman she is. Donatello erased her hairline by gluing a strap to her forehead so precisely as to intensify the perception of Holofernes as a sordid case of lust.[7] This verdict must have been instinctual in the city of Absalom, all the more so since Holofernes is not only naked and extraordinarily hairy, but also sits on plush pillows which rest upon a frieze of orgiastic putti drunk on wine.[8] The stacking of all these elements conjured up dreams of Luxury, sitting naked on cushions and furs while combing her hair, waiting for the night to get wild.[9]

This association did not require much mental work in the Florence of Girolamo Savonarola, the leading preacher at the time.[10] He routinely railed against what he called the city of vice. He implored Florentines to change their lives, exhorting them to purify their actions and undertake what he saw as a divinely ordained mission. He roared that a New Jerusalem was possible and, in less than five years of preaching, convinced

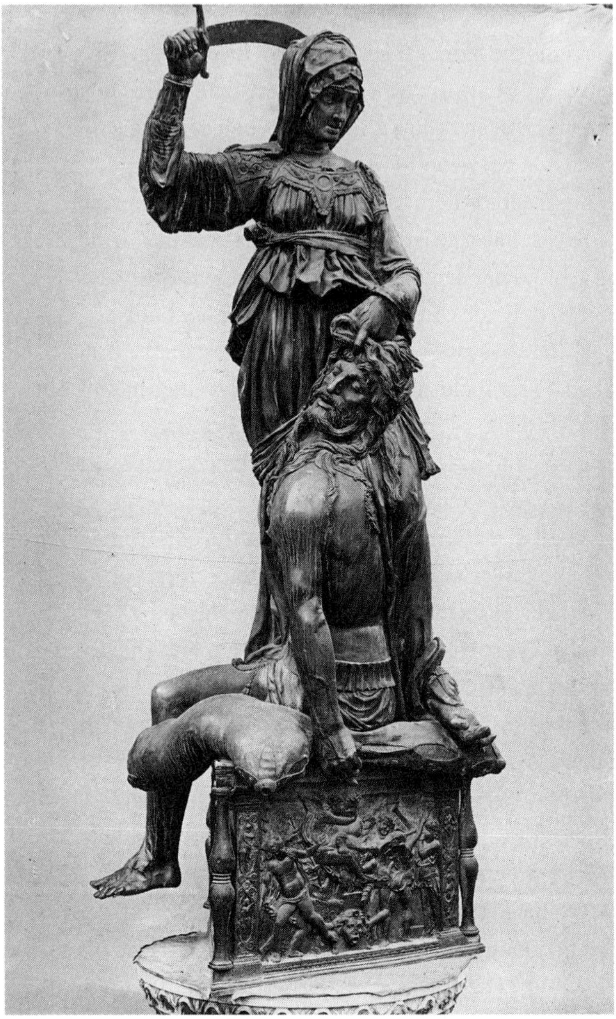

Figures 10.1a–c (above, facing). Donatello, *Judith and Holofernes*. Palazzo della Signoria, Florence.

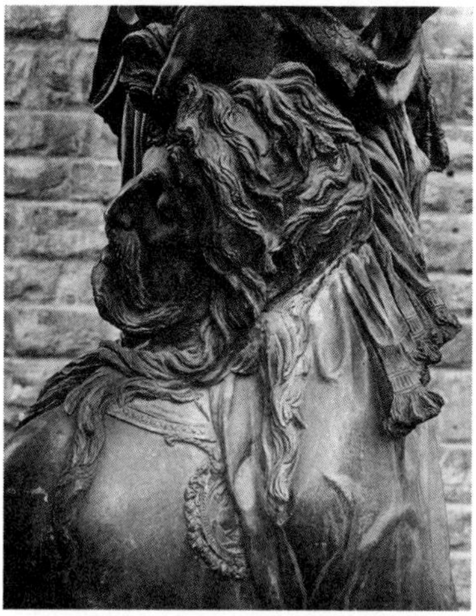

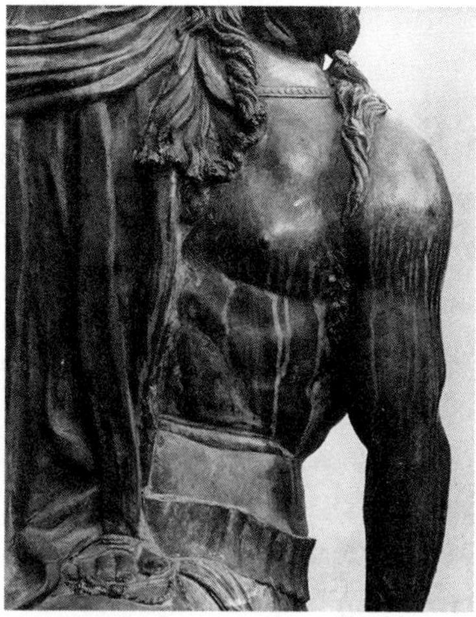

many that it was so, thus creating a base of supporters who backed anti-Medicean measures and the writing of a new constitution.[11]

Savonarola achieved all this by also criticizing hair care. He also attacked Florentines' excessive love of gold and of fashion excesses. Yet hair played a fundamental role in his tirades.[12] "My Florence, do penitence . . . and as I said, take away the hairstyles and the kids' *zazzere* [plate 31], together with all the vanities and offenses to the eye."[13] He understood the effectiveness of these critiques early in his career, and never stopped. He told mothers: "The children are your garden. When they are young and virginal, weed starts eating the grass if you [. . .] make them indulge in luxury. And this is why I have told you many times: [. . .] Cut their hair!"[14] He chastised long, full hair as being so immoral that he blessed the children who went against the will of their depraved parents.[15] This was in the summer of 1495, a few months before Donatello's Judith was moved to the city square, and almost a year after Savonarola had ordered "that all girls veil their heads so that no one could see their hair."[16]

Savonarola was not the first to consider hair care as a sign of a lesser life. In this book we have encountered many of the predecessors from whom he learned how to execrate it. Yet his energy was different: his audiences were bigger, his tones louder.[17] "You, women who pride yourselves of your beauty. I'm telling you: you are all ugly," he shouted.[18] He shamed widows for "walking about clean and fresh with veils and bands over their heads, ironed and pleated."[19] He even attacked Pope Alexander VI, lover of pomp: "Barbers will come to shave Italy up to the bones. [. . .] They will shave you to such an extent that not even a hair of your beard will remain."[20] Savonarola had an arsenal of razor-sharp maxims: "Shave yourself, Italy! One thing is to cut and trim, but another thing is to go bald. [. . .] Your chin will be shaven, and your head too." As the expression risked sounding cryptic, he quickly added: "You don't occupy yourself with anything besides prostitutes and luxuries. [. . .] You live like pigs. [. . .] Go bald, Italy! When the eagle ages, its feathers fall. So your feathers will be plucked from you, and your hair will be ripped from your head."[21]

If I draw from so many of Savonarola's sermons, cobbling together expressions that he recited weeks apart, it is to foreground the density by which he clung to hair. Density matters here. Savonarola was not interested in the theological quibbles of Augustine and Thomas Aquinas. That was not how you transformed the hearts of a city. The pace had to be fast, the associations self-evident, the thinking provided in blocks. "Cut your hair and throw it away."[22] *It's not rocket science, people!*

But after years of preaching, Savonarola realized that words were not enough. So, shortly after Donatello's Judith was moved out of the Medici palace, he commanded actions: "You who have homes full of vanities [. . .] and books like *Il Morgante* [. . .], bring them to me so that we can burn them in sacrifice to God. And you, mothers, who adorn your daughters with so much vanity and superfluous headgear, bring them to me, so that when his Day of Wrath comes, he won't find them in your houses."[23]

The request may have reminded Savonarola's audience of a time sixty years earlier, when Bernardino da Siena had ordered the building of straw sheaf. Florentines had stacked their vanities on it: playing cards, mirrors, perfumes, and wigs, which went up in flames as people's materialistic crazes vanished with them.[24] Some attendees must have also heard about the bonfires the Franciscan Bernardino da Feltre had organized in cities just outside the Florentine state, where he "publicly burned many hair extensions and books that he reputed to be useless."[25]

Savonarola was reviving friars' most spectacular rituals, to galvanize people into renouncing material goods.

The bonfire, however, was but a phase in a robust attempt to reorganize society. Savonarola instituted squads—some two thousand children joined them—to collect alms and harass gamblers, blasphemers, and girls (he encouraged boys to tip their little precious tiaras over).[26] Some people blamed Savonarola for giving his followers a free hand, but others were genuinely impressed, as they saw the squads as embodying a spiritual transformation that seemed to be possible. They were the proof that boys who "looked like they were sporting the hairstyles not just of women but of prostitutes" could be turned into Christians who had "shed every superfluity of clothing, hairstyles, purses, and other vanities."[27] Those boys came to be held in such high respect that an impressive number of adults gave up on books, wigs, and false beards. They piled them up on pyres and burned them, together with paintings, combs, and mirrors.[28] Note what was burned: books, paintings, beauty tools, and hair.[29] These were objects that gave meaning to one another: links in a chain of values that Savonarola wanted to not only break, but melt for good. They also constituted most of the material evidence for this book.

According to the friar Placido Cinozzi, whose report helps us reconstruct the logistics of the bonfires, these spectacles marked a dramatic transformation in the folds of society.[30] Over the years, however, historians have grown less sensationalist. They debate whether the drop in Florentine consumption of luxury goods could have been caused by other factors. After the Medici fled, after all, Florence was low on money: no major building campaign took off; only a few altarpieces were commissioned.[31] Those who replaced the Medici had limited interest in the arts and classical literature. You could say that they inhabited a different culture, with alternative interests and reference points. It is often said that Botticelli's world almost vanished, even if it may be more correct to say that it decreased in size and changed in form. This may explain why he felt the need to adjust his style: so that his paintings could appeal to different values, and he could keep on working.[32]

Perhaps Botticelli too fell under Savonarola's spell.[33] But this is where history's attempt to own its sources falls short.[34] The evidence is inconclusive: we do not know whether a change of heart ever happened in Botticelli. He spent time with Savonarola's critics but also frequented his supporters; his own brother was one of them.[35] Some of Botticelli's paintings do illustrate the apocalyptic visions Savonarola described: an angelic ring-around-the-rosy now in London's National Gallery; a crucifixion standing out against a sky crossed by a river of blood, now at Harvard University. Yet it is unsure whether he believed in what he painted, or merely seconded the wishes of new patrons.[36]

Fifteenth-century art stood in a dubious relationship to power, as it did to necessity and time. The artistic labor of the Renaissance was much more similar to work as we know it than to art as it is today. Back then, artists were paid by the size of their works, the time spent making them, and the materials employed.[37] Botticelli had to clock in the hours to earn a living, and needed to paint more than he had in the past, if his commissions were as small as the two panels I have just mentioned. Also: while the Medici were still in power, Savonarola criticized Botticelli's style. He said that any one of his Madonnas "dressed like a whore," by which he meant that Botticelli appealed to the Florentines' basest desires rather than challenging them, as pious images ought to do.[38] And even if Savonarola never mentioned Botticelli by name—his attacks were hardly personal, which is why those in power tolerated them—Botticelli surely got the hint.

If, under the Medici, Botticelli had built a career on giant paintings of Venuses, portraits of moneyed merchants, altarpieces set in luxurious settings, and saints who looked like prostitutes, he now dedicated his craft to edifying tales, devotional panels, and reparatory works.[39] His refashioning of himself as a painter of substance happened immediately after Lorenzo de' Medici's death. A Florentine—we do not know his name—described Botticelli's style to the Duke of Milan as "virile," which in the vernacular of the time meant both "adult" and "manly," in the sense of "distant from feminine frivolities."[40] The transformation is corroborated by the ways Botticelli transformed his take on Judith. Twenty years earlier, he had given her an elaborate coiffure in line with her Biblical characterization as an "exceedingly beautiful" woman of

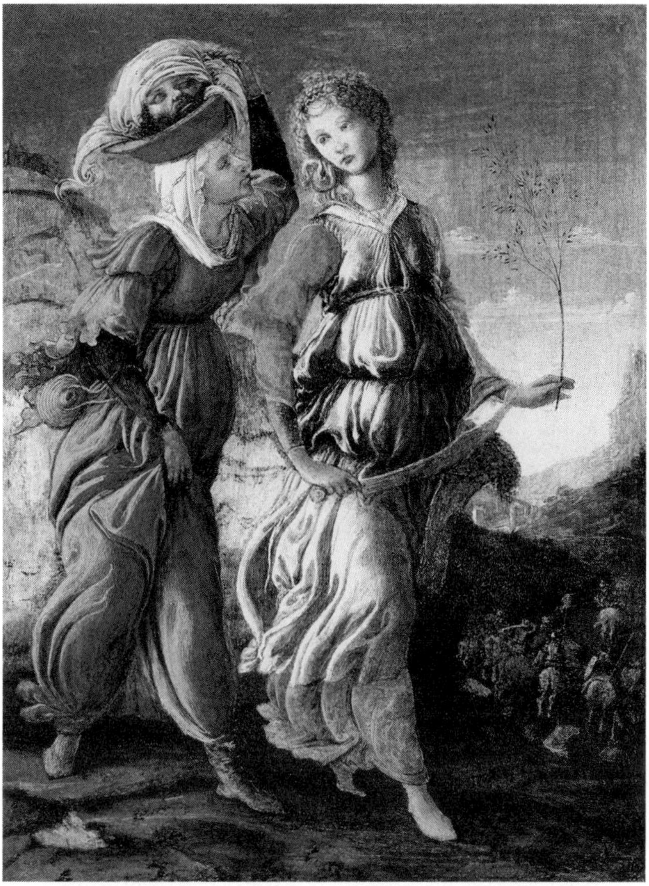

Figure 10.2a. Sandro Botticelli, *Judith with the Head of Holofernes.* Cincinnati Art Museum.

means (figure 10.2a).[41] But after Savonarola told his followers to keep hair "to measure," Botticelli shifted his attention to another biblical descriptor and painted Judith as a widow, hiding her hair under a scarf that, while looking expensive, remained orthodox (figure 10.2b).[42]

It is around this time that Botticelli also executed the *Allegory of Calumny,* his last and most sophisticated reflection on the power of hairstyling (plate 32). In it, two women work on the hair of Slander—in the

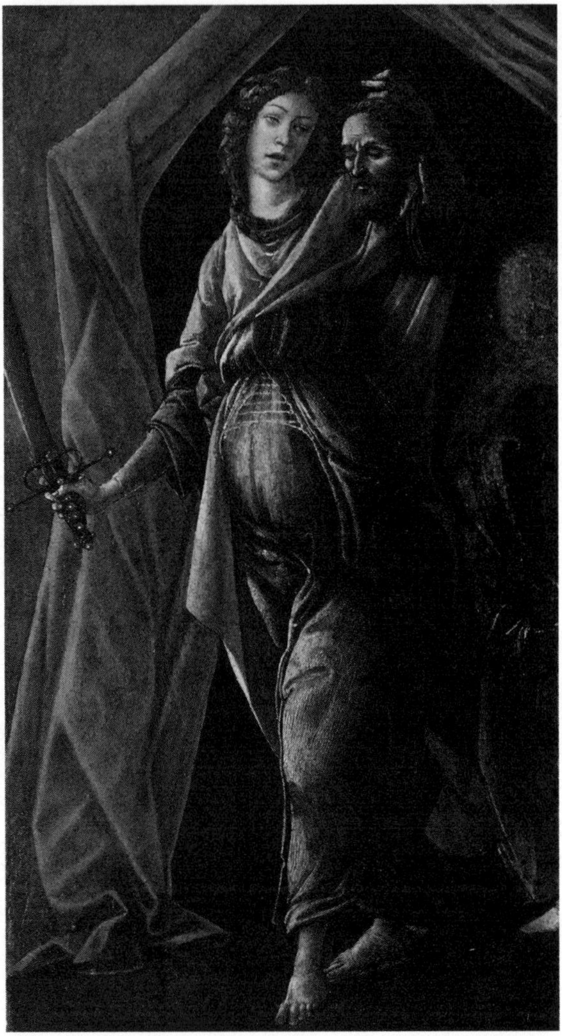

Figure 10.2b. Sandro Botticelli, *Judith with the Head of Holofernes*. Rijksmuseum, Amsterdam.

center, holding a torch—as a way to sway the judge of the case, who sits on the right. The women are not just generic maids, but are Treachery and Deceit, according to the Greek satirist Lucian, whose description of a painting by the great Apelles served as the model for Botticelli's allegory.[43]

Hairstyling dominates many corners of the picture. The mane of naked Truth, on the left, flutters diagonally, echoing the course of her chastising sash. To emphasize its looseness, Botticelli represents the outermost figure on the other side—the blond adviser whispering in the judge's hairy ears—with a tight bun. Botticelli's thematization of hair is not generic. Rather, he turns it into the means by which figures interact with one another. While Slander's hair is being done, she drags the accused by it. Given how much of his career Botticelli had devoted to the painting of hair until then, and how little he did so afterward, his emphasis on it in the *Allegory of Calumny* gives the panel the sense of a goodbye.

If pivoting a painting on the point of hairstyling feels like a reexamination of Botticelli's career, however, it is because in the painting he reemploys past formulas. In the golden relief above the prince, a centaur is also dragged by his hair, echoing the gesture of his earlier Pallas (see figure 5.3). In *Calumny*, Truth is a double of his famous Venus (plate 1), perhaps in an attempt to salvage it by retroactively changing it from being perceived as an erotic goddess to being seen as a personification of pure, honest beauty.[44] I would go as far as to call *Calumny* an act of repentance, given that by associating hairdressing with deception, Botticelli aligned himself with all those for whom hairstyling stood for the decorative (Boccaccio, Cicero, Pico della Mirandola, just to remind you of a few).[45] The repentance also chimes with Savonarola's attacks.

A couple of winters before Botticelli painted *Calumny*—or maybe just one winter, since we are not sure when he painted it—Savonarola lashed out against the mothers who let their daughters go to mass without veils.[46] Florentines were familiar with the criticism: it dated back to when Pierozzi had been bishop.[47] Yet, while Pierozzi had seen the habit as a generic expression of vanity, Savonarola insisted it was harmful. He revived the medieval assertion that hairstyles steal gazes, to deduce that a woman needed to cover her head "out of respect for the angels and the priests who are in the church so that none of them would be caught by her beauty."[48]

Notice that Savonarola did not speak about women's eyes. He probably thought it was unlikely that officiants could be distracted by them, since women were routinely reminded to direct their gaze to the ground, like guilt-ridden convicts.[49] If we take the etiquette manuals of the time at face value, we need to imagine women as avoiding the gaze of anyone while on their way to church and, once the ceremony started, fixing their eyes on liturgical books.[50] But even if the meeting of eyes was avoided, women's hair, all the more visible because their heads were bent, must have been a menace for the officiating priest. This is why Savonarola claimed that it entrapped men's gazes like a magical lasso. And that is what Botticelli's *Calumny* shows: the visual entrapment of a princely judge, seated on the elevated platform like a priest on the chancel, losing his focus because of a hairdo. Behind him, holding a sword, is the gilded statue of Saint Paul, the main detractor of female coiffures, as Savonarola knew well.[51] Paul looks away, as if his warning against trickeries has gone unheard by the king, whose ears are filled with gossip.

Botticelli is so precise in his correspondences and so eloquent in his details because he knows how to control gazes. His portrait of Simonetta Vespucci (plate 10) is a magisterial application of the mechanics of visual entrapment as much as *Calumny* is its commanding deconstruction. It is even a confession, if you will, as the panel exposes how a man is bound to fall for a woman because of her labyrinthine hairstyle. Her hair is a stratagem Botticelli exposes from a sobering distance, like a film director who pulls the camera away from the set to remind viewers that what they have been watching is an illusion.[52]

This distance reveals that Botticelli developed an awareness of the politics of Florentine hair. I do not mean it in the sense that Botticelli took hair as political by default. I do not think he was sitting in his studio sketching out his own politics, since politics were not the motive of his art. Rather, hair had become political because it was intensely scrutinized by Florentine society, which relied on it to play out its many divisions and express its unspeakable fears: the demise of civic traditions, death's sneak attack on life, and the irrational, self-destructive pull of desire.

This book has delved into many sources to reconstruct how late-fifteenth-century Florentines approached hair: which features they valued, and which they ignored. The idea has been to immerse you in the net of their beliefs about hair, to make you feel their hold and, conversely, to appreciate the boldness of those who tried to escape them. The interconnectedness in my presentation of those beliefs—the tightness of the knots—is meant to produce a different experience of hair, since hair is not a feature that Renaissance Florence shared with us. I think it is important to stress this difference because there is an immediacy in encountering hair that makes people believe it can cut through cultures and times. I do not share that view. For me, this way of approaching hair mistakes its naturalness for egalitarianism—it implies that, because most of us have hair, we all view it the same way, and thus share an entry point to life and the past. I find this to be perhaps the most pernicious aspect of hair—something so insidious that it takes an army of thinkers to dismantle it.[53]

So this is why this book has reconstructed the hair of people in late-fifteenth-century Florence as a foreign substance: to delay your experience of it. This is also why the evidence drawn upon for this book has been limited to what was available in one city for roughly two decades. Travel to fifteenth-century Milan, and hair is straightened and gummed to the scalp.[54] Look at sixteenth-century paintings, and hair changes into something feathery or textile-like.[55] Read the advice of Catholic zealots of a few decades after that, and you find a preoccupation with hair dyeing that is nowhere to be found in the Florence of one hundred years earlier.[56] Change cities or skip generations, and you will find that hair is labored into different materials, and different notions of anatomy. Well-being, gender, age, morals, and history are reshuffled into a different order. This book is not about those other outcomes, as I see few connections between them and what fifteenth-century Florence took for granted. For the citizens of Florence, hair was a receptacle of visual desire, a filthy mass in constant need of reordering; and this was as true as the fact that the sky was blue and Christ died on the cross with parted hair falling over his shoulders.[57] So, as a last gesture in this book, I ask you to believe all the associations I have unpacked in the previous chapters as being no longer in need of any explanation because in fifteenth-century Florence, everyone took hair, with all its peculiar associations, at face value.

The straightforwardness of hair is what made it powerful. Savonarola referred to hair extensively in his sermons because it allowed him to reach the hearts of the widest audience and reach them straight away. Attacking hair was not like condemning gold, a metal to which most Florentines had no real connection—something they saw from a distance, on the clothes of their lords and on the altars of churches. Hair was a part of them. It grew on their feet and on the backs of their hands. Its experience required no special status: hair was just there, even when you paid no attention to it. And it was such relatability that turned hair into a political element.

We could say that politics was invested in hair because it was a fundamental site for the construction of gender, class, and age stereotypes. If the work of Botticelli and other artists created dreamscapes that pivoted on hair transformations, it is because they identified hair as a key element in the maintenance of cultural divisions. Yet it is not that people with money and power imposed such divisions simply because they profited from them. They developed their sense of the human self in relation to such beliefs as they learned—from their families and confessors, from their doctors and teachers, from the treatises in natural philosophy, and from chatter in the street—that hair was the element that gave away everyone's identity immediately.

When Amerigo Vespucci, the famous navigator and cousin-in-law of Simonetta (see plate 10), recounted his first encounter with native Americans, he described their hair: "They have no hair on their body but for long black hair on their heads, the women especially, which makes them beautiful. They are not very fair of countenance, for they have broad faces somewhat reminiscent of the Tartars, they do not allow any hair to grow on their brows or eyelids, nor in any other part, except the head, because they consider bodily hair an ugly thing."[58] Vespucci was not the sole writer to rely on hair to signal the natives' otherness. Another Florentine living in Cadiz, Giovan Battista Strozzi, described "many brown men . . . with hair extending to the middle of their shoulders."[59] And both Vespucci and Strozzi noted the natives' hair because they knew their correspondents would read it as an index of the natives' morality.

By insisting that native men had long hair, Strozzi put them on the same plane with Florentine women. And by insisting that the length of native women's hair was exceptional, Vespucci presented them as exceedingly feminine, which is why he called them "beautiful." The "New World," in other words, was a continent without men, which meant a continent with no sense of justice, governed by the drive to be "inordinately lustful."[60] The evocation of a community of people with long, loose hair—a typology that Florentines encountered every day in Donatello's Holofernes (figure 10.1a)—was enough to arouse the disturbing sense of a depraved, uncivilized society.

You may shake your head at the violence of these derogations, but the belief that hair gives away modes of conduct is still within us. Its capacity to express human fear, for instance, was articulated by Leon Battista Alberti in the fifteenth century, Giovanni Paolo Lomazzo in the sixteenth, and Charles Darwin in the nineteenth—and has been described in the same way by many psychologists today, as if no time ever passed.[61] Art criticism has played a particularly important role in maintaining these biases. Darwin's work was viewed as instrumental by the criminologist Cesare Lombroso, who argued that the type of hair could reveal whether a person had a delinquent nature.[62] And both Darwin and Lombroso inspired the connoisseur Giovanni Morelli, who assumed that Renaissance artists never put any thought into their depictions of hair.[63] Hair, Morelli claimed, was one of painters' stylistic twitches. He assumed that it was rendered mechanically, and thus took it as a useful characteristic through which to recognize an artist's hand and attribute an artwork. Morelli expected in artistic hair a passivity similar to that which scientists attributed to real hair, and many art historians have embraced his method. Even today, paintings are included in or expelled from Leonardo da Vinci's corpus because of the way their figures' hair is painted.[64] In a way, there is a kind of eloquence to hair: it speaks where Leonardo and other artists remained reticent about their choices.

Yet, after researching the ways art critics and historians carried on with one way of looking at hair, I have come to the conclusion that it is a mistake to present its passivity as descending linearly from Darwin to Lombroso and Morelli. Considering hair unimportant because of its immediacy was not an attitude shared by a small group of people who could be named individually. Rather, it was as pervasive as it was unnoticed. The attitude can be found in the writings of Johann Joachim Winckelmann, who taught that the hairstyles of classical busts only served to identify their subjects.[65] It returns in the lectures on aesthetics by Wilhelm Friedrich Hegel, an admirer of Winckelmann. Even if Hegel no longer lived in a world where doctors assumed the existence of bodily humors, he did not challenge the symptomatic nature of hair. Quite the opposite, he stated that hair had "the character of a plant production rather than of an animal one"—a sentence that could have been plucked from a fifteenth-century Florentine treatise. "It is a sign of weakness rather than a proof of the organism's strength," he insisted.[66]

How could anyone have possibly felt the need to speak of hair positively when so many authoritative voices described it as valueless, and saw value in its inferiority? Such voices date back to historians as ancient as Tacitus, who looked at the hair of British barbarians to classify their ethnic provenance.[67] They were ratified by Seneca, who differentiated between freeborn boys with straight hair and enslaved kids with curls.[68] So I am hardly surprised when I read that a connoisseur of the stature of Bernard Berenson considered one of Leonardo's hairless profiles, and not one of his detailed coiffures, as the most exquisite drawing of the Renaissance.[69] His judgment passes for admiration of a masterful sobriety that appears valid to his readers even today, because it is sustained by the patriarchal moralism that has shaped much history writing and art criticism.[70]

The belittling of hair is the only element of continuity in the ever-changing notions about hair. The attitude has been so pervasive that, though anthropologists and sociologists have exposed its cultural constructedness since the 1950s, it has taken almost forty years for art historians to turn hair into a subject worth studying.[71] Some of the research for this book has been developed in relation to their thought and findings.[72] Yet their focused disciplinary approaches—their interests in documenting religious bans, or in exploring the expressive possibilities of hair in painting—do not acknowledge the density from which hair eventually derived its cultural might and political utility.[73] It is the connectedness of hair—the knots it has formed between culture and what is attributed to nature—that reveal it to be a fundamental element of life.

In searching for connections, this book has also inquired into what has been left out. This is a matter not only of asking which aspects of artworks have been neglected, but of questioning the silences that sustain our notions of beauty. For many centuries, critics and viewers shared one another's biases, and thus maintained the idea that the beauty of the past did not exist only in the past. In the nineteenth century, when Botticelli's paintings began to be revalued, French actresses began styling their hair *à la Botticelli*.[74] It was an artificial move, pushed by a growing body of opinion leaders who insisted that Botticelli had given form to a supreme form of attractiveness. To notice this kind of pressure means to face the way in which the market and cultural politics have dominated aesthetics. I find it hard to believe that something appears beautiful simply because it is beautiful. I have carried this skepticism with me while researching the many voices that decried hair as a product of hell in the fifteenth century, and while noticing an echo of those voices in the words being written today on that period. This is why in this book I have included some sentences in italics; they serve as reminders of the murmuring of a patronizing chorus, confident in its knowledge and thus unaware of the political load of its judgment. Can we ever shake off the Christian morality that has validated notions of aesthetic success? If the beauty ascribed to Botticelli's work depends on a patriarchal takedown of women as sinfully enticing, where does this leave us? When I think about all this, I suddenly become weary, like a patient who discovers not only that the therapy he has endured is ineffective, but that he will have no choice but to endure it again.

In response to the reinscription of past judgments into today's narratives about the past, this book has tried to recover the voices of a few who offered an alternative approach to hair. Their points were whispered and short-lived. They were not shared by most Florentines, who took the relevance of hair to be as thin as its width, as superficial as its rooting in the skin, as painless as its cutting. To disregard hair was as natural as shedding it; caring for hair meant flirting with the devil. The disparaging of hair not only was sexist, but hit all the targets of religious patriarchy: young rebels, who were dismissed as effeminate, and foreigners, seen as lecherous and barbaric.[75] By showing their care for hair, these groups failed to subscribe to the hegemonic idea that the worth of hair lay in its capacity to negate itself. But such a refusal never turned into open defiance. I have found not a single fifteenth-century source that indulged in the pleasure of hairstyling completely. Even when reading Boccaccio's *Comedy of the Florentine Nymphs* or exploring Botticelli's career, I have encountered U-turns that brought me back to safe moralizing grounds. Even the most daring passages by Apuleius and Ovid are followed by conclusions that insist that in the end, hair does not matter. Such repudiation expresses hair's singularly dissociative way of being, according to which it can draw attention to itself only insofar as it becomes something else. This further explains its metamorphoses into fire, sunbeams, streams of water, foliage, and even architectural elements. Metaphoric thinking found a most fertile ground in hair because hair itself was constitutively in denial. In a way, this whole book has articulated the unique processes of transfiguration and assimilation that hair triggered because of its self-negation. Hairstyles can be appreciated only momentarily and out of context. Aesthetically, they emerge as beautiful only if you look at them up close and forget about the rest.

The distance required to appreciate hairstyling may explain why it was Leonardo who first revalued Botticelli's heads. Living for most of his life in Milan, from which place he could only hear a muffled version of Savonarola's attacks, Leonardo was far enough removed to approach Botticelli's work without indulging in its moralization. The encounter took place around 1503, when Leonardo was in Rome and went to look at a fresco Botticelli had painted in the Sistine Chapel some twenty years earlier (figure 10.3a).[76] The scene shows Moses defending two women from two shepherds who have unjustly seized the well that the women set up. The episode is a turning point in Moses's life, since it was in this defense that he first revealed the nobility and perceptiveness of a true leader.[77] "Aren't you ashamed?" he shouted to the shepherds, "You are masses of long hair and lumps of flesh, not men. The girls are working like boys and shirk none of their duties, while you young men go daintily like girls. Away with you: give place to those who were here before you to whom the water belongs!"[78] After which Moses punched the shepherds.

But Botticelli is not interested in the aggression of Moses, which he places in the background. He instead pivots the fresco upon what happens next: Moses attentively pouring water for the women, who look at each other in disbelief. *What has just happened?* Botticelli places the women right in the center, showing one of them from behind to reveal her elaborate hairstyle (figure 10.3b). They are not peasants but

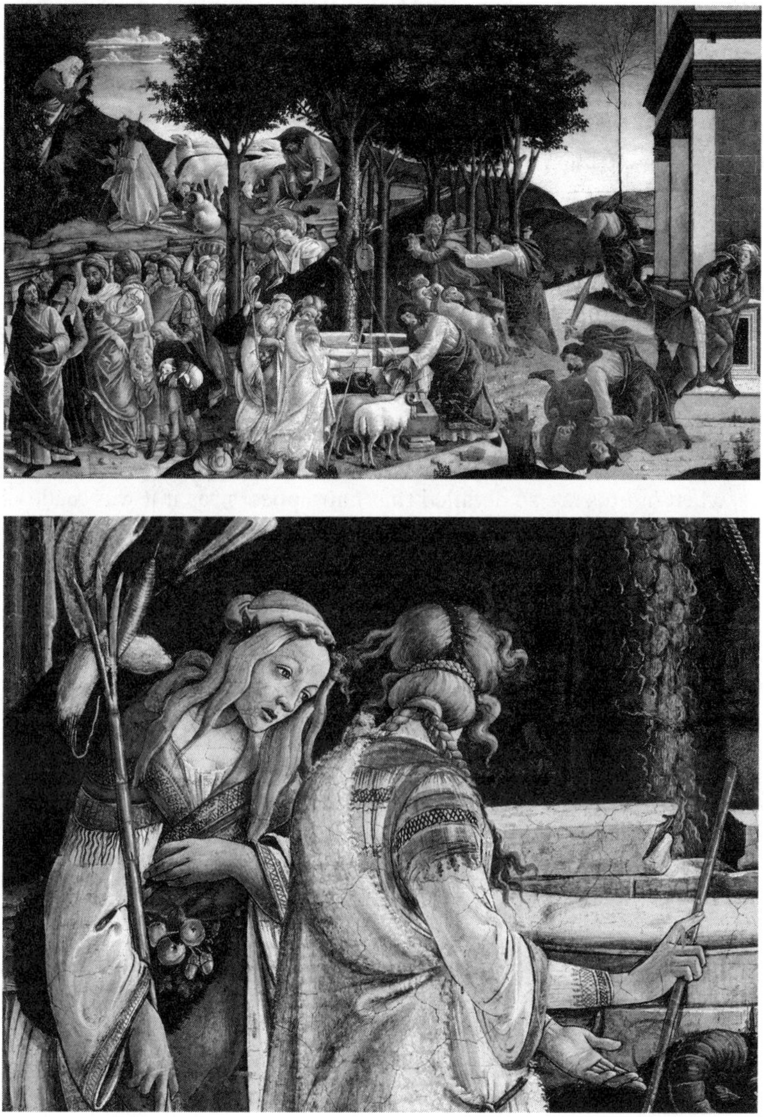

Figures 10.3a and 10.3b. Sandro Botticelli, *Life of Moses*. Sistine Chapel, Vatican City.

the daughters of a respected priest, and as usual, hairstyling serves as a pointer to status here. For Botticelli, however, it is also a means to an erotic atmosphere. It is the pictorial equivalent of lighting a scented candle, to use a cheap analogy. The priests gathering in the Sistine Chapel knew, after all, that the woman would become Moses's wife; so Botticelli simply had to turn her head and expose her hair to hint at the ensuing romance.

Leonardo took notice. In a note he wrote to himself after his visit, he criticized Botticelli for not getting the proportions of his figures in the middle and background right.[79] He was correct: Botticelli's Moses, which returns multiple ways in the fresco, hardly changes in size even when he is sitting in a faraway field, removing his shoe. But Leonardo also praised Botticelli for what he termed foreground painting—that is, when figures are so detailed that hair appears "as if it was made of threads" (*disfilar capegli*).[80]

Unlike his teacher Filippo Lippi, and unlike other Florentine artists who used their craft to capture the ribbons and veils that gave an arresting form to a female head, Botticelli tended to showcase hair's naked versatility. He often reduced the amount of embellishment and took hair as both a holding knot and a thing to hold. His work in the Sistine Chapel confirms this. There, he added only one accessory to the woman's head: a string of red beads, as glossy as summer cherries, pinned along a line that cuts through the back of her head. But it is less the beads than the hair that attracts the eye: four symmetrical ponytails stick out of two balloons of hair that are tightened by braids. Leonardo sketched the hairstyle on a sheet of paper (figure 10.4).

The fluttering curls and strong vertical parting of Leonardo's coiffure leave little doubt about its model. By adding knots and spirals, however, he took Botticelli's hairstyle to new heights, creating a composition so intricate that if it were transcribed into a painting it would have expressed lascivious intentions, as no hairstyle with this level of workmanship was socially acceptable outside wedding ceremonies. This reasoning supports the opinion that this drawing served as the preparatory sketch for a now lost painting of Leda.[81] (And Leda was the nymph who, according to Boccaccio, seduced Jupiter, rather than the

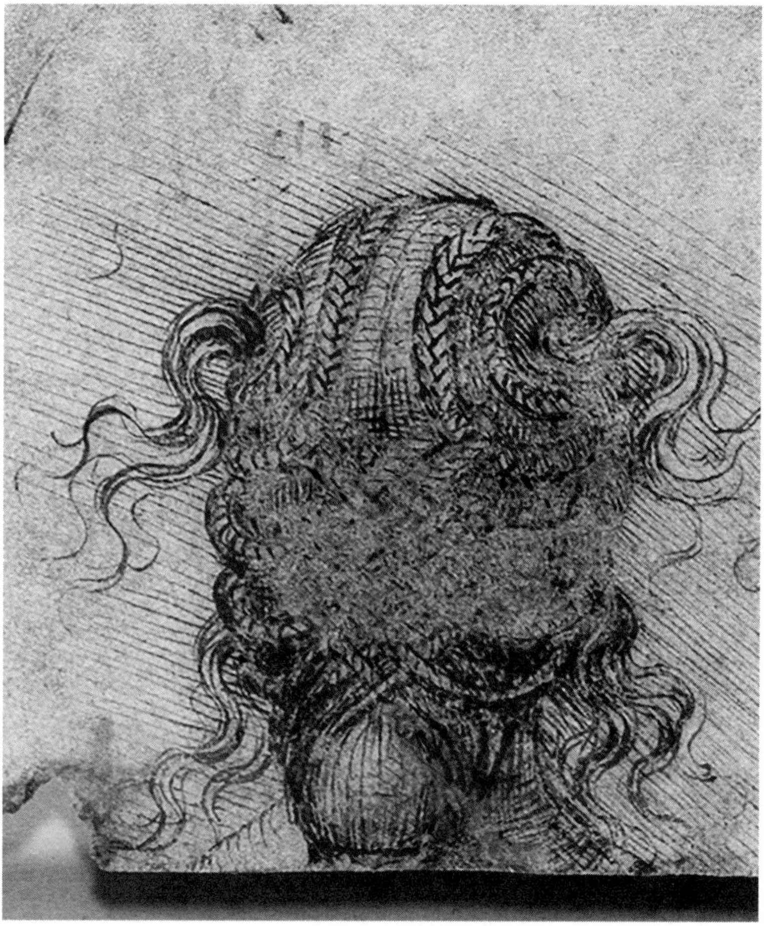

Figure 10.4. Leonardo da Vinci, hairstyle (detail). Windsor Castle, Windsor.

other way around.)[82] And yet I wonder if Leonardo developed an interest in hair not because of what it could signify, but because it represented the crux for figurative painting: that precarious space in which the ideal of depiction confronted its own dissolution. That tension must have resonated with Leonardo, for whom hair existed as the very limit of representation.

In reading about physiology, Leonardo came to see hair as the layer

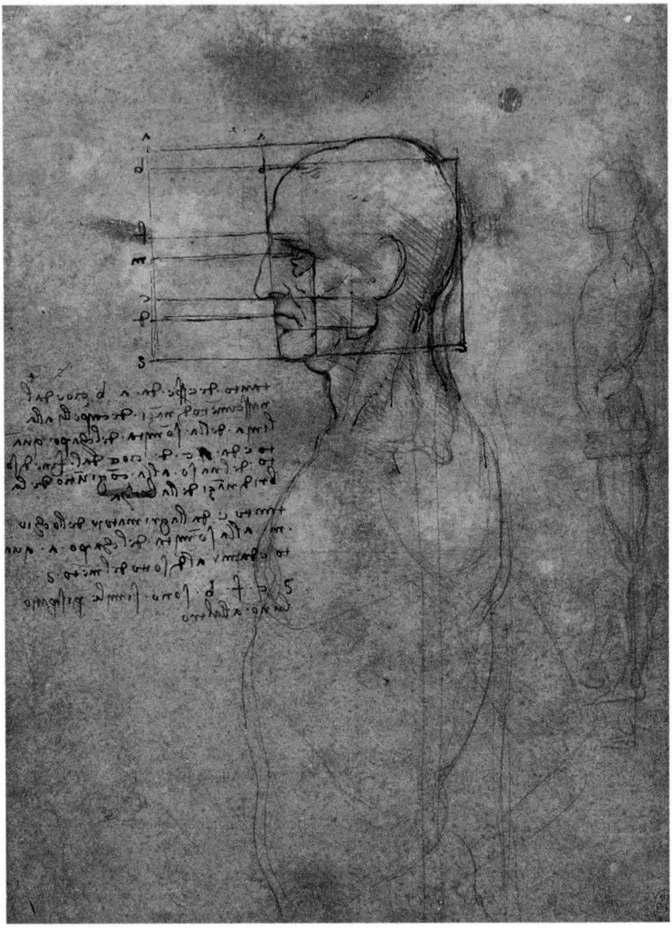

Figure 10.5. Leonardo da Vinci, proportions of the head. Windsor Castle, Windsor.

of dried skin that detaches itself from living flesh (see figure 3.2). In studying human proportions, he identified the hairline as the point from which one starts measuring (figure 10.5), as if everything above it existed outside harmony or even knowledgeability.[83] He believed all this because he had learned in Florence how hair served as the divider between chaos and order. It was the furrow that separated a land of virtue from a territory of vice, the fold between utility and fashion, the gate that opened from life onto the abyss of death. In a way, hair was less a threshold than the tenuous string that held the contradictions of human existence together. Thus, it captivated any artist who sought to explore its full breadth by making works with the ambition of being both immediately clear and impossible to contain.

APPENDIX: MAPS

MAP I

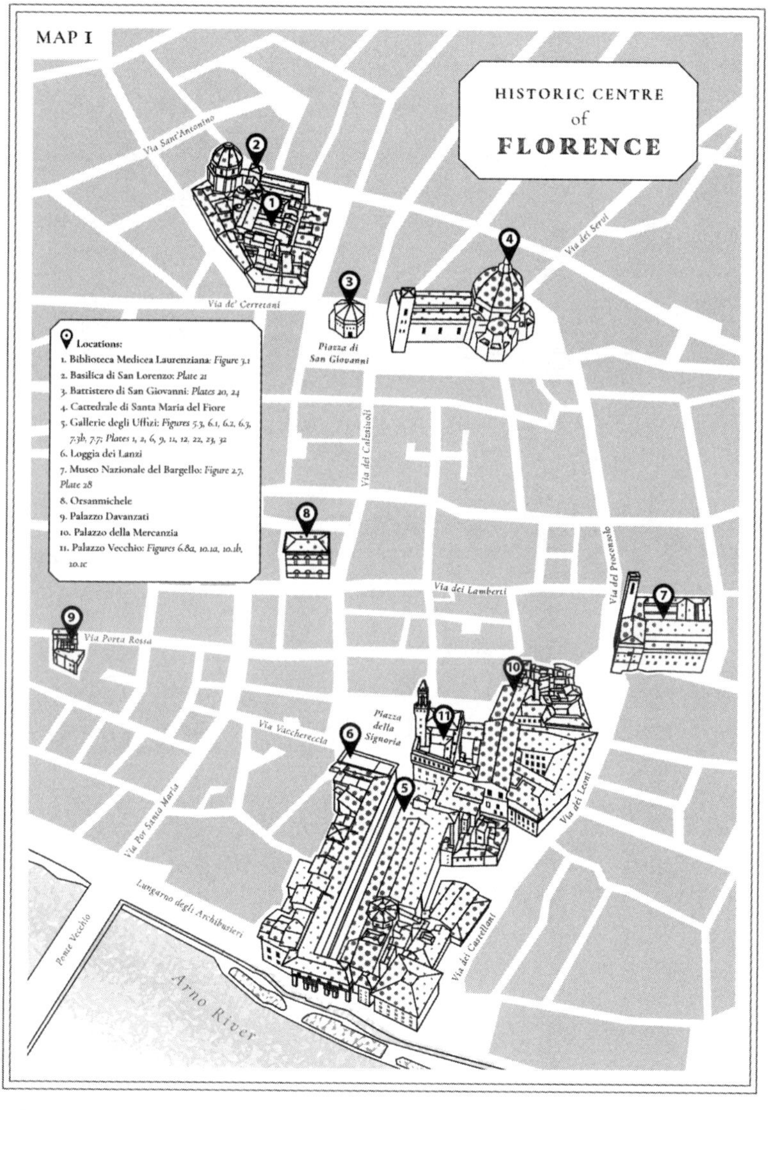

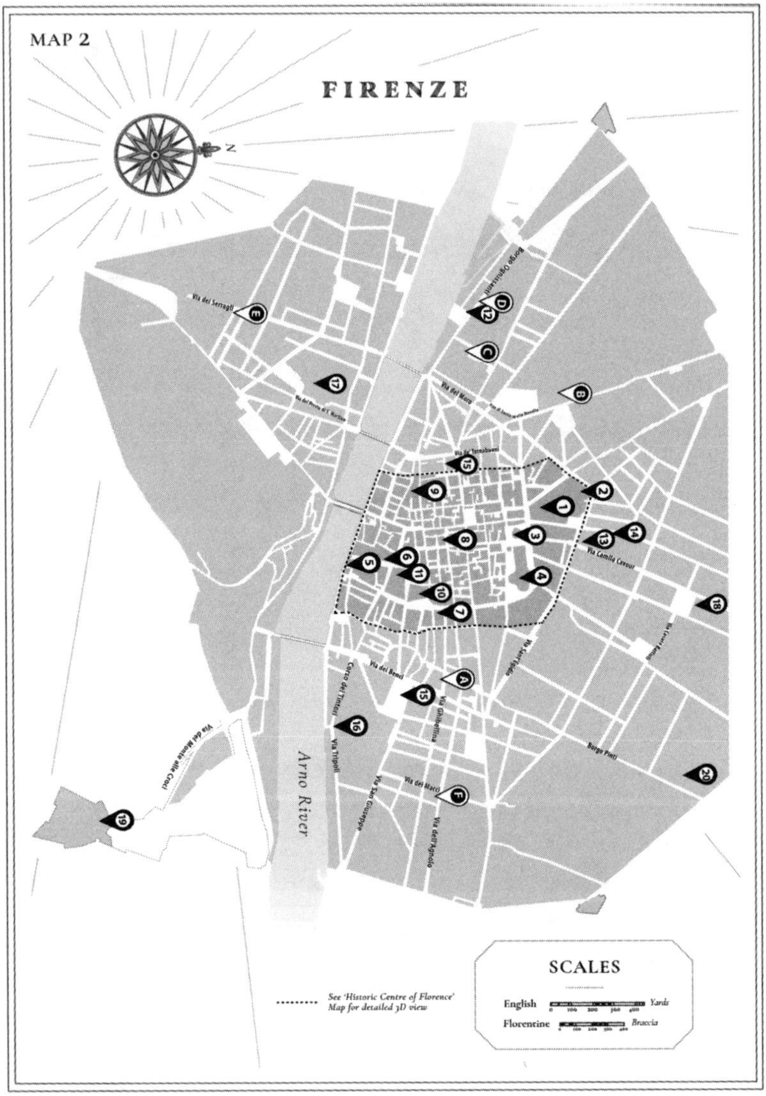
MAP 2
FIRENZE
N
Borgo Ognissanti
Via dei Serragli
Via del Moro
Via de' Tornabuoni
Via Camillo Cavour
Via dei Benci
Corso dei Tintori
Via Ghibellina
Via Tripoli
Via dei Malcontenti
Via San Giuseppe
Via dei Marmi
Via dell'Agnolo
Borgo Pinti
Via del Monte alle Croci
Arno River
See 'Historic Centre of Florence' Map for detailed 3D view
SCALES
English
Yards
Florentine
Braccia

MAP 2

FIRENZE

MAP LEGEND:

Currently located in Florence:

1. Biblioteca Medicea Laurenziana: *Figure 3.1*
2. Basilica di San Lorenzo: *Plate 21*
3. Battistero di San Giovanni: *Plates 20, 24*
4. Cattedrale di Santa Maria del Fiore
5. Gallerie degli Uffizi: *Figures 5.3, 6.1, 6.2, 6.3, 7.3b, 7.7; Plates 1, 2, 6, 9, 11, 12, 22, 23, 32*
6. Loggia dei Lanzi
7. Museo Nazionale del Bargello: *Figure 2.7, Plate 28*
8. Orsanmichele
9. Palazzo Davanzati
10. Palazzo della Mercanzia (Gucci Museum)
11. Palazzo Vecchio: *Figures 6.8a, 10.1a, 10.1b, 10.1c*
12. Chiesa di San Salvatore in Ognissanti
13. Palazzo Medici Riccardi: *Figure 8.4*
14. Biblioteca Riccardiana: *Figure 7.5*
15. Piazza di Santa Croce
16. Biblioteca Nazionale Centrale di Firenze
17. Basilica di Santo Spirito: *Figure 9.8*
18. Museo di San Marco: *Figures 5.1c, 7.6*
19. Abbazia di San Miniato al Monte
20. Palazzo Scala-della Gherardesca (Four Seasons Hotel)

No longer located in Florence:

A. Le Stinche Prison
B. Santa Maria Novella Library
C. Sandro Botticelli's Workshop
D. Amerigo Vespucci's family residence
E. Santa Elisabetta delle Convertite
F. Andrea del Verrocchio's Workshop

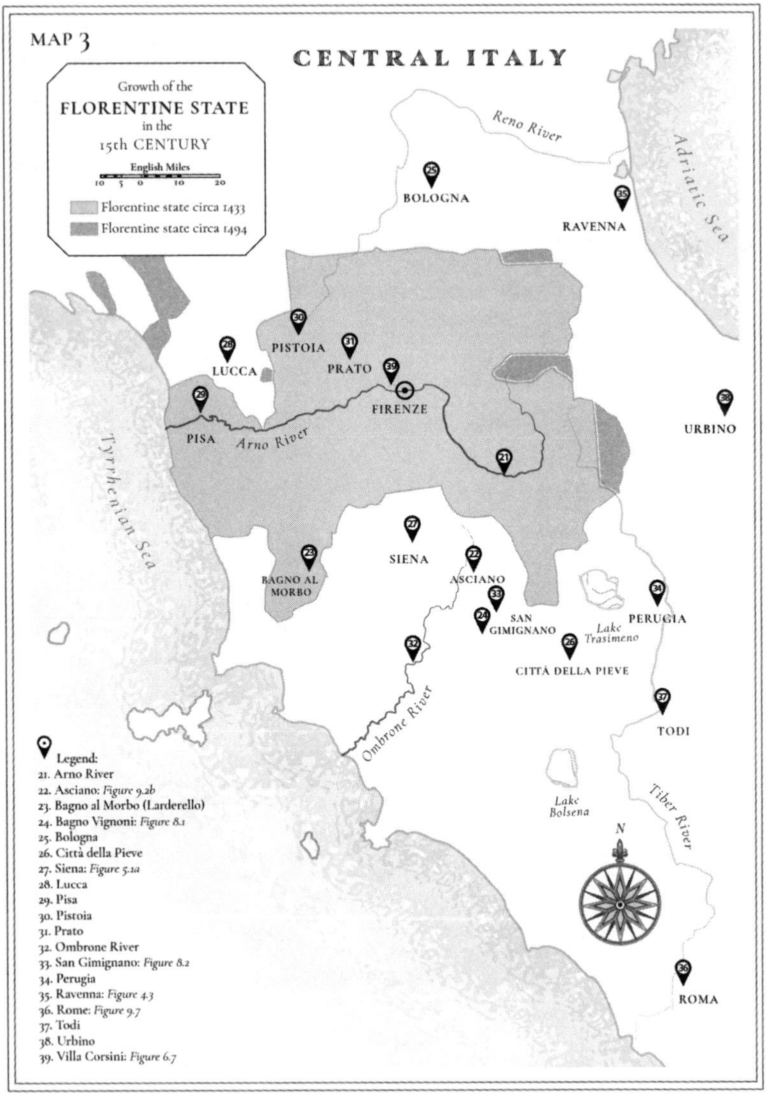
MAP 3
CENTRAL ITALY
Growth of the
FLORENTINE STATE
in the
15th CENTURY
English Miles
10 5 0 10 20
Florentine state circa 1433
Florentine state circa 1494
Reno River
Adriatic Sea
BOLOGNA
RAVENNA
PISTOIA
LUCCA
PRATO
FIRENZE
PISA
Arno River
URBINO
Tyrrhenian Sea
SIENA
ASCIANO
BAGNO AL
MORBO
SAN
GIMIGNANO
PERUGIA
Lake
Trasimeno
CITTÀ DELLA PIEVE
Ombrone River
TODI
Lake
Bolsena
Tiber River
N
ROMA
Legend:
21. Arno River
22. Asciano: *Figure 9.2b*
23. Bagno al Morbo (Larderello)
24. Bagno Vignoni: *Figure 8.1*
25. Bologna
26. Città della Pieve
27. Siena: *Figure 5.1a*
28. Lucca
29. Pisa
30. Pistoia
31. Prato
32. Ombrone River
33. San Gimignano: *Figure 8.2*
34. Perugia
35. Ravenna: *Figure 4.3*
36. Rome: *Figure 9.7*
37. Todi
38. Urbino
39. Villa Corsini: *Figure 6.7*

ACKNOWLEDGMENTS

The research for this book spanned fifteen years. I started collecting information sometime in 2007, when I was working as an adjunct at a fashion school in London. By 2010 I had completed my first article on Renaissance hair, which I sent to an academic journal. I still have the cover letter, which is full of confidence: "Dear Prof. Lang: Herein enclosed is an essay of mine, 'The Metamorphoses of Hair.'" After nine months, I got two rejections from peer reviewers. I ran home, cried a bit, and got annoyed with Michal (who was not yet my husband), because he did not understand how defeated I felt. But Michal's puzzlement was sobering, and the rejections were just; the essay was a mess. I simply clustered Florentine sources. I did not see the knots that tied them together. It took many people and reviews (from other journals, which eventually started publishing my research) to make me realize the need for this book. And while it is impossible to name everyone who helped shape it, I would like to acknowledge those who contributed to it directly with intelligent questions, reading suggestions, or a helping hand:

Damiano Acciarino, Albert Russell Ascoli, Hannah Baader, Harleen Bagga, Vincent Barletta, Fabio Barry, Susanna Berger, James Boaden, Lina Bolzoni, Francesca Borgo, Emilia Calbi, Stephen J. Campbell, BuYun Chen, Philippe Cordez, Arnold Coonin, Virginia Cox, Patrick Crowley, Pele Cox, Susan Dackerman, Shane Dawson, Rowan Dorin,

Chad Elias, Marzia Faietti, Aileen Feng, Erik Gustafson, Fiona Griffith, Kimeron Hardin, Christie Harner, Linden J. Hill, Helen Hills, Elizabeth Horodowich, Elis Imboden, Meagan Khoury, Joan Kee, Herbert Kessler, Dorothy Ko, Pavle Levi, Rodolfo Maffeis, Jean Ma, Alexander Marr, Michele Matteini, Jody Maxmin, Timothy McCall, Richard Meyer, Laura Mendez, Mitchell B. Merback, Federica Missere Fontana, Maria Giuseppina Muzzarelli, Jonathan Nelson, Alessandro Nova, Vivian Nutton, Anna Ottani Cavina, Katharine Park, Aleesa Pitchamarn Alexander, Sarah Prodan, David Reilly, Jessica Richardson, Michael Rocke, Pat Rubin, Barbara Spackman, Victor Stoichita, Ann Marguerite Tartsinis, Stéphane Toussaint, Marvin Trachtenberg, Nancy J. Troy, Camille Utterback, Michele Vescovi, Samuel Vitali, Hanna Vorholt, Jacquelyn Williamson, Gerhard Wolf, Edward Wouk, Usha Iyer, and Rebecca Zorach.

Four of my Stanford colleagues—Paula Findlen, Richard Vinograd, Marci Kwon, and Alexander Nemerov—deserve extra praise for reading the manuscript and offering advice as well as support. As usual, I owe much to John Gagné for talking me through my thoughts, Marina Cotugno for finding all the pictures and clearing their rights, Renaldo Migaldi for many precious suggestions on the text, and Randoph Petilos, my editor at the University of Chicago Press, for being such a cool guy. Edward Zhang helped me research the history of hair combs and the things fifteenth-century Florentines thought to be antiquities. Michelle Liu is the talented designer behind the maps.

The book is dedicated to my mother, who had Snow White's hair when I started looking at Botticelli's painting for the first time, and is sporting Joan of Arc's bob as I send this manuscript to press.

ILLUSTRATION CREDITS

FIGURES

Figure 2.1. Leonardo da Vinci, *Madonna of the Carnation*, about 1475. Bayerische Staatsgemäldesammlungen—Alte Pinakothek, Munich. CC BY-SA 4.0.

Figure 2.2. Andrea del Verrocchio with assistants, *Tobias and the Angel*, about 1470–75. National Gallery, London.

Figure 2.3. Andrea del Verrocchio with assistants, *Madonna and Child with Two Angels*, about 1476–78. National Gallery, London.

Figure 2.4. Leonardo da Vinci, *Naked Mona Lisa*, about 1514–16. Musée Condé, Château de Chantilly.

Figure 2.5. Sandro Botticelli, *Four Scenes from the Early Life of Saint Zenobius*, about 1500. National Gallery, London.

Figure 2.6. Andrea del Verrocchio, *Bust of a Woman*, about 1460–70. Frick Collection, New York. © The Frick Collection.

Figure 2.7. Desiderio da Settignano, *Bust of a Woman*, about 1460. Museo del Bargello, Florence. By permission of Ministero della Cultura—Museo Nazionale del Bargello. Photo by Victor Coonin.

Figure 3.1. Bartholomeus Anglicus, *De proprietatibus rerum*, Ms. Conv. Soppr. 462, f. 1v. Biblioteca Medicea Laurenziana, Florence. By permission of Ministero della Cultura (MiC); further reproduction prohibited.

Figure 3.2. Leonardo da Vinci, the layers of the scalp and the cerebral ventricles, RCIN 912603, about 1490–92. Windsor Castle, Windsor. Royal Collection Trust © Her Majesty Queen Elizabeth II 2021.

Figure 4.1. Unknown artist, *The Beautiful Simonetta*, about 1475–1500. Ashmolean Museum, Oxford. © Ashmolean Museum.

Figure 4.2. Giovanni Boccaccio, *Comedy of the Florentine Nymphs* (aka *Ameto*), 1478. 4 Inc.c.a. 112 m, f. 2r, Bayerische Staatsbibliothek, Munich.

Figure 4.3. Sandro Botticelli, *Triumph of Love*, about 1470–75. Ms 143, f. 141v. Istituzione Biblioteca Classense, Ravenna.

Figure 4.4. Sandro Botticelli, illustration to Inferno 27 in Dante's *Divine Comedy*, about 1481–88. Kupferstichkabinett, Staatliche Museen, Berlin. © bpk Bildagentur / Staatliche Museen, Berlin / Phillip Allard / Art Resource, NY.

Figure 4.5. Luca della Robbia, *The Month of April*, about 1450–56. © Victoria and Albert Museum, London.

Figure 5.1a. *Death of Absalom*, after a drawing by Piero del Minella, about 1447. Duomo di Siena. Opera della Metropolitana di Siena.

Figure 5.1b. Florentine artist, death of Absalom, about 1370–90. From *Speculum humanae salvationis*, Ms 43-1950, f. 10r. © The Fitzwilliam Museum, Cambridge.

Figure 5.1c. Fra Angelico and workshop, *Crucifixion*, about 1438–43. Cell 42, Museo di San Marco, Florence. By permission of Ministero della Cultura, Direzione Regionale Musei della Toscana, Firenze.

Figure 5.2. Jean Pucelle, *Breviarium ad usum Ecclesiae Parisiensis*, about 1347–80. Ms Latin 1052 f. 232r, Bibliothèque nationale de France, Paris.

Figure 5.3. Sandro Botticelli, *Pallas and the Centaur*, about 1480–85. Gallerie degli Uffizi, Florence. By permission of Ministero della Cultura; further reproduction prohibited.

Figure 5.4. Fra Angelico, *Ordination of Saint Lawrence*, about 1448–49. Cappella Niccolina, Vatican City. © Governatorato SCV—Direzione dei Musei.

Figure 5.5. Comb bearing depiction of the legend of Saint Eustache, France, third quarter of the fourteenth century. Inv. 149/AV, Museo Civico d'Arte Antica, Palazzo Madama, Turin. By concession of Fondazione Torino Musei.

Figure 6.1. Piero del Pollaiuolo, *Charity*, 1469–70. Gallerie degli Uffizi, Florence. By permission of Ministero della Cultura; further reproduction prohibited.

Figure 6.2. Filippo Lippi, *Madonna and Child with Two Angels*, about 1460–65. Gallerie degli Uffizi, Florence. By permission of Ministero della Cultura; further reproduction prohibited.

Figure 6.3. Piero del Pollaiolo, *Prudence*, 1469–72. Gallerie degli Uffizi, Florence. By permission of Ministero della Cultura; further reproduction prohibited.

Figure 6.4. Andrea del Verrocchio (attr.), *Scipio*, about 1475. Musée du Louvre, Paris. Photo by Tony Querrec. © RMN-Grand Palais / Art Resource, NY,

Figure 6.5. Unknown artist, two busts of warriors facing each other, 1470–80. Bibliothèque nationale de France, Paris. RESERVE EA-19-BOITE, Gisèle Lambert 198.Hind A.I.57.

Figure 6.6. Francesco di Giorgio, *Entablature on the Human Form*, about 1476. Ms. Saluzzo 148, f. 21v. Biblioteca Reale, Turin. ©MiC—Musei Reali/ Biblioteca Reale.

Figure 6.7. Roman caryatid, late first century BCE. Villa Corsini a Castello. Florence. Photo by Sailko; Wikimedia Commons CC-BY 3.0. By permission of Museo Archeologico Nazionale di Firenze—Direzione regionale Musei della Toscana; further reproduction prohibited.

Figure 6.8a. Benedetto da Maiano, portal of the Hall of Lilies, about 1480. Musei Civici Fiorentini, Palazzo Vecchio, Florence.

Figure 6.8b. Sandro Botticelli, decorative border, about 1480–85. British Museum, London. © The Trustees of the British Museum.

Figure 7.1. Leonardo da Vinci, studies of water, about 1512–13. Windsor Castle, Windsor. RCIN 912579. Royal Collection Trust / © Her Majesty Queen Elizabeth II 2021.

Figure 7.2. *Head of Oceanus*, third century CE. Musée National du Bardo, Tunis. Photo by Giorgio Lotti © Mondadori Portfolio / Art Resource, NY.

Figure 7.3a. Mariano Taccola, dam mechanism, about 1427–41. From *De ingeneis*, clm 197.II, f. 114v, Bayerische Staatsbibliothek, Munich.

Figure 7.3b. Leonardo da Vinci, water flowing under a bridge. Inv. GDSU 447 E, Gabinetto dei Disegni e delle Stampe degli Uffizi, Florence. By permission of Ministero della Cultura; further reproduction prohibited.

Figure 7.4a. Workshop of Sandro Botticelli, *Venus*, about 1490. Gemäldegalerie, Berlin. © bpk Bildagentur / Gemäldegalerie, Staatliche Museen, Berlin / Jörg P. Anders / Art Resource, NY.

Figure 7.4b. Workshop of Sandro Botticelli, *Venus*, about 1496–97. Private collection, Geneva. Photo by Bibliotheca Hertziana. CC BY-NC.

Figure 7.4c. Workshop of Sandro Botticelli, *Venus*, about 1485–90. Galleria Sabauda, Turin. ©MiC—Musei Reali / Galleria Sabauda.

Figure 7.5. Attavante degli Attavanti, head of Medusa, about 1450–1550. Ms Ricc. 2056, f. 1r, Biblioteca Riccardiana, Florence. By permission of Ministero della Cultura.

Figure 7.6. Fra Angelico, *Lamentation of Christ*, about 1438–43. Cell 5, Museo di San Marco, Florence. By permission of Ministero della Cultura, Direzione Regionale Musei della Toscana, Firenze.

Figure 7.7. Sandro Botticelli, *Madonna of the Magnificat*, about 1483. Gallerie degli Uffizi, Florence. By permission of Ministero della Cultura; further reproduction prohibited.

Figure 7.8. Andrea del Castagno, *David with the Head of Goliath*, about 1450–55. Courtesy of the National Gallery of Art, Washington.

Figure 8.1. Thermal pool of Bagno Vignoni, Province of Siena. Photo by Matteo Vinattieri. Wikimedia Commons, public domain.

Figure 8.2. Memmo di Filippuccio, two people bathing, about 1300–1310. Camera del Podestà, Palazzo Comunale, San Gimignano. Photo by Roberto Sigismondi. By concession of Musei Civici di San Gimignano.

Figure 8.3. Ricciardo di Nanni, *Apollo and Daphne*, last quarter of the fifteenth century. Ms. VITR/22/4, f. 13r, Biblioteca Nacional de España, Madrid.

Figure 8.4. Benozzo Gozzoli, *Procession of the Magi*, about 1459–60. Medici Chapel, Palazzo Medici Riccardi, Florence.

Figure 8.5. Antonio Grifo, Petrarch turning into a laurel, 1470. Illustration in Petrarch, *Canzoniere* and *Triumphs*. Inc. G.V.15, f. 7r, Biblioteca Queriniana, Brescia.

Figure 9.1. Pope John XXI, *Thesaurus pauperum*, 1497, f. 1r. Wellcome Collection, London. CC 0.

Figure 9.2a. Benozzo Gozzoli, *Bust of a Woman*, about 1458. Cleveland Museum of Art, Cleveland. CC 0.

Figure 9.2b. Francesco di Valdambrino, *Annunciation*, about 1410–11. Palazzo Corboli, Asciano. Photo by the author. By authorization of Soprintendenza Archeologia, Belle Arti e Paesaggio per le province di Siena, Grosseto e Arezzo; further reproduction prohibited.

Figure 9.3. *Ortus sanitatis*, 1491. Wellcome Collection, London. CC 0.

Figure 9.4. Workshop of Mino da Fiesole, bust of young woman in frame of door mirror, about 1470. Cabinet des médailles et antiques, Bibliothèque Nationale de France, Paris.

Figure 9.5. Comb, about fourteenth or fifteenth century. Walker Art Gallery, National Museums, Liverpool. Bridgeman Images.

Figure 9.6. Comb bearing image of the Annunciation. Musée national du Moyen Age, Thermes de Cluny, Paris. Photo by Jean-Gilles Berizzi © RMN-Grand Palais / Art Resource, NY.

Figure 9.7. Giovanni Boccaccio, *Labyrinth of Love (Corbaccio)*, 1487. 70.3.F.11, f. 1, Biblioteca Nazionale Centrale "Vittorio Emanuele II," Rome.

Figure 9.8. Domenico di Zanobi, *Madonna del Soccorso*, about 1475–85. Velluti Chapel, Basilica di Santo Spirito, Florence.

Figures 10.1a, 10.1b, and 10.1c. Donatello, *Judith and Holofernes*, about 1455–60. Palazzo della Signoria, Florence. Photo courtesy of Fondazione Zeri.

Figure 10.2a. Sandro Botticelli, *Judith with the Head of Holofernes*, about 1469–70, Cincinnati Art Museum, Ohio. © Cincinnati Art Museum / John J. Emery Endowment / Bridgeman Images.

Figure 10.2b. Sandro Botticelli, *Judith with the Head of Holofernes*, about 1497–1500. Rijksmuseum, Amsterdam. CC 0.

Figures 10.3a and 10.3b. Sandro Botticelli, *Life of Moses*, about 1481–82. Sistine Chapel, Vatican City. © Governatorato SCV—Direzione dei Musei.

Figure 10.4. Leonardo da Vinci, *The Head of Leda*, about 1505–08. RCIN 912516, Windsor Castle, Windsor. Royal Collection Trust / © Her Majesty Queen Elizabeth II 2021.

Figure 10.5. Leonardo da Vinci, proportions of the head and a standing nude, about 1490. RCIN 912601, Windsor Castle, Windsor. Royal Collection Trust / © Her Majesty Queen Elizabeth II 2021.

PLATES

Plates 1 and 2. Sandro Botticelli, *The Birth of Venus*, about 1486. Gallerie degli Uffizi, Florence. By permission of Ministero della Cultura; further reproduction prohibited.

Plates 3 and 4. Andrea del Verrocchio, head of a woman with elaborate coiffure, about 1475. British Museum, London. © The Trustees of the British Museum.

Plate 5. Leonardo da Vinci, *Portrait of Ginevra de' Benci*, about 1474–78. Courtesy of the National Gallery of Art, Washington.

Plates 6, 11, and 12. Sandro Botticelli, *Primavera*, about 1486. Gallerie degli Uffizi, Florence. By permission of Ministero della Cultura; further reproduction prohibited.

Plates 7 and 8. Piero del Pollaiolo, *Portrait of a Lady*, about 1470. Poldi Pezzoli Museum, Milan.

Plate 9. Piero and Antonio Pollaiolo, *Prudence*, 1469–72. Gallerie degli Uffizi, Florence. By permission of Ministero della Cultura; further reproduction prohibited.

Plate 10. Sandro Botticelli, *Portrait of Simonetta Vespucci*, about 1480. Städel Museum, Frankfurt. CC BY-SA 4.0.

Plate 13. Ricciardo di Nanni, *Triumph of Love*, last quarter of the fifteenth century. Ms VITR/22/4, f. 12v, Biblioteca Nacional de España, Madrid.

Plate 14. Sandro Botticelli and Filippino Lippi, *Mary Magdalene Listening to Christ Preach*, about 1484. Cat. 44, John G. Johnson Collection, Philadelphia Museum of Art.

Plate 15. Sandro Botticelli and Filippino Lippi, *Mary Magdalene Receives Last Communion from Saint Maximinus*, about 1484. Cat. 47, John G. Johnson Collection, Philadelphia Museum of Art.

Plates 16 and 17. Francesco Pesellino, *The Death of Absalom*, 1445–50. Musée de Tessé, Le Mans. Photo by the author. © Musées du Mans, achat vente Fouret en 1863, inv. 10.21.

Plate 18. Cenni di Francesco, *Martyrdom of Saints John the Baptist and Lawrence,* about 1385. Inv. 1290, John G. Johnson Collection, Philadelphia Museum of Art.

Plate 19. Filippino Lippi, *The Life of Virginia*, about 1475–1500. Musée du Louvre, Paris. Photo by Daniel Arnaudet © RMN-Grand Palais / Art Resource, NY.

Plate 20. Vittore Ghiberti, frame of south door of the Florence baptistry, about 1452–56. Battistero di San Giovanni, Opera di Santa Maria del Fiore. Photo by the author.

Plate 21. Donatello, *Passion Pulpit*, about 1460. Basilica di San Lorenzo, Florence. Photo courtesy of Fondazione Zeri. By permission of Parrocchia di San Lorenzo; further reproduction prohibited.

Plate 22. Sandro Botticelli, *Fortitude*, about 1470. Gallerie degli Uffizi, Florence. By permission of Ministero della Cultura; further reproduction prohibited.

Plate 23. Piero del Pollaiolo, *Justice*, 1469–72. Gallerie degli Uffizi, Florence. By permission of Ministero della Cultura; further reproduction prohibited.

Plate 24. Capital on the south side of Florence's baptistery. Battistero di San Giovanni, Opera di Santa Maria del Fiore. Photo by the author.

Plate 25. Workshop of Piero del Pollaiolo, *The Triumph of Aemilius Paulus*, about 1472–73. Musée Jacquemart-André, Institut de France, Paris. Photo by the author.

Plates 26 and 27. The so-called Farnese Cup, about second century BCE. Museo Archeologico Nazionale, Naples. Photo by Giorgio Albano. By permission of Ministero della Cultura.

Plate 28. Comb bearing image of Susanna and the Elders, about 1500–30. Museo Nazionale Del Bargello, Florence. By permission of Ministero della Cultura—Museo Nazionale del Bargello.

Plates 29 and 30. Matteo di Giovanni, *Massacre of the Innocents*. Museo di Capodimonte, Naples. Photos by the author. By permission of Ministero della Cultura; further reproduction prohibited.

Plate 31. Gherardo di Giovanni del Fora, *Portrait of Piero de Medici*, 1488. Ms SQ XXII K 22, f. 2v. Biblioteca Nazionale "Vittorio Emanuele III," Naples. By permission of Ministero della Cultura. © Biblioteca Nazionale di Napoli.

Plate 32. Sandro Botticelli, *Allegory of Calumny*, about 1496–97. Gallerie degli Uffizi, Florence. By permission of Ministero della Cultura; further reproduction prohibited.

NOTES

CHAPTER ONE

1. Raymond Firth, *Symbols: Public and Private* (New York: Routledge, 1973), 269–70.
2. Michel Foucault, "The Subject and Power," *Critical Inquiry* 8, no. 4 (1982): 777–95. See also Johan Galtung, "Cultural Violence," *Journal of Peace Research* 27, no. 3 (1990): 291–305.
3. On psychosocial methods to inculcate ways of seeing and judging, see Louis Althusser, "Ideology and Ideological State Apparatuses (Notes towards an Investigation)," in id., *Lenin and Philosophy and Other Essays* (New York: Monthly Review Press, 2001), 85–126.
4. Niklas Luhmann, "Klassische Theorie der Macht. Kritik ihrer Prämissen," *Zeitschrift für Politik* 16 (1969): 149–70, esp. 150. Foucault also problematized a search for an origin "because it is an attempt to capture the exact essence of things, their purest possibilities, and their carefully protected identities." Michel Foucault, "Nietzsche, Genealogy, History," in *Aesthetics, Methods, and Epistemology: Essential Works of Michel Foucault*, 2 vols. (London: Penguin, 2000), vol. 2, 371.
5. On hegemony, Antonio Gramsci, *Quaderni del carcere*, ed. Valentino Gerratana, 4 vols. (Turin: Einaudi, 2014), vol. 3, 2010–34.
6. Niccolò Machiavelli first voiced this interpretation in his much-commented-upon *Discourses on the First Decade of Titus Livius*, 1.52. The Medici were linked by marriage to more families than their rivals, and thus served as a link between different Florentine communities. John F. Padgett and Christopher K. Ansell, "Robust Action and the Rise of the

Medici, 1400–1434," *American Journal of Sociology* 98, no. 6 (1993): 1259–1319. On Machiavelli's relationship with the Medici, see John M. Najemy, "Machiavelli and the Medici: The Lessons of Florentine History," *Renaissance Quarterly* 35, no. 4 (1982): 551–76.

7. Nicolai Rubinstein, *The Government of Florence under the Medici (1434 to 1494)* (Oxford, UK: Oxford University Press, 1997), 69–76; Dale Kent, *Cosimo de Medici and the Florentine Renaissance: The Patron's Oeuvre* (New Haven, CT, and London: Yale University Press, 2000), 348–51; Riccardo Fubini, *Italia quattrocentesca: Politica e diplomazia nell'età di Lorenzo il Magnifico* (Milan: Francoangeli, 1994), 62–86 and 220–52.
8. Guido Ruggiero, *The Renaissance in Italy: A Social and Cultural History of the Rinascimento* (Cambridge, UK: Cambridge University Press, 2015), 205–7. On the various meanings of "humanism," Riccardo Fubini, *L'umanesimo italiano e i suoi storici* (Milan: F. Angeli, 2001), 15–72. For a reexamination of humanism, Sylvia Wynter, "Unsettling the Coloniality of Being/Power/Truth/Freedom: Towards the Human, after Man, Its Overrepresentation; An Argument," *New Centennial Review* 3, no. 3 (2003): 257–337.
9. Andrew S. Wilson and Desmond Tobin, "Hair after Death," in *Aging Hair*, ed. Ralph Trüeb and Desmond Tobin (Berlin: Springer, 2010), 249–61.
10. Aristotle, *De generatione animalium* 5.3–5.
11. More precisely, long-haired girls were compared to cows: "Donne, fate che le vostre fanciulle non siano vacche. Fate che le vadino coperte el petto, non portino la coda come le vacche, non abbino le corna come le vacche; fatele posare queste veliere." Girolamo Savonarola, *Prediche sopra Amos e Zaccaria*, ed. Paolo Ghiglieri, 3 vols. (Rome: Angelo Belardetti, 1971–72), vol. 1, 324.
12. Eviatar Zerubavel, *Taken for Granted: The Remarkable Power of the Unremarkable* (Princeton, NJ: Princeton University Press, 2018), 14–15. I'm grateful to Elizabeth Horodowich for this suggestion.
13. Helen E. Longino, *The Fate of Knowledge* (Princeton, NJ: Princeton University Press, 2002), 120.
14. Alexander Nagel and Christopher S. Wood, *Anachronic Renaissance* (New York: Zone Books, 2010), 45–50.
15. To get a sense of the range of dates attributed to Botticelli's works, read the entry for his London Adoration (assigned to almost any year between 1468 and 1480) in Ronald Lightbown, *Sandro Botticelli: Life and Work*, 2 vols. (Berkeley and Los Angeles: University of California Press, 1978), vol. 2, 25–26.

16. Svetlana Alpers, *The Vexations of Art: Velázquez and Others* (New Haven, CT, and London: Yale University Press, 2005), 219.
17. Karl R. Popper, *The Poverty of Historicism* (Boston: Beacon Press, 1957), 105–11 and 152–59.
18. Emanuele Lugli, "The Hair Is Full of Snares: Botticelli's and Boccaccio's Wayward Erotic Gaze," *Mitteilungen des Kunsthistorischen Institutes in Florenz* 61, no. 2 (2019): 203–33.
19. On historians and art historians' obsession with change, see Judith M. Bennett, *History Matters: Patriarchy and the Challenge of Feminism* (Philadelphia: University of Pennsylvania Press, 2006), 54–81; Thomas Crow, "The Practice of Art History in America," *Daedalus* 135, no. 2 (2006): 70–90.
20. Alfred Gell, *Art and Agency: An Anthropological Theory* (Oxford, UK: Clarendon Press, 1998), 16.
21. Jose Ortega y Gasset, *Obras completas*, 10 vols. (Madrid: Revista de Occidente, 1957–69), vol. 9, 56–63. See also John T. Graham, *The Social Thought of Ortega y Gasset* (Columbia and London: University of Missouri Press, 2001), 221.
22. Michael Baxandall, *Giotto and the Orators: Humanist Observers of Painting in Italy and the Discovery of Pictorial Composition 1350–1450* (New York: Oxford University Press, 1971), 1–8. On the perils of reading Florentine artworks only through art patronage, Patricia Rubin, *Images and Identity in Fifteenth-Century Florence* (New Haven, CT, and London: Yale University Press, 2007), xix.
23. Joan Wallach Scott, *On the Judgment of History* (New York: Columbia University Press, 2020), 82–88.
24. Florentines were familiar with the image of a downward-pointing sword suspended by a horse hair over the head of a ruler to visualize the lethal insecurity of politics. The image is described in the popular book *Fior di virtù*. See *The Florentine Fior di Virtù of 1491*, tr. Nicholas Fersin (Philadelphia: E. Stern, 1953), 78–79. On its success, Paul F. Grendler, "Form and Function in Italian Renaissance Popular Books," *Renaissance Quarterly* 46, no. 3 (1993): 451–85, esp. 455–61.
25. Walter Johnson, "On Agency," *Journal of Social History* 37, no. 1 (2003): 113–24, esp. 116.
26. The elements of the past that continue to be culturally active within the present, even if in less legible ways, are called "residual" in Raymond Williams, *Marxism and Literature* (Oxford, UK: Oxford University Press, 1977), 121–27.

CHAPTER TWO

1. In 1472, Leonardo was recorded as a member of the Compagnia di San Luca, the Florentine painters' guild. In Florence, a painter's training lasted between three and six years, which means that Leonardo started his apprenticeship sometime between 1466 and 1469. In 1469 Leonardo is recorded as a dependent ("boca," literally "mouth to feed") in the tax record of his grandfather in Vinci, on which Luca Beltrami, *Documenti e memorie riguardanti la vita e le opere di Leonardo da Vinci* (Milan: Treves, 1919), 2n3. While a tax record does not prove residence, many scholars have taken this document as evidence that Leonardo moved to Florence later in that year. Pietro C. Marani, *Leonardo: Catalogo completo dei dipinti* (Florence: Cantini, 1989), 12–18.
2. David A. Brown, *Leonardo da Vinci: Origins of a Genius* (New Haven, CT, and London: Yale University Press, 1998), 7 and 128–38. It is the sixteenth-century biographer Giorgio Vasari who first connected Leonardo's interest in hair to his apprenticeship under Verrocchio, "some of whose drawings depict heads of women with fine characters [*arie*] and hairstyles, which, because of their beauty, Leonardo da Vinci constantly imitated." ("Sono alcuni disegni di sua [Verrocchio's] mano nel nostro libro fatti con molta pacienza e grandissimo giudizio, in fra i queli sono alcune teste di femina con bell'arie et acconciature di capegli, quali per la sua bellezza Lionardo da Vinci sempre imitò.") Giorgio Vasari, *Le vite de' più eccellenti pittori scultori e architettori nelle redazioni del 1550 e 1568*, ed. Rosanna Bettarini, 6 vols. (Florence: Sansoni and SPES, 1966–87), vol. 3, 538. On the translation of *aria* as "character," Michael Baxandall, *Painting and Experience in Fifteenth-Century Italy: A Primer in the Social History of Pictorial Style* (Oxford, UK: Oxford University Press, 1988, 1st. ed. 1972), 110.
3. David A. Brown, "Leonardo apprendista," *Lettura Vinciana* 39 (2000):, 17.
4. Antonio Natali, *Lo sguardo degli angeli: Verrocchio, Leonardo a il "Battesimo di Cristo"* (Ciniello Balsamo, Italy: Silvana, 1998), 66–68; Christina Neilson, *Practice and Theory in the Italian Renaissance Workshop: Verrocchio and the Epistemology of Making Art* (Cambridge, UK: Cambridge University Press, 2019), 268n36.
5. Numerous studies of hairstyling have been attributed to Verrocchio's pupils, such as Biagio d'Antonio (Florence: Gabinetto Disegni e Stampe degli Uffizi, inv. 1254 E), Lorenzo di Credi (Karlsruhe: Staatliche Kunst-

halle, #409), and Perugino. On d'Antonio, see Luciano Bellosi and Alessandro Angelini, *Sassetta e i pittori toscani tra XIII e XV secolo* (Florence: SPES, 1986), 58–61; Roberta Bartoli, *Biagio d'Antonio* (Milan: Motta, 1999), 36–37. On di Credi, see Gigetta Dalli Regoli, *Lorenzo di Credi* (Milan: Edizioni di Comunità, 1966), 31–33 and 124–25. On Perugino, see Brown, *Leonardo: Origins*, 34 and 128.

6. "Delle oscurità delle ombre, o voi dire chiarezze de' lumi. Benché li pratichi mettino in tutte le cose infuscate, come alberi, prati, capelli, barbe e peli, di 4 sorte chiarezze nel contraffare un medesimo colore [. . .] a me pare che esse varietà sieno infinite sopra una quantità continua, la quale in sé è divisibile in infinito." *Il Codice Atlantico di Leonardo da Vinci nella Biblioteca Ambrosiana di Milano*, ed. Augusto Marinoni, 12 vols. (Florence: Giunti, 1975–1980), vol. 3, 534v. See also Jean-Paul Richter, *The Literary Works of Leonardo da Vinci*, 2 vols. (London: Oxford University Press, 1939), vol. 1, 330n548.

7. On these three subjects (landscape, drapery, and hair), Gigetta Dalli Regoli, "Leonardo e Sandro all'inizio degli anni Settanta: La forma degli alberi," in *"Tutte le opere non son per istancarmi": Raccolta di scritti per i settant'anni di Carlo Pedretti*, ed. Fabio Frosini (Rome: Edizioni Associate, 1998), 59–76; Françoise Viatte, "The Early Drapery Studies," in *Leonardo da Vinci: Master Draftsman*, ed. Carmen C. Bambach (New York: Metropolitan Museum of Art, 2003), 111–20; Viatte, "Verrocchio et Leonardo da Vinci: À propos des 'têtes idéales,'" in *Florentine Drawing at the Time of Lorenzo the Magnificent*, ed. Elizabeth Cropper (Bologna: Nuova Alfa, 1992), 52–53. Viatte's account expanded on André Chastel, "Les capitaines antiques affrontés dans l'art florentine du quinzième siècle," *Mémoires de la Société nationale des Antiquaires de France* 3 (1954): 279–89.

8. Alexander Nagel, "Leonardo and Sfumato," *RES: Anthropology and Aesthetics* 24 (1993): 7–20; Francesca Fiorani, *The Shadow Drawing: How Science Taught Leonardo How to Paint* (New York: Farrar, Straus and Giroux, 2020), 146–64.

9. Four of the drawings that Leonardo took to Milan in 1482 record hairstyles. *Codex Atlanticus*, 10:888r: "una testa in faccia di giovane co[n] una bella capellatura [. . .] Una testa di proffilo con bella capellatura [. . .] Una testa di putta con trezie rannodate. Una testa con un'acconciatura." Richter, *The Literary Works*, vol. 1, 387–88n680.

10. Verrocchio trained as a goldsmith, but his artistic interests were wide. Giovanni Rucellai called him "sculptor and painter" in a 1457 entry of

his journal, and a "book illustrator" in 1463. Alessandro Perosa, *Giovanni Rucellai ed il suo Zibaldone*, 2 vols. (London: Warburg Institute, 1960–81), vol. 1, 23–24; Neilson, *Practice and Theory*, 16–25. In Florence, goldsmiths commonly worked in other media. See Katalin Prajda, "Goldsmiths, Goldbeaters and Other Gold Workers in Early Renaissance Florence: 1378–1433," in *Craftsmen and Guilds in Medieval and Early Modern Periods*, ed. Eva Jullien and Michel Pauly (Stuttgart, Germany: Franz Steiner, 2016), 197–221.

11. "Fa' che 'l pennello non sia mai troppo carico. La ragione: che ti verrà fatto i tuoi lavori come capelli sottili che è più vago lavoro." Cennino Cennini, *Il libro dell'arte*, ed. Franco Brunello (Vicenza, Italy: Pozza, 1971), 157. The version I refer to is Florence, Biblioteca Medicea Laurenziana, Plut. 78.23. The date and location are revealed in the colophon: "Finito libro referamus gratis Christi, 1437, a dì 31 di Luglio. Ex Stinchharum f[ecit]." Modern editions integrate this version with the text of a seventeenth-century manuscript in Florence's Riccardiana library (Ms. 2190) which contains seventeen more chapters and is not regarded as a direct derivation of Plut. 78.23. Verrocchio's approximate date of birth is derived from tax declarations, but the evidence is inconclusive: in 1446 Verrocchio was said to be twelve years old, but in 1457 he declared himself to be twenty-one, not twenty-three. Dario A. Covi, *Andrea del Verrocchio: Life and Work* (Florence: L.S. Olschki, 2005), 265 and 268.
12. Michelle O'Malley, *The Business of Art: Contracts and the Commissioning Process in Renaissance Italy* (New Haven, CT: Yale University Press, 2005), 3–12.
13. Baxandall, *Painting and Experience*, 23–28; Michelle O'Malley, *Painting under Pressure: Fame, Reputation and Demand in Renaissance Florence* (New Haven, CT: Yale University Press, 2013), 64–75.
14. Cennini, *Libro*, 4: "Fui informato nella detta arte XII anni da Agnolo di Taddeo da Firenze mio maestro, il quale imparò la detta arte da Taddeo suo padre; il quale suo padre fu battezzato da Giotto, e fu suo discepolo anni XXIIII." Cennini's claim was accurate since his master, Agnolo Gaddi, was the son of one of Giotto's pupils. Some art historians think, however, that Cennini's technique was no longer representative of Giotto's. Miklós Boskovits, "Cennino Cennini: Pittore nonconformista," *Mitteilungen des Kunsthistorischen Institutes in Florenz* 17, no. 2–3 (1973): 204–7. On Giotto's fame in the fifteenth century (he was almost a "synonym" for painting itself), Baxandall, *Giotto and the Orators: Hu-*

manist Observers of Painting in Italy and the Discovery of Pictorial Composition 1350–1450 (New York: Oxford University Press, 1971), 66–78; Robert Brennan, *Painting as a Modern Art in Early Renaissance Italy* (London: Harvey Miller, 2019), 220–28, 242, and 263. I thank Robert Brennan for sharing an advance copy of his book with me.

15. On the attribution of figure 2.3, *Verrocchio: Master of Leonardo*, ed. Francesco Caglioti and Andrea de Marchi (Venice: Marsilio, 2019), 128–31.

16. "Perché giova ad exercitarsi nel ochio in vedere cose minute e guardare cose luminose e similmente zova al audito ascoltar i suoni occulti [. . .] Affaticandosi adonque l'occhio e l'audito nelle cose extreme poi meglio sentono l'obiecto mediocre et ha[n]no poi migliore operatione." Girolamo Manfredi, *Liber de homine / Libro del perché* (Bologna: 1474), f. 13r. On its popularity, Charles Singer, *Studies in the History and Method of Science* (Oxford, UK: Clarendon Press, 1917), 101; Antònia Carré and Lluís Cifuentes, "Girolamo Manfredi's *Il Perché*: The *Problemata* and Its Medieval Tradition," *Medicina & Storia* 10 (2010): 17–18.

17. Pliny's *Natural History* is among the five books that Leonardo declared himself to own in a note of 1487–90. Carlo Vecce, *La biblioteca perduta: I libri di Leonardo* (Rome: Salerno, 2017), 65. It is also a book that Leonardo could read, since it had been translated into Italian by Cristoforo Landino in 1476. Riccardo Fubini, "Cristoforo Landino, le *Disputationes Camaldulenses* e il volgarizzamento di Plinio: Questioni di cronologia e di interpretazione," in *Studi in onore di Arnaldo d'Addario*, ed. Luigi Borgia and others (Lecce, Italy: Conte, 1995), 535–60; Ugo Rozzo, "La fortuna della *Naturalis Historia* di Plinio nell'editoria del XV secolo," *Archives internationales d'histoire des sciences* 61 (2011): 92–99.

18. Pliny, *Natural History* 34.19.

19. Pliny, *Natural History* 35.36. On the role of the line for Pliny, see David Rosand, "Una linea sola non stentata," in *Linea I: Grafie di immagini tra Quattrocento e Cinquecento*, ed. Marzia Faietti and Gerhard Wolf (Venice: Marsilio, 2008), 17–28, esp. 17–20.

20. Cennini, *Libro*, 69–72. The pelt of pig (*porco*) and squirrel (*vaio*) was also recommended in Giovanni Battista Armenini, *De' veri precetti della pittura* (Ravenna: 1587), 110, thus making a case for the continuity of these brushes over two centuries. Armenini specifies that pig hair brushes were employed for frescoes, and squirrel hair brushes for oil painting and final touches. He states, however, that only a few painters constructed them from scratch in his time, as brushes could easily be bought in

apothecaries' shops. On the making of small brushes, see also François Quiviger, "The Brush in Poetry and Practice: Agnolo Bronzino's *Capitolo del pennello* in Context," in *Poetry on Art: Renaissance to Romanticism*, ed. Thomas Frangenberg (Donington, UK: Shaun Tyas, 2003), 101–3.

21. "Fallo ben sodetto e punzìo, e che la punta esca poco poco fuor del bocciuolo. Poi intigni poca cosa della punta in nel mordente, e lavora i tuo' adornamenti e i tuo' fregi. E, come ti dico, fa' che 'l pennello non sia mai troppo carico. La ragione: che ti verrà fatto i tuoi lavori come capelli sottili che è più vago lavoro. Cennini," *Libro*, 156–57.
22. On this innovative modeling, Neilson, *Practice and Theory*, 152–56.
23. On the practice of using assistants as models, Claire Van Cleave, *Master Drawings of the Italian Renaissance* (Cambridge, MA: Harvard University Press, 2007), 20–21. This convention offers the only basis for the belief that Leonardo modeled for Verrocchio's *David*, as popularized by Charles Nicholl, *Leonardo da Vinci: Flights of the Mind* (New York: Viking, 2004), 74; Ross King, *Leonardo and the Last Supper* (New York: Walker & Company, 2012), 25; and Walter Isaacson, *Leonardo da Vinci* (New York: Simon & Schuster, 2017), 35–36.
24. Vecce, *La biblioteca perduta*, 65.
25. "'E' parevon di Danne [Daphne] i suoi crin d'oro." Luigi Pulci, *Morgante* 15.99–101.
26. Luigi Pulci, the author of *Morgante*, was an avid reader of medieval poetry and continued many of its narrative topoi. Antea's love for the knight Rinaldo, for instance, is described as being a result of her being hit by Cupid's flaming arrow, a medieval trope (*Morgante* 16.21.8: "e par che fiamme Amor nel suo cor fiocchi"). I mention this episode in preparation for chapter 4, in which I discuss the burning nature of desire.
27. Maria Giuseppina Muzzarelli, *Gli inganni delle apparenze: Disciplina di vesti e ornamenti alla fine del Medioevo* (Turin: Scriptorium, 1996), 180; Stefan Hanß, "Face-Work: Making Hair Matter in Sixteenth-Century Central Europe," *Gender & History* 33, no. 2 (2021): 314–45.
28. Jill Dunkerton and Luke Syson, "In Search of Verrocchio the Painter: The Cleaning and Examination of 'The Virgin and Child and Two Angels,'" *National Gallery Technical Bulletin* 31 (2010): 23.
29. More precisely, Oxford, UK: Christ Church Picture Gallery, A.5; Berlin: Staatliche Museen, Kupferstichkabinett, 5095; Florence: Uffizi, Gabinetto dei Disegni e delle Stampe, 130E.
30. Covi, *Andrea del Verrocchio*, 221–22.

31. A case in point is offered by the ending of Matteo Maria Boiardo's epic *Orlando in Love*, in which the woman warrior Bradamante, sporting short hair after an injury, is mistaken for a man by the Spanish princess Fiordespina. The shearing of Bradamante's hair and her consequent virilization are described at 3.8.61 ("Benché convenne le chiome tagliare / Per la ferita, che era grande e strana / Le chiome li tagliò come a garzone / Poi li donò la sua benedizione"). Michelle DeCoste, "Knots of Desire: Female Homoeroticism in Orlando Furioso 25," in *Queer Italia: Same-Sex Desire in Italian Literature and Film*, ed. Gary Cestaro (New York: Palgrave, 2004), 55.
32. Elizabeth Walmsley, "Leonardo's Portrait of Ginevra de' Benci: A Reading of the X-Radiographs and Infrared Reflectographs," in *Leonardo da Vinci's Technical Practice: Paintings, Drawings, and Influence*, ed. Michel Menu (Paris: Hermann, 2014), 56–71, esp. 60–64.
33. Pricking returns in Leonardo's portrait of Isabella d'Este. *I disegni di Leonardo da Vinci e della sua cerchia nelle collezioni pubbliche in Francia*, ed. Pietro C. Marani (Florence: Giunti, 2008), 72–73. The *Mona Lisa* was also made the same way, see Pascal Cotte and Lionet Simonot, "Mona Lisa's *spolvero* revealed," *Journal of Cultural Heritage* 45 (2020): 1–9: https://doi.org/10.1016/j.culher.2020.08.004.
34. Elisabetta Gnignera, *I soperchi ornamenti: Copricapi e acconciature femminili nell'Italia del Quattrocento* (Siena, Italy: Protagon, 2010), 11–12; Patricia Simons, "Giovanna and Ginevra: Portraits for the Tornabuoni Family by Ghirlandaio and Botticelli," *I Tatti Studies in the Italian Renaissance*, 14/15 (2011–12): 104–6 and 116–20. On Florence's growing wealth, Richard A. Goldthwaite, *The Economy of Renaissance Florence* (Baltimore: Johns Hopkins University Press, 2009), 381–83.
35. On the treaty of Lodi, signed on April 9, 1454, see Pierluigi Majocchi, "Francesco Sforza e la Pace di Lodi, 9 aprile 1454," *Archivio storico lodigiano* 127 (2008): 141–204. Leonardo was born on April 15, 1452.
36. In the 1430s, Florence's tax revenue amounted to an average of 549,637 florins per year. After 1454 it was 121,959. Elio Conti, *L'imposta diretta a Firenze nel Quattrocento (1427–1494)* (Rome: Istituto storico italiano per il Medio Evo, 1984), 340; Giovanni Ciappelli, *Fisco e società a Firenze nel Rinascimento* (Rome: Edizioni di storia e letteratura, 2009), 136–37.
37. Peter Howard, "The Language of Luxury in Renaissance Florence," in *Luxury and the Ethics of Greed in Early Modern Italy*, ed. Catherine Kovesi (Turnhout, Belgium: Brepols, 2018), 58–64. Cf. Catherine Kovesi, "Lux-

ury in the Renaissance: A Contribution to the Etymology of a Concept," in *Renaissance Studies in Honor of Joseph Connors*, ed. Machtelt Israëls and Louis A. Waldman, and Guido Beltramini, 2 vols. (Cambridge, MA: Harvard University Press, 2013), vol. 2, 239–40.

38. The Florentine Gregorio (Goro) Dati (1362–1435) proudly celebrated the "marvelous wealth" (*maravigliosa ricchezza*) that the Florentines displayed on the feast day of Saint John the Baptist, patron of Florence: "E per tutto è pieno di donne giovani, e fanciulle vestite di seta, e ornate di gioie, e di pietre preziose, e di perle." Goro Dati, *Istoria di Firenze* (Florence: Giuseppe Manni, 1735), 86. Florentines' ostentation on the feast day of 1475 is also remarked upon in a letter by the notary Piero Cennini, published in Girolamo Mancini, "Il bel S. Giovanni e le feste patronali di Firenze descritte nel 1475 da Piero Cennini," *Rivista d'arte* 6 (1909): 220–27. Generally, on the feast day: Richard Trexler, *Public Life in Renaissance Florence* (New York: Academic Press, 1980), 240–63.

39. "Oggi, nel mezo della observanzia cristiana, le vergini publicamente, a cavallo, ornate quanto più possono, et dipincte d'ogni lascivia, colle trombe inanzi chiamando il popolo a vedere la sfrenata audacia del meritricidio ardire, ne portano al campo della disiderata giostra; intorniando le piaze [going around the squares] et facendo monstra, ne vanno a non essere più vergini." Matteo Palmieri, *Vita Civile*, ed. Gino Belloni (Florence: Sansoni, 1982), 114.

40. The metaphor comes from Baldesar Castiglione, *Libro del cortegiano* 2.8: "E porrà cura d'aver cavallo con vaghi guarnimenti, abiti ben intesi, motti appropriati, invenzioni ingeniose, che a sé tirino gli occhi de' circonstanti, come calamita il ferro." I am grateful to Victor Stoichita for directing me to this passage.

41. Alessandra Strozzi, whose correspondence has survived to us, reveals a detachment toward her daughters after they married and became financially separated from her. See Ann M. Crabb, *The Strozzi of Florence: Widowhood and Family Solidarity in the Renaissance* (Ann Arbor: University of Michigan Press, 2000), 89.

42. Christiane Klapisch-Zuber, *Women, Family, and Ritual in Renaissance Italy* (Chicago: University of Chicago Press, 1985), 213–46. The necessity of dowry for Florentine marriages is made evident by the establishment of a city's dowry fund. Julius Kirshner and Anthony Molho, "The Dowry Fund and the Marriage Market in Early Quattrocento Florence," *Journal of Modern History* 50, no. 3 (1978): 404–38.

43. On the role of architecture in constructing gender divides, see Mark Wigley, "Untitled: The Housing of Gender," in *Sexuality and Space*, ed. Beatriz Colomina (New York: Princeton Architectural Press, 1992), 327–89, esp. 332–51. Wigley focuses on Leon Battista Alberti, who, in his book on family management, recommended locking women up. Leon B. Alberti, *I libri della famiglia*, ed. Ruggiero Romano and Alberto Tenenti (Turin: Einaudi, 1969), 265: "Difenda la donna serrata in casa le cose e sè stessa con ozio, timore e suspizione."
44. Goldthwaite, *Economy of Renaissance Florence*, 382; Klapisch-Zuber, *Women, Family*, 227. On the inextricable linkage between capitalism and women's oppression, Silvia Federici, *Caliban and the Witch* (New York: Autonomedia, 2004), 61–75.
45. Timothy McCall, *Brilliant Bodies: Fashioning Courtly Men in Early Renaissance Italy* (University Park, PA: 2022), 33–43.
46. These definitions date to the Middle Ages as demonstrated in Isidore of Seville, *Etymologiarum libri* 19.24.8. They were also legally binding, as argued in *De patria potestate* by Angelo degli Ubaldi (1325–1400), who states that married women "debent ire facie semicoperta," whereas unmarried women "debent stare in capillo, non capite velato." Osvaldo Cavallar, "Il velo nel diritto comune: Tra metafora e negazione della moda," in *Il velo in area mediterranea fra storia e simbolo*, ed. Maria Giuseppina Muzzarelli, Maria Grazia Nico Ottaviani, and Gabriella Zarri (Bologna: Il Mulino, 2014), 58–60.
47. On the role of female guardians, Patrizia Bettella, *The Ugly Woman: Transgressive Aesthetic Models in Italian Poetry from the Middle Ages to the Baroque* (Toronto: University of Toronto Press, 2005), 45–52.
48. Giovanni da Capistrano, *Trattato degli ornamenti, specie delle donne*, ed. Aniceto Chiappini (Siena: Cantagalli, 1956), 119: "I motivi per cui le donne devono velarsi, cioè in segno della prevaricazione e di sudditanza e per ovviare alla libidine." I think Capistrano took it from Peter Lombard's commentary on Saint Paul's first letter to the Corinthians. Petrus Lombardus, *Opera Omnia*, Patrologia Latina 191, 2 vols. (Paris: Migne, 1854), vol. 2: col. 1634: "Et ideo mulier debet habere velamen super caput, scilicet ad significandum quod sensualitas debet subjici rationi."
49. A woman could take her veil off for her husband's funeral, a right that all other attending women were denied by law. *Statuti della Repubblica Fiorentina*, ed. Romolo Caggese, 2 vols. (Florence: Tipografia Galileana and E. Ariani 1910–21), vol. 1, 223 ("nulla mulier debeat se scapigliare vel

supra bendam elevare, nisi uxor defuncti"). The concession was not an invitation to seduce. On the contrary, a widow was required to pull her hair in desperation, as explained in Capistrano, *Trattato degli ornamenti*, 118–19.

50. A female veil was called "curtain" (*curtina*) by Giovanni da Capistrano in his *Trattato degli ornamenti*, 118.

51. Students read that the Roman consul Gaius Suplicius Gallus divorced his wife because he caught her outdoors without a veil in Valerius Maximus, *Facta et dicta memorabilia* 6.3.10. On Valerius Maximus's fame in the fifteenth century, Marijke Crav, *Exemplary Reading: Printed Renaissance Commentaries on Valerius Maximus* (1470–1600) (Zurich: Lit, 2015), 2. Little does it matter that Valerius Maximus did not draw an accurate picture of Roman history, as the episode returned in Flavio Biondo, *Romans triumphans* 8, as one of the reasons to repudiate a wife. See Maria Agata Pincelli, "*Librariis certatim transcribere contendentibus*: Sulla tradizione manoscritta e la prima ricezione della *Roma triumphans* di Biondo Flavio," in *The Invention of Rome: Biondo Flavio's* Roma Triumphans *and Its Worlds*, ed. Frances Muecke and Maurizio Campanelli (Geneva: Droz, 2017), 199–208.

CHAPTER THREE

1. My description is a mashup of passages. The metaphor of digestion as a form of putrefaction is found in Girolamo Manfredi, *Liber de homine / Libro del perché* (Bologna: 1474), f. 1v ("Troppo mangiare e bevere [. . .] putressano de che nasce un caldo putredinale"). The comparison between the body and a chimney is from ibid., f. 27v ("Perché adonque l'huomo e di statura drita tutti li fumi del corpo ascendono al capo come al camino"). I took the description of digestion as a form of cooking from Avicenna, *Canon*, 4.2, where Avicenna explains that it takes place in the liver, from which veins carry nutrients to the tissues. Avicenna is also responsible for the dissemination of Galen's belief that arteries carry vital spirits in the blood as they stem from the heart, the seat of the soul. Nancy G. Siraisi, *Medieval and Early Renaissance Medicine: An Introduction to Knowledge and Practice* (Chicago: University of Chicago Press, 1990), 78–114.

2. Mondino de' Liuzzi, *Hanothomya del corpo humano*, ed. Maria Rosaria D'Anzi (Rome: Aracne, 2012), 39.18. Written c. 1316 and much copied until

1478, when it was printed in Pavia, de' Liuzzi's manual defined fifteenth-century medicine as argued in Nancy G. Siraisi, *Taddeo Alderotti and His Pupils: Two Generations of Italian Medical Learning* (Princeton, NJ: Princeton University Press, 1981), 66–69. Before 1500, Avicenna's medical magnum opus, the so-called *Canon*, mostly circulated as abridgments and lecture material. See Nancy G. Siraisi, *Avicenna in Renaissance Italy: The Canon and Medical Teaching in Italian Universities after 1500* (Princeton, NJ: Princeton University Press, 1987), 49–56.

3. Oskar Cameron Gruner, *A Treatise on the Canon of Medicine of Avicenna* (London: Luzac., 1930), 91–92.
4. This description also returned in a nonmedical work: Cristoforo Landino, *Comento sopra la Comedia*, ed. Paolo Procaccioli, 4 vols. (Rome: Salerno, 2001), vol. 3, 1414–15. Landino claimed that he relied not only on Avicenna but on anatomical descriptions by Galen, Aristotle, and Albert the Great.
5. Michael Boylan, "The Digestive and "Circulatory" Systems in Aristotle's Biology," *Journal of the History of Biology* 15, no. 1 (1982): 89–118. Doctors openly acknowledged these differences. For instance, Mondino de' Liuzzi discussed Aristotle's and Galen's differences in his *Hanothomya* 32.41–42.
6. Manfredi, *Liber de homine*, f. 1r: "El cibo che puro nutrimento è così vinto e transmutato dal corpo nostro che non transmuta il corpo. Anzi si converte in substantia nostra et de questo chi ne piglia troppo, la natura non lo può digestire. Unde generasi di molte superfluità."
7. Valentin Groebner, "Complexio/Complexion," in *The Moral Authority of Nature*, ed. Lorraine Daston and Fernando Vidal (Chicago: University of Chicago Press, 2003), 361–83. At p. 367, Groebner recalls Jacopo da Forlì's teaching on complexions in 1360s Florence. Today's historians are quick at stressing the connection between immaterial complexions and the body's four humors (blood, black bile, yellow bile, and phlegm), but the latter were often considered vehicles of, rather than equivalent to, complexions, as argued in Siraisi, *Medieval and Early Renaissance Medicine*, 101–6. Many fifteenth-century texts that circulated in Florence did not mention the humors, as they did not rely on the Hippocratic-Galenic corpus that cemented their importance. See Jacques Jouanna and Neil Allies, "The Legacy of the Hippocratic Treatise 'The Nature of Man': The Theory of the Humors," in *Greek Medicine from Hippocrates to Galen*, ed. Philip van der Eijk, Jacques Jouanna, and Neil Allies (Leiden, Netherlands: Brill, 2012), 335–60. In Florence such a corpus was known in frag-

ments, which were systematized only in the sixteenth century. Vivian Nutton, "Hippocrates in the Renaissance," *Sudhoffs Archiv Zeitschrift für Wissenschaftsgeschichte* 27 (1989): 420–39; Nancy G. Siraisi, *The Clock and the Mirror: Girolamo Cardano and Renaissance Medicine* (Princeton, NJ: Princeton University Press, 1997), 119–45. Aristotle's *De generatione et corruptione* (II.3, 330b) made no mention of the four humors either.

8. Pantegni, in *Omnia Opera Ysaac in hoc volumine contenta* (Lyon: 1515), f. 3v: "In sicco et calido [corpore] nigri et crispi [pili] sunt; in frigido et umido [sunt] lenes et flavi." On this printed edition, the first of a text that had circulated since the eleventh century, see Mark Jordan, "The Fortune of Constantine's Pantegni," in *Constantine the African and 'Alī Ibn Al-'Abbās Al-Maǧūsī: The Pantegni and Related Texts*, ed. Charles Burnett and Danielle Jacquart (Leiden, Netherlands: Brill, 1994), 286–302.

9. Aristotle, *The History of Animals* 1.6 and 3.10: "In some animals the hair goes on gradually hardening into bristle until it no longer resembles hair but spine, as in the case of the hedgehog." Translated by John A. Smith and William D. Ross in vol. 4 of *The Works of Aristotle* (Oxford, UK: Clarendon Press, 1910), 517b. The same point returns in Aristotle, *On the Generation of Animals* 5.3.

10. Cameron Gruner, *A Treatise*, 265–66.

11. *De secretis mulierum*, ch. 27: "Capilli eorum sunt extensi et longi, sive sint nigri sive albi, et sunt subtiles." The four complexions are described in chs. 26–29. On the popularity of this treatise, often attributed to Albert the Great, see Helen Rodnite Lemay, *Women's Secrets: A Translation of Pseudo-Albertus Magnus' De Secretis Mulierum with Commentaries* (Albany: State University of New York Press, 1992), 7–16.

12. Florence was very energetic in translating Galen's writings. The professor of theoretical medicine Lorenzo Laurenzi (whom Botticelli portrayed in a painting that today is in Philadelphia) translated Galen's comments to Hippocrates' *Aphorisms* in 1494, and announced his intention to translate all of Galen's other works in a letter he wrote in 1500. Armando F. Verde, *Lo Studio fiorentino 1473–1503*, 6 vols. (Florence: Istituto nazionale di studi sul Rinascimento, 1973–2010), vol. 2, 160–63.

13. "Nude autem pilis frigide omnes complexiones, sive igitur inmesurate habent humiditates sive mensurate." Galen, *De Complexionibus* 2.5. For the Latin text available in the fifteenth century, see *Galenus Latinus*, vol. 1: *Burgundio of Pisa's Translation of Galen's Peri kraseon, "De complexionibus,"* ed. Richard J. Durling (Berlin and New York: De Gruyter, 1976),

75–76. On the growing popularity of Galen, see Giorgio Cosmacini and Martino Menghi, *Galeno e il galenismo: Scienza e idee della salute* (Milan: F. Angeli, 2012), 130–31.

14. *Galenus Latinus*, 76: "Et igitur quod in terra quidem siccum sine humectatione ultime est, quod autem in hominis corpore et similter homini animalium non sine humiditate et aptum maxime omnium ad generationem pilorum." Which is followed by the fish example (among others): "Ex ostracodermis quidem enim et malacosarcis, ut puta ostreis et caravis et cancris, et quecunque folidota animalium sunt, ut serpentes, aut squamea, ut pisces, non posset nasci pilus."

15. Aristotle, *De historia animalium* 3.10: "Hair differs in quality also according to the relative heat or warmth of the locality." The translation is by Smith and Ross.

16. Suzanne Conklin Akbari, "The Diversity of Mankind in the Book of John Mandeville," in *Eastward Bound: Travel and Travellers 1050–1500*, ed. Rosamund Allen (Manchester, UK: Manchester University Press, 2004), 156–76.

17. Tacitus, *Agricola* 11; Strabo 7.1.2; Isidore of Seville, *Etymologiarum libri* 19.24.7; Pliny, *Natural History* 7.2. I could add other examples, such as Galen, *De temperamentis* 2.5: "The hair of the Egyptians, Arabs, Indians, and in general of all peoples who inhabit hot, dry places, has poor growth and is black, dry, curly and brittle"; Diodorus Siculus, *The Library of History* 5.28: "The Gauls' hair is not only blonde by nature, but they also seek to augment artificially this natural color. [. . .] They wear it drawn up from their forehead over the top of their heads to the back of the necks so that their appearance resembles satyrs and pans." Generally, see Elizabeth Bartman, "Ethnicity in Roman Portraiture," in *Cultural Identity in the Ancient Mediterranean*, ed. Erich S. Gruen (Los Angeles: Getty Research Institute, 2011), 222–54.

18. Andrea da Barberino, *Guerino detto il Meschino*, ed. Giuseppe Berta (Milan: Guglielmini e Radaelli, 1841), 62: "Queste genti sono belle . . .] ed hanno i capelli biondi, quando poi s'invecchiano diventano negri. [. . .] In questa città [in Albania] maschi e femmine hanno i capelli lunghi." Verrocchio probably purchased a copy of the 1473 edition printed in Padua, where he worked, as the title is listed in his 1484 inventory. Christina Neilson, *Practice and Theory in the Italian Renaissance Workshop: Verrocchio and the Epistemology of Making Art* (Cambridge, UK: Cambridge University Press, 2019), 258n122. Guerino's story was popular in

Florence. Marco Villoresi, "Tra Andrea da Barberino e Luigi Pulci: La letteratura cavalleresca a Firenze nel Quattrocento," in *Paladini di carta: Il modello cavalleresco fiorentino*, ed. Villoresi (Rome: Bulzoni, 2006), 12–14.

19. Ethiopian curls were explained not only by stressing that skin pores could be shaped like screws but by reminding readers of the African heat, since "hair, in proximity to a fire, immediately curls." *Galenus Latinus*, 79: "Etenim quid oportet corrigias recordari ipsos capillos videntes, si approprinquant igni, mox eversos? Ita quidem igitur Ethiopes omnes crispi." Physical description was never far from moral judgment. Michael Scot considered curls indicative of narrow-mindedness, since he thought they were caused by occluded pores, which inhibited the brain's ventilation. Michael Scot, *Liber physiognomiae* (Venice: 1483), ch. 59: "Cuius capilli sunt mixtim cirspi significant hominem duri ingenii aut multi simplicitatis sive utrumque." It is difficult to know what geographical area the Florentines had in mind when speaking about Ethiopians. See Matteo Salvadore, *The African Prester John and the Birth of Ethiopian-European Relations*, 1402–1555 (New York: Routledge, 2017), 1–17; Alessandro Bausi and Paolo Chiesa, "The 'Ystoria Ethyopie' in the 'Cronica Universalis' of Galvaneus de la Flamma (d. c.1345)," *Aethiopica* 22 (2019): 45–46.

20. Albert the Great, *Questions concerning Aristotle's "On Animals,"* tr. Irven M. Resnick and Kenneth F. Kitchell Jr. (Washington: Catholic University of America Press, 2008), 554: "For hair is generated from the vapor and humor in the skin and by the heat pushing it out. In addition, hair is generated from the work of the third digestive power, which is evident from the fact that hair can be generated in every part." Generally, on the mapping of races in the late Middle Ages, see Geraldine Heng, *The Invention of Race in the European Middle Ages* (Cambridge, UK: Cambridge University Press, 2018), 34–42.

21. Paul of Aegina, *De re medica* (Paris: 1532), 3.1: "Etenim calvitium humidi penuria fieri consuevit." Though not printed until the sixteenth century, *De re medica* was known among Florentine doctors of the fifteenth. Katharine Park, *Doctors and Medicine in Early Renaissance Florence* (Princeton, NJ: Princeton University Press, 1985), 226.

22. Celsus, *De Medicina* (Florence: 1478), 6.1. Celsus stated that hair could be made stronger by regular shaving, a myth of which I was still reminded when I was growing up in Italy. His treatise, written in the first century, was rediscovered in Italy in 1426–27. See Dionisio Ollero Granados,"New Light on Celsus' 'De Medicina,'" *Sudhoffs Archiv* 62, no. 4 (1978): 359–

77, esp. 364. On alopecia, see also *Pantegni*, f. 95, and Isidore of Seville, *Etymologiarum libri* 4.8.1.

23. In a story by Poggio Bracciolini, two girls shout at a man because he is bald, calling him "deforme per le calvizie." Poggio Bracciolini, *Facezie* (Rome: A. Sommaruga, 1885), 208–9. Completed by 1438, Bracciolini's *Facetiae* quickly became famous throughout Europe. By the 1470s the text was available in eleven editions, on which see Lotte Hellinga, *Text in Transit: Manuscript to Proof and Print in the Fifteenth Century* (Leiden, Netherlands: Brill, 2014), 168–200. Leonardo had read it by 1487, when he copied many of Bracciolini's words into his notebook known as the *Codex trivulzianus* (at f. 43r). Bracciolini's humorous story was inspired by the abuses Julius Caesar had suffered because of his baldness. See Suetonius, *Histories of Twelve Caesars*, tr. Philemon Holland and ed. John H. Freese (New York: Routledge, 1930), 32: "The deformity of his bald head was oftentimes subject to the scoffs and scorns of backbiters and slanderers."

24. 2 Kings 2. Florentines could spot Elisha among the prophets of Lorenzo Ghiberti's *Gates of Paradise*, on which see Patricia Rose, "Bears, Baldness, and the Double Spirit: The Identity of Donatello's Zuccone," *Art Bulletin* 63, no. 1 (1981): 31–41, esp. 35–36.

25. I am thinking of Synesius of Cyrene's *Eulogy of Baldness*, cited by the philosopher Pico della Mirandola in his letter to Ermolao Barbaro (June 3, 1485) and reproduced in Gianfranco Contini, *Letteratura italiana del Quattrocento* (Florence: Sansoni, 1976), 78–80.

26. Hippocrates (*Aphorisms* 1.3) defines health as the shunning of extremes. In his *Nature of Man* (ch. 9), he suggests curing a disease by prescribing a measure opposed to it, in line with Aristotle's belief that to stop a vice "we must drag ourselves away to the contrary extreme" (*Nicomachean Ethics* 2.9). Generally, see Paolo Crivelli, "Aristotle's Logic," in *The Oxford Handbook of Aristotle*, ed. Christopher J. Shields (New York: Oxford University Press, 2012), 126–29. We encountered such a search for the mean also in chapter 2, in reading *The Book of Why* on how to improve vision. *The Book of Why* belongs to the genre of Aristotelian *Problemata*, according to which "each excess of defects reduces the other to the mean" (*Problemata* 1.2).

27. Manfredi, *Libro de homine*, f. 31r: "Non havendo adunque la femina testiculi exteriori, e similmente l'uomo castrato, a loro caldo naturale non può avere tal refezione da essi testicoli al cuore et cussi non se fortifica nella sua maniera ma spargessi a le parti inferiore et il caldo disperso è

molto più debile che l'unito." On women's hair as revelatory of their sex life, see also Seneca, *Epistles* 95.20–21.

28. Aristotle, *The History of Animals* 3.11: "The hairs in the eyelashes do not grow, but fall off, when sexual activity begins, and the more the greater this activity is."
29. Manfredi, *Libro de homine*, f. 31v: "El coito rifreda et desecca molto il capo: unde deseccando l'humido de la parte anteriore del capo et sottigliando la sua viscosità per la quale teneva fermati li capelli, se vengono a cadere essi capelli."
30. Aristotle, *The History of Animals* 3.11: "For no boy ever gets bald, no woman, and no castrated man. In fact, if a man be castrated before reaching puberty, the later growths of hair never come at all."
31. Heat could produce an overabundance of hair in women. Albert the Great, *Questions*, 133: "Sometimes women like this [that is, women in whom heat abounds] produce a beard and, similarly, hair on the other parts, like in the armpits, the groin, and around the mouth or the opening of the vulva, owing to the strong heat resulting from the striking of the penis against the vulva during intercourse."
32. On Botticelli's classical sources, see Ronald Lightbown, *Sandro Botticelli: Life and Work*, 2 vols. (Berkeley and Los Angeles: University of California Press, 1978), vol. 1, 87.
33. *Pantegni*, f. 4r: "Calidiores et sicciores sunt masculi. Femine frigiores et humidiores: quod ex pilis constat."
34. Lorraine Daston and Fernando Vidal, introduction to *The Moral Authority of Nature* (Chicago: University of Chicago Press, 2003), 1–20, esp. 2–3.
35. Marsilio Ficino, *De vita*, ed. Albano Biondi and Giuliano Pisani (Pordenone, Italy: Biblioteca dell'immagine, 1991), 32: "Si quid spermatis supra quam natura toleret coitu profluat, obesse magis quam si quadragies tantundem sanguinis emanarit."
36. Albert the Great, *Questions*, 132–33.
37. Bartholomeus Anglicus, *De proprietatibus rerum* 5.66. *De proprietatibus rerum* was written in Magdeburg in the 1240s. See Michael C. Seymour, *Bartholomaeus Anglicus and His Encyclopedia* (Aldershot, UK: Variorum, 1992), 29–35. The dual terminology (*crines/capilli*) may derive from Isidore of Seville, *Etymologiarum libri* 11.1.28–31.
38. Sixtus IV, "Etsi dominici gregis," in Baptista de Salis, *Summa casuum conscientiae* (Nuremberg: 1488), f. 279r–a.
39. In 1489, friar Tommaso Sardi catalogued the library of Santa Maria No-

vella; it had 717 volumes. S. Orlandi, *La biblioteca di S. Maria Novella in Firenze dal sec. XIV al sec. XIX* (Florence: Il Rosario, 1952), 15. The Dominican library in Bologna could count 700 volumes in 1496, but that was also an exceptional case, as most libraries only had books in double-digit amounts. Luigi Frati, "La biblioteca del convento dei domenicani in Bologna," *Archiginnasio* 5 (1910): 217–33, esp. 218–20. Sardi catalogued the Florentine copy of Bartholomew's book as #374 (Orlandi, *La biblioteca*, 45). Today the manuscript is identified as Florence: Biblioteca Medicea Laurenziana, Conv. Soppr. 462. The sections on "pilis" and "capillis" are at ff. 57r–v. Gabriella Pomaro, "Censimento dei manoscritti della biblioteca di S. Maria Novella. Parte I: Origini e Trecento," *Memorie domenicane* 11 (1980): 325–470, esp. 330, and 449–50.

40. For the location of the books, see Orlandi, *La biblioteca*, 45 (#376, *Pantegni*) and 52 (#489–490, Isidore of Seville's *Etymologiarum libri*).

41. Seymour, *Bartholomaeus Anglicus*, 23–25. Bartholomew was at the University of Paris between 1224 and 1231. It is thus not surprising that his work references medical textbooks that were part of the curriculum there, such as Galen's commentary to Hippocrates' *Aphorisms*, Galen's so-called *Ars Parva*, the *Pantegni*, and the *Viaticum*. Paul O. Kristeller, "Bartholomaeus, Musandinus and Maurus of Salerno and Other Early Commentators of the 'Articella,' with a Tentative List of Texts and Manuscripts," *Italia medievale e umanistica* 19 (1976): 58–87.

42. The famous doctor Aldobrandino da Siena described hair as made of a "hot and dry smoke" (*materia fumosa, calda e secca*), thus playing down the role of humidity. Aldobrandino da Siena, *Del conservare i capelli e i denti*, ed. Francesco Zambrini (Imola: I. Galeati, 1876), 1. This edition transcribes the translation made by the Florentine notary Zucchero Bencivenni in 1310 known as *La santà del corpo*, whose original is in Florence: Biblioteca Medicea Laurenziana Pl. LXXIII 47. Rossella Baldini, "Zucchero Bencivenni, 'La Santà del Corpo,' volgarizzamento del 'Régime du corps' di Aldobrandino da Siena (a. 1310) nella copia coeva di Lapo di Neri Corsini (Laur. Pl. LXXIII 47)," *Studi di lessicografia italiana* 15 (1998): 21–293; S. Baggio, "Sulla tradizione dello scrivere medicina in volgare," *Rivista italiana di dialettologia* 12 (1988): 209–16.

43. Plato, *Timaeus* 76b–c.

44. Until Marsilio Ficino translated it around 1469 and printed it in 1484, Plato's *Timaeus* was mostly available through two partial versions by Cicero and Calcidius, on which see Irene Caiazzo, "La materia nei com-

menti al Timeo del secolo XII," *Quaestio: Annuario di storia della metafisica* 7 (2007): 245–64. See also James Hankins, *Plato in the Italian Renaissance*, 2 vols. (Leiden, Netherlands: Brill, 1990), vol. 1, 4 and 300–301. On Ficino's access to manuscripts, see Gijsbert Jonkers, *The Textual Tradition of Plato's Timaeus and Critias* (Leiden, Netherlands: Brill, 2017), 355–61.

45. On the ten layers, see Mondino, *Hanothomya* 39.16: "Il numero delle parte, le quale secondo la sentenzia di Avicenna, in nella prima fen del tertio Canone al primo capitulo, sono in tutto diece." The ten layers started with (1) the hair, and were then identified as (2) the scalp, (3) muscular flesh, and (4) the cranium. By cracking the cranium open, you would then find (5) the so-called dura mater, followed by (6) the pia mater and (7, 8) two dense lattices of vessels that protected (9) the final substance, the brain, from (10) the skull. On Leonardo as reader of Mondino, see Carlo Pedretti, *Il tempio dell'anima: L'anatomia di Leonardo da Vinci fra Mondino e Berengario* (Foligno, Italy: Cartei & Bianchi, 2007), 63.

46. "Settu taglieraj vna cipolla per lo mezo potra vedere e nvmerare tutte le uesste over schorze che cie[n]tro dessa cipolla circularme[n]te vesstivano." Kenneth D. Keele and Carlo Pedretti: *Leonardo da Vinci, Corpus of Anatomical Studies in the Collection of Her Majesty the Queen*, 3 vols. (London: Johnson Reprint Company, 1978–80), vol. 1, 70.

47. Alessandro Nova, "Valore e limiti del metodo analogico nell'opera di Leonardo da Vinci," in *Leonardo da Vinci. Metodi e tecniche per la costruzione della conoscenza*, ed. Pietro C. Marani and Rodolfo Maffeis (Busto Arsizio, Italy: Nomos, 2016), 25–36.

48. Plato, *Timaeus* 76d; Aristotle, *The History of Animals* 1.6, 3.11.

49. "Capilli et ungues non sunt sicut caetera membra corporis, quia membra alia habent virtutes naturales quibus reguntur: capillorum autem et unguium nullu[m] est, sed generatio sola." Elbukassen Elmutar (Ibn Butlan), *Tacuinum sanitatis* (Strasbourg: 1531); "Tacuinum aegritudinum," 16.6. I am citing from a sixteenth-century edition of the *Tacuinum sanitatis*, but this health manual started circulating in Italy in the middle of the thirteenth century and spread in the early fifteenth. Cathleen S. Hoeniger, "The Illuminated *Tacuinum sanitatis* Manuscripts from Northern Italy ca. 1380–1400: Sources, Patrons, and the Creation of a New Pictorial Genre," in *Visualizing Medieval Medicine and Natural History, 1200–1550*, ed. Jean A. Givens, Karen M. Reeds, and Alain Touwaide (Aldershot, UK: Taylor and Francis, 2016), 51–81, esp. 54–55; Maurizio Tuliani, *Il Tacuinum sanitatis di Bevagna: Un prontuario medico del XIV secolo* (Perugia, Italy: Fabbri, 2015), 15–24.

50. Michael Scot, *Liber physiognomiae* (Venice: 1483), ch. 59: "Capilli plani et extensi in colore albi vel blundi si sint subtiles et molles signant hominem naturaliter timidum: corde debilem et viribus. Pacificum in societatibus [. . .] Capilli grossi et eritti ac breves significant hominem naturaliter fortem, securum, audacem." Scot's *Liber physiognomiae* is the third part of his *Liber introductorius*. Leonardo knew it, as he writes in the Madrid Codex II (f. 3r). Carlo Vecce, *La biblioteca perduta: I libri di Leonardo* (Rome: Salerno, 2017), 199. Leonardo returned to the passage when writing a section of his *Book on Painting* (ch. 178), in which he discusses hair in relation to human moods. Domenico Laurenza, *De figura umana: Fisiognomica, anatomia ed arte in Leonardo* (Florence: L. S. Olshki, 2001), 69–70.
51. Carlo Ginzburg, "Clues: Roots of a Scientific Paradigm," *Theory and Society* 7, no. 3 (1979): 273–88.
52. "Si pili multi et nigri sunt in pectore vel in confinitate pectoris: calorem significant cordis. Si non contrarium. Si pauci et lenes sunt pili: humidiatem significant. Si multi et asperi siccitatem." *Pantegni* f. 3r, ch. 1.15. On the same folio, see also ch. 1.13: "Si pili super ventre et pectine multi sunt: significant calorem epatis. Si non, contrarium." Hair as revelatory of the state of specific organs is also in Galen, "Ars medica," in *Opera omnia*, ed. Carl G. Kühn, 22 vols. (Leipzig, Germany: Karl Knobloch, 1821–33), vol. 1, 331–37.
53. Galen had considered the stance later embraced by Savonarola, but ultimately rejected it. *Galenus latinus* 2.6: "Scilicet quod oportet scrutari hominum complexiones, unamquamque particulares scrutantem per se ipsam, et non existimare, si cui pilosus thorax, universum ex necessitate huac corpus siccius et caladium existere, sed in corde quidam caladium esse plurimum, ideoque et irascibile."
54. Michele Savonarola, *Speculum physionomiae*, Ms V, f. 62r(b)–v(a). Cited in Gabriella Zuccolini, *Michele Savonarola, medico humano: Fisiognomica, etica e religione alla corte estense* (Bari, Italy: Edizioni di Pagina, 2018), 164. Generally on Savonarola's treatise, which was written in 1442, pp. 117–206.
55. Michele Savonarola, *Practica maior* (Venice: 1547), 1.1: "Capilli rusi, et eorum multitudo [. . .] somni multitudo: res sanguini attinentes somniare;" 4.1: "Quod si fuerit ex melancholia gravitas multa, vigilie imaginationes corrupte, capilli nigri, et similia signa de melancholia supra in principio operis."
56. Pietro Ispano, *Il tesoro dei poveri / Thesaurus pauperum: Ricettario medico*

del XIII secolo, ed. Luca Pescante (San Sepolcro, Italy: Aboca, 2007), 14; Ilaria Zamuner and Eleonora Ruzza, *I ricettari del codice 52 della Historical Medical Library di New Haven* (*XIII sec. U.Q.*) (Florence: L. S. Olschki, 2017), vii. On the *Viaticum*, see Mary Frances Wack, *Lovesickness in the Middle Ages: The "Viaticum" and Its Commentaries* (Philadelphia: University of Pennsylvania Press, 1990), 35.

57. Michele Savonarola, *Pratica de egritudinibus a capite usque ad pedes* (Colle val d'Elsa, Italy: Bono Gallo, 1479).

CHAPTER FOUR

1. "Primo segno di amore e crini svelsi." Lorenzo de' Medici, "Ambra," in *Tutte le opere*, ed. Paolo Orvieto, 2 vols. (Rome: Salerno, 1992), vol. 2, 909.
2. Francis W. Kent, *Lorenzo de' Medici and the Art of Magnificence* (Baltimore: Johns Hopkins University Press, 2004), 41–42. On the fortune of Lorenzo's poetry, see Federico Sanguineti, "Documenti e giudizi critici" in Lorenzo il Magnifico, *Poesie* (Milan: BUR, 1992), 26–44.
3. André Rochon, *La jeunesse de Laurent de Médicis (1449–1478)* (Paris: Les Belles Lettres, 1963), 310–30.
4. Stefano Carrai, "La lirica toscana nell'età di Lorenzo," in *La lirica di Corte nell'Italia del Quattrocento*, ed. Marco Santagata and Stefano Carrai (Milan: Francoangeli, 1993), 96–144.
5. Lorenzo regarded Landino as one of the most accomplished teachers of the university and, when reforming the institution, he increased Landino's salary from one hundred to three hundred florins. Armando F. Verde, *Lo Studio fiorentino 1473–1503*, 6 vols. (Florence: Istituto nazionale di studi sul Rinascimento, 1973–2010), vol. 1, 298; Bruce McNair, *Cristoforo Landino: His Works and Thought* (Leiden, Netherlands: Brill, 2019), 4–5 and 19–27. Landino taught a course on Petrarch in 1467, but we only know its opening oration, in which he praises Petrarch's vernacular poetry. Roberto Cardini, *La critica del Landino* (Florence: Sansoni, 1973), 113–166; and McNair, *Landino*, 33–36.
6. I am thinking of six passages, which I take from Francesco Petrarca, *Canzoniere*, ed. Marco Santagata (Milan: Mondadori, 2004): "Tra le chiome de l'òr nascose il laccio, al qual mi strinse, Amore" (59.4–5, at p. 307); "Dico le chiome bionde, e 'crespo laccio, / che sì soavemente lega et stringe / l'alma" (197.9–11, at p. 855); "Son questi i capei biondi,

et l'aureo nodo—dich'io—ch'ancor mi stringe" (198.3–4, at p. 859); "O chiome bionde di che 'l cor m'annoda / Amor" (253.3–4, at p. 1025); "E i tuoi lacci nascondi / fra i capei crespi et biondi [. . .] spargi co le tue man' le chiome al vento, / ivi mi lega, et puo' mi far contento," (270.56–60, at p. 1095); and "Le chiome stesse / lega 'l cor lasso" (359.56–57, at p. 1369). On hair in the *Canzoniere*, see Giuseppe Mazzotta, *The Worlds of Petrarch* (Durham, NC: Duke University Press, 1993), 60–68.

7. "Perché l'arco e li stral' di man m'estorse, e mi legò co' suoi biondi capelli." Lorenzo de' Medici, *Tutte le opere*, 1:169.

8. "Dicitur autem amor ad amo verbo quod significat capere vel capi. Nam qui amat captus est cupidinis vinculis aliumque desiderat suo capere hamo." Andrea Capellano, *Trattato d'amore*, ed. Salvatore Battaglia (Rome: Perrella, 1947), 13. On the diffusion of Capellano's text in fifteenth-century Florence, pp. xxxv–xxxxvi; Pio Rajna, "Tre studi per la storia del Libro di Andrea Capellano," *Studi di filologia romanza* 5 (1889) 205–24; and Orazio Croce, "Influssi del De amore di Andrea Cappellano nella Scuola poetica siciliana: Una revisione critica" (PhD dissertation, Università di Catania 2010), 249–55.

9. Today Petrarch is mostly known for his *Rime*, but fifteenth-century inventories reveal that his *Trionfi* enjoyed greater popularity, especially among merchants. Simona Brambilla, "I mercanti lettori del Petrarca" *Verbum* 7:1 (2005), 185–219: 196–97; Christian Bec, *Les marchands écrivains: Affaires et humanisme à Florence, 1375–143* (Paris: La Haye, Mouton & Co., 1967) 411–13 and 152–55; Vittorio Fanelli, "I libri di messer Palla di Nofri Strozzi (1372–1462)," *Convivium* 18 (1949): 57–73. Petrarch's *Trionfi* went through thirty-four printed editions in the last thirty years of the fifteenth century (his poems went through twenty-three). Amedeo Quondam, "La letteratura in tipografia," in *Letteratura italiana*, vol. 2: *Produzione e consumo*, ed. Alberto Asor Rosa (Turin: Einaudi, 1983), 598 and 643. Petrarch's sonnets started enjoying greater popularity toward the end of the fifteenth century, but it was only in the sixteenth, during which they went through 120 printed editions, that they became famous. Luca Verrelli, "Il Proemio del Commento di Francesco Filelfo ai *Rerum Vulgarium Fragmenta*: Ipotesi preliminari," *Medioevo e Rinascimento* 28 (2014): 96; Carlo Dionisotti, "Fortuna del Petrarca nel Quattrocento," in id., *Scritti di storia della letteratura italiana*, 4 vols. (Rome: Edizioni di storia e letteratura, 2008–16), vol. 3, 93–136; Luigi Balsamo, "Chi leggeva le cose volgari del Petrarca nell'Europa del '400 e '500," *La bibliofilia* (2002):

247–66, esp. 247; Michele Feo, *Codici latini del Petrarca nelle biblioteche fiorentine* (Florence: Le lettere, 1991), 69.

10. Petrarch, *Triumphs* 1.90 (Caesar and Cleopatra), 1.151–52 (Mars and Venus), and 1.159 (Jupiter).
11. Diane Wolfthal, "The Woman in the Window: Licit and Illicit Sexual Desire in Renaissance Italy," in *Sex Acts: Practice, Performance, and Perversion in Early Modern Italy*, ed. Allison Levy (Farnham, UK: Ashgate, 2010), 57–75.
12. The preacher was friar Cherubino, and his sickening prohibitions are highlighted in Angela Giallongo, *L'avventura dello sguardo: Educazione e comunicazione visiva nel Medioevo* (Bari: Dedalo, 1995), 219–21.
13. Natalie Tomas, *A Positive Novelty: Women and Public Life in Renaissance Florence* (Clayton, Australia: Monash Publications in History, 1992), 30–31.
14. The definition of Florence as pathologically sexist comes from Richard C. Trexler, *Power and Dependence in Renaissance Florence*, 3 vols. (Binghamton, NY: Center for Medieval & Renaissance Studies, 1993), vol. 2, 2. On men's perception of violence as ethical, see Susanne L. Wofford, "The Social Aesthetics of Rape: Closural Violence in Boccaccio and Botticelli," in *Creative Imitation: New Essays on Renaissance Literature in Honor of Thomas M. Greene*, ed. David Quint and others (Binghamton, NY: Center for Medieval and Renaissance Studies: 1992), 189–238.
15. "Ballata giovincella dirai a quella ch'ha la bionda trezza ch'Amor, per la sua altezza, m'ha comandato i' sia servente d'ella." Lapo Gianni, *Rime*, ed. E. Lamma (Imola, Italy: I. Galeati, 1895), 13.
16. "Io guardo i crespi e li biondi capelli de' quali ha fatto per me rete Amore; d'un fil di perle e quando d'un bel fiore per me' pigliar i' trovo che gli adesca." Fazio degli Uberti, Canzone 3, in *Poeti minori del Trecento*, ed. Natalino Sapegno, (Milan: Ricciardi, 1952), 93. Still useful is Rodolfo Renier, *Liriche edite ed inedite di Fazio degli Uberti* (Florence: Sansoni, 1883), 27.
17. "Omè, ch'io sono all'amoroso nodo / legato con due belle trecce bionde / e strettamente ritenuto, a modo / d'uccel ch'è preso al vischio fra le fronde; [. . .] Aiutami, Pietà, che n' hai valore; / ché, sanza l'altre gran bellezze molte, / solo coi be' capei m'uccide Amore." Cino da Pistoia, *Rime*, ed. G. Zaccagnini (Geneva: L. S. Olschki, 1925), 43.
18. The sitter was identified as Simonetta Cattaneo by Aby Warburg in a 1893 essay, translated in English as "Sandro Botticelli's Birth of Venus and Spring," in *The Renewal of Pagan Antiquity*, tr. David Britt (Los Angeles:

Getty Research Institute, 1999), 133. The identification is supported by a passage from Giorgio Vasari's 1568 *Vite* in which Botticelli is said to have portrayed the woman loved by Giuliano de' Medici, brother of Lorenzo. Giorgio Vasari, *Le vite de' più eccellenti pittori scultori e architettori nelle redazioni del 1550 e 1568*, ed. Rosanna Bettarini, 6 vols. (Florence: Sansoni and SPES, 1966–87), vol. 3, 519. For much of the nineteenth century, Simonetta's portrait was identified with a painting in Florence's Pitti palace, on which see Joseph A. Crowe and Giovan Battista Cavalcaselle, *A History of Painting in Italy*, 3 vols. (London: J. Murray, 1864–66), vol. 2, 424 and 427. The identification was popularized by Alfred von Reumont, *Lorenzo de' Medici: Il Magnifico*, 2 vols. (Leipzig, Germany: Duncker & Humblot, 1874), vol. 2, 218, a book that was translated into English (1876) and Italian (also 1876), and reprinted in German (1888). When John Ruskin lectured on Simonetta's portrait—transcribed in *Ariadne Florentina* (New York: Wiley, 1875), p. 258—he was thinking of the Pitti portrait. It is only with Warburg that the Frankfurt portrait was recognized as Simonetta's and the Pitti painting was taken as reproducing the likeness of Fioretta Gorino, a lower-class lover of Lorenzo de' Medici's brother, Giuliano. On this demotion, see *I dipinti della Galleria Palatina e degli Appartamenti Reali: Le scuole dell' Italia centrale, 1450–1530*, ed. Serena Padovani (Florence: Giunti, 2014), 144–48. Warburg's attribution was accepted by Giovanni Morelli in *Kunstkritische studien über italienische malerei: Die galerie zu Berlin* (Leipzig, Germany: F. A. Brochaus, 1893, 1st ed. 1880), 11; and by Hermann Ullmann in *Sandro Botticelli* (Munich: Verlagsanstalt für Kunst und Wissenschaft, 1893), 54–56.

19. "Intorno al col suo bianco treccia avolga, / degli ardenti amator' dura catena / e forte laccio che già mai si sciolga." Lorenzo de' Medici, *Tutte le opere*, 2:849.

20. "Le chiome sciolte intorno a quella gola, / onde vien quel parlare umano e tardo, / che l'anima, ascoltando, e il cor m'invola." Giusto de' Conti, *La bella mano*, ed. Giuseppe Gigli (Lanciano, Italy: Carabba, 1916), 146.

21. On Lorenzo's knowledge of Conti's *La bella mano*, Emilio Bigi, *Dal Petrarca al Leopardi: Studi di stilistica storica* (Milan: R. Ricciardi, 1954), 29. *La bella mano* was particularly important in Florence, as it was there that Conti wrote it in 1440. Italo Pantani, *L'Amoroso messer Giusto da Valmontone: Un protagonista della lirica italiana del XV secolo* (Rome: Salerno, 2018), 178–79. On the importance of Conti in Florence, see also Cecil Grayson, *Studi su Leon Battista Alberti* (Florence: L. S. Olschki, 1998), 106.

The compilation I mention is known to specialists as the "Raccolta Aragonese." It was sent to Naples in 1477, and contained a preface on Tuscan poetry signed by Lorenzo de' Medici, even if composed by Angelo Poliziano, the scholar, translator, and tutor of Lorenzo's eldest son. Michele Barbi, "La Raccolta Aragonese," in id., *Studi sul canzoniere di Dante* (Florence: Giunti, 1915), 215–338; Domenico de Robertis, "Lorenzo Aragonese," *Rinascimento* 34 (1993): 3–14.

22. "E ricciute le vette de' capegli, / che vi pare attaccati mill'anegli." I'm quoting from the so-called "V" version of the poem known as *Nencia di Barberino*. Lorenzo de' Medici, *Opere*, ed. Attilio Simioni (Bari: Laterza, 1914), vol. 2, 152. On the many versions of this poem, Lorenzo, *Tutte le opere*, 2:673–84.
23. Lorenzo, *Tutte le opere*, 2:893–910. It may be enough to highlight two verses: "et queste trecce bionde / qual'in man porto con dolore acerbo" (36.5–6, at p. 907) and "primo segno di amore e crini svelsi" (46.5, at p. 909). On the medieval topos of hair as a memento of loved ones, see Virtus Zallot, *Sulle teste nel medioevo: Storie e immagini di capelli* (Bologna, Italy: Il Mulino, 2021), 161–64.
24. The chronicler Benedetto Dei introduces Renaissance lords by comparing them to the sons of gods in his *La Cronica*, ed. Roberto Barducci (Monte Oriolo, Italy: Papafava, 1984), 57, 73, and 131. See also Judith Bryce, "Performing for Strangers: Women, Dance, and Music in Quattrocento Florence," *Renaissance Quarterly* 54, no. 4 (2001): 1074–1107, esp. 1093n; Alison Brown, "Piero in Power, 1492–1494: A Balance Sheet for Four Generations of Medici Control," in *The Medici: Citizens and Masters*, ed. Robert D. Black and John E. Law (Florence: Villa I Tatti, the Harvard University Center for Italian Renaissance Studies, 2015), 113–27, esp. 117; and Timothy McCall, *Brilliant Bodies: Fashioning Courtly Men in Early Renaissance Italy* (University Park: Pennsylvania State University Press, 2022), 4 and 105.
25. Giorgio Agamben, *The Adventure* (Cambridge, MA: MIT Press, 2018), 43–64; Katherine A. Porter, "St. Augustine and the Bullfight," in *Collected Stories and Other Writings* (New York: Library of America, 2008), 808–9.
26. Michael Camille, *The Medieval Art of Love: Objects and Subjects of Desire* (London: L. King, 1998), 69–71.
27. Simonetta Vespucci died in 1476. Lorenzo de' Medici praised her beauty in *Tutte le opere*, 1:376: "per la bellezza che così morte forse più che mai alcuna viva mostrava."

28. On shirts with embroidered bands (*trina ad reticellas*), Rosita Levi Pisetzky, *Storia del costume in Italia*, 5 vols. (Milan: Istituto editoriale italiano, 1964–75), vol. 2, 285; Egidia Polidori Calamandrei, *Le vesti delle donne fiorentine nel Quattrocento* (Rome: Multigrafica, 1973, 1st ed. 1924), 101.
29. Shirts were basically undergarments. In 1448 Caterina Strozzi, married to the wealthy silk merchant Marco Parenti, ordered, as part of her dowry, "XVII camice lavorate." The information comes from Caterina's mother correspondence. Alessandra Strozzi, *Lettere di una gentildonna fiorentina*, ed. Cesare Guasti (Florence: Sansoni, 1877), 15. See also Levi Pistezky, *Storia del costume*, 2:76.
30. In his manual on female etiquette, Francesco da Barberino tells the story of Guglielmo da Folcacchieri's gorgeous daughter, in whom an Austrian duke lost interest after she accidentally exposed her leg while falling. Francesco da Barberino, *Reggimento e costumi di donna*, ed. Giuseppe E. Sansone (Turin: Loescher, 1957), 13.
31. The fabulously expensive jewel is known as the "Seal of Nero" and is today in Naples's Archaeological Museum. In the fifteenth century it traveled across the Italian peninsula, until Lorenzo de' Medici bought it in 1487. Melissa M. Bullard and Nicolai Rubinstein. "Lorenzo de' Medici's Acquisition of the *Sigillo di Nerone*," *Journal of the Warburg and Courtauld Institutes* 62 (1999): 283–86. The seal, however, had been known in Florence since at least 1428, when the sculptor Lorenzo Ghiberti provided it with a new mount, as he records in his *Commentarii*, ed. Julius von Schlosser, 2 vols. (Berlin: J. Bard, 1912), vol. 1, 47. Ghiberti made some copies of the gem, which circulated in Florence, on which Nicole Dacos, "Le rôle des plaquettes dans la diffusion des gemmes antiques: Le cas de la collection Médicis," *Studies in the History of Art* 22 (1989): 71–91, esp. 72–73. Architect Filarete described the seal in his 1464 *Trattato di architettura*, ed. Anna Maria Finoli and Liliana Grassi, 2 vols. (Milan: Il Polifilo), vol. 2, 679. It was also replicated by the medal maker Cristoforo di Geremia and the sculptor Isaia di Pisa. See Francesco Caglioti and Davide Gasparotto, "Lorenzo Ghiberti, il 'Sigillo di Nerone' e le origini della placchetta 'antiquaria,'" *Prospettiva* 85 (1997): 2–38.
32. A lady sporting feathers appears in a Florentine engraving representing "The Fight for the Breeches," on which see Aby Warburg, "Artistic Exchanges between North and South in the Fifteenth Century," in *The Renewal of Pagan Antiquity*, 275–76. Another woman wearing two sheaves

of feathers is in Luca della Robbia's tondo in Florence's Bargello museum. Simonetta's feathers are often taken to refer to a Medici device. See Adrian W. B. Randolph, *Engaging Symbols: Gender, Politics, and Public Art in Fifteenth-Century Florence* (New Haven, CT: Yale University Press, 2002), 111–13. Yet the Medici feathers are three rather than four, as in the Frankfurt portrait, and of different colors (green, red, and white/silver). I am grateful to Samuel Vitali for this observation.

33. For the sanctions against pearls, issued in 1464 and repeated in 1472, see Curzio Mazzi, *Due provvisioni suntuarie fiorentine (29 novembre 1464, 29 febbraio 1471 [1472]): Per nozze Olschki-Finzi* (Florence: Aldino, 1908), 5–7, and Ronald E. Rainey, "Sumptuary Legislation in Renaissance Florence" (PhD dissertation, Columbia University, 1985), 516–19.

34. Elisabetta Gaetani, a nun in Pisa's convent of San Matteo, wrote to Lucrezia on behalf of a Genoese friend married to a Pisan, "who does not dress according to the statutes and wears surcoats and brocades and pearls, and after she was made aware of it, has not left her house" ("perché non va secondo gli statuti e porta cotte e brocati e perle; e da poi che lli fu ditto questo, non è uscita di casa"). In her letter of October 19, 1473, Elisabetta asks Lucrezia if the statutes apply to a foreigner and whether her friend could get a license. Lucrezia Tornabuoni, *Lettere*, ed. Patrizia Salvadori (Florence: L. S. Olschki, 1993), 125.

35. This *frenello* is recorded in a 1456 inventory of the possessions of Piero de' Medici, Lucrezia's husband. See Maria Sframeli, *I gioielli dei Medici: Dal vero e in ritratto* (Livorno, Italy: Sillabe, 2003), 11.

36. In 1458 Bartolomea Diotisalvi received a *frenello* with 274 pearls from her husband Bernardo Rivieri. Iodoco del Badia, *Miscellanea Fiorentina di erudizione e storia*, 2 vols. (Florence: Landi, 1902), vol. 1, 191. See also Brucia Witthoft, "Marriage Rituals and Marriage Chests in Quattrocento Florence," *Artibus & Historiae* 3, no. 5 (1982): 43–59, esp. 55n21.

37. The wedding took place on May 9, 1468; the bride was Bona of Savoy. For a description of her outfit, see Levi Pisetzky, *Storia del costume in Italia*, 2:192.

38. The Florentine joust took place on January 29, 1475, as stated by the chronicler Giusto d'Anghiari. Nerida Newbigin, "I Giornali [1437–1482] di Ser Giusto Giusti d'Anghiari," *Letteratura italiana antica* 3 (2002): 41–246, esp. 184. While celebrating a political alliance, the joust also served to cement Lorenzo's cultural politics. By funding communal festivities, the Medici tacitly appropriated them, blurring the boundaries between

republic and tyranny, and electing family members and associates to the rank of civic heroes. Richard C. Trexler, *Public Life in Renaissance Florence* (Ithaca, NY: Cornell University Press, 1991), 423. The outfits of the joust are described by numerous sources, on which see Paola Ventrone, "La giostra 'classica' di Giuliano del 1475," in *Le Temps revient / Il Tempo si rinnova: Feste e spettacoli nella Firenze di Lorenzo il Magnifico*, ed. Ventrone (Cinisello Balsamo, Italy: Silvana, 1982), 189–205; Maurice Javion, "La 'giostra' Florentine de 1475," *Ecrire à la fin du moyen-âge, le pouvoir et l'écriture en Espagne et en Italie: 1450–1530* (Aix and Marseille: Université de Provence, 1990), 93–105.

39. "Erano le perle circha dieci; con esso giostrò et tucte si perderono." The chronicler is Rodolfo Gonzaga, son of the Marquis of Mantua, writing to his mother Barbara on January 31, 1475. Ruggero M. Ruggieri, *L'umanesimo cavalleresco italiano: Da Dante al Pulci* (Rome: Edizioni dell'Ateneo, 1962), 166.

40. On the arrival of the drawing in England, see Mark Evans, "Whigs and Primitives: Dante and Botticelli in England from Jonathan Richardson to John Flaxman," in *Botticelli Past and Present*, ed. Ana Debenedetti and Caroline Elam (London: UCL Press, 2019), 96.

41. Lorenza Melli, "Botticelli als Zeichner: Seine Kopfstudien," in *Botticelli: Bildnis, Mythos, Andacht*, ed. Andreas Schumacher (Frankfurt am Main: Städel Museum, 2009), 103–6.

42. Victoria Kirkham and Paul F. Watson, "*Amore e Virtù*: Two Salvers Depicting Boccaccio's *Comedia delle Ninfe Fiorentine* in the Metropolitan Museum," *Metropolitan Museum Journal* 10 (1975): 35–50, esp. 38.

43. The copy owned by Giovanni di Antonio Minerbetti starts with an inscription: "Pay respect to this book and, for God's charity, return it quickly" (*Chi lo legie lo riguardi, e rendalo presto in charità di Dio*). Florence: Biblioteca Riccardiana, Ms 1051, recto of front endpaper (*guardia*). A similar instruction ("Per che ti prego, quando l'arai letto, tu mel rimandi, ch'è cosa dovuta") is in Florence, Biblioteca Medicea Laurenziana, Ashburnham 1346, f. 1v.

44. The Sienese merchant Ghinozzo di Tommé Allegretti transcribed a copy in his own hand. Florence: Biblioteca Medicea Laurenziana, Plut. 90 sup. 102. Generally, see Bec, *Les marchands écrivains*, 407–15; Rhiannon Daniels, *Boccaccio and the Book: Production and Reading in Italy 1340–1520* (London: Modern Humanities Research Association and Maney Publishing, 2009), 18–24; Marco Cursi, "Fare scrivere il Boccaccio: Codici e co-

pisti 'a prezzo' fra Bologna e Firenze all'inizio del sec. XV," *Studi sul Boccaccio* 30 (2002): 321–34. For a recension of the twenty-eight manuscripts of the *Comedy*, Vittore Branca, *Tradizione delle opere di Giovanni Boccaccio* (Rome: Edizioni di storia e letteratura, 1958), 13–14. In the 1991 revision of his book, Branca added three more manuscripts (at p. 23).

45. At the end of the manuscript, Morelli wrote that copying the text gave him pleasure: "Schritto per mano di me Girolamo Morelli per la moria del 1449, per mio piacere." Florence: Biblioteca Riccardiana, Ms 1071 (R. III. 1), f. 25r. The inscription at the beginning of this book, *Knots*, is a homage to his search for pleasure during hard times. On the mutilated manuscript, see Salomone Morpurgo, *I manoscritti della R. Biblioteca Riccardiana di Firenze: Manoscritti italiani*, 9 vols. (Rome and Prato: Giacchetti, 1900), vol. 1, 59. The *moria* was the eighteen-month plague that struck Florence in 1448, on which see Ann G. Carmichael, *Plague and the Poor in Renaissance Florence* (Cambridge, UK: Cambridge University Press, 1986), 69. Morelli served as Lorenzo's correspondent in Milan in the late 1470s, about which see Pier Giorgio Ricci and Nicolai Rubinstein, *Censimento delle lettere di Lorenzo di Piero de' Medici* (Florence: L. S. Olschki, 1964), 29.

46. As I stated in the introduction, the *Comedy* was first printed in 1478. A second edition came out the following year. Jane Tylus, "On the Threshold of Paradise (*Comedia delle ninfe fiorentine*, or *Ameto*)," in *Boccaccio: A Critical Guide to the Complete Works*, ed. Victoria Kirkham, Michael Sherberg, and Janet L. Smarr (Chicago: University of Chicago Press, 2013), 133.

47. "I biondi capelli, con vezzose ciocche sparti sopra le candide spalle, ristretti da fronzuta ghirlanda di ghiandifera quercia discerneli; e rimirandola tutta con occhio continuo, tutta in sé la loda." Giovanni Boccaccio, *Comedia delle ninfe fiorentine* 5.3. Unless otherwise noted, all English translations of the *Comedia* are from Giovanni Boccaccio, *L'Ameto*, tr. Judith Powers Serafini-Sauli (New York: Garland, 1985).

48. Boccaccio states it plainly: Ameto "enjoys training his eyes no less than his hearing," and, at every new song, "he takes from it what he can, without ever averting his gaze from the newcomers" ("Ameto, il quale non meno l'occhio che l'audito diletta di esercitare, quello che puote prende della canzone, senza dalle nuovamente venute levare la vista"). Boccaccio, *Comedia* 12.6.

49. "E di quella i biondi capelli, a qualunque chiarezza degni d'assomigliare,

sanza niuno maesterio, lunghissimi, parte ravvolti alla testa nella sommità di quella, con nodo piacevole d'essi stessi, vede raccolti; e altri più corti, o in quello [nodo] non compresi, fra le verdi frondi della laurea ghirlanda più belli sparti vede e raggirati; e altri dati all'aure, ventilati da quelle, quali sopra le candide tempie e quali sopra il dilicato collo ricadendo, più la fanno cianciosa." Boccaccio, *Comedia* 12.7. I have changed the last word of Serafini-Sauli's translation, as in Neapolitan *cianciosa* is "graceful," and not Serafini-Sauli's "delightful." Boccaccio learned the term in Naples, where he lived for ten years before returning to Florence and writing the *Comedia*. Giovanni Boccaccio, *Decameron, Filocolo, Ameto, Fiammetta*, ed. Enrico Bianchi, Carlo Salinari, and Nataliano Sapegno (Florence: Ricciardi, 1952), 931–32.

50. I am thinking of Mathieu Vendôme's *Ars versificatoria* 1.56, as published in Edmond Faral, *Les arts poétiques du XIIe et du XIIIe siècle: Recherches et documents sur la technique littéraire du Moyen Age* (Paris: H. Champion, 1923), 129–30. Another writing manual was Geoffrey of Vinsauf's *Poetria nova*, which, at vv. 567–600, describes women from the hair down. Ernest Gallo, *The "Poetria nova" and Its Sources in Early Rhetorical Doctrine* (The Hague: Mouton, 1971), 44. Boccaccio owned a copy of the *Poetria nova*—on which see Antonia Mazza, "L'inventario della 'Parva libraria' di Santo Spirito e la biblioteca del Boccaccio," *Italia medievale e umanistica* 9 (1966), 1–74: 16 and 61—and reworked one of Vendôme's tales into *Decameron* 7.9. Generally, on the importance of the *Ars versificatoria* for Italian poets, see Mario Marti, *Storia dello Stil nuovo*, 2 vols. (Lecce, Italy: Milella, 1973), vol. 1, 127–35.

51. Guillaume de Lorris, *Roman de la Rose*, 521–70. We know that a copy of the *Roman* was sold in Florence in 1367. Bec, *Les marchands écrivains*, 411. On the fortune of this poem in fifteenth-century Italy, see Luigi Foscolo Benedetto, *Il "Roman de la Rose" e la letteratura Italiana* (Halle, Germany: Max Niemeyer, 1910), 186–95.

52. An important source for Boccaccio's hair descriptions is Cino da Pistoia, whose lectures on law Boccaccio attended in Naples. Cino was a famed jurist, not just a respected poet. Boccaccio reworked Cino's "Omè, ch'io sono all'amoroso nodo" into his poem "Se quelle trecce d'or che m'ànno il core." Martina Mazzetti, "Boccaccio e Cino: la costruzione di una poetica tra riscritture, echi e (false) parodie," in *Cino da Pistoia nella storia della poesia italiana*, ed. Rossend Arqués Corominas and Silvia Tranfaglia (Florence: Franco Cesati, 2016), 209–32.

53. "E particularmente come l'altre mirandola, vede i suoi capelli a' quali appena comparazione di biondezza puote in sé trovare, e di quelli grandissima parte, sovra ciascuna orecchia ravolti in lunga forma con maestrevole mano, riguarda; e degli altri ampissime trecce composte vede sopra l'estremità del collo ricadere; e quindi, l'una verso la destra parte e l'altra verso la sinistra incrocicchiate, risalire al colmo del biondo capo; i quali, ancora avanzati ritornando in giù, in quello medesimo modo nascondere vede le loro estremità sotto le prime salite; e quelle con fregio d'oro lucente e caro di margherite istrette stanno ne' posti luoghi. Né d'alcuna parte un sol capello fuori del comandato ordine vede partire." Boccaccio, *Comedia* 12.18–20.

54. Boccaccio, *Esposizioni sopra il Dante* 18: "Egli [the labyrinth] fu—e ancora è—un monte tutto dentro cavato e tutto fatto ad abituri quadri a modo che camere, e ciascuna di queste camere ha quattro usci, in ciascuna faccia uno, i quali vanno ciascuno in camere simiglianti a queste, e così poco si puote avanti andare che l'uomo vi si smarrisce entro senza saperne fuori uscire se per avventura non è."

55. "Valle incantata [. . .] porcile di Venere." Giovanni Boccaccio, *Corbaccio*, ed. Pier Giorgio Ricci (Turin: Einaudi, 1977), 13. Today the book is better known as *Corbaccio*, but its first Florentine edition (1487, figure 9.7) had a triple title: *Invectiua di Messer Giouanni Boccaccio contra una malvagia donna:. Decto laberinto damore et altrimente il Corbaccio.* At p. 18 of Ricci's edition, Boccaccio defines the labyrinth as the place where one gets stuck: "Laberinto, perché cosi in essa gli uomini, come in quello già faceano, senza saperne mai riuscire, s'avviluppano."

56. On Boccaccio's labyrinths, see Penelope Reed Doob, *The Idea of the Labyrinth from Classical Antiquity through the Middle Ages* (Ithaca, NY: Cornell University Press, 1990), 167–71; and Italo Calvino, *Una pietra sopra: Discorsi di letteratura e società* (Turin: Einaudi, 1980), 96.

57. That is how Boccaccio (*Comedia* 9.13) describes Lia's hairstyle: "lunghissimi, parte ravvolti alla testa nella sommità di quella, con nodo piacevole d'essi stessi, vede raccolti."

58. Boccaccio, *Comedia* 15.24: "I biondi capelli da velo alcuno non coperti mostrava, de' quali, non so come legati."

59. Boccaccio, *Comedia* 5.4.

60. In his treatise on love, Andreas Capellanus defines it as a force that empowers as much as it imprisons. Capellano, *Trattato d'amore*, 28–33 and 187. The definition returns in Boccaccio's *Corbaccio*, which defines lovers

as those who both speak about love and only listen to love laments: "Sono i miseri . . . del fallace amore inretiti: le voci de' quali, in quanto di così fatto amore favellino, Niuno altro suono hanno negli orecchi." Boccaccio, *Corbaccio* (ed. Ricci), 18. Interestingly, a vulgarization of Capellanus's treatise follows Boccaccio's *Comedia* in a Medici manuscript.See Florence: Biblioteca Medicea Laurenziana, Plut. 41.36, ff. 1–50 (Boccaccio's *Comedia*) and 51–78 (Capellanus' *De amore*).

61. Charles Dempsey, *The Early Renaissance and Vernacular Culture* (Cambridge, MA: Harvard University Press, 2012), 97; Rainey, "Sumptuary Legislation," 450–53; and Elisabetta Gnignera, *I soperchi ornamenti: Copricapi e acconciature femminili nell'Italia del Quattrocento* (Siena, Italy: Protagon, 2010), 181–200.

62. Simonetta married Marco Vespucci, son of Lorenzo de' Medici's ambassador in Piombino, at the age of sixteen. Rachele Farina, *Simonetta: Una donna alla corte dei Medici* (Turin: Bollati Boringhieri, 2001), 28–29.

63. At one point, Boccaccio writes that Ameto "riguarda, esamina, distingue e conferma in sé delle venute ninfe la mira bellezza." It is a play on the four stages of scholastic reasoning, and their inclusion marks the moment Ameto enters philosophical inquiry as argued in Jonathan Usher, "Boccaccio's Experimentation with Verbal Portraits from the 'Filocolo' to the 'Decameron,'" *Modern Language Review* 77, no. 3 (1982), 585–96, esp. 592.

64. "Vede che sieno le ninfe, le quali più all'occhio che allo 'ntelletto erano piaciute, e ora allo 'ntelletto piacciono più che all'occhio." Boccaccio, *Comedia* 46.3.

65. "Questo libro conpilato per messere Giovanni Bocchacci nonn è libro di nimphe, chome è intitolato, ma è libro di virtù. Amen." Florence: Biblioteca Riccardiana, Ms 1051, f. 78v.

66. *The Golden Ass* is the title by which Apuleius's *Metamorphoses* was known, as it still is. It was printed in 1469, one of the first books to be published in Italy. Robert H. F. Carver, *The Protean Ass: The Metamorphoses of Apuleius from Antiquity to the Renaissance* (Oxford, UK: Oxford University Press, 2007), 163. The fame of Apuleius's tale, however, preceded its printed edition—especially among Florentines, who had access to so many manuscripts that they could compare multiple versions of Apuleius's text, something impossible for many other books. Julia Haig Gaisser, *The Fortunes of Apuleius and the Golden Ass: A Study in Transmission and Reception* (Princeton, NJ: Princeton University Press, 2008), 130–32 and 144–45.

67. Apuleius, *The Metamorphoses* 2.8–9, translated by Edward J. Kenney (London: Penguin, 2004). In this passage, Apuleius seems to refer to Propertius: "What avails it, my love, to step out with coiffured hair and flutter the sheer folds of a Coan dress? What avails it to drench your locks with Syrian perfume and to vaunt yourself in foreign finery, to destroy your natural charm with purchased ornament, preventing your figure from displaying its own true merits? Believe me, there is no improving your appearance: Love is naked." Propertius, *Elegies*, ed. George P. Goold (Cambridge, MA: Harvard University Press, 1990), 41–43. The "bald Venus" passage was well known in the fifteenth century. Francesco Barbaro cited it in his treatise *De re uxoria*, which he presented to Lorenzo de' Medici the Elder (younger brother of Lorenzo de' Medici's grandfather) in 1416. Cristina Fenu, "Una Venere calva: Paradossi visivi tra allusività letteraria e mondanità veneziana nel 'De re uxoria' di Francesco Barbaro," *Archivum mentis* 4 (2015): 15–40, esp. 32–33.

68. Gaisser, *The Fortunes of Apuleius*, 99–121; Carver, *The Protean Ass*, 127–41.

69. For instance, Boccaccio's *Comedia* 31.3–7 followed Apuleius's retelling of the Judgment of Paris (*Metamorphoses* 10.30–34), which emphasizes the goddesses' nudity. Apuleius's description of Psyche's deception (*Metamorphoses* 5.9–10) is reworked by Boccaccio into Agapes' tale (*Comedia* 32.8–43), which ends with a direct reference to Psyche. On this borrowing, see Carver, *The Protean Ass*, 129 and 213–14. On Apuleian influences in Boccaccio's other works, see Claudio Moreschini, "Sulla fama di Apuleio nel Medioevo e nel Rinascimento," in *Studi filologici, letterari e storici in memoria di Guido Favati*, ed. Giorgio Varanini and Palmiro Pinagli (Padua, Italy: Antenore, 1977), 469–71.

70. "A quelli con intero animo Ameto pensando, conosce i lunghi, biondi e copiosi capelli essere della donna speziale bellezza; de' quali se essa Citerea, amata nel cielo, nata nell'onde e nutricata in quelle, bene che d'ogni altra grazia piena, si vegga di quelli nudata, appena potrà al suo Marte piacere. Adunque tanta estima la degnità de' capelli alle femine quanta, se, qualunque si sia, di preziose veste, di ricche pietre, di rilucenti gemme e di caro oro circundata proceda, sanza quelli in dovuto ordine posti, non possa ornata parere; ma in costei essi, disordinati, più graziosa la rendono negli occhi d'Ameto." Boccaccio, *Comedia* 12.8–9.

71. "In a nutshell, hair is so important that whatever adornments a woman may appear in—gold, jewels, fine clothes—unless she's made the most

of her hair, you can't call her properly dressed." Apuleius, *Metamorphoses* 2.9. The *ordinatus/ornatus* pairing appears just before, at 2.8.

72. Apuleius, *Metamorphoses* 2.8.
73. "So with my head once more completely shaved and not covering or veiling my baldness, I entered joyfully on my duties as a member of this ancient college, founded in the time of Sulla." Apuleius, *Metamorphoses* 11.30.
74. "Sommamente desiderosa d'essere guatata." Boccaccio, *Corbaccio* (ed. Ricci), 55. The session of hairstyling is described at pp. 51–54.
75. Giovanni Boccaccio, *Genealogie deorum gentilium libri*, ed. Vincenzo Romano, 2 vols. (Bari, Italy: Laterza, 1951), vol. 1, 497–98.
76. Boccaccio repeats his version of Medusa's story in *De claris mulieribus*. Giovanni Boccaccio, *Famous Women*, ed. and tr. Virginia Brown (Cambridge, MA: Harvard University Press, 2003), 43–45.
77. Boccaccio had access to alternative versions of the story. Ovid, for instance, describes Medusa as victim of rape in his *Metamorphoses* (4.753–803). This is not, however, how Boccaccio chose to tell the story.
78. "De Gorgone meretrice, quod crinita serpentibus fuerit." Isidore of Seville, *Chronicon Maius*, Patrologia Latina 83 (Paris: Migne, 1850), col. 1027. Leonardo da Vinci owned a copy of Isidore's chronicle, which he listed in both his Codex Atlanticus (f. 559r) and Codex Madrid II (f. 2v). By 1482 there were three editions available (Ancona 1477, Cividale del Friuli 1480, and L'Aquila 1482), on which see Romain Descendre, "La biblioteca di Leonardo," in *Atlante della letteratura italiana*, ed. Sergio Luzzatto and Gabriele Pedullà, 3 vols. (Turin: Einaudi, 2010), vol. 1, 529–95.
79. Yael Even, "The Emergence of Images of Sexual Violence in Quattrocento Florentine Art," *Fifteenth-Century Studies* 27 (2002): 113–28; Diane Wolfthal, *Images of Rape: The "Heroic" Tradition and Its Alternatives* (Cambridge, UK: Cambridge University Press, 1999), 80–82 and 127–50; Sharon T. Strocchia, *Nuns and Nunneries in Renaissance Florence* (Baltimore: Johns Hopkins University Press, 2009), 180–82.
80. On Boccaccio's misogyny, Deanna Shemek, "Doing and Undoing: Boccaccio's Feminism (*De mulieribus claris*)" in *Boccaccio: A Critical Guide to the Complete Works*, 195–204.
81. "Medusa . . . habuit . . . crines non solum flavos, sed aureos, quorum splendore captus Neptumnus cum ea concubuit in templo Minerve . . . quam ob rem rubata Minerva . . . crines Meduse mutavit in angues. [. . .] Medusam crines habuisse aureos ideo fictum reor, ut intelligamus eam

fuisse ditissimam, cum per crines summantur substantie temporales propter has autem substantias Neptunnus, id est exterus homo, ut fuit Perseus, in concupiscentiam eius trahitur." Boccaccio, *Genealogie deorum*, 1:497.

82. "Ama maximamente e capegli, cioè el superfluo. . . . Et Minerva gli muta e capegli begli in serpicelle, perché la sapientia finalmente scuopre simili fraude, et dimostra el veleno loro." Cristoforo Landino, *Comento sopra la Comedia*, ed. Paolo Procaccioli, 4 vols. (Rome: Salerno, 2001), vol. 2, 553.
83. "Decore presertim in crinibus, quoniam ornamentis (que per crines significantur, qui sunt, ut demonstrat Apulegius, precipuum mulierum decus. Nam si tollantur, nulla fuerit adeo pulcra, quin turpissima videatur)." Coluccio Salutati, *De laboribus Herculis*, ed. Berthold L. Ullman, 2 vols. (Zurich: Artemis, 1951), vol. 2, 417. It is unclear when Salutati and Boccaccio met but in their first epistolary exchange (the year was 1367 and Salutati was thirty-five), the tone is friendly. Coluccio Salutati, *Epistolario*, ed. Francesco Novati, 5 vols. (Rome: Istituto storico italiano, 1891–1911), vol. 1, 48–49.
84. Salutati's copy has been identified in London: British Library, Ms 4838. Gaisser, *The Fortunes of Apuleius*, 135. Salutati considers Medusa a personification of rhetoric, since rhetoric eclipses concepts with excessive decoration. See also Carver, *The Protean Ass*, 144.
85. Apuleius, *Metamorphoses* 2.9.
86. "Avea cosí dolce ed attrattive maniera, che tutti quegli, che con lei avevano qualche domestichezza e notizia, credevano sommamente essere amati da lei." Lorenzo de' Medici, *Comento de' miei sonetti,* ed. Tiziano Zanato (Florence: L. S. Olschki, 1991), 155–56. The Medici owned two copies of *The Golden Ass*, one made in 1425 by Antonio di Mario (Florence: Biblioteca Medicea Laurenziana, Plut. 54.12) and one made for Lorenzo's father in the 1450s and decorated by Francesco d'Antonio del Chierico (Florence: Biblioteca Medicea Laurenziana, Plut 54.13).
87. "Di insuperabile bellezza e gentilezza." Lorenzo de' Medici, *Comento*, 155.
88. Dante, *Convivio*, ed. Franca Brambilla Ageno, 2 vols. (Florence: Le Lettere, 1995), vol. 2, 149: "Lo quale amore poi, trovando la mia disposta vita al suo ardore, a guida di fuoco, di picciolo in grande fiamma s'accese."
89. "Il cuore per questo [Amore] era di tante fiamme circundato, che li pareva impossibile assopportare lo affanno che dal suo ardente desiderio nasceva." Lorenzo de' Medici, *Comento*, 185.
90. Zöllner also emphasizes the shimmering breastplate that Simonetta

wears over her shirt (and under her braids) as indicative of chastity. See Frank Zöllner, *Sandro Botticelli* (Munich, London, and New York: Prestel, 2015), 55–57.

91. Botticelli's *Chastity* is taken to represent Semiramide Appiani, bride of Pierfrancesco Medici, Mercury's alter ego. For Botticelli's *Primavera* as a wedding gift and an interpretation of downward flames as symbol of love, see Mirella Levi d'Ancona, *Botticelli's Primavera: A Botanical Interpretation Including Astrology, Alchemy, and the Medici* (Florence: L. S. Olshki, 1983), 54–57.
92. On the pervasiveness by which the Medici symbolized love through flames, see Salvatore Settis, "Citarea 'su una impresa di bronconi,'" *Journal of the Warburg and Courtauld Institutes* 34 (1971): 135–77, esp. 143–44 and 157.
93. Petrarch, *Triumphs* 3.181: "come nell'ossa il suo foco si pasce."
94. Annarosa Garzelli, "Un 'Trionfo dell'Amore' di ambito botticelliano," *Prospettiva*, 33–36 (1983–84): 83–92, esp. 84.
95. On Ricciardo di Nanni, Annarosa Garzelli, *Miniatura fiorentina del Rinascimento: 1440–1525; Un primo censimento* (Florence: La Nuova Italia, 1985), 55–66.
96. On Botticelli's illustrations for the *Divine Comedy*, see Ronald Lightbown, *Sandro Botticelli: Life and Work*, 2 vols. (Berkeley and Los Angeles: University of California Press, 1978), vol. 1, 147–56; and, specifically on figure 4.4, vol. 2, 181–82. Botticelli's drawings are often said to have been popularized through the the engravings decorating some editions of Cristoforo Landino's commentary to the *Divine Comedy*, but this view has been recently challenged by Alessandra Baroni in "L'autore delle incisione del *Comento* e la controversa figura di Baccio Baldini," in *Per Cristoforo Landino lettore di Dante: Il contesto civile e culturale, la storia tipografica e la fortuna del Comento sopra la Comedia*, ed. Lorenz Böninger and Paolo Procaccioli (Florence: Le Lettere, 2016), 153–69.
97. Isidore of Seville, *Etymologies* 3.71.16–17: "A comet (*cometa*) is a star, so named because it spreads out the 'hair' (*coma*) of its light. When this type of star appears it signifies plague, famine, or war. Comets are called *crinitae* in Latin because they spread their flames like hair (*crines*)." The translation is by Stephen A. Barney and others (Cambridge, UK: Cambridge University Press, 2006).
98. Luigi Pulci, *Morgante* 15.36: "Era già sera, e 'l sol verso la Spagna nell'oceàn tuffava i suoi crin d'oro."

99. Pulci, *Morgante* 25.74: "O Febo, come hai tu que' be' crin d'oro così lasciato fulminare adesso."

100. John Pope-Hennessy, *Catalogue of Italian Sculpture in the Victoria and Albert Museum*, 3 vols. (London: Victoria and Albert Museum, 1964), vol. 1, 104–12; Rab Hatfield, "Some unknown descriptions of the Medici Palace in 1459," *Art Bulletin* 52 (1970): 232–49. The decoration of the Medicis' study room is described in Filarete, *Trattato*, 2:696. Filarete's last recorded visit to Florence was in 1456. It is then possible that the palace was finished by then. The iconography of the months is based on Columella's *De Re Rustica*, a copy of which was made for Piero de' Medici, Lorenzo's father, by 1458. It is Florence: Biblioteca Medicea Laurenziana, Ms 53.32, on which see Francis Ames-Lewis, *The Library and Manuscripts of Piero di Cosimo de' Medici* (New York: Garland, 1984), 16, item 71.

101. The Neapolitan friend was Diomede Carafa. He requested the drawing in 1468. Eve Borsook, "A Florentine Scrittoio for Diomede Carafa," in *Art, the Ape of Nature: Studies in Honor of H. W. Janson*, ed. Moshe Barash and others (New York: H. N. Abrams, 1981), 91–96. Diomede Carafa, count of Maddaloni, assembled a stupendous collection of antiquities and was the beneficiary of Lorenzo de' Medici's many gifts. Bianca de Divitiis, "New Evidence for Diomede Carafa's Collection of Antiquities," *Journal of the Warburg and Courtauld Institutes* 73 (2010): 335–53.

102. "Quia per crines viros inflammare cupiunt vel consueverunt." Johannes Nyder, *Formicarius* 5.10.85. The *Formicarius* was written in the 1430s and first printed in 1475. The passage entered the *Malleus Maleficarum*, completed in 1486, on which *The Hammer of Witches: A Complete Translation of the Malleus Maleficarum*, tr. Christopher S. Mackay (Cambridge, UK: Cambridge University Press, 2009), 417. The passage is also a reworking of William of Auvergne's thirteenth-century *De Universo* 2.3.25 in Guilelmi Auverni, *Opera Omnia*, 2 vols. (Paris: Thierry, 1674), vol. 1, col. 1072bE.

103. Angelo Poliziano, *Stanze cominciate per la giostra di Giuliano de' Medici*, ed. Vincenzo Pernicone (Turin: Loescher, 1954), 19: "Tosto Cupido entro a' begli occhi ascoso, al nervo adatta del suo stral la cocca, poi tira quel col braccio poderoso, tal che raggiugne e l'una e l'altra cocca; [. . .] ah come al giovinetto corse il gran foco in tutte le midolle!"

104. Consider, for instance, the letter that Francesco Accolti wrote to Poliziano in Carlo Oliva, *Poesia italiana: Il quattrocento* (Milan: Garzanti, 1978), 17. We have already encountered the trope in Pulci, *Morgante* 16.21: "gli tenea drieto gli occhi / e par che fiamme Amor nel suo cor fiocchi."

105. Boys could serve as pegs too. Angelo Poliziano admired the curls of the boy Crisocomo, whose name is a calque of the Greek words χρυσός and κόμη ("golden hair"). Angelo Poliziano, *Epigrammi greci*, ed. Anthos Ardizzoni (Florence: La Nuova Italia, 1951), 18–19. The poem dates to 1481. When the printed version appeared in 1498, after Poliziano's death, all the homosexual references became heterosexual. Alessandro Perosa, *Studi di filologia umanistica*, 3 vols. (Rome: Edizioni di storia e letteratura, 2000), vol. 1, 43.
106. Conti, *La bella mano*, 27: "a mia voglia arsi e non soffersi morte."
107. This new title is inspired by a verse by Lorenzo de' Medici, "Selve d'Amore," in *Tutte le opere*, 1:584: "Così dentro allo specchio del mio core si queta questo bel foco amoroso." Poems also served as "mirrors" to project and construct one's image, as argued in Lina Bolzoni, "Tra parole e immagini: Per una tipologia cinquecentesca del lettore creativo," *Lettere italiane* 48, no. 4 (1996): 527–58, esp. 556.

CHAPTER FIVE

1. "Che si metterà in capo una donna per ornare i capelli cento fiorinate d'oro e più. Or che è questo? E' poveri cattivi non hanno pure il necessario coprimento, né che mangino: e quel sacco di letame tiene in ornamenta cento ov[v]ero dugento fiorinate d'oro in capo, e mariti isventurati consentono a cciò, e perdonne l'anima co[n] lloro insieme. Dovrebbersene far grandi statuti e bandi di ta' vanitadi, se gli uomini fossero chente dovrebbero essere. Non vi maravigliate, che questi soperchi che fanno le donne è una de le cagioni intra l'altre de la morte e de la distruzione di questa cittade, cerciò che Dio abomina e ha in dispetto le cose disordinate e soperchie." *Racconti esemplari di predicatori del Due e Trecento*, ed. Giorgio Varanini and guido Baldassarri, 3 vols. (Rome: Salerno, 1993), vol. 2, 375–76. Translated by Katherine L. Jansen in *The Making of the Magdalen: Preaching and Popular Devotion in the Later Middle Ages* (Princeton, NJ: Princeton University Press: 2000), 157.
2. The statement may sound hyperbolic, but clothes were expensive in the fifteenth century. A Florentine made an average of 208 florins (net) per year, according to David Herlihy and Christiane Klapisch-Zuber, *Tuscans and Their Families: A Study of the Florentine* Catasto *of 1427* (New Haven, CT: Yale University Press, 1485), 95. And yet a family could spend more than two florins just for having a garland sewn (that is, aside from the

cost of materials); on which see Carole Collier Frick, *Dressing Renaissance Florence: Families, Fortunes, and Fine Clothing* (Baltimore: Johns Hopkins University Press, 2002), 46. For a garland made of peacock feathers, Marco Parenti spent sixty florins, an amount that could sustain a family of four for a year. See Valeria Pinchera, "Vestire la vita, vestire la morte: Abiti per matrimoni e funerali, XIV–XVII secolo," in *La moda*, Storia d'Italia 19, ed. Carlo M. Belfanti and Fabio Giusberti (Turin: Einaudi, 1978), 240–41; Carole Frick Collier, "Cappelli e copricapi nella Firenze nel Rinascimento: L'emergere dell'identità sociale attraverso l'abbigliamento," in *Moda e moderno: Dal Medioevo al Rinascimento*, ed. Eugenia Paulicelli (Rome: Meltemi, 2006), 127–28n26. Such extravagances could probably be afforded by only 2 percent of Florentine households, according to estimates by Herlihy and Klapish-Zuber, *Tuscans*, 74, 95, and 124.

3. A contemporary Dominican, Hugo de Prato Florido (1262–1322) also wrote: "Capilli enim corporis superfluitates sunt per quod bona temporalia designantur." Cited in Jansen, *The Making of the Magdalen*, 157, note 45.
4. Enzo Fagiolo, "L'arte del medico nel pensiero di Tommaso d'Aquino," *Medicina nei secoli* 19, no. 3 (2007): 783–96.
5. "Videtur quod capilli et ungues in homine non resurgent. Sicut enim capilli et ungues ex superfluitatibus cibi generantur; ita urina, sudor, et aliae hujusmodi faeces. Sed haec non resurgent cum corpore. Ergo nec capilli et ungues." Thomas Aquinas, *Summa theologiae* 3.Supp., q. 80, a.2. The supplement to the third part of Aquinas's *Summa* was compiled by his students by assembling together passages from his earlier writings. Indeed, this passage returns in Thomas Aquinas, *Scriptum super sententiis* 44.2.2. On the dissemination of the *Summa*, see Paul J. Griffiths, "Catholic Traditions," in *The Cambridge Companion to the Summa Theologiae*, ed. Philip McCosker and Denys Turner (Cambridge, UK: Cambridge University Press, 2016), 292–96.
6. Marie-Dominique Chenu, *Toward Understanding Saint Thomas* (Chicago: H. Regnery, 1964), 58–69.
7. Luke 21:18.
8. Deuteronomy 32:4.
9. Augustine of Hippo, Psalm 52. Augustine also discusses hair and its ornaments in one of his letters (245). See Augustine, *Select Letters*, Loeb Classical Library 239 (Cambridge, MA: Harvard University Press, 1930), 478–81.
10. "Capilli et ungues sunt dati in ornamentum homini. Sed corpora homi-

num, praecipue electorum, debent resurgere cum omni ornatu." Aquinas, *Summa theologiae* III.Supp., q. 80, a. 2. In an earlier draft of this book, I had introduced Augustine as one "one of the four doctors of the Church," but the institution of the four doctors dates to 1298, after Aquinas's death in 1274. Victor Saxer, "Il culto dei martiri romani durante il Medioevo centrale nelle basiliche Lateranense, Vaticana e Liberiana," in *Roma antica nel Medioevo: Mito, rappresentazioni, sopravvivenze nella Respublica Christiana dei secoli IX–XIII* (Milan: Vita & Pensiero, 2001), 155.

11. Sergio Simonetti, *L'anima in S. Tommaso d'Aquino* (Rome: Armando, 2007), 131–33.
12. Aquinas, *Summa theologiae* III.Supp., q. 80, a. 2.
13. 1 Timothy 2:9–10. The concept returns in 1 Peter 3:3: "Your beauty should not come from outward adornment, such as elaborate hairstyles and the wearing of gold jewelry or fine clothes."
14. Dominican novices also needed to learn the Psalms and the Gospel of Matthew. Benedict M. Ashley, *The Dominicans* (Collegeville, MN: 2009), 52. All three texts had been commented upon by Saint Dominic. A. T. Drane, *The History of St. Dominic, Founder of the Friars Preachers* (London: Longmans, 1891), 475.
15. Aquinas (1225–74) took the habit in Naples in 1244, or a few years earlier. Jean-Pierre Torrel, *Saint Thomas Aquinas: The Person and His Work*, 2 vols. (Washington: Catholic University of America Press, 1996), 1:8–9; Raimondo Spiazzi, *San Tommaso d'Aquino: Biografia documentata* (Bologna: ESD, 1995), 41–42.
16. Vatican City: Biblioteca Apostolica Vaticana, Ms Lat. 4691, f. 114r.
17. Augustine of Hippo, *Sermones* 99.13: "Capilli mulieris, superfluae possessiones. Tergat capillis, tergat prorsus, operetur misericordiam: et cum terserit, osculetur; accipiat pacem, ut habeat caritatem."
18. Jansen, *The Making of the Magdalen*, 184–94.
19. The depiction of Mary Magdalen's loose hair covering her body encouraged the practice of repenting by wearing hair shirts. The Florentine Antonia Pulci dramatized the role of such shirts in her play *Santa Guglielma*, in which the protagonist puts on a hair shirt after retiring to a hermitage. Antonia Pulci, *Florentine Drama for Convent and Festival*, ed. James W. Cook and Barbara C. Cook (Chicago: University of Chicago Press, 1996), 133. Florentines expected hermits to look disheveled after reading works such as Domenico Cavalca, *Vite de' Santi Padri*, ed. Carlo Delcorno, 2 vols. (Florence: Edizioni del Galluzzo, 2009), vol. 2, 682 and 983–84. Cavalca's

work enjoyed tremendous success, as is explained in Delcorno's preface, xi–xiii. For representations of the Magdalene in which her hair does not cover her arms and feet, see Alison Wright, "Pollaiuolo's 'Elevation of the Magdalen's Altar-Piece and an Early Patron," *Burlington Magazine* 139 (1997): 444–51.

20. Giordano of Pisa's sermon, from which I quoted at the beginning of this chapter, offers a relevant example here. This may be the right time to point out that it was composed for the feast of Mary Magdalene (July 22).

21. Bernardino da Siena, *Le prediche volgari*, ed. Ciro Cannarozzi, 5 vols. (Florence: Libreria editrice fiorentina, 1940–58), vol. 5, 182: "Terzo modo di peccare si fu co' capegli; imperò ch' ell' [Mary Magdalene] aveva cossì bel capo e sempre avea che fare di stare a imbiondire e di stare al sole a seccare, e nulla cosa di vanità non lassa di fare." Bernardino gave this Lenten sermon on March 29, 1425. Filippo Lippi was born in 1406 and entered the Carmelite order in 1421; on which see Megan Holmes, *Fra Filippo Lippi: The Carmelite Painter* (New Haven, CT: Yale University Press, 1999), 14. Historical sources say that "everyone" attended Bernardino's sermons, a claim that may not be an exaggeration. See Cynthia L. Polecritti, *Preaching Peace in Renaissance Italy: Bernardino of Siena and His Audience* (Washington: Catholic University of America Press, 2000), 39–46.

22. "Grande malignità e peccato è, credetemi, el portare tanta robba in capo; ché avete imparato ognuno e ognuna a portare una balla [. . .] O donna, pon mente al mio dire. Del tuo capo tu n'hai fatto un Iddio, e così ne fai tu, madre, del capo de la tua figliuola." Bernardino da Siena, *Le prediche volgari dette nella piazza del campo l'anno 1427*, ed. Luciano Bianchi, 3 vols. (Siena, Italy: Tipografia arciv. San Bernardino, 1880–88), vol. 3, 268–69.

23. This is the opinion that friar Roberto Caracciolo (1425–95) expressed in his sermon "De Santo Bernardino predicatorum nostri temporis prinicipe" in *Sermones de laudibus sanctorum* (Reutlingen: 1495), ff. 199r–202v, esp. 201v.

24. Giovanni da Capistrano, *Trattato degli ornamenti, specie delle donne*, ed. Aniceto Chiappini (Siena, Italy: Cantagalli, 1956), 114–15. His reasoning builds on Matthew 5:36 ("For you cannot make one hair white or black"), a passage that was also commented upon by Augustine of Hippo (*De doctrina Christiana* 4.21) and Bernardino da Siena (*Opera omnia*, Venice: Poletti, 1745, 3:256a and 260b). On Capistrano's treatise, see Massimo Baldini, *I filosofi, le bionde e le rosse* (Rome: Armando, 2005), 88, and

Maria Consiglia de Matteis, "Gruppi sospetti o emarginati nella visione della società di S. Giovanni da Capestrano," in *San Giovanni da Capestrano nella chiesa e nella società del suo tempo*, ed. Edith and Lajos Pásztor (L'Aquila: Arti grafiche aquilane, 1989), 112.

25. Girolamo Savonarola, *Prediche sopra Aggeo*, ed. Luigi Firpo (Rome: Belardetti, 1964), 19–20: "O voi che avete le case vostre piene di vanità e di figure e cose disoneste e libri scellerati e el Morgante e altri versi contra la fede, portateli a me questi, per farne fuoco e uno sacrificio a Dio. E voi, madre che adornate le vostre figliuole con tante vanità e superfluità a capellature, portatele tutte qua a noi per mandarle al fuoco, acciò che, quando verrà l'ira di Dio, non trovi queste cose nelle case vostre."
26. Savonarola gave the sermon in 1494.
27. The book is Siena, Italy: Biblioteca Comunale degli Intronati, Ms U.V.7. Dionisio Pacetti, "Codici autografi di S. Bernardino da Siena della Vaticana e della Comunale di Siena," *Archivum Franciscanum historicum* 27 (1934): 224–58 and 565–84, esp. 238–41.
28. Carlo Delcorno, "L'Osservanza francescana e il rinnovamento della predicazione," in *Frati osservanti e la società in Italia nel sec. XV* (Spoleto, Italy: Centro italiano di studi sull'Alto Medioevo, 2013), 3–53.
29. Maria Giuseppina Muzzarelli, "Veli e copricapi fra norma e prassi," in *Il velo in area mediterranea fra storia e simbolo*, ed. Muzzarelli, Maria Grazia Nico Ottaviani, and Gabriella Zarri (Bologna: Il Mulino, 2014), 20.
30. Florentine literacy was low. In 1427 only 5,111 heads of households, out of a population of around 37,000, declared themselves to be literate. Robert Black, *Education and Society in Florentine Tuscany: Teachers, Pupils and Schools, c. 1250–1500* (Leiden, Netherlands: Brill, 2007), 42. On Florence's population, Herlihy and Klapish-Zuber, *Tuscans*, 57.
31. The norm was part of six constitutions that Malabranca issued on September 30, 1279, while being papal legate for a territory (*latere*) that included Tuscany. Andrea Tilatti, "'Legatus de latere domini pape': Il cardinale Latino e le costituzioni del 1279," in *Scritti in onore di Girolamo Arnaldi offerti dalla Scuola nazionale di studi medioevali*, ed. Andrea Degrandi and others (Rome: Scuola nazionale di studi medievali, 2001), 513–43.
32. The punishment pertained to canon law, but the correct legal course was unclear, especially in Bologna, where Malabranca issued his constitutions. See Virpi Mäkinen and Heikki Pihlajamäiki, "The Individualization of Crime in Medieval Canon Law," *Journal of the History of Ideas* 65, no. 4 (2004): 525–42.

33. Salimbene de Adam, *Cronica*, ed. Giuseppe Scalia, 3 vols. (Bari, Italy: Laterza, 1966), vol. 1, 246 and 474–75. Salimbene's description depends on Ecclesiastes 7:26 ("And I find more bitter than death the woman, whose heart is snares and nets, and her hands as bands"), which shows once more that what historians call "primary sources" were pervasively shaped by the scriptures.
34. The ban on silk braids, prescribed in 1326, is reported in Giovanni Villani, *Nuova Cronica*, ed. Giuseppe Porta, 3 vols. (Parma, Italy: Guanda, 1990–91), vol. 2, 537. Peacock feathers were prohibited in 1439, on which see Egidia Polidori Calamandrei, *Le vesti delle donne fiorentine nel Quattrocento* (Florence: La voce, 1924), 83. Special occasions warranted exceptions, such as the headpiece decorated with peacock feathers that Marco Prenti bought for his wife in 1447, on which see note 2 above.
35. This law is from 1456: "Item non possino portare cappucci, cappellecti, nè corna." Francesco C. Pellegrini, *Nozze Mancini-D'Achiardi* (Livorno, Italy: Giusti, 1898).
36. The regulation of crowns and "ghirlande" dates to 1355. *Legge suntuaria fatta dal comune di Firenze l'anno 1355 e volgarizzata nel 1356 da ser Andrea Lancia*, ed. Pietro Fanfani (Florence: Società tipografica sulle Logge del grano, 1851), 10–11. Crowns could cost a maximum of two florins, and had to be registered. Lorenzo Tanzini, *Statuti e legislazione a Firenze dal 1355 al 1415: Lo statuto cittadino del 1409* (Florence: L. S. Olschki, 2004), 69–73. Verrocchio started his career as a goldsmith, as he declared in the cadastre of 1457. Dario A. Covi, *Andrea del Verrocchio: Life and Work* (Florence: L. S. Olschki, 2005), 24. He registered as a painter in 1472. David A. Brown, *Leonardo da Vinci: Origins of a Genius* (New Haven, CT, and London: Yale University Press, 1998), 24. On Botticelli's brother, see Ronald Lightbown, *Sandro Botticelli: Life and Work*, 2 vols. (Berkeley and Los Angeles: University of California Press, 1978), vol. 1, 17. Generally, see Marco Ciatti, "Considerazioni sull'oreficeria e le altre arti," in *L'arte a Firenze nell'età di Dante*, ed. Angelo Tartuferi and Mario Scalini (Florence: Giunti, 2004), 157.
37. Compare Florence to Perugia, where the sumptuary laws were issued by Cardinal Domenico Capranica in an ordinance of 1445. The punishment for violating them was harsh (excommunication, for instance), which speaks to the power the bishop had in a city with strong ties to the papacy. Ariodante Fabretti, "Statuti e ordinamenti suntuarii intorno al vestire degli uomini e delle donne in Perugia dall'anno 1266 al 1536,"

Memorie della Reale Accademia di Scienze di Torino 38 (1886): 137–232, esp. 189–90. And now consider Terni, whose government issued directives against consumption in 1444 after hearing the sermons of Giacomo della Marca, a renowned Franciscan friar who also influenced policies in Recanati and Fermo. Alberto Ghinato, "Apostolato religioso e sociale di San Giacomo della Marca in Terni," *Archivum Franciscanum historicum* 49 (1965): 106–42 and 352–90; Maria Giuseppina Muzzarelli, *Guardaroba medievale: Vesti e società dal XIII al XIV Secolo* (Bologna: Il Mulino, 1999), 200–201.

38. Andrea Zorzi, "Aspetti e problemi dell'amministrazione della giustizia penale nella Repubblica fiorentina: II: Gli assetti quattrocenteschi e dell'ultimo periodo repubblicano," *Archivio storico italiano* 145, no. 4 (1987): 527–78, esp. 551–52. See also Richard C. Trexler, *Public Life in Renaissance Florence* (Ithaca, NY: Cornell University Press, 1991), 409–10, which argues that Lorenzo's sumptuary laws served to prevent Florentine families from using their wealth to enlist allies.

39. Ronald E. Rainey, "Sumptuary Legislation in Renaissance Florence" (PhD dissertation, Columbia University, 1985), 429–31 and 517; Jane Bridgeman, "'Pagare le Pompe': Why Quattrocento Sumptuary Laws Did Not Work," in *Women in Italian Renaissance Culture and Society*, ed. Letizia Panizza (Oxford, UK: Legenda, 2000), 209–26.

40. A first attempt to create a policing body for sumptuary laws failed in 1427. The city tried to keep it alive until 1467 by shifting its responsibility to different offices. In 1439 the task fell to the Ufficiali della Notte, the newly minted corps to prosecute sodomy; in 1449 it went to the Camera del Comune, the city's accountants, and in 1459 to the Conservatori delle Leggi. Rainey, "Sumptuary Legislation," 457–64.

41. Florence's sumptuary laws also went against the interests of the *conservatori*—that is, the very people who should have enforced them. By 1459 the *conservatori* were appointed by the Cento, a council which in the 1470s aligned with the *ottimati*, the wealthy Florentines whose habits the sumptuary laws tried to curb. Nicolai Rubinstein, *The Government of Florence under the Medici (1434 to 1494)* (Oxford, UK: Clarendon Press, 1997), 114 and 206–7.

42. Rainey, "Sumptuary Legislation," 518–21. The law of 1472 reads: "A tutte le donne et huomini . . . sia prohibito portare vestiti o ornamenti con oro o ariento o chermisi . . . et sia prohibito portare gioie et perle d'ongni ragione, et zibellini, lattitiji et ermellini . . . et sia prohibito portare pelli

o drappi frappati. [. . .] Sia, non obstante le prohibitioni sopradecte, pemesso alle donne di qualunque età portare una brocchetta di quella qualità vorranno, et insino in tre anella con pietre o perle. Et havere cintola come vorranno fornita o d'ariento biancho o d'oro." In Curzio Mazzi, "Due provvisioni suntuarie fiorentine," *Rivista delle biblioteche e degli archivi* 19 (1908): 42–52, esp. 49.

43. Florentine women seem to have been resourceful when working around such bans. Prevented from wearing silver necklaces, they went for longer-than-usual silver belts, which were lawful, and wrapped them around their necks to make them look like chains. Rainey, "Sumptuary Legislation," 522–23.

44. Roberto Bizzocchi, *Chiesa e potere nella Toscana del Quattrocento* (Bologna: Il Mulino, 1987), 76.

45. Rainey, "Sumptuary Legislation," 461.

46. Mazzi, "Due provvisioni," 48–49: "Quanto danno risulta alla città [. . .] per le spese et ornamenti che si fanno [. . .] et per infamia." On infamy, see Elena Brambilla, "Confessione, casi riservati e giustizia 'spirituale' dal XV secolo al concilio di Trento," in *Fonti ecclesiastiche per la storia sociale e religiosa d'Europa*, ed. Cecilia Nubola and Angelo Turchini (Bologna: Il Mulino, 1999), 500–503. On second thought, this norm seems designed to minimize the role of the bishop in shaping the juridical ties between Florentine families.

47. The best biography of Antonino Pierozzi is, in my opinion, Raoul Morçay, *Saint Antonin archevêque de Florence (1389–1459)* (Tours, France: Mame, 1914). Son of the notary Niccolò di Pierozzo, Antonino became prior of the Dominican convent of San Marco, the penitential retreat of Lorenzo's grandfather, and ascended to the episcopal see in 1446. Bizzocchi, *Chiesa e potere*, 209; Dale Kent, *Cosimo de' Medici and the Florentine Renaissance* (New Haven, CT: Yale University Press, 2000), 149–59. Pierozzi remained bishop until Lorenzo was eight years old. Even after Pierozzi's death, however, Lorenzo continued dealing with his legacy, as is shown in his letters. Lorenzo de' Medici, *Lettere I: 1460–1474*, ed. Riccardo Fubini (Florence: Giunti, 1977), 299–300.

48. Pierozzi's manual was divided into three parts, which circulated independently under the titles of *Defecerunt*, *Omnis mortalium cura*, and *Curam illius habe*. Gilberto Aranci, "I 'confessionali' di S. Antonino Pierozzi e la tradizione catechistica del '400," *Vivens homo* 3 (1992): 273–92; Odd Langholm, *The Merchant in the Confessional: Trade and Price in*

the Pre-Reformation Penitential Handbooks (Leiden, Netherlands: Brill, 2003), 132–35. The three confessionals are attested by 285 copies between manuscripts and incunabula, 23 of which were made in fifteenth-century Florence. Sandro Bertelli, "Appunti sulla tradizione manoscritta dei confessionali di Sant'Antonino," in *Antonino Pierozzi OP (1389–1459): La figura e l'opera di un santo arcivescovo nell'Europa del Quattrocento*, ed. Luciano Cinelli and Maria Pia Paoli (Florence: Nerbini, 2013), 274–75.

49. "Secunda ratio quare illud vitium magis reperitur in mulieribus est ex eos quia sicut magnanimus omnia ista temporalia parva estimat, et ipsam gloriam temporalem, unde de ea modicam curam habet, ita econtra pusillanimis parva magna estimat, et ipsam gloriam mundi magnum bonum reputat. Mulier autem comiter parvi animi est, et debilioris cognitionis quam vir, unde et gloriam temporalem magnum quod arbitratur. Et eum non valeat apparere vel exaltari in magnis negociis quia nec in regimine, nec in docendo, vel negociando, et huiusmodi, saltem in apparentia pulchritudinis querit gloriam consequi, quae tamen est quid vanum et transitorium." Antoninus Florentinus, *Summa maior* 2.4.5 (Lyon, France: Cleyn, 1506).

50. "Duplex autem ratio poteste assignari quare istud vitium immodestiae et superflui ornatus magis reperitur in mulieribus quam in viris. Prima est, quia ipse ornatus mulieris ultra vitium immodestie est provocativus ad lasciviam, quod aspicientes ex eo, qua adijcit ad apparentiam pulchritudinis, quae quanto maior est, tanto plus elicit, et excitat concupiscentia hominis, cum autem mulier sit caput peccati, et arma diaboli." Antoninus, *Summa maior* 2.4.5.

51. Pierozzi pairs hair to breasts in his *Ominis mortalium cura* (Florence: 1470), ff. 25r–v: "Portando . . . o le corne o ricci o capegli morti . . . mostrano le mammelle."

52. "Unde et de quaedam comitissa habetur [. . .] quod cum esset multum liberale ad pauperes, et orationibus dedita, sed multum vana in ornatu, et praecipue capillorum, post mortem apparuit cuiusdam sibi familiari devotae mulieri, et interroganti de statu suo, respondit se fore dannatam praecipue propter ornatum capitis, et capillorum, unde et vidit misericorditer illam caput illud habere plenum serpentibus mordentibus ipsum loco capillorum in poenam illius vanitatis." Antoninus, *Summa maior* 2.4.5.

53. Antoninus, *Ominis mortalium cura* (1470), ff. 12v–13r: "La persona apertamente extima e pensa quello che desidera da che procede chel superbo

ha falsa extimatione di se medesimo reputandosi di maggiore excellentia che a esso non conviene secondo la ragione."

54. Gregory the Great (*Moralia in Iob* 31.45) defined pride as the source of all sins. Other theologians, however, considered it to be on the same level of vainglory. Thomas Aquinas addressed their differences in his *Summa* 2.2, q. 162, in which he defined pride as an inordinate search for excellence and thus separated it from vainglory, an outward show of excellence.

55. Aquinas, *Summa* 2.2 q. 16. On Pierozzi's relationship to Aquinas, see Noel Denholm-Young and Hermann Kantorowicz, "De Ornatu Mulierum: A Consilium of Antonius De Rosellis with an Introduction on Fifteenth-Century Sumptuary Legislation," *La bibliofilía* 35, no. 8/9 (1933): 315–35, esp. 327 and 329. The same points return in Giovanni da Capistrano, *Trattato degli ornamenti*, 170. Generally, on fifteenth-century notions of vanity, see Maria Giuseppina Muzzarelli, "'Let the Great Evil of These Vanities Be Known': Preaching against Luxury and Futility. An Analysis of Italian Fifteenth-Century Sermons," *Przegląd Tomistyczny* 22 (2016): 233–49.

56. Antoninus, *Summa maior* 2.4.5: "Gemmas pendentes in frontes, [. . .] vittae sunt quibus capillos ligant vel colligunt ne defluant, et si suos non habent ligant alienos, zona cingulum est quod nunc sit de serico intexto, et ornamenti auri, et argenti. Crines capilli crispati, vel tricati flavi facti." Before being included in Pierozzi's *Summa*, this treatise circulated independently with the title *De ornatu mulierum*. It is reproduced in Thomas Kaeppeli, *Scriptores ordinis praedicatorum medii aevi*, 4 vols. (Rome: Istituto storico domenicano, 1970–1993), vol. 1, 87–89.

57. Pierozzi participated to the Bolognese summit organized by Cristoforo di San Marcello, bishop of Rimini, on whose relationship to the pope, see Joachim W. Stieber, *Pope Eugenius IV, the Council of Basel and the Secular and Ecclesiastical Authorities in the Empire* (Leiden, Netherlands: Brill, 1978), 36. This meeting led Pierozzi to write *De ornatu mulierum*. Thomas M. Izbicki, "The Origins of the *De ornatu mulierum* of Antoninus of Florence," *Modern Language Notes* 119, no. 1 (2004): 142–61, esp. 143. As the minutes report, the assembly banned headgear ("balicos siue mittras in capite"), a measure somewhat softer than what Pierozzi proposed.

58. Antoninus, *Summa maior* 2.4.5: "Crines capilli crispati, vel tricati flavi facti, cum frequenti humectatione, et solis desiccatione, et inde capitis lesione."

59. Pierozzi served as the confessor of many high-standing women. Morçay,

Saint Antonin, 180–97; Enzo Maurri, *Un fiorentino tra Medioevo e Rinascimento: Sant'Antonino* (Turin: Edizioni paoline, 1989), 134–37.

60. "Absalon, il quale remase appiccato ad una quercia per li capelli, che erano lunghi, e poi fu ucciso da' suoi nemici." Antoninus, *Opera a ben vivere*, ed. Francesco Palermo (Florence: Cellini, 1858), 120. To which Pierozzi added: "By being tied to some small sins, which is what hair stands for, our spiritual enemies, that is demons, easily beat us up and kill us. Similarly, we read that Samson also lost his strength after losing his hair and was then blinded by his enemies." ("Essendo legato a certi peccati minuti, i quali s'intendeno per li capelli, leggiermente poi i nostri nimici spirituali, cioè le demonia, ci percuotono e uccidono. Così anco leggiamo che Sansone, perduti i capelli, perdette simiglintemente la forza, e fu poi acciecato da' suoi nimici.")

61. In Florence, David was seen less as a fighter of tyranny than as a repented sinner. Horst W. Janson, *The Sculpture of Donatello* (Princeton, NJ: Princeton University Press, 1963), 5–7. In his *Comedy*, Dante took David as a model of conversion. Theresa Federici, "Dante's Davidic Journey: From Sinner to God's Scribe," in *Dante's Commedia: Theology as Poetry*, ed. Vittorio Montemaggi and Matthew Treherne (Notre Dame, IN: University of Notre Dame Press, 2010), 180–209. Cf. Teodolina Barolini, *Dante's Poets: Textuality and Truth in the Comedy* (Princeton, NJ: Princeton University Press, 1984), 275–79.

62. Chretien de Troyes, *Le Roman de Perceval*, 4791–92.

63. "Ché, chi lui mira, dice ch'è Assalonne; innamorar ben fa uomin e donne." Aldo F. Massera, *Sonetti burleschi e realistici dei primi due secoli*, 2 vols. (Bari, Italy: Laterza, 1920), vol. 2, 27.

64. "E vi credete più bel ch'Ansalone / Come sovente le farfalle al foco / Credete trar le donne dal balcone." Dino Compagni, *Non vi si monta per iscala d'oro*, vv. 9–11 in Claudio Giunta, "La giovinezza di Guido Cavalcanti," *Cultura neolatina* 55, no. 3–4 (1995): 149–78, esp. 152–53.

65. 2 Samuel 14:25–26.

66. Wilfred G. E. Watson, *Classical Hebrew Poetry: A Guide to Its Techniques* (London: T & T Clark, 2005), 316–21.

67. The floor mosaic, designed by Pietro del Minella in 1447, carries an inscription: "ABSALON VIDI PENDER PE' CHAPELLI, POI CHE FEDÒ LA CHAMERA PATERNA E TUTCO ERA [IN]FILZATO DI QUADRELLI." The sentence comes from Domenico da Monticchiello's *Triumphus contra amorem*, written for the Visconti family, Milanese ally of the Sienese government. Domenico

da Montichiello, *Rime*, ed. Guido Mazzoni (Rome: Metastasio, 1887), 44; Marilena Caciorgna, *Il naufragio felice: Studi di filologia e storia della tradizione classica nella cultura letteraria e figurativa senese* (Sarzana, Italy: Agorà, 2004), 102–4. The comparison of Absalom to a hangman comes from Landino's commentary to Dante's *Comedy*, which features Absalom in *Inferno* 28.137: "Et dipoi nella fuga passando sobto una quercia rimase apiccato a' rami per la chioma; et da Ioab uno de' capitani di David fu morto." Cristoforo Landino, *Comento sopra la Comedia*, ed. Paolo Procaccioli, 4 vols. (Rome: Salerno, 2001), vol. 2, 938.

68. "Absalon . . . et postea per capillos suspensos interfectus fuit," cited in Jansen, *The Making of the Magdalen*, 158. Another example comes from the Florentine poet Francesco Malecarni's *Trionfo d'amore*: "E Assalonne a cui costar si care / le bionde chiome che fuggendo avanti / a' filistei, lo vero appeso stare." Cited in Francesco Flamini, "La lirica toscana del rinascimento anteriore ai tempi del Magnifico," *Annali della Reale Scuola Normale Superiore di Pisa: Filosofia e filologia* 8 (1891): 28. In describing Absalom's death, the Bible (2 Samuel 18:9) does not mention his hair. It simply says that Absalom's head was caught in the boughs of a tree. It is Jospehus's first-century *Antiquities of the Jews* (7.238–239) that first identifies Absalom's hair as the cause of his entrapment. Yet, speculations about his death multiplied for centuries. Peter Lombard, for instance, proposed that Absalom was caught by his neck (*Commentaria in Psalmos* 191.0077C: "ramis cuius circumnectentibus collum eius").

69. "Quamvis enim Absalon patrem suum inique persequebatur, tamen per eum Christus propter aliquas similitudines designatur; non ideo, quia Absalon inique contra patrem suum agebat. Sed quia pulcherrimus fuit et in arbore supsensus erat; Christus enim erat speciosus forma prae filiis hominum et in arbore crucis suspensus, emisit spiritum." *Speculum humanae salvationis*, ed. Jules Lutz and Paul Perdrizet, 2 vols. (Mühlhausen, Germany: Ernest Meininger, 1907–9), vol. 1, 3. On the tremendous popularity of this text (more than 350 manuscripts survive to this day), Adrian Wilson and Joyce Lancaster Wilson, *A Medieval Mirror: Speculum Humanae Salvationis 1324–1500* (Berkeley and Los Angeles: University of California Press, 1985), 25–29.

70. Today the manuscript is split into two volumes: Paris: Bibliothèque Nationale, Ms. lat. 9584 and Cambridge, UK: Fitzwilliam Museum, Ms 43-1950. The two are reproduced together in Montague R. James and Bernard Berenson, *Speculum Humanae Salvationis: Being a Reproduction of*

an Italian Manuscript of the Fourteenth Century (Oxford, UK: John Jonson, 1926). For its attribution to a Florentine artist, see pp. 45–58. Its iconography was known throughout Tuscany, as Absalom hanging from the tree returns in the "Aristotle Room" of Asciano's Palazzo Corboli.

71. The little we know about this panel is summarized in Nathaniel E. Silver, "Francesco di Stefano, called Il Pesellino: The Artistic Identity of a Renaissance Painter" (PhD dissertation, University College London, 2012), 284–85. Its iconography returns in a drawing (London: British Museum 1889,0527.61) attributed to Baccio Baldini or Maso Finiguerra. Sidney Colvin, *A Florentine Picture Chronicle* (London: B. Quaritch, 1898); Aby Warburg, "The Picture Chronicle of a Florentine Goldsmith (1899)," in *The Renewal of Pagan Antiquity*, tr. David Britt (Los Angeles: Getty Research Institute, 1999), 165–68.

72. Marco Assirelli, "L'immagine dello 'stolto' nel Salmo 52," in *Il Codice miniato: Rapporti tra codice, testo e figurazione*, ed. Melania Ceccanti e Maria Cristina Castelli (Florence: L. S. Olschki, 1992), 32–33. Hair care was taken as expressing wickedness in Lorenzo de' Medici's Florence. For instance, Poliziano described Francesco de' Pazzi, the murderer of Lorenzo's brother Giuliano, as devoted to his mane: "Statura fuit brevi, gracili corpunsculo, colore sublivido, candida coma, cuius et in cultu nimium ferebatur occupatus." Angelo Poliziano, *Coniurationis commentarium / Commentario alla congiura dei Pazzi*, ed. Leandro Perini (Florence: Firenze University Press, 2012), 10. Poliziano's description is drawn from Julius Caesar's accusations of foppishness. Christina Shuttleworth Kraus, "Hair, Hegemony, and Historiography: Caesar's Style and Its Earliest Critics," in *Aspects of the Language of Latin Prose*, ed. Tobias Reinhardt, Michael Lapidge, and J. N. Adams (Oxford, UK: Oxford University Press, 2005), 105.

73. Antoninus, *Summa maior* 2.6.6.

74. Parallels between Absalom and Judas are in Peter Lombard, *Commentaria in Psalmos* 191.0077D, and Peter Damian, *Episolae* 144, 0284A.

75. In Paolo Uccello's Battle of San Romano triptych, many horses have their tails cropped or tied in knots, as is the case in a drawing of a charger by Pisanello (Louvre's Codex Vallardi, n. 2444r).

76. Pulci, *Morgante* 19.11: "e' be' capelli avea dietro alle spalle."

77. "E certo io sarei pur da lui scampata; ma, nel fuggire, a un ramo s'avvolse la bella treccia, e tutta avviluppata: giunse costui, e per forza la svolse; quivi mi prese." Pulci, *Morgante* 19.13.

78. "Le belle chiome mie tra mille sterpi rimason, de' pensar, tutte stracciate, tra boschi e tra burrati e lupi e serpi, che fur, come Absalon, mal fortunate." Pulci, *Morgante* 19.15. In another episode (26.145–46), Pulci comments on how Orlando defeats an enemy by grasping his hair, an effect of the latter's carelessness.
79. A popular text in Florence, Iacopo Passavanti's *Specchio di vera penitenza*, tells the story of a coal miner who claimed to have seen a dark knight chasing a naked woman and pulling her by her hair. *Racconti esemplari,* 2.549–53.
80. In a reversal of power dynamics, the witch Morgana invites the knight Orlando to grab her by her hair in Matteo Maria Boiardo, *Orlando innamorato* 2.8.58. For a reading of this request as an allegory of Fortune, who must be seized by her forelock, see David Quint, *Epic and Empire: Politics and Generic Form from Virgil to Milton* (Princeton, NJ: Princeton University Press, 1993), 260–61.
81. Fighting children also appear on a tray painted by Lo Scheggia, today in Florence's Palazzo Davanzati, which art historians have interpreted as expressing a desire for male progeny. *Art and Love in Renaissance Italy*, ed. Andrea Bayer (New Haven, CT: Yale University Press, 2008), 158.
82. Gabriella Piccinni, "'Svelate' e afferrate per i capelli. Le donne e le loro chiome tra immaginario erotico, violenza fisica e violenza psicologica," in *Eretico ed erotico nel medioevo*, ed. Christian Grasso and Massimo Miglio (Rome: Istituto storico italiano per il Medio Evo, 2019), 127–30.
83. "Si quis studiose percusserit aliquem vacuis manibus, aut calce, vel capillos extraxerit, vel alapam ei dederit, vel spinserit, vel alio simili modo offendiderit, et ex tali offensa sanguis exiverit condemnetur per Dominum Potestatem in libris quinquaginta. Si vero sanguis non exiverit in libri viginti quinque." *Statuta populi communis Florentiae 1415*, 3 vols. (Fribourg, Switzerland: Michael Kluch, 1778–83), vol. 1, 324.
84. On hair pulling in the Middle Ages, see Virtus Zallot, *Sulle teste nel medioevo: Storie e immagini di capelli* (Bologna: Il Mulino, 2021), 165–90.
85. Sharon T. Strocchia, *Nuns and Nunneries in Renaissance Florence* (Baltimore: Johns Hopkins University Press, 2009), 15–18. On the average age of Florentine girls entering conventual life (17.6 years), see Anthony Molho, *Marriage Alliance in Late Medieval Florence* (Cambridge, MA: Harvard University Press, 1994), 306–7.
86. To describe Cecilia Gonzaga's taking the habit, Vespasiano da Bisticci simply wrote: "She had her hair cut" *(tagliò i capegli)*. Vespasiano da

Bisticci, *Vite di uomini illustri*, ed. Ludovico Frati, 3 vols. (Bologna: Romagnoli dall'acqua, 1892–93), vol. 3, 297. Benozzo Gozzoli represented the cutting of Santa Rosa's hair to indicate her entrance to conventual life in the now lost frescoes depicting her life in the church of the Poor Claires in Viterbo. See Lorenza Melli, *I disegni italiani del Quattrocento nel Kupferstich-Kabinett di Dresda* (Florence: Centro Di, 2006), 99–103.

87. Saint Paul (1 Corinthians 11:3–15) asserts that God gave long hair to women as a form of veiling. He then reasons that if women ever cut their hair, they needed to replace it with a veil to respect God's will. Gabriella Zarri, "Il velo delle monache: Repertori di costume degli ordini religiosi (secoli XV–XVIII)," in *Il velo in area mediterranea*, 196–97. Pauline associations of hair and veil abound in medieval sermons. Giordano da Pisa praised the Magdalene for making "a lovely white kerchief of her hair to wash those blessed feet of Christ." Cited in *Racconti esemplari*, 2:375–76.

88. Isidore of Seville, *De ecclesiasticis officiis* 2.4. In his influential history of Christian rites, Isidore defined tonsure as "a certain kind of sign that is symbolized in the body but is performed in the soul, so that by this sign in religion vices might be curtailed and we might cast off the crimes of our flesh just like our hairs. Then, senses, like wild locks of hair, having been made new, we might shine forth." The translation is by Thomas L. Knowbel (New York: Newman Press, 2008), 70–71.

89. Gregory the Great, *Moralia in Iob* 1.2.82.

90. Tonsures became a clerical obligation with the Lateran council of 1215. "Clerics [. . .] must have a becoming crown and tonsure and apply themselves diligently to the study of the divine offices and other useful subjects. [. . .] They are not to use . . . anything else indicative of superfluity." Henry J. Schroeder, *Disciplinary Decrees of the General Councils: Text, Translation and Commentary* (St. Louis: B. Herder, 1937), 257. The norm entered Pope Gregory IX's decretals (3.1.15) and was required of Western clerics until 1917 (*Codex Iuris canonici*, 136). On the pre-1215 history of the tonsure, see Louis Trichet, *La tonsure: Vie et mort d'une pratique ecclésiastique* (Paris: Editions du Cerf, 1990), 58–67 and 69–75. In Italy the tonsure has been documented since the so-called "Collection of Five Books" composed between 1014 and 1023. *Collectio canonum in V libris*, ed. Massimo Fornasari (Turnhout, Belgium: Brepols, 1970), III.199 and 202–5.

91. "Ex hac enim magna capitis sacerdotum rasura conspicio non solum pilos abradi, sed etiam conscientiam et virtutem." Poggio Bracciolini, *Opera omnia*, ed. Riccardo Fubini, 4 vols. (Turin: Bottega d'Erasmo, 1964–69),

vol. 4, 4. The letter is dated July 10, 1432. See also Anthony F. D'Elia, *The Renaissance of Marriage in Fifteenth-Century Italy* (Cambridge, MA: Harvard University Press, 2005), 120.

92. That was in 1455: "Per questa constitutione noi facciamo ammonitione [. . . a] tutti e ciaschuno cherico o persona ecclesiastica della nostra città e diocesi, presenti e futuri constituti negl'ordini minori o prima tonsura, se vogliono godere e retinere il privilegio clericale, portino l'abito e tonsura decente ad tale ordine e stato suo." In Richard C. Trexler, *Church and Community, 1200–1600: Studies in the History of Florence and New Spain* (Rome: Edizioni di Storia e Letteratura, 1987), 461 (rule 33). Pierozzi's efforts were not isolated. In 1438 the bishop of Pistoia asked the *podestà* of Prato to identify the clerics without tonsure. Bizzocchi, *Chiesa e potere*, 272–73.

93. "Essendo condecente cosa che i cherici, come nella tonsura, esi etiandio nell'abito siano diferenti da' secolari, e perciò debbono essere alieni da ongni vanità, dexiderando noi risecare alchune male usanze intorno a cciò, ordiniamo che niuno chericho usi diportare zazzera, ma usi capelli tondi per insino ad mezzo gl'orecchi. E disopra porti la cherica non troppo piccola, per modo che appena si possa vedere, nè ancora troppo grande, acciò di non paia monachale." Trexler, *Church and Community*, 463. For the definition of "condecente" as "proper," *Vocabolario degli Accademici della Crusca*, 3 vols. (Florence: Accademici della Crusca, 1691, 3rd ed.), vol. 2, 377.

94. The norm was inserted in a set of constitutions promulgated in the 1450s that remained valid until 1509, when archbishop Cosimo Pazzi suspended them. Trexler, *Church and Community*, 441–66. The constitutions are preserved in Florence: Biblioteca Medicea Laurenziana, Ms Antinori 18, ff. 1–11. The dating of this manuscript is debated. At the end of the text (norm 60, at p. 466 of Trexler's edition) is written "1455," but Trexler thinks the dating should be pushed to 1458, as the rulings deal with issues Pierozzi faced toward the end of the decade. On the cathedral doors as billboard, Rubinstein, *The Government of Florence*, 111.

95. On the fresco, painted in 1448–49, see Laurence B. Kanter and Pia Palladino, *Fra Angelico* (New Haven, CT: Yale University Press, 2006), 207–14. Poggio knew Tommaso Parentucelli before his election as Pope Nicholas V in 1447. Poggio traveled with the curia, including to Rome, until 1453, on which see Ernst Walser, *Poggius Florentinus: Leben und Werke* (Berlin: Teubner, 1914), 189–90. On Pierozzi's visits to Rome in 1455 and 1459, Morçay, *Saint Antonin*, 228–29 and 269–70.

96. Guillaume Durand, *Rationale divinorum officiorum* (Lyon, France: Jacques

Maillet, 1497), f. 43r (book 4, ch. 3): "Tertio pectinatur caput. Nam per capillos superflue cogitationes et cura terrene sollicitudinis per caput mens et intentio, quae cunctis animae actibus sicut caput caeteris membris supereminet significantur. Congrue igitur pectine capilli complanantur, et ordinantur et evulsi separantur ad notandum quod tunc specialiter mores componere et superfluas cogitationes a se repellere debet." Durand composed the *Rationale* in the thirteenth century, but its popularity increased after its first edition in 1459.

97. The definition of mass as a spiritual fight comes from Honorius Augustodunensis's *Gemma animae*, on which see Michele Tomasi, "Note su due avori gotici del Museo Civico d'Arte Antica," *Palazzo Madama: Studi e notizie* 3, no. 2 (2012–13): 16–27, esp. 20–21.
98. Alfred Gell, *Art and Agency: An Anthropological Theory* (Oxford, UK: Clarendon Press, 1998), 16.

CHAPTER SIX

1. The councillors met on December 18, 1469. Lorenzo's father, Piero di Cosimo, died on December 2. On the evolution of the Mercanzia from an independent trade organization to city magistracy, see Richard A. Goldthwaite, *The Economy of Renaissance Florence* (Baltimore: Johns Hopkins University Press, 2009), 109–14.
2. The earliest document attesting to the commission dates to August 18, 1469; its first payment was recorded on September 27. Alison Wright, *The Pollaiuolo Brothers: The Arts of Florence and Rome* (New Haven, CT: Yale University Press, 2005) 561–62.
3. Antonella Astorri and David Friedman, "The Florentine Mercanzia and Its Palace," *I Tatti Studies in the Italian Renaissance* 10 (2005): 11–68.
4. Verrocchio's drawing is often identified with an allegory of Faith today in Florence: Gallerie degli Uffizi, Gabinetto dei disegni e delle stampe, 208E. On its attribution, see Dario A. Covi, *Andrea del Verrocchio: Life and Work* (Florence: L. S. Olschki, 2005), 237–39. On Verrocchio's work for the Mercanzia, ibid., 71–77; and Andrew Butterfield, "Verrocchio's Christ and Saint Thomas: Chronology, Iconography, and Political Context," *Burlington Magazine* 134 (1992): 225–33.
5. This hypothesis is exposed in Michelle O'Malley, *Painting under Pressure: Fame, Reputation and Demand in Renaissance Florence* (New Haven, CT: Yale University Press, 2013), 28–34.
6. Jacques Mesnil, "Appunti d'Archivio dai libri dell'Arte dei Medici e

Speziali," *Rivista d'Arte* 4 (1906): 131–36; Alessandro Cecchi, "Piero o Antonio? Considerazioni sulle Virtù del Tribunale della Mercanzia e le altre opere degli Uffizi alla luce dei restauri," in *La stanza dei Pollaiuolo: I restauri, una mostra, un nuovo ordinamento*, ed. Antonio Natali and Angelo Tartuferi (Florence: Centro Di, 2007), 41–53.

7. Giovanni Fetti's relief of Fortitude has adorned the top of the Loggia dei Lanzi since the late fourteenth century, when the building was still known as the Loggia dei Priori. The loggia changed its name around 1541, when Duke Cosimo I de' Medici repurposed it as the headquarters of his lancers (*lanzi*). Carl Frey, *Die Loggia dei Lanzi zu Florenz* (Berlin: Wilhelm Hertz, 1885), 96–97. Frey's dating rests on a sixteenth-century song transcribed in Florence: Biblioteca Riccardiana, Ms 1052, on which see Salomone Morpurgo, *I manoscritti della R. Biblioteca Riccardiana di Firenze: Manoscritti italiani*, 9 vols. (Rome and Prato: Giacchetti, 1900), vol. 1, 48. Around 1435 in the cathedral of Prato, the Florentine painter Paolo Uccello also frescoed an allegory of Fortitude holding a column.

8. Robert Ross Holloway, "The Lady of the Denarius," *Numismatica e Antichità Classiche* 24 (1995): 207–16. On collecting coins in Florence, Roberto Weiss, "The Study of Ancient Numismatics during the Renaissance (1313–1517)," *Numismatic Chronicle* 8 (1968): 177–87.

9. Pearls were banned as solitaires. Clusters of pearls were tolerated for a maximum of six *once* (that is, around a quarter of a pound) at the value of ten florins per *oncia*. Curzio Mazzi, "Due provvisioni suntuarie fiorentine," *Rivista delle biblioteche e degli archivi* 19 (1908): 42–52, esp. 44: "Per la adorneza del capo, possino portare oncie 6 di perle in fruscholi o in qualunque altra cosa parrà loro per adorneza di detto capo: et sieno di pregio di fiorini dieci l'oncia o meno: et più possino portare uno vespaio et grillanduza di perle di conto, come a loro parrà." For the definition of "fruscoli," see Elisabetta Gnignera, *I soperchi ornamenti: Copricapi e acconciature femminili nell'Italia del Quattrocento* (Siena, Italy: Protagon, 2010), 45 and 147; on "vespaio," see Ronald E. Rainey, "Sumptuary Legislation in Renaissance Florence" (PhD dissertation, Columbia University, 1985), 450–53. Generally on regulations concerning pearls, see Maria Giuseppina Muzzarelli, "Reconciling the Privilege of a Few with the Common Good: Sumptuary Laws in Medieval and Early Modern Europe," *Journal of Medieval and Early Modern Studies* 39, no. 3 (2009): 597–617; and Rainey, "Sumptuary Legislation," 516–19. Pearls were not just markers of distinction, but the means by which the wealthy tried to materially outshine everyone else. Timothy McCall, "Brilliant Bodies:

Material Culture and the Adornment of Men in North Italy's Quattrocento Courts," *I Tatti Studies in the Italian Renaissance* 16 (2013): 445–90.

10. On the mirror as a symbol of self-knowledge and circumspection, Remo Bodei, "Prudenza," in *Le virtù cardinali: Prudenza, temperanza, fortezza, giustizia* (Rome and Bari: Laterza, 2017), 4.

11. Portraits of brides against a blue sky became more common after around 1465, the date attributed to Alesso Baldovinetti's portrait in London's National Gallery, usually taken as the prototype for Piero's portraits (including plate 7). *Antonio e Piero del Pollaiuolo: "Nell'argento e nell'oro, in pittura e nel bronzo,"* ed. Andrea di Lorenzo and Aldo Galli (Milan: Skira, 2014), 240–53. The dating of Baldovinetti's painting still rests on evidence exposed in Ruth Wedgwood Kennedy, *Alesso Baldovinetti: A Critical and Historical Study* (New Haven, CT: Yale University Press, 1938), 133. The Pollaiuolo brothers worked with Baldovinetti for the cardinal of Portugal's chapel at San Miniato al Monte. Wright, *The Pollaiuolo Brothers*, 119–29.

12. On the busts of Florentine women, Arnold Victor Coonin, "The Most Elusive Woman in Renaissance Art: A Portrait of Marietta Strozzi," *Artibus et Historiae* 30 (2009): 41–64.

13. I am well aware that both mirror and snake are "positive" attributes in the iconography of Prudence, where the former stands for a symbol of reflection and the latter as the embodiment of wisdom (as in Matthew 10:16, "Be as shrewd [*prudentes* in the Vulgate] as snakes"). Those meanings are discussed in Emile Mâle, *The Gothic Image: Religious Art in France of the Thirteenth Century* (New York: 1972, 1st English ed. 1913), 21 and 120. Still, I wonder if their meanings could be opened up to accommodate a critique of Botticelli's iconoclastic take on Fortitude.

14. On the importance of the Herculean dilemma for Florentines, see Ronald G. Witt, *Hercules at the Crossroads: The Life, Works, and Thought of Coluccio Salutati* (Durham, NC: Duke University Press, 1983), 215–21. Generally, see Victoria A. Kahn, *Rhetoric, Prudence, and Skepticism in the Renaissance* (Ithaca, NY, and London: Cornell University Press, 1985).

15. For numerous cases of knights recognized by their insignia, see Matteo Maria Boiardo, *Orlando innamorato*, ed. Luigi Garbato, 2 vols. (Milan: Marzorati, 1970), vol. 1, 72 ("per insegna portava il cavalliero / nel scudo azuro una gran stella d'oro") and 73 ("porta nel blavo la luna de argento, sir di Bordella, nomato Angelino"), and vol. 2, 243 ("Quel cavallier avea nome Ariante, che per insegna le corne portava").

16. "Turritum tortis caput adcumularat in altum crinibus, extructos augeret

ut addita cirros congeries celsumque apicem frons ardua ferret." *Prudentius,* ed. and tr. H. J. Thomson, 2 vols. (Cambridge, MA: Harvard University Press, 1949–53), vol. 1, 292–93.

17. Three manuscripts of Prudentius's *Psychomachia* certainly circulated in fifteenth-century Florence: Biblioteca Riccardiana, Ms 418, ff. 1r–18v; Biblioteca Medicea Laurenziana: Plut. 91.4 and Ms AD 343, which belonged to Francesco Nelli, Petrarch's pen friend and secretary of the bishop of Florence. Jennifer O'Reilly argued in her *Studies in the Iconography of the Virtues and Vices* (New York: Garland, 1988), 1–59, that the poem was read moralistically. Ricc. Ms 418, however, seems to have been used to learn Latin, given that some comments explain words, and the manuscript is bound together with a grammar book. See also Robert Black, *Humanism and Education in Medieval and Renaissance Italy: Tradition and Innovation in Latin Schools from the Twelfth to the Fifteenth Century* (Cambridge, UK: Cambridge University Press, 2004), 225–32 and 258.
18. Franco Sacchetti, *Il Trecentonovelle,* ed. Antonio Lanza (Florence: Sansoni, 1984), 313–16 (novella CL).
19. Valentin Groebner, *Who Are You? Identification, Deception, and Surveillance in Early Modern Europe* (New York: Zone Books, 2007) 31–53. On legal procedures of identification at the time, see also Patricia L. Rubin, *Images and Identity in Fifteenth-century Florence* (New Haven, CT: Yale University Press, 2007), 108–19.
20. On the demise of chivalric values, Amedeo Quondam, *Cavallo e cavaliere: L'armatura come seconda pelle del gentiluomo moderno* (Rome: Donzelli, 2003), 80.
21. Brunetto Latini, *Tresor* 5.62: "Simia è una bestia che di molte cose somiglia l'uomo, e volentieri contraffà quello che la vede fare all'uomo." Generally, see Horst W. Janson, *Ape and Ape Lore in the Middle Ages and the Renaissance* (London: Warburg Institute, 1952), 73–106. For the metaphor in fifteenth-century Florence, Kenneth Gouwens, "Erasmus, 'Apes of Cicero,' and Conceptual Blending," *Journal of the History of Ideas* 71, no. 4 (2010): 523–45, esp. 530–33. On the ludic dimension of monkeys, see Jean Wirth, "Les singes dans les marges à drôleries des manuscrits gotiques," *Micrologus* 8, no. 2 (2000): 429–44; and Felice Moretti, *Dal ludus alla laude: Giochi di uomini, santi e animali dall'alto Medioevo a Francesco d'Assisi* (Bari, Italy: Edipuglia, 2007), 58–62.
22. In his search for an alternative crest, Sacchetti's knight went to two painters, in Florence and Ferrara. I find it interesting that Sacchetti attri-

butes the transformation of the bear to a painter (*dipintore*) rather than an armor maker, and I wonder if his choice should be read as a critique of painters' cunning, or in relation to the geopolitics of the art market. By statute, armor makers could not work outside their cities. Mario Scalini, "Novità e tradizione nell'armamento bassomedievale toscano," in *Guerra e guerrieri nella Toscana del Rinascimento*, ed. Franco Cardini and Marco Tangheroni (Florence: Edifir, 1990), 164. Boccaccio compares apes to artists in his *Genealogia deorum gentilium* 14.17, on which see Janson, *Ape and Ape Lore*, 290–93.

23. Nicoletta Pons, *Botticelli* (Milan: Rizzoli, 1989), 15; David A. Brown, "Verrocchio and Leonardo: Studies for the *Giostra*," in *Florentine Drawing at the Time of Lorenzo the Magnificent*, ed. Elizabeth Cropper (Bologna: Nuova Alfa, 1992): 99–109; Francesco Caglioti, "Andrea del Verrocchio e i profili di condottieri antichi per Mattia Corvino," in *Italy and Hungary: Humanism and Art in the Early Renaissance*, ed. Péter Farbaky and Louis A. Waldman (Milan: Officina libraria, 2011), 504–51.
24. Wright, *The Pollaiuolo Brothers*, 54–55. The knight was Benedetto Salutati and the joust took place in 1469. Piero's other documented commission is for work in the cardinal of Portugal's chapel, on which see Frederick Hartt, Gino Corti, and Clarence Kennedy, *The Chapel of the Cardinal of Portugal, 1434–1459, at San Miniato in Florence* (Philadelphia: University of Pennsylvania Press, 1964), 159–61. In 1472, Antonio made a silver helm, a gift to the Duke of Urbino, for the Florentine government. Wright, *The Pollaiuolo Brothers*, 534.
25. Wright (*The Pollaiuolo Brothers*, 55) calculated that Pollaiuolo was paid some 540 florins for chivalric trappings, more than four times the price of the six Mercanzia virtues. On the armors used in battle, see Lionello G. Boccia and Eduardo T. Coelho, *L'arte dell'armatura in Italia* (Milan: Bramante, 1967), 149–50; Helmut Nickel, Stuart W. Phyrr, and Leonid Tarassuk, *The Art of Chivalry: European Arms and Armor from the Metropolitan Museum of Art* (New York: Metropolitan Museum of Art, 1982), 29.
26. On the relief reproduced as figure 6.4, see Patricia L. Rubin and Alison Wright, *Renaissance Florence: The Art of the 1470s* (London: National Gallery Publications, 1999), 274–75; *Verrocchio: Master of Leonardo*, ed. Francesco Caglioti and Andrea de Marchi (Venice: Marsilio, 2019), 100.
27. On the accumulation of motifs, André Chastel and Peter Murray, *L'arte del Rinascimento italiano, La civiltà del Rinascimento: Storia e cultura 2* (Rome: Laterza, 1991), 108. On the decline of aristocracy as registered by

the fifteenth-century writer Matteo Maria Boiardo, see David Quint, *Epic and Empire: Politics and Generic Form from Virgil to Milton* (Princeton, NJ: Princeton University Press, 1993), 256–61.

28. Arthur M. Hind, *Early Italian Engraving*, 7 vols. (London: M. Knoedler, 1938–48), vol. 1, 48 (A.I.57). Hind reads the two knights as Romulus and Remus because of the inscription "RO/SPQR/RV" on the central shield. The point is repeated in Giséle Lambert, *Les premières gravures italiennes: Quattrocento-début du Cinquecento; Inventaire de la collection du département des estampes et de la photographie* (Paris: Editions de la Bibliothèque nationale de France, 1999), inv. 198.
29. Ippolita di Majo, "Qualche considerazione su un dipinto napoletano di Matteo di Giovanni: La Strage degli Innocenti di Santa Caterina a Formello," in *Matteo di Giovanni: Cronaca di una strage dipinta*, ed. Cecilia Alessi and Alessandro Bagnoli (Asciano: Ali edizioni, 2006), 130–45.
30. On the "courtization" of warriors, Norbert Elias, *Power & Civility* (New York: Pantheon Books, 1982), 258–70.
31. "Prima est, quia ipse ornatus mulieris ultra vitium immodestie est provocativus ad lasciviam, quod aspicientes ex eo, qua adijcit ad apparentiam pulchritudinis, quae quanto maior est, tanto plus alicit, et excitat concupiscentia hominis, cum autem mulier sit caput peccati, et arma diaboli secundum Originem [. . .] ideo diabolus [. . .] instigat ipsam mulierem ad se ornandum ad hoc, ut talis armatura eius sive gladius sit acutior." Antoninus Florentinus, *Summa maior* 2.4.5. On women's bellicosity, see also Giovanni Boccaccio, *The Corbaccio*, tr. Anthony K. Cassell (Urbana: University of Illinois Press, 1975), 43.
32. Giorgio Agamben, "On the Limits of Violence," *Diacritics* 39, no. 4 (2009): 103–11, 105.
33. On the use of brooches in hairstyling, Elisabetta Gnignera, *I soperchi ornamenti:Copricapi e acconciature femminili nell'Italia del Quattrocento* (Siena, Italy: Protagon, 2010), 195–98.
34. For the attribution of the painting to Pollaiuolo, see Raimond van Marle, *The Development of the Italian Schools of Painting*, 19 vols. (The Hague: M. Nijhoff, 1923–38), vol. 11, 420. Van Marle's reasoning is challenged by Carlo Gamba, "Due tavole del Museo Jacquemart-André," *L'arte* 21 (1957): 3–4 (Gamba attributes the panel to Verrocchio's workshop) and Laurence Kanter, *Leonardo: Discoveries from Verrocchio's Studio; Early Paintings and New Attributions* (New Haven, CT: Yale University Art Gallery, 2018), 48–57.
35. "Capitulo volutas uti capillamento concrispatos cincinnos praependentes

dextra ac sinistra conlocaverunt et cymatiis et encarpis pro crinibus dispositis frontes orneverunt." Vitruvius, *De architectura* 4.1.7.

36. The dating of Francesco di Giorgio's drawings is unclear, even if scholars agree that they must have been executed after Pollaiuolo's virtues. The Codex Saluzzianus 148, in Turin's Royal Library (which includes figure 6.6) is dated to 1475–80 by Scaglia and to 1482–86 by Mussini. Gustina Scaglia, *Francesco di Giorgio Martini: Checklist and History of Manuscripts and Drawings in Autographs and Copies from ca. 1470 to 1687 and Renewed Copies (1764–1839)* (Bethlehem, PA: Lehigh University Press, 1992), 25, 154–59, and 189–91; Massimo Mussini, "La trattatistica di Francesco di Giorgio: Un problema critico aperto," in *Francesco di Giorgio architetto*, ed. Francesco. P. Fiore and Manfredo Tafuri (Milan: Electa, 1994): 360–62 and 382–85. An equivalent sketch in Florence: Biblioteca Medicea Laurenziana, Ashburnam 361, f. 13v is dated by both around 1480–82. The debate is summed up in *La traduzione del De Architectura di Vitruvio dal ms. II.I.141 della Biblioteca Nazionale Centrale di Firenze*, ed. Marco Biffi (Pisa: Scuola normale superiore, 2002), lvi. Cf. Marina de Franceschini, "Villa Adriana and a Great Artist of the Renaissance: Francesco di Giorgio Martini," in *Leonardo e l'antico*, ed. Andrea Bruciati (Rome: L'Erma di Bretschneider, 2021), 125–26. De Franceschini argues that Francesco di Giorgio's Florentine drawings include sketches he made at Villa Adriana in 1465 and then reworked as the drawings now in Turin. The drawings were previously discussed by Arnold Nesselrath in "I libri di disegni di antichità: Tentativo di una tipologia," in *Memoria dell'antico nell'arte italiana*, ed. S. Settis (Turin: Einaudi 1986), vol. 3, 87–147, esp. 120–21. Francesco di Giorgio may have been in touch with the Pollaiuolo brothers after his trip to Florence in 1463. Ralph Toledano, *Francesco di Giorgio Martini: Pittore e scultore* (Milan: Electa, 1987), 38–41.

37. Before being published in 1485, Alberti's treatise circulated in manuscript form for some thirty years. Anthony Grafton, *Leon Battista Alberti: Master Builder of the Italian Renaissance* (New York: Hill and Wang, 2000), 266.

38. "Nextrum appellant apud nos Etruscos victam pertenuem, qua capillum virgines vinciant atque innectant; fasciolam idcirco, quae quasi regula circumflexa pro anulo columnae calcem obambit, si ita licet, nextrum appellemus." Leon Battista Alberti, *L'architettura (De re aedificatoria)*, ed. Giovanni Orlandi, 2 vols. (Milan: Il Polifilo, 1966), vol. 2, 525.

39. "Fingere idcirco oportet vocabula, ubi usitata non suppeditant." Alberti, *L'architettura*, 1:525.

40. "Vitruvium [. . .] ut par sit non scripsisse hunc nobis, qui ita scripserit, ut non intelligamus." Alberti, *L'architettura*, 2:441.
41. "Per achonciatura il chrocefisso." Siena: Biblioteca Comunale, A.I.5, ff. 28r-29r.
42. Respectively: Luca da Panzano, "Ricordanze" in *"Brighe, Affanni, Volgimenti di Stato": Le ricordanze quattrocentesche di Luca di Matteo di Messer Luca dei Firidolfi da Panzano*, ed. Anthony Molho and Franek Sznura (Florence: SISMEL Edizioni del Galluzzo, 2010), 78 ("Achonciatura di poçço"); Pèleo Bacci, *Documenti toscani per la storia dell'arte*, 2 vols. (Florence: Gonnelli, 1910), vol. 2, 41 ("Demo a dì 30 di dicembre a Filippo orafo per achonciatura le chrocie dell'ariento e'l rischiarare"); Sacchetti, *Il Trecentonovelle*, 138–39 ("dell'acconciatura [of pig skins] poi gli pagò quello se ne venìa").
43. Cornelio von Fabriczy, "Andrea del Verrocchio ai servizi dei Medici," *Archivio storico dell'arte* 1 (1895): 163–75, esp. 168 ("Per achonciatura di tutte le teste chotalie che sono sopra gli uscij del cortile in Firenze"). The note is dated 1496. The idea to decorate the doors of the Medici palace with the heads of emperors and illustrious women came to Lorenzo de' Medici after he received two marble busts from Pope Sixtus IV in 1471. Osano Shigetoshi, "Due 'Marsia' nel giardino di Via Larga: La ricezione del 'decor' dell'antichità romana nella collezione medicea di sculture antiche," *Artibus et Historiae* 17, no. 34 (1996): 95–120, esp. 96.
44. The expression "pietre conce" is first documented in Florence in 1376 and returns in numerous documents of the fifteenth century. Roberto Gargiani, *Princìpi e costruzione nell'architettura italiana del Quattrocento* (Rome: Laterza, 2003), 79–80.
45. The idea of a return is also what separates the verb "achonciare" from "conciare."
46. Giovanni Boccaccio, *Amorosa visione*, ed. Vittore Branca (Florence: Sansoni, 1944), 104: "Spesso il suo' cape' con ordinato / stile acconciava, e della sua bellezza / prima l'occhio allo specchio consigliato, adorna venia innanzi alla mattezza bestiale, e quivi parea che dicesse 'Agraditi la mia piacevolezza?'" This much-quoted edition by Branca is known to modernize Boccaccio's language. The text read by fifteenth-century Florentines was slightly different. For instance, in a manuscript (Florence: Biblioteca Medicea Laurenziana, Plut. 90.93), I read at f. 42r: "Spesso li suoi capelli con hordinato / stilo acionciava." On Branca's modernization, see Carlo Caruso, "L'edizione Branca dell'Amorosa vi-

sione (1944) e la nuova filologia," in *Caro Vitto: Essays in Memory of Vittore Branca*, ed. Jill A. Kraye and Laura Lepschy (Reading, UK: Italianist, 2007), 28–48.

47. Francesco da Barberino, *Reggimento e costumi di donna*, ed. Giuseppe E. Sansone (Rome: Zauli, 1995), 168: "Poi domandato, perchè dunque pettinava ella i suoi capelli: 'Perch'ella volea mostrare che femina era, di chui natura d'acconciarsi.'"

48. The caryatid seen in figure 6.7 was probably purchased in Rome by Jacopo Salviati, Lorenzo de' Medici's son-in-law. See *L'Antiquarium di Villa Corsini a Castello*, ed. Fabrizio Paolucci and Antonella Romualdi (Florence: Polistampa, 2010), 52. It is difficult to know what caryatids Botticelli may have observed, as we know little about his travels. On caryatids visible between the fifteenth and the early sixteenth centuries, see Christian Hülsen, *Il libro di Giuliano da Sangallo, Codice Vaticano Barberiniano Latino 4424* (Leipzig: Harrassowitz, 1910), 18–20; and Kathleen W. Christian, "Raphael's Vitruvius and Marcantonio Raimondi's Caryatid Facade," in *Marcantonio Raimondi: Raphael and the Image Multiplied*, ed. Edward H. Wouk (Manchester, UK: Manchester University Press, 2016), 66–83. The Florentine sculptor Agostino di Duccio included caryatidic braids in reliefs he made around 1455, on which see Pier Giorgio Pasini, *Il tempio malatestiano: Splendore cortese e classicismo umanistico* (Milan: Skira, 2000), 56.

49. Sarah B. McHam, "Structuring Communal History through Repeated Metaphors of Rule," in *Renaissance Florence: A Social History*, ed. Roger J. Crum and John T. Paoletti (Cambridge, UK: Cambridge University Press, 2006), 111–21. Benedetto da Maiano employed the classical motif for other architectural furnishings, such as the lavabo in the St John the Evangelist Sacristy of Loreto's Casa Santa, which is dated between 1482 and 1490 in Carl Doris, *Benedetto da Maiano: A Florentine Sculptor at the threshold of the High Renaissance* (Turnhout: Brepols, 2006), 276.

50. The refitting of the Hall of the Lilies started in 1469, the same year as the Mercanzia commission. Nicolai Rubinstein, *The Palazzo Vecchio, 1298–1532: Government, Architecture, and Imagery in the Civic Palace of the Florentine Republic* (Oxford, UK: Clarendon Press, 1995), 32–33 and 58–61.

51. Ronald Lightbown, *Sandro Botticelli: Life and Work*, 2 vols. (Berkeley and Los Angeles: University of California Press, 1978), vol. 2, 45–46.

52. Adriana Cavarero, *Inclinazioni: Critica della rettitudine* (Milan: Raffaello Cortina, 2013), 76.

CHAPTER SEVEN

1. Leonardo employed such a level in many of his water engineering projects. Leonardo da Vinci, *Del moto e della misura dell'acqua* (Bologna: Francesco Cardinali, 1828), 306.
2. "Nota il moto del livello dell'acqua, il quale fa a uno de' capelli, che hanno due moti, de' quali l'uno attende al peso del vello, l'altro al liniamento delle sue volte; così l'acqua ha le sue volte revertiginose, delle quali una parte attende all'impeto del corso principale, l'altra attende al moto incidente e refresso." Windsor Castle, Royal Library: RL 12579r. For Leonardo's definitions of "moto refresso" and "moto incidente," see Edmondo Solmi, *Nuovi studi sulla filosofia naturale di Leonardo da Vinci* (Mantua: Mondovi, 1905), 59.
3. Quintilian, *Institutio oratoria* 8.2.7. Quintilian's text became influential after the book-hunter Poggio Bracciolini rediscovered it in 1416. Furio Murru, "Poggio Bracciolini e la riscoperta dell'Istitutio Oratoria di Quintiliano (1416)," *Critica Storica* 20 (1983): 621–26. On the importance of Quintilian in the fifteenth century, see Jean Cousin, *Recherches sur Quintilien: Manuscrits et éditions de l'Institution Oratoire* (Paris: Les Belles lettres, 1975). Also, Aristotle mentions the vertex when describing the anatomy of the skull in *History of Animals* 1.7.
4. Pliny, *Natural History* 9.15; Albertus Magnus, *On Animals: A Medieval Summa Zoologica*, tr. Kenneth F. Kitchell Jr. (Baltimore: Johns Hopkins University Press, 1999), 1681. A fifteenth-century copy of Albert's treatise is in Florence: Biblioteca Medicea Laurenziana, Cod. Fiesolano 67. On Leonardo's interest in zoology, see Domenico Laurenza, *De figura umana: Fisiognomica, anatomia e arte in Leonardo* (Florence: Leo S. Olschki, 2001), 178–79. On Leonardo as reader of Albert, see Martin Kemp, *Leonardo da Vinci: The Marvellous Works of Nature and Man* (Oxford, UK: Oxford University Press, 2006), 83–84.
5. Veronica Shue-Ron Shi, "Omo (quasi) sanza lettere: Leonardo's Quest to Teach Himself Classical Latin," in *Leonardo's Library: The World of a Renaissance Reader*, ed. Paula Findlen (Stanford, CA: Stanford Libraries, 2019), 28–41.
6. In his discussion of metaphors, Ricoeur stresses the preeminence of imagination over words. He deplores that "imagination has not yet been considered under its sensible, quasi-optic aspect but under its quasi-verbal aspect. However, the latter is the condition of the former." Paul

Ricoeur, "The Metaphorical Process as Cognition, Imagination, and Feeling," *Critical Inquiry* 5, no. 1 (1978): 143–59, esp. 149.

7. On Leonardo's analogical thinking, see Alessandro Nova, "Valore e limiti del metodo analogico nell'opera di Leonardo da Vinci," in *Leonardo da Vinci: Metodi e tecniche per la costruzione della conoscenza*, ed. Pietro C. Marani and Rodolfo Maffeis (Busto Arsizio, Italy: Nomos, 2016), 25–36. See also Ernst Gombrich, "Leonardo da Vinci's Method of Analysis and Permutation: The Form of Movement in Water and Air," in *The Heritage of Apelles: Studies in the Art of the Renaissance* (Ithaca, NY: Cornell University Press, 1976): 39–56; Martin Kemp, "From 'Mimesis' to 'Fantasia: the Quattrocento Vocabulary of Creation, Inspiration and Genius in the Visual Arts," *Viator* 8 (2006): 347–98; Leslie A. Geddes, *Watermarks: Leonardo da Vinci and the Mastery of Nature* (Princeton, NJ: Princeton University Press, 2020), 103.

8. Isidore of Seville, *Etymologies* 1.37.4. The translation is by Stephen A. Barney and others (Cambridge, UK: Cambridge University Press, 2006).

9. Isidore (*Sententiae* 3.13.1) argued that pagan fables incited the mind to lust. In his *Differentiae* (1.preface), he also accused classical poetry of bastardizing the meaning of words because of metrical requirements. This was well known in Leonardo's time. The friar Girolamo Savonarola, for instance, cites Isidore in his attacks on pagan poetry. Girolamo Savonarola, *Apologetico: Indole e natura dell' arte poetica*, ed. Antonino Stagnitta (Rome: Armando, 1998), 98. Augustine's passage is *De Doctrina Christiana* 3.7.11. Augustine claims that the metaphor was popular in his time. On Augustine's notion of metaphor, see Erich Auerbach, *Scenes from the Drama of European Literature* (Manchester, UK: Manchester University Press, 1959), 37–43.

10. Pauline Voute, "Notes sur l'iconographie d'Océan: A propos d'une fontaine à mosaïques découverte à Nole (Campanie)," *Mélanges de l'École française de Rome: Antiquité* 84, no. 1 (1972), 639–74. See also Fabio Barry, "The Mouth of Truth and the Forum Boarium: Oceanus, Hercules, and Hadrian," *Art Bulletin* 93, no. 1 (2011): 7–37, esp. 13–14.

11. Isidore, *Etymologies* 1.37.4.

12. The emphasis of each author, however, is different. Aristotle speaks of "transference" in *Poetics* 1459a 7–8, and of a process that discloses something that was not evident previously in *Rhetoric* 1411b 9ff–1412a 13. Cicero (*Orator* 3.39, 157) defines metaphor as a misplaced simile. Quintilian follows Cicero in *Instituto oratoria* 8.6.8, but comments on it as the ingenious

activity of the mind in another passage (10.1.130). Generally, see Umberto Eco, *Semiotica e filosofia del linguaggio* (Turin: Einaudi, 1984), 141–98.

13. Ernesto Grassi, *Renaissance Humanism: Studies in Philosophy and Poetics* (Binghamton, NY: Center for Medieval and Early Renaissance Studies, 1988), 50–57; Massimo Cacciari, *La mente inquieta: Saggio sull'umanesimo* (Turin: Einaudi, 2019), 33–41, where Cacciari argues that scholars defined the philosophy of the Renaissance as a reflection on the possibility of words and thus turned it into a form of philology. On the similarities between philosophy and philology, see also Eugenio Garin, *Italian Humanism: Philosophy and Civic Life in the Renaissance* (New York: Harper & Row, 1965), 4.
14. Salutati was a reader of Boccaccio. Margherita Morreale, "Coluccio Salutati's *De Laboribus Herculis* and Enrique de Villena's *Los Doze Trabajos de Hercules*," *Studies in Philology* 51, no. 2 (1954): 95–106, esp. 97. The two corresponded, and may have also met in Florence in 1352. Berthold L. Ullman, *The Humanism of Coluccio Salutati* (Padua, Italy: Antenore, 1963), 41.
15. Grassi, *Renaissance Humanism*, 31–36.
16. "Oportet enim [. . .] ex his omnibus aliquid invenire, [. . .] iudicare super inventis, [. . .] eligere, [. . .] optime pronuntiare." Coluccio Salutati, *De laboribus Herculis*, ed. Berthold L. Ullman, 2 vols. (Zurich: Artemis, 1951), vol. 1, 45.
17. Salutati was a notary, and chancellor of Florence. He wrote letters on behalf of the government, compiled the city's official history, and was consulted on diplomatic matters. On his many duties, see Demetrio Marzi, *La Cancelleria della Repubblica fiorentina* (Rocca San Casciano, Italy: Cappelli, 1910), 131–52. On his important cultural role, see Ronald G. Witt, *Coluccio Salutati and His Public Letters* (Geneva: Droz, 1976), 288.
18. This is Angelo Poliziano's recommendation: "Fabellae [. . .] non rudimentum sed et instrumentum quandoque philosophiae sunt." Angelo Poliziano, *Le selve e la strega: Prolusioni nello Studio fiorentino* (1482–1492), ed. Isidoro del Lungo (Florence: Sansoni, 1925), 184.
19. Grassi, *Renaissance Humanism*, 39 and 102; Luca d'Ascia, "Pandolfo Collenuccio e Lorenzo Valla," *Giornale critico della filosofia italiana* 77, no. 2 (1998): 189–93.
20. Lorenzo de' Medici, *Ambra* 12: "L''orribil barba, ch'è pel ghiaccio rigida / fan gli occhi, e'l naso un fonte, e l' cielo lo 'nfrigida." Consider also stanza 15, in which Ocean's description ("di fronde fluvial le tempie") recalls Augustine's metaphor.

21. Filarete, *Treatise on Architecture*, ed. John R. Spencer, 2 vols. (New Haven, CT: Yale University Press, 1965), vol. 2: fol. 94r ("questi archi sono alti dalla pelle dell'acqua braccia ventotto") and fol. 97r ("La pila di mezzo è venti braccia grossa, e sarà alta dalla pelle dell'acqua braccia quaranta"). Filarete worked for Piero de' Medici and dedicated to him a copy of his architectural treatise (the so-called Codex Magliabechianus), between 1465 and 1469.
22. Frank D. Prager and Gustina Scaglia, *Mariano Taccola and His Book "De Ingeneis"* (Cambridge, MA: MIT Press, 1972), xi.
23. Elizabeth Cropper, introduction to *Florentine Drawing at the Time of Lorenzo the Magnificent*, ed. ead. (Bologna: Nuova Alfa, 1994), ix–xv; David Rosand, "Una linea sola non stentata," in *Linea I: Grafie di immagini tra Quattrocento e Cinquecento*, ed. Marzia Faietti and Gerhard Wolf (Venice: Marsilio, 2008), 17–28, esp. 21–26.
24. Still, the concept of *disegno* was far from being standardized at the end of the fifteenth century. See Renzo Baldasso, "Filarete's "Disegno," *Arte Lombarda* 155, no. 1 (2009): 39–46.
25. "Sustineat similes fluctibus illa sinus." Ovid, *Ars amatoria* 3.148. The inventory of hairstyles is at 3.133–68. On the speed that characterizes Ovid's lists, see Italo Calvino, *Perché leggere i classici* (Milan: Mondadori, 1995), 32. What I term Ovid's "conclusion" is *Ars amatoria* 3.151: "Nec mihi tot positus numero comprendere fas est." He repeats the point at 3.135 ("Nec genus ornatus unum est").
26. If you do not readily recognize these mythological figures, you are in good company. In a manuscript of Ovid's *Ars amatoria* (Florence: Biblioteca Riccardiana, Ms 1543, f. 6.v), a fifteenth-century reader left comments with information about every character mentioned in the text: "Leodamia: fu nata di Tessaglia, figliuola di Tasso [. . .] fu bella donna et chasta la quale molto comanda Ovidio in una sua epistola."
27. Ronald Lightbown, *Sandro Botticelli: Life and Work*, 2 vols. (Berkeley and Los Angeles: University of California Press, 1978), vol. 2, 121–22.
28. Advice to copy the facial features of ancient masterworks comes from Pliny, *Natural History* 34.19, and Ovid, *Metamorphoses* 10.248–49. On artists' merging features from different works, see Ernst Kris and Otto Kurz, *Legend, Myth, and Magic in the Image of the Artist* (New Haven, CT: Yale University Press, 1979), 44.
29. Robert Black, *Humanism and Education in Medieval and Renaissance Italy: Tradition and Innovation in Latin Schools from the Twelfth to the Fifteenth*

Century (Cambridge, UK: Cambridge University Press, 2004), 247. Black recalls that between 1401 and 1403, the friar Giovanni Dominici deplored the fact that the youth were reading Ovid's lascivious poems, such as his *Ars amatoria*, which was available in Italian. Its translation is attributed to the notary Andrea Lancia (doc. 1297–1357). Vanna Lippi Bigazzi, *I volgarizzamenti trecenteschi dell'*Ars Amandi *e dei* Remedia Amoris, 2 vols. (Florence: Accademia della Crusca, 1987), vol. 2, 909–17; Egidio Bellorini, *Note sulle traduzioni italiane dell'"Ars Amatoria" e dei "Remedia amoris" d'Ovidio anteriori al Rinascimento* (Bergamo, Italy: Cattaneo, 1892), 12–15. It may be worth stressing that some Florentines encountered the text paired with Boccaccio's *Comedia delle ninfe fiorentine*, as in Florence: Biblioteca Medicea Laurenziana, Plut. 41.36. Reading one text after the other turns Boccaccio's hairstyles into applications of Ovid's idea of hair as the first means to love. Ovid's *Ars amatoria* was first printed in Venice in 1472, the year after Ovid's *Metamorphoses*, which was published in both Bologna and Rome. Ovid's *Metamorphoses* was followed by twenty-three other editions before the turn of the century. Grundy Steiner, "Source-Editions of Ovid's Metamorphoses (1471–1500)," *Transactions and Proceedings of the American Philological Association* 82 (1951): 219–31.

30. Nandini B. Pandey, "Female Hair as Symbolic Vehicle of Domination in Ovidian Love Elegy," *Classical Journal* 113, no. 4 (2018): 454–88.

31. "Solverat effusos quoties sine lege capillos, infesta est trepidis visa Diana feria; sive iterum adductos fulvum collegit in aurum, compta cytheriaco est pectine visa Venus." Angelo Poliziano, *Prose volgari inedite e poesie latine e greche edite e inedite*, ed. Isidoro Del Lungo (Florence: Barbera, 1867), 240. The girl was fifteen-year-old Albiera degli Albizzi. She died from pneumonia on July 14, 1473. Rita degl'Innocenti Pierini, "L'epicedio di Angelo Poliziano per Albiera degli Albizi: Tradizione classica e contaminazione di generi," in *Angelo Poliziano: Dichter und Gelehrter*, ed. Thomas Baier, Tobias Dänzer, and Ferdinand Stürner (Tübingen, Germany: Attempto, 2015), 1–27. The cited passage borrows from Ovid, *Ars amatoria* 3.143–47. It is also a play on Tibullus, *Corpus* 4.2.9–10: "Seu solvit crines, fusis decet esse capillis, / seu compsit, comptis est veneranda comis."

32. "So' anco di quelle che hanno piú capi che 'l diavolo; ogni dì rimutano uno capo di nuovo. El diavolo n'ha sette, e ci è tale che n'ha anco più; che di quello ch'io mi ricordo da quindici anni in qua, tanti modi, tante forge, ch'io trasecolo. [. . .] Io veggo tale che porta il capo a trippa, chi il porta

a frittella, chi a taglieri, chi a frappole, chi l'aviluppa in su, chi in giù. Oh, egli è il mal segno tante forge! Ponetele giù, vi dico. Così a voi, donne, ponete giù tante vanità: che se voi vi vedeste [. . .] voi parete pure civette e barbagianni e locchi." Bernardino da Siena, *Prediche volgari sul campo di Siena 1427*, ed. Carlo DelCorno, 2 vols. (Milan: Rusconi, 1989), vol. 2, 1093.

33. Bernardino da Siena, *Le prediche volgari inedite, Firenze 1424, 1425, Siena 1425*, ed. Dionisio Pacetti (Siena, Italy: Cantagalli, 1935), 197: "che ti separi da' libri de Ovidio e dagli altri libri d'innamoramenti [. . .] ché, sotto quella coverta del m[i]ele, v'è il veleno." See also Marco Agosti, "La pedagogia di San Bernardino da Siena," in *S. Bernardino da Siena: Saggi e ricerche pubblicati nel quinto centenario della morte* (1444–1944) (Milan: Vita e pensiero, 1945), 413–14.

34. Leon Battista Alberti, *On Painting and On Sculpture: The Latin Texts of "De pictura" and "De statua,"* ed. Cecil Grayson (London: Phaidon, 1972), 87. For Alberti the movements of hair are seven, because Quintilian wrote that there are seven types of motion. Anthony Grafton, *Leon Battista Alberti: Master Builder of the Italian Renaissance* (New York: Hill and Wang, 2000), 118–20.

35. Aby Warburg, "Sandro Botticelli's Birth of Venus and Spring," in *The Renewal of Pagan Antiquity* (Los Angeles: Getty Research Institute, 1999), 93–107; Spyros Papapetros, *On the Animation of the Inorganic: Art, Architecture, and the Extension of Life* (Chicago: University of Chicago Press, 2012), 45 and 66–69. Berenson speaks of Botticelli's hair as "life-communicating" in Bernard Berenson, *Florentine Painters, The Drawings of Florentine Painters*, 2 vols. (London: J. Murray, 1903), vol. 1, 71–74. On the limited circulation of *De pictura*, completed by 1435 but known through only three fifteenth-century manuscript copies, see Alison Wright, *The Pollaiuolo Brothers: The Arts of Florence and Rome* (New Haven, CT: Yale University Press, 2005), 227–50; and Patricia L. Rubin, *Images and Identity in Fifteenth-Century Florence* (London: Yale University Press, 2007), 95–96. It is only in the nineteenth century that Alberti's treatise started receiving scholarly attention. D. R. Edward Wright, *Il "De pictura" di Leona Battista Alberti e i suoi lettori* (Florence: L. S. Olshki, 2010), 239–42. On the three surviving fifteenth-century manuscripts, see also Lucia Bertolini, "Sulla precedenza della redazione volgare del *De pictura* di Leon Battista Alberti," in *Studi per Umberto Carpi*, ed. Marco Santagata and Alfredo Stussi (Pisa, Italy: ETS, 2000), 181–210.

36. Georges Didi-Huberman, "The Imaginary Breeze: Remarks on the Air of

the Quattrocento," *Journal of Visual Studies* 2 (2003): 275–89, esp. 277; Alessandro Nova, *Il libro del vento: Rappresentare l'invisibile* (Genoa: Marietti, 2007), 69.

37. Alberti learned how to approach hair through Latin literature. Virgil's description of Venus (*Aeneid* 1.319) speaks of hair spread by the wind ("dederatque comam diffundere ventis"), as does Ovid's description of Daphne (*Metamorphoses* 1.529: "et levis impulsos retro dabat aura capillos"). Petrarch also drew from both to describe Laura's "capei d'oro a Laura sparsi." Giuseppe Mazzotta, *The Worlds of Petrarch* (Durham, NC: Duke University Press, 1993), 62.

38. The cup was valued at ten thousand florins, according to an inventory drawn in 1492 (known through a 1512 copy). There it is described as "una schodella di sardonio e chalcidonio e aghata, entrovi più fighure, et di fuori una testa di Medusa." Laurie Fusco and Gino Corti, *Lorenzo de' Medici: Collector and Antiquarian* (Cambridge, UK: Cambridge University Press, 2006), 380.

39. Lorenzo received the cup in 1471, as he records in his diary: "In September of 1471 I was elected ambassador to Rome for the coronation of Pope Sixtus IV, where I was honored, and from there [. . .] I took away our dish of carved chalcedony [that is, the cup] along with many other cameos and coins." In Fusco and Corti, *Lorenzo*, 6 (the translation is by the two authors). On the cup's placement in Lorenzo's study, see Luke Syson, "The Medici Study," in *At Home in Renaissance Italy*, ed. Marta Ajmar-Wollheim and Flora Dennis (London: Victoria and Albert Museum, 2006), 288–93. In recounting Cardinal Raffaele Riario's visit to Lorenzo's study in 1478, Poliziano said that his collection was displayed "in promptuarium"—that is, on open shelves. Angelo Poliziano, *Della congiura dei Pazzi*, ed. Alessandro Perosa (Padua, Italy: Antenore, 1958), 25–27, note 6.

40. In a letter, dated 1480, to the Duke of Ferrara Ercole d'Este, Antonio da Montecatini writes that Giovanni d'Aragona visited the Palazzo Medici and saw "una schudella scholpita dentro de tante varie figure, che era una cosa digna, fu reputata da valuta da quatromila ducati." Fusco and Corti, *Lorenzo*, 323.

41. Kim J. Hartswick, "The Gorgoneion of the Aigis of Athena: Genesis, Suppression, and Survival," *Revue archéologique* 2 (1993): 269–92, esp. 275–78.

42. Eugene J. Dwyer, "The Temporal Allegory of the Tazza Farnese," *American Journal of Archaeology* 96, no. 2 (1992): 255–82.

43. Angelo Poliziano, "In pateram egregiam Laurentii Medicis," in Fusco and Corti, *Lorenzo*, 340. The original is in Florence: Biblioteca Medicea Laurenziana, Plut. 90 sup. 37, ff. 127v–128r.
44. The images decorate Jacopo Bracciolini's translation of Bartolomeo Facio's *De origine belli inter Gallos et Britannos historia*. Melania Ceccanti, *Il sorriso della sfinge: L'eredità del mondo antico nelle miniature riccardiane* (Florence: Polistampa, 2009), 152–55; Annarosa Garzelli, *Miniatura fiorentina del Rinascimento, 1440–1525: Un primo censimento*, 2 vols. (Florence: La Nuova Italia, 1985), vol. 1, 80 and 195. Attavante was known for studying medals, intaglios, and ancient cameos. Leah R. Clark, *Collecting Art in the Italian Renaissance Court: Objects and Exchanges* (Cambridge, UK: Cambridge University Press, 2018), 84–95.
45. Bertoldo replicated the cup's shallow relief in his medal of Mehmed II, cast around 1480. He also reproduced the cup's Nile figure as the judge in the stucco relief of Florence's Palazzo Scala-della Gherardesca. James D. Draper, *Bertoldo di Giovanni, Sculptor of the Medici Household* (Columbia: University of Missouri Press, 1992), 26, 100, and 237. See also Alessandro Parronchi, "The Language of Humanism and the Language of Sculpture: Bertoldo as Illustrator of the *Apologi* of Bartolomeo Scala," *Journal of the Warburg and Courtauld Institutes* 27 (1964): 108–36, esp. 126.
46. Andrew Butterfield, ed., *Verrocchio: Sculptor and Painter of Renaissance Florence* (Washington: National Gallery of Art, 2019), 127–29. The Medusa of Giuliano de' Medici's bust by Verrocchio is often said to mimic the Farnese cup, but I do not see the similarities. A more apt term of comparison for Verrocchio's gorgon, it seems to me, is offered by the Medusa heads of the so-called Trophies of Marius, visible in Rome since at least 1140. Francis M. Nichols, ed., *Mirabilia Urbis Romae*, ed. Francis M. Nichols (London: Ellis and Elvey, 1889), 107n1. On Giuliano's bust, see Keith Christiansen and Stefan Weppelmann, eds., *The Renaissance Portrait: From Donatello to Bellini* (New York: Metropolitan Museum of Art, 2011), 174.
47. Toby E. S. Yuen, "The *Tazza Farnese* as a Source for Botticelli's *Birth of Venus* and Piero di Cosimo's *Myth of Prometheus*," *Gazette des Beaux Arts* 74 (1969): 175–78; Paul Holberton, "Classicism and Invention: Botticelli's Mythologies in Our Time and Their Time," in *Botticelli Past and Present*, ed. Ana De Benedetti and Caroline Elam (London: UCL Press, 2019), 68.
48. The drawing is reproduced and discussed in Ronald Lightbown, *Sandro Botticelli: Life and Work*, 2 vols. (Berkeley and Los Angeles: University of

California Press, 1978), vol. 2, 162. To my knowledge, this connection has gone undetected until now.

49. The friar Giovanni da Fiesole was first called "angelicus" in Domenico da Corella's *Theotocon*, written around 1464. Lorenzo Amato, "L'*Angelicus pictor* e il confratello poeta Domenico di Giovanni da Corella," in *Angelicus Pictor: Ricerche e interpretazioni sul Beato Angelico*, ed. Alessandro Zuccari (Milan: Skira, 2008), 67–69.
50. Magnolia Scudieri, "Il ciclo affrescato nel convento di San Marco a Firenze," in *Beato Angelico: L'alba del Rinascimento*, ed. Alessandro Zuccari, Giovanni Morello, and Gerardo de Simone (Milan: Skira, 2009), 109–23.
51. Eugenio Marino, *Beato Angelico: Umanesimo e teologia* (Rome: Atena, 1984), 493–96.
52. This reflection was inspired by the description of sculptures in Michael Baxandall, *The Limewood Sculptors of Renaissance Germany* (New Haven, CT: Yale University Press, 1980), 192.
53. Miklós Boskovits and David A. Brown, *Italian Paintings of the Fifteenth Century* (Washington: National Gallery of Art, 2003), 3–7.
54. Rolf Bagemihl, "The Trevisan Collection," *Burlington Magazine* 135 (1993): 559–63, esp. 561. Trevisan also invited Donatello to study his collection. Horst W. Janson, *The Sculpture of Donatello* (Princeton, NJ: Princeton University Press, 1963), 123–25. Trevisan received the Farnese cup from the King of Naples, who had purchased it from a merchant in the early 1450s. After Trevisan's death in 1465, the cup passed to the pope, from whom Lorenzo bought it.
55. Coins bearing images of the gorgoneion ranged from the common *denarii* of Lucius Plautius Plancus to the rare *aureii* of Caracalla. I am grateful to Federica Misserere Fontana for telling me about the numismatic interest of Angelo Poliziano. Federica Misserere Fontana, "Raccolte numismatiche e scambi antiquari a Bologna fra Quattrocento e Seicento," *Bollettino di numismatica* 25 (1995): 161–209, esp. 163–64.
56. Stephen R. Wilk, *Medusa: Solving the Mystery of the Gorgon* (Oxford, UK: Oxford University Press, 2000), 235.
57. "Ama maximamente e capegli, cioè el superfluo [. . .] Et Minerva gli muta e capegli begli in serpicelle, perché la sapientia finalmente scuopre simili fraude, et dimostra el veleno loro." Cristoforo Landino, *Comento sopra la Comedia*, ed. Paolo Procaccioli, 4 vols. (Rome: Salerno, 2001), vol. 2, 553. I wonder if the hidden snakes in Medusa's hair offered Botticelli the idea of shaping Simonetta's hair like flames, as discussed in chapter 4.

58. Isidore of Seville, *Etymologies* 1.37.4.
59. Galen, *De usu partium* 14.6. Galen sees hair as decorative for both men and women. Yet he states that hair serves for women's protection, whereas in men it evacuates their abundant humors.
60. Thomas Aquinas, *Summa theologica* III.Supp. q. 80, a.2.
61. The full passage reads: "Per i capelli [Dante meant] le sustanze mondane, e meritamente, perciocchè i capelli in sè non hanno alcuno umore, né altra cosa la quale alla nostra corporal salute sia utile; sono solamente alcuno ornamento al corpo, e per questo ne son dati dalla natura: e così dirittamente sono le sustanze temporali, le quali per sé medesime alcuna cosa prestar non possono alla salute dell'anima nostra, ma prestano alcuno ornamento a' corpi: e perciò dirittamente sentono coloro, i quali intendono per i capelli le predette sustanze: risurgerano adunque i prodighi co' crin mozzi a dimostrare, come essi stoltamente e con dispiacere a Dio diminuiscono le loro temporali ricchezze." Giovanni Boccaccio, *Il comento di sopra la "Divina commedia" di Dante Alighieri*, 3 vols. (Florence: Ignazio Moutier, 1831–32), vol. 2, 148. He is discussing Dante, *Inferno* 7.46–57. Boccaccio gave his lectures on Dante's *Comedy* in the church of Santo Stefano in Badia every weekday, starting on October 23, 1373. He stopped at canto 17.
62. "Verse wishes its very words to be graceful in appearance [. . .] Metre desires to appear as a handmaid with hair adorned." Geoffrey of Vinsauf, *Poetria Nova*, tr. Margaret F. Nims (Toronto: Pontifical Institute of Mediaeval Studies, 1967), 83.
63. Cicero, *Epistulae ad Atticum* 2.1.1: "quamquam tua illa (legi enim libenter) horridula mihi atque incompta [that is, disheveled] visa sunt, sed tamen erant ornata hoc ipso quod ornamenta neglexerant."
64. Peter Godman, *From Poliziano to Machiavelli: Florentine Humanism in the High Renaissance* (Princeton, NJ: Princeton University Press, 1998), 35. On this treatise, see Letizia Panizza, "Pico della Mirandola e il *De genere dicendi philosophorum* del 1485: L'encomio paradossale Dei "Barbari" e la loro parodia," *I Tatti: Studies in the Italian Renaissance* 8 (1999): 69–103.
65. "Profecto quod Synesius de adolescente, de oratione dici commode potest. Comatam orationem semper cinaedam. Quare nos nostram malumus capillis hirtam, globosam, inexpeditam, quam cum impuritatis vel nota vel suspicione belle comatam." Giovanni Pico della Mirandola, "De genere dicendi philosophorum," in *Prosatori Latini del Quattrocento*, ed. Eugenio Garin (Turin: Einaudi, 1976), 810.

66. Giorgio Agamben, *The Use of the Bodies* (Stanford, CA: Stanford University Press, 2015), 264.
67. Giovanni Boccaccio, *On Poetry*, ed. and tr. Charles G. Osgood (New York: Liberal Arts Press, 1956), 104. Boccaccio reflected on the art of poetry in the last two books of his *Genealogy*, which he wrote in response to moralists' attacks. One of his critics, the famous miracle-working Carthusian monk Pietro Petroni, dreamed of Boccaccio's death and urged him to give up his secular studies to prepare his soul for God. Guido Traversari, "Il beato Pietro Petroni senese e la conversione del Boccaccio," *Rassegna pugliese di scienze, lettere ed arti* 22 (1905): 76–82. On the complex genesis of Boccaccio's *Genealogy*, see Salomon's introduction in Giovanni Boccaccio, *Genealogy of the Pagan Gods*, ed. Jon Solomon, 2 vols. (Cambridge, MA: Harvard University Press, 2011–2017), vol. 1, viii–x.
68. Apuleius, *Metamorphoses* 2.8–9. See also note 67 in chapter 4.
69. Boccaccio, *On Poetry*, 104.
70. Botticelli was not the only Florentine to challenge moralists. Even before he was born in 1445, a group of humanists were accused of holding anticlerical, even heretical, views. See Arthur Field, *The Intellectual Struggle for Florence: Humanists and the Beginnings of the Medici Regime, 1420–1440* (Oxford, UK: Oxford University Press, 2017), 75–126.

CHAPTER EIGHT

1. This text is known as *Dell'adornamento delle donne* (sometimes *Dell'adornamento delle femmine*). It is the Florentine vulgarization of "De ornatu mulierum" section of the medieval compilation known as *Trotula*. *The Trotula: A Medieval Compendium of Women's Medicine*, ed. and tr. Monica H. Green (Philadelphia: University of Pennsylvania Press, 2001), 166–91. On the manuscript tradition of "De Ornatu Mulierum," which circulated in three versions, Monica H. Green, "The Development of the Trotula," *Revue d'histoire des textes* 26 (1996): 119–203, esp. 139–43. The Florentine translation is printed as *Libro degli adornamenti delle donne*, ed. Giuseppe Manuzzi (Florence: 1863). On this turbulent, posthumous publication, as well as its manuscript sources, see Rossella Mosti, "Per un'edizione critica di quattro trattatelli medici del primo Trecento," *Studi di lessicografia italiana* 31 (2014): 45–73.
2. "Acciò chella femina sia scavissima e piena e sanza peli inutili dal capo a' piedi: In prima mente vada al bagno." Florence: Biblioteca Medicea

Laurenziana, Plut. 73.51, f. 56v. The word *soave* means "pleasing to the senses." It is often used in reference to waves and breezes; hence its use as synonym for the adjectives "light," "moderate," and "delightful," as explained by Dante in *Convivio* 88: "Soave è tanto quanto suaso, cioè abbellito, dolce, piacente, e dilettoso."

3. Lorenzo planned to stay at Bagno Vignoni for two weeks in May 1490, as he wrote in a letter sent from there. Didier Boisseuil, "Les Médicis aux bains: Le thermalisme dans le territoire siennois au Quattrocento, entre fonctions thérapeutiques et pratiques diplomatiques," in *L'ultimo secolo della Repubblica di Siena: Arti, cultura e società*, ed. Mario Ascheri and Fabrizio Nevola (Siena, Italy: Accademia senese degli Intronati, 2007), 429n72 and 448 (for a list of letters referring to Bagno Vignoni). On the Medici as spa regulars, see Gaetano Pieraccini, *La stirpe de' Medici di Cafaggiolo*, 3 vols. (Florence: Vallechi, 1924), vol. 1, 60–65 and 120–22; Ingeborg Walter, *Lorenzo il Magnifico e il suo tempo* (Rome: Donzelli, 2005), 25–26. On Bagno a Morba (in today's Larderello), Medici's preferred spa, see Janet Ross, *The Lives of the Early Medici as Told in Their Correspondence* (London: Chatto & Windus, 1910), 111–18, 179–86, and 255.
4. In 1334 Jacopo Tondi left a description of Bagno Vignoni. See his "Visita nell'antico stato della Repubblica di Siena," in Alessandro Lisini, "Notizie delle miniere della Maremma Toscana e leggi per l'estrazione dei metalli nel Medioevo," *Bullettino senese di storia patria* 6, no. 3 (1935): 185–256, esp. 218. For remarks on how crowded it was, Federigo Melis, "La frequenza alle terme nel basso medioevo," in *Primo congresso italiano di studi storici termali* (Fidenza, Italy: Mattioli, 1963), 42.
5. I took the detail of the garland from a letter that Poggio Bracciolini wrote in 1416. There he also complained of the many friars who bathed immodestly. Eugenio Garin, *Prosatori latini del Quattrocento* (Turin: Einaudi, 1976), 227. On the covered bridge at Bagno Vignoni, see Didier Boisseuil, *Le thermalisme en Toscane à la fin du Moyen Âge: Les bains siennois de la fin du XIIIe siècle au début du XVIe siècle* (Rome: Ecole française de Rome, 2002), 145 and 158n13.
6. David S. Chambers, "Spas in the Italian Renaissance," in *Reconsidering the Renaissance*, ed. Mario A. di Cesare (Binghamton, NY: Medieval & Renaissance Texts & Studies, 1992), 25–26.
7. Katharine Park, "Natural Particulars: Medical Epistemology, Practice, and the Literature of Healing Springs," in *Natural Particulars: Nature and the Disciplines in Renaissance Europe*, ed. Anthony Grafton and Nancy G.

Siraisi (Cambridge, MA: MIT Press, 1999), 347–67; Gabriella Zuccolin, "Ruolo ed evoluzione della balneoterapia nel pensiero scientifico-medico in Italia dal XII al XVI secolo," in *Il calore della terra: Contributo alla storia della geotermia in Italia*, ed. Marco Ciardi and Raffaele Cataldi (Pisa: ETS, 2005), 110.

8. This superstition is criticized, and thus recorded, in Ugolino da Montecatini, *Tractatus de balneis*, ed. Michele G. Nardi (Florence: L. S. Olschki, 1950), 36.
9. Chambers, "Spas in the Italian Renaissance," 14–15.
10. Bartolomeo della Scala wrote a Latin poem centered on the nymph Amorba while at Bagno a Morba. He sent it to Lorenzo de' Medici on April 25, 1484. Ross, *Lives of the Early Medici*, 256–58.
11. Lucrezia Tornabuoni restored Bagno a Morba. Yvonne Maguire, *The Women of the Medici* (London: Routledge, 1927), 82–87 and 100–109; Chambers, "Spas in the Italian Renaissance," 18–19. On spa architecture in Tuscany, Charles R. Mack, "The Renaissance Spa: Testing the Architectural Waters," *Southeastern College Art Conference Review* 11, no. 3 (1988): 193–200.
12. Maria Bendinelli Predelli, "Tirant lo Blanc e gli affreschi erotici di San Gimignano," *Filologia e critica* 15 (1990): 508–20; Jean C. Campbell, *The Game of Courting and the Art of the Commune of San Gimignano, 1290–1320* (Princeton, NJ: Princeton University Press, 1997), 107–90. On steam baths, see Georges Vigarello, *Concepts of Cleanliness: Changing Attitudes in France since the Middle Ages* (Cambridge, UK: Cambridge University Press, 1988), 22. In Italy, *stufe* or saunas became popular after the Council of Constance (1414–18). Anna Esposito, "Stufe e bagni pubblici a Roma nel Rinascimento," in *Taverne, locande e stufe a Roma nel Rinascimento* (Rome: Roma nel Rinascimento, 1999), 79. From Constance, Pope Martinus V brought to Rome one spa manager. We even know his name: Angelinus de Bolzana de Alamania.
13. "Esse nonne fosse usata, faccia questa stufa in questo modo: togli tegoli e pietre vive, e siano bene calde nel fuoco, e sieno poste nella stufa sì che la femmina sudi nella detta stufa." Florence: Biblioteca Medicea Laurenziana, Plut. 73.51, f. 56v.
14. Michel Pastoureau, *The Devil's Cloth: A History of Stripes and Striped Fabric* (New York: Columbia University Press, 2001), 114n74. The Duke of Ferrara Borso d'Este took fabric pavilions ("pavalguni de tela da campo") with him when he went to the spas in Abano. Thomas J. Tuohy, "Stud-

ies in Domestic Expenditure at the Court of Ferrara, 1451–1505: Artistic Patronage and Princely Magnificence" (PhD dissertation, Warburg Institute / University of London, 1982), 148. Boccaccio dramatizes the logistics of baths (mattresses being unrolled, towels prepared) in *Decameron* 8.10.

15. On bathing as an aristocratic pursuit, Vigarello, *Concepts of Cleanliness*, 23–24.
16. "Ad quod balneum vadunt multe sterile ut in usu illius possint esse prolifice [. . .] multa mulieres ex huius usu factas prolificas." Ugolino da Montecatini, *De balneis*, 88–89.
17. Lucrezia Tornabuoni to Lorenzo Medici on June 8, 1477. Ross, *Lives of the Early Medici*, 182–83.
18. Katharine Park, *Doctors and Medicine in Early Renaissance Florence* (Princeton, NJ: Princeton University Press, 1985), 39–41, 114–17, and 216–18.
19. On the popularity of thermal guidebooks, whose number increased from the middle of the fourteenth century, see Didier Boisseuil, Marylin Nicoud, and Laurence Moulinier, "Il *De balneis* di Francesco da Siena: Uno sguardo sul termalismo Italiano all'inizio del Quattrocento," in *Die Renaissance der Heilquellen in Italien und Europa von 1200 bis 1600*, ed. Didier Boisseuil and Hartmut Wulfram (Frankfurt am Main: Peter Lang, 2012), 129–62. Scholars often cite those texts from a compilation, printed in 1533 in Venice, with the title *De balneis*, and I follow this convention. On this important publication, see Ugo Stefanutti, "Un capolavoro dell'idrologia medica e della balneoterapia: La collezione *De balnesis*," in *Primo congresso italiano di studi storici termali*, 457–66.
20. "Capillos prolixos et claros facit." Giovanni Elisio, "Breve compendium de totius Campaniae Balneis," in *De balneis* (Venice: 1533), f. 210v.
21. On the variety of people who took an interest in the body (healers, astrologers, barbers, apothecaries, and street fraudsters), and even claimed to treat its diseases, see Katharine Park, "Medical Practice," in *The Cambridge History of Science*, volume 2: *Medieval Science*, ed. David C. Lindberg and Michael H. Shank (Cambridge, UK: Cambridge University Press, 2013), 611–29; Nancy G. Siraisi, *Medieval and Early Renaissance Medicine: An Introduction to Knowledge and Practice* (Chicago: University of Chicago Press, 1990), 79.
22. "De Balneo Fontis [. . .] sanat omnes plagas, et mirabiliter extrahit ferrum . . . sanat scabiem, facit capillos prolixos et pulchros" Elisio, "Breve Compendium," 212r.

23. The *Trotula* includes five recipes for depilatory treatments, all of which rely on quicklime, arsenic, or a combination of both. *Trotula*, ed. Green, 166–69, 174–75, and 190–91. On ivory as a paragon for female skin, Avinoam Shalem, *The Oliphant: Islamic Objects in Historical Context* (Leiden, Netherlands: Brill, 2004), 82–84.
24. Esposito, "Stufe e bagni pubblici a Roma," 88. Boccaccio describes the stripping of hair and its cutting with a piece of glass in *Corbaccio*, ed. Pier Giorgio Ricci (Turin: Einaudi, 1977), 51: "pelando le ciglia e le fronti, e col vetro sottigliando le gote, e del collo assottigliando la buccia, e certi peluzzi levandone."
25. "Onda a coloro a cui caggion i capelli . . . sì loro conviene usare buone vivande, calde e umide, che si cuocono leggiermente allo stomaco e bene nodriscono, e ch'elle non siano salate." Aldobrandino da Siena, *Del conservare i capelli e i denti*, ed. Francesco Zambrini (Imola, Italy: Galeati, 1876), 3. This publication is an excerpt from Aldobrandino da Siena's *Régime du corps*, a manual on well-being that today is known through seventy-three manuscripts. Nicolò Premi, "Le Régime du corps et les environnements textuels de ses manuscrits," *Medioevi* 5 (2019):, 127–40, esp. 128–30. The text from which I cite is the fourteenth-century translation by Zucchero Bencivenni, a Florentine. See note 42 in ch. 3.
26. "Dopo che elli [hair, which is plural in Italian] sono ingenerati, si possono cadere per li pertugi della carne ond'elli vegnono, sì come d'essere troppo aperti o vero troppo chiusi: perciò che quand'elli sono troppo aperti, il fummo se ne va troppo fuori, e quand'elli sono troppo chiusi, il fumo non ne puote uscire." Aldobrandino da Siena, *Del conservare i capelli*, 1–2.
27. *Problemata* 1.16, 2.6, 2.10, 10.22–23, and 10.62–64. In *The Complete Works of Aristotle: The Revised Oxford Translation*, 2 vols., ed. Jonathan Barnes (Princeton, NJ: Princeton University Press 1984), 2.
28. Maaike van der Lugt, "Aristotle's Problems in the West: A Contribution to the Study of the Medieval Latin Tradition," in *Aristotle's Problemata in Different Times and Tongues*, ed. Pieter De Leemans and Michèle Goyens (Leuven, Netherlands: Leuven University Press, 2006), 73–75.
29. Ann M. Blair, "The *Problemata* as a Natural Philosophical Genre," in *Natural Particulars*, 171–204.
30. The papal copy, dated 1454, is Biblioteca Apostolica Vaticana: Ms. Vat. Lat. 2111. John Monfasani, "The Pseudo-Aristotelian 'Problemata' and Aristotle's 'De animalibus' in the Renaissance," in *Natural Particulars*, 205–47, esp. 206. Among those who relied on Gaza's version was Gaza's pupil Angelo Poliziano. This is demonstrated by Poliziano's notes for his

course on Ovid's *Fasti* given in 1481–82. Francesco Lo Monaco, "Introduzione," in *Commento inedito ai Fasti di Ovidio* (Florence: L. S. Olschki, 1991), xxxiii. Before Gaza, the text of the *Problemata* was mostly known through a translation by Bartolomeo of Messina, on which see Josef Brams, *La riscoperta di Aristotele in Occidente* (Milan: Jaca Book, 2003), 89–103; and Gerardo Marenghi, "Un capitolo dell'Aristotele medievale: Bartolomeo da Messina, traduttore dei *Problemata physica*," *Aevum* 36 (1962): 268–83. Bartolomeo's translation did not disappear after the publication of Gaza's. It was printed in 1475, and again in 1482. Much of its success came from its commentary by the great scholar Pietro d'Abano, on which see Nancy G. Siraisi, "The Expositio Problematum of Peter of Abano," *Isis* 61 (1970): 321–39.

31. Enthusiasm for Gaza's translation is proved by the manuscripts copied even before it was printed in 1473. Most of the critiques came from George of Trebizond, who also translated the *Problemata* and published his version in 1454. John Monfasani, "George of Trebizond's Critique of Theodore Gaza's Translation of the Aristotelian Problemata," in *Aristotle's Problemata in Different Times and Tongues*, 275–94. Poliziano also criticized Gaza's adaptation in his *Miscellaneorum centuria prima*. John Monfasani, "Angelo Poliziano, Aldo Manuzio, Theodore Gaza, George of Trebizond, and chapter 90 of the *Miscellaneorum centuria prima*," in *Interpretations of Renaissance Humanism*, ed. Angelo Mazzocco (Leiden, Netherlands: Brill, 2006), 243–65.
32. Monfasani, "The Pseudo-Aristotelian 'Problemata,'" 205–47.
33. Aristotle, *De historia animalium* 3.10. Other references to hair are at 1.7 and 2.1. The title is usually translated as "The History of Animals," but this is misleading, given that in premodern Europe the term "historia" expresses a form of knowledge which unfolds as description of its parts without explaining their causes. Gianna Pomata and Nancy Siraisi, introduction to *Historia: Empiricism and Erudition in Early Modern Europe*, ed. Siraisi (Cambridge, MA: MIT Press, 2005), 1–38.
34. Aristotle, *De generatione animalium* 5.5–7.
35. On this division, known as hylomorphism, see Charlotte Witt, "Hylomorphism in Aristotle," *Apeiron* 22 (1989): 141–58. Notice that Aldobrandino da Siena is being Aristotelian when he states that hair loss can be prevented by intervening on either hair "matter" or the "openings" that give shape to it. Aldobrandino da Siena, *Del conservare i capelli*, 2: "possono i capelli cadere [. . .] per diffalta di matera o per lo difetto de' pertugi."
36. The bronze sphere example is in Aristotle, *Physics* 2.3. See also Aristotle,

Metaphysics 8.1045a. On the medieval reception of the bronze sphere example and Aristotle's emphasis of form over substance, see Gabriele Galluzzo, *The Medieval Reception of Book Zeta of Aristotle's Metaphysics*, 2 vols. (Leiden, Netherlands: Brill, 2012), vol. 1, 98–101. Generally, Sarah Broadie, "Nature and Craft in Aristotelian Teleology," in *Aristotle and Beyond: Essays in Metaphysics and Ethics* (Cambridge, UK: Cambridge University Press, 2010), 85–100.

37. "The principal cause of thickness and thinness [of hair] is the skin, for this is thick in some animals and thin in others, rare in some and dense in others. The different quality of the included moisture is also a helping cause, for in some animals this is greasy and in others watery. For, generally speaking, the substratum of the skin is of an earthy nature; being on the surface of the body, it becomes solid and earthy as the moisture evaporates." Aristotle, *On the Generation of the Animals* 5.3–5. The translation is by Arthur Platt (Oxford, UK: Clarendon Press, 1910). See also, Stefano Perfetti, *Aristotle's Zoology and Its Renaissance Commentators, 1521–1600* (Leuven, Belgium: Leuven University Press, 2000), 11–28.

38. The point returns in Aristotle, *De anima* 1.5: ". . . for all the parts of the animal body which consist wholly of earth such as bones, sinews, and hair seem to be wholly insensitive and consequently not perceptive even of objects earthy like themselves, as they ought to have been," and 3.13: "That is why we have no sensation by means of bones, hair, etc., because they consist of earth." Both translations are by John A. Smith (Oxford, UK: Clarendon Press, 1931). The passages were discussed by Thomas Aquinas in *Commentary on Aristotle's De Anima*, ed. Kenelm Foster and Silvester Humphries (London: Routledge 1951), 12 and 184; and by Albertus Magnus, *Summa de creaturis* 2.33.3, in id., *Opera omnia*, ed. Auguste Borgnet, 38 vols. (Paris: Vivès, 1890–1899), vol. 35, 289b. This characterization returns in *Problemata* 2.10. Hippocrates, *Oeuvre complètes*, ed. and tr. Emile Littré, 10 vols. (Paris, Baillière, 1839–61), vol. 7, 507–11; and vol. 8, 564–65.

39. Thomas de Garbo, *Summa medicinalis* (Venice, 1506), ff. 32r–33r: "Utrum pili sint animati, et utrum eorum materia sit calida vel frigida." On the fortune of this treatise, see Park, *Doctors and Medicine*, 202–9.

40. Plato, *Protagoras*, in *Complete Works*, ed. John. M. Cooper (Indianapolis, IN: Hackett, 1997), 767. The translation is by Stanley Lombardo and Karen Bell.

41. "Tagliati non rimettono in su la tagliatura, come rimettono l'herbe,

ma escon in fuori dalla radice." Pliny, *Natural History* 11.37. I am quoting from the Venetian edition of 1543, itself a reprint of the first edition (1476) by Nicholas Jenson, also printed in Venice, on which see Martin Lowry, *Nicholas Jenson and the Rise of Venetian Publishing in Renaissance Europe* (Oxford, UK: Blackwell, 1991), 130–32. The translation was by Cristoforo Landino. Nicoletta Marcelli, "La *Naturalis historia* di Plinio nel volgarizzamento di Cristoforo Landino," *Archives internationales d'Histoire des sciences* 61 (2011): 137–61.

42. "That the process is not a withering, that the hair does not whiten as grass does by withering, is shown by the fact that some hairs grow grey from the first, whereas nothing springs up in a withered state. Many hairs also whiten at the tip, for there is least heat in the extremities and thinnest parts." Aristotle, *On the Generation of the Animals* 5.5. The translation is by Arthur Platt.

43. Because of its thoroughness, it is worth transcribing a longer section of the passage: "Et nimirum opinabitur quis, sicut in terra sicca herbis inpossibile est et nasci et augmentari et nutriri, secundum eandem rationem et in cute capillis. Habet autem non ita: terra quidem enim ut terra sicca dicitur, cutis autem ut cutis. Et igitur quod in terra quidem siccum sine humectatione ultime est, quod autem in hominis corpore et similiter homini animalium non sine humiditate et aptum maxime omnium ad generationem pilorum." Galen, *De complexionibus* 2.5, in *Galenus Latinus*, vol. 1: *Burgundio of Pisa's Translation of Galen's Peri kraseon*, ed. Richard J. Durling (Berlin and New York: De Gruyter, 1976), 76.

44. "Generatio enim utique hiis non qualis herbis, sed qualis arboribus secundum primam rationem a nature operatis, non ex necessitate sequentibus complexiones." Galen, *De complexionibus* 2.5.

45. Lucretius, *De rerum naturae* 5.788; Corniolo della Cornia, *La divina villa* 7.6. It is not certain that Lucretius's poem was as popular in Florence as Stephen Greenblatt claims in *The Swerve: How the Renaissance Began* (London: Bodley Head, 2011), 219–41. Yet the text was known to Leonardo. Marco Beretta, "Leonardo and Lucretius," *Rinascimento* 49 (2009): 341–72; Alison Brown, "Natura idest? Leonardo, Lucretius, and Their Views of Nature," in *Leonardo da Vinci on Nature: Knowledge and Representation*, ed. Fabio Frosini and Alessandro Nova (Venice: Marsilio, 2013), 153–79.

46. Girolamo Manfredi, *Liber de homine / Libro del perché* (Bologna: 1474), f. 31v.

47. Albertus Magnus, *Questions Concerning Aristotle's 'On Animals,'* ed. Irven M. Resnick and Kenneth F. Kitchell Jr. (Washington: Catholic University of America Press, 2008), 312. Albert read Thomas Scot's translation of Aristotle's treatise.
48. Leon Battista Alberti, *L'architettura (De re aedificatoria)*, ed. Giovanni Orlandi, 2 vols. (Milan: Il Polifilo, 1966), vol. 1, p. 113.
49. According to Isidore of Seville's etymological manual, plants took their names from human hair and not the other way round. Isidore of Seville, *Etymologies* 17.10.4: "The cyme [*cyma*] is so called as if the word were *coma* ["hair"], for this term means the crown of vegetable plants or trees, in which is located the natural power to make plant life." The translation is by Stephen A. Barney and others (Cambridge, UK: Cambridge University Press, 2006).
50. Angelo Poliziano, *Stanze cominciate per la giostra di Giuliano de' Medici*, ed. Vincenzo Pernicone (Turin: Loescher-Chiantore, 1954), 34: "né mai le chiome del giardino eterno / tenera la brina o fresca neve imbianca."
51. Ovid, *Metamorphoses* 10.98.
52. Ricciardo di Nanni represented Daphne's metamorphosis twice, on which see Annarosa Garzelli, *Miniatura fiorentina del Rinascimento, 1440–1525: Un primo censimento*, 2 vols. (Florence: La Nuova Italia, 1985), vol. 1, 130, and illustration 188. On nails and hair as vegetative, see Augustine of Hippo, *De Civitate Dei* 7.23: "Varro in eodem de diis selectis libro tres [that is, his *Divine Antiquities*] esse adfirmat animae gradus in omni universaque natura: unum, quod omnes parte corporis, quae vivunt, transit et non habet sensum, sed tantum ad vivendum valetudinem; hanc vim in nostro corpore permanare dicit in ossa, ungues, capillos; sicut in mundo arbores sine sensu aluntur et crescunt et modo quodam suo vivunt." The idea became a tenet of Platonism, according to which the cosmos is divided between vegetative souls (trees, nails, bones, hair), sensitive souls, and intellectual souls. Claudio Moreschini, *Apuleio e il platonismo* (Florence: L. S. Olschki, 1978), 6.
53. Pliny, *Natural History* 15.39.
54. Generally, on this painting, see David A. Brown, *Leonardo da Vinci: Origins of a Genius* (New Haven, CT, and London: Yale University Press, 1998), 101–22.
55. Mary D. Garrard, "Who Was Ginevra de' Benci? Leonardo's Portrait and Its Sitter Recontextualized," *Artibus et historiae* 27, 53 (2006): 23–56, esp. 29. Ginevra's chastity was praised in poems by Bernardo Bembo, Cristo-

foro Landino, and Alessandro Braccesi, on which see *Virtue and Beauty: Leonardo's Ginevra de' Benci and Renaissance Portraits of Women*, ed. David A. Brown (Washington: National Gallery of Art, 2001), 201n14.

56. *De materia medica* 1.88: "peruncto ante coitum genitali, abortiuum fieri constat." For the reception of *De materia medica* in the fifteenth century, see John M. Riddle, "Dioscorides," in *Catalogus Translationum et Commentariorum IV*, ed. Ferdinand Edward Cranz and Paul O. Kristeller (Washington: Catholic University of America Press, 1980), 1–143. On the use of juniper (*juniperus communis*) as a contraceptive, see Carlo Flamigni, *Il controllo della fertilità: Storia, problemi e metodi dall'antico Egitto a oggi* (Turin: UTET, 2006), 118 and 294. Juniper was often mixed up with cedar, as in Pliny, *Natural History* 24.36.

57. Galen, *De simplicium medicamentorum temperamentis ac facultatibus* 6.2.15, in Galen, *Opera omnia*, ed. Carl G. Kühn, 22 vols. (Leipzig, Germany: Karl Knobloch, 1821–33), vol. 11, 854. On Galen and abortion, see John M. Riddle, "Oral Contraceptives and Early-Term Abortifacients during Classical Antiquity and the Middle Ages," *Past & Present* 132 (1991): 3–32, esp. 13–14.

58. Gabriella Zarri, "Introduzione," in *Velo e* velatio: *Significato e rappresentazione nella cultura figurativa dei secoli XV–XVII*, ed. Zarri (Rome: Edizioni di storia e letteratura, 2014), viii–ix; Adrian W. B. Randolph, *Engaging Symbols: Gender, Politics, and Public Art in Fifteenth-Century Florence* (New Haven, CT: Yale University Press, 2002), 108–37.

59. Elizabeth Cropper, "The Beauty of Woman: Problems in the Rhetoric of Renaissance Portraiture," in *Rewriting the Renaissance: The Discourses of Sexual Difference in Early Modern Europe*, ed. Margaret W. Ferguson, Maureen Quilligan, and Nancy J. Vickers (Chicago: University of Chicago Press, 1986), 187–89. On the associations of Laura and laurel, see Robert M. Durling, "Petrarch's 'Giovene donna Sotto un Verde Lauro,'" *MLN* 86, no. 1 (1971): 1–20.

60. Petrarch, *Nel dolce tempo della prima etate*, 42–44. On this canzone (*RVF* 23), Leonard Barkan, "Diana and Actaeon: The Myth as Synthesis," *English Literary Renaissance* 10, no. 3 (1980): 317–59, esp. 335–38; Nicholas Mann, "From Laurel to Fig: Petrarch and the Structures of the Self," *Proceedings of the British Academy* 105 (2000): 17–42.

61. Grifo illustrated what is a copy of the *editio princeps* of Petrarch's *Rime* (Venice: 1470) during his exile in Milan between 1491 and 1497, the year of his death. We know that Leonardo designed a costume that Grifo wore

at the wedding of the Duke of Milan, Lodovico il Moro, and Beatrice d'Este (the drawing is London: British Library, Arundel 263, f. 250r). Giordana Mariani Canova, "Antonio Grifo: Illustratore dell'incunabulo Queriniano G.V.15," in *Illustrazione libraria, filologia e esegesi petrarchesca tra Quattrocento e Cinquecento*, ed. Giuseppe Frasso, Ennio Sandal, and Giordana Mariani Canova (Padua, Italy: Antenore, 1990), 157–59; Joseph B. Trapp, "Petrarch's Laura: The Portraiture of an Imaginary Beloved," *Journal of the Warburg and Courtauld Institutes* 64 (2001): 55–192, esp. 82–85.

62. Sara Sturm-Maddox, *Petrarch's Laurels* (University Park: Pennsylvania State University Press, 1992), 6–7. On fifteenth-century representations of Daphne's metamorphosis generally, see Yves Giraud, *La fable de Daphne: Essai sur un type de métamorphose végétale dans la littérature et dans les arts jusqu'à a la fin du XVIIe siècle* (Geneva: Droz, 1968), 150–63.

63. Lorenzo de' Medici also imagined turning into laurel branches, out of which his loved one would make a garland. Lorenzo de' Medici, "Selve," in *Tutte le opere*, ed. Paolo Orvieto, 2 vols. (Rome: Salerno, 1992), vol. 1, 542–43.

64. Francesco da Barberino, *Reggimento e costumi di donna*, ed. Giuseppe E. Sansone (Turin: Loescher, 1957), 343: "E se ghirlanda porta lodo che sia pur una giuliva, e piccioletta, ché, como voi sapete, grossa cosa è tenuta portar fastella in luogo di ghirlande."

65. "Ut pompe Florentinorum tollantur in quas occasione ornamentorum et vestium lescive didicerunt incurrere, ob quas indecentes expensas temere subierunt, provisum et ordinatum est quod nulla mulier cuiuscumque condictionis vel dignitatis existat, ferat vel teneat in capite seu dorso aliquod ornamentum de perlis vel aliquam perlam nec coronam de auro vel argento vel etiam contrafactam nec aliquam ghirlandam vel rete de auro vel argento." *Statuti della Repubblica Fiorentina*, ed. Romolo Caggese, 2 vols. (Florence: Tipografia galileana and E. Ariani, 1910–21), vol. 1, 227. This norm, from the *Statuto del capitano del popolo* of 1322–25, was repeated in 1355 and 1409. See *Legge suntuaria fatta dal comune di Firenze l'anno 1355 e volgarizzata nel 1356 da ser Andrea Lancia*, ed. Pietro Fanfani (Florence: Società tipografica sulle Logge del grano, 1851), 10–11; *Statuti e legislazione a Firenze dal 1355 al 1415: Lo statuto cittadino del 1409*, ed. Lorenzo Tanzini (Florence: L. S. Olschki, 2004), 69–73.

66. The origin of the nickname is explained in Giorgio Vasari, *Le vite de' più eccellenti pittori scultori e architettori nelle redazioni del 1550 e 1568*, ed.

Rosanna Bettarini, 6 vols. (Florence: Sansoni and SPES, 1966–87), vol. 3, 475–76. On the creations by Tommaso Bigordi (Ghirlandaio's father), *Ghirlandaria: Un manoscritto di ricordi della famiglia Ghirlandaio*, ed. Lisa Venturini (Florence: L. S. Olschki, 2017), 199. Generally, on *ghirlandai*, see Carole Collier Frick, *Dressing Renaissance Florence: Families, Fortunes, and Fine Clothing* (Baltimore: Johns Hopkins University Press, 2002), 26–27; Frick, "Cappelli e copricapi nella Firenze nel Rinascimento: L'emergere dell'identità sociale attraverso l'abbigliamento," in *Moda e moderno: Dal Medioevo al Rinascimento*, ed. Eugenia Paulicelli (Rome: Meltemi, 2006), 127–28n26.

67. Angelo Poliziano speaks of the ways in which garlands protected faces from the sun in *Stanze* 5: "e 'l volto difendea dal solar raggio, con ghirlanda di pino o verde faggio." Boccaccio also speaks twice of the screening function of garlands. Giovanni Boccaccio, *Ninfale fiesolano*, ed. Pier Massimo Forni (Milan: Mursia, 1991), 55: "L'altra [ninfa] che stava in piè colse due frondi, e d'esse una ghirlanda si facea, poi sopra suoi capelli crespi e biondi la si ponea, perché'l sol l'offendea;" Boccaccio, *Comedia delle ninfe fiorentine*, 5.25, in *Tutte le opere*, ed. Vittore Branca, 10 vols. (Milan: Mondadori, 1964–98), vol. 2, 692: "le ghirlande della fronzuta quercia, ritenenti [. . .] l'accese luci di Febo."

68. Lorenzo de' Medici, "Innamoramento di Lorenzo (Corinto)," in *Tutte le opere*, vol. 2, 866. The making of a garland and the kiss that came with it culminate a day spent caressing, dancing, and tossing flower petals ("diversi fiori e sopra il viso tuo li farei piovere").

69. For me, the most precise accounts of garlands can be found in Luigi Pulci's *Morgante*. Pulci describes women making them (14.85; 19.9), explains them as social markers (28.138), and presents them as gifts worthy of kings (25.88). Among the harshest critics of garlands was Bernardino da Siena, who criticized widows and orphans for wearing them at mass. Bernardino da Siena, "Quadragesimale de christiana religione," in *Opera omnia*, ed. Pacifico M. Perantoni, 9 vols. (Florence: Quaracchi, 1950), vol. 2, 95: "Mirabile equidem videtur si mulier in morte sponsi vel patris ad missam pergeret caput florbis adornata."

70. On the visual richness of garlands, Giovanni Boccaccio, *Amorosa visione*, ed. Vittore Branca (Florence: Sansoni, 1944), 6: "di molte fronde, di vermiglie rose e di bianche e d'altri fiori adorna legata con rilucente oro." In Boccaccio's *Ninfale fiesolano* (ed. Forni, p. 162), one of the garlands is made to smell nice and to feel comfortable on the head ("e la seconda

cominciò a far, d'alquanti fior più belli, mescolando con essi alcuna fronda d'odoriferi e gentili albuscelli"). On garlands as evoking spring, see Dino Compagni, "Al novel tempo e gaio del pascore," in *Lirica antica italiana*, ed. Eugenia Levi (Florence: Bemporad and Seeber, 1908), 3.

71. On Botticelli's garlands in relation to Ovid's *Fasti* and Roman traditions, see Lew Andrews, "Botticelli's 'Primavera,' Angelo Poliziano, and Ovid's 'Fasti,'" *Artibus et historiae* 32, no. 63 (2011): 73–84, esp. 74–76; Rebekah Compton, "Botticelli's Garlands," *Source: Notes in the History of Art* 35, no. 4 (2016): 283–92.

72. A fifteenth-century description of the benefits of *ranno* can be found in Giovanni Dominici, *Il libro d'amore di carità*, ed. Antonio Ceruti (Bologna: Romagnoli-Dall'Acqua, 1889), 117–18: "Il capo si vuole sgrassare col ranno e sapone, e mondarlo dalle schianze [scab] col forte aceto e nera filigine, e liberarlo da' superchi capelli col tagliente rasoio." Outside of Florence, *ranno* was often called "lascivia" or "lexivia." See, for instance, *Trotula,* 168–71. Aldobrandino da Siena (*Del conservare i capelli*, 4) simply speaks of "filtered water," but his Florentine translator rendered it as "ranno."

73. Pier de' Crescenzi, *De agricoltura volgare* (Venice: 1519), f. 100r: "Se si porrà spessamente la cienere con la lasciva intorno al suo pedale, renderà questo arbore [pomegranate] fructuoso et allegro." I cite from a Venetian edition (hence the term "lascivia"; see note 72), but Pier de' Crescenzi's treatise, originally in Latin, was first printed in Florence in 1478. Concetta Bianca, "La diffusione manoscritta e a stampa degli *Scriptores rei rusticae* nel Quattrocento," *Schede umanistiche* 21, no. 1 (2007): 91–106, esp. 98–101. Bianca recalls that in 1469 the Florentine Benedetto Maffei bought Pier de' Crescenzi's book, known as *Liber ruralium commodorum*, for three ducats. Today, it is Vatican City: Biblioteca Apostolica Vaticana, Ms Ottob. Lat. 1569.

74. Maidenhair plays a crucial role in a story told in Francesco da Barberino, *Reggimento*, 234: "La reina di Francia avea maritata una sua figliuola al re d'Inghilterra, la quale avea pochi cavelli, e quelli tutto dì le cadeano; e per questo maritaggio si facea pace d'una gran guerra. Il re d'Inghilterra udendo questo difetto non la volea. La madre, ciò saputo, facea raccogliere del capelvenero e seccare e poi ardere, e faceva mattere la cenere in un drappo a bollire in la liscia [another term for *ranno*], per mantenere i capelli e moltipricare; con la qual liscia la facea lavare sicché non tocasse dove pelo non volea."

75. Pier de' Crescenzi, *De agricoltura volgare*, f. 132v.

76. Francesco da Barberino, *Reggimento*, 234–35: "E [the queen] faevale [that is, to her daughter] usare lo pettine dell'avorio risiegato largo, che tenea netta la testa sicché i pori stavano stretti e tenevano i cavelli."

77. "Verum ubi iam puro discrimine pectita tellus, deposito squalore nitens sua semina poscet." I am referring to the verses 94–95 of the carmen that follows book 10 of Columella's *De re rustica*. Columella's text had been known for most of the fifteenth century. It was first printed in Rome in 1471, but only one copy of that edition survives at Cambridge, UK. It was then reprinted as part of *Scriptores rei rusticae* (Venice: Nicolaus Jenson, 1472), which is the edition I checked. There, Columella's conclusive poem is identified as book 11; not 10, as in most modern editions.

78. Pier de' Crescenzi (*De agricoltura volgare*, ff. 25r-28v) recalls how farmers burnt dry bushes, branches, and leaves to fertilize the ground. He also recommends the use of pig dung. P. Nanni, "Agricolture a agricoltori nelle terre di Francesco di Marco Datini (XIV–XV secolo)," *Rivista di storia dell'agricoltura* 1, no. 2 (2010): 3–33, esp. 22. Pliny also speaks of ash and dung as hair anointments. Pliny, *Natural History* 29.34: "Alopecias replet fimi pecudum cinis cum oleo cyprio et melle, item ungularum muli vel mulae ex oleo myrteo, praeterea, ut Varro noster tradit, murinum fimum, quod item muscerdas appellat." The popular *Thesaurus Pauperum* (ch. 1) suggests burning the feces of pigeons or goats and using the ashes to make a hair-fortifying *ranno*.

79. Sandra Cavallo, "Health, Beauty and Hygiene," in *At Home in Renaissance Italy*, ed. Marta Ajmar-Wollheim and Flora Dennis (London: Victoria & Albert Museum, 2006): 176–77.

80. The passage reads: "The feathers grow upon birds and change every year; hair grows upon animals and changes every year, except a part such as the hair of the beard in lions and cats and creatures like these. The grass grows in the fields, the leaves upon the trees, and every year these are renewed in great part. So then we may say that the Earth has a spirit of growth, and that its flesh is the soil; its bonds are the successive strata of the rocks which form the mountains; its cartilage is the tufa stone; its blood the springs of its waters." Cited from William A. Emboden, "The Spirit of Growth," *Achademia Leonardi Vinci* 1 (1988), 70–75. The original is Codex Leicester, f. 34r. I'm grateful to Francesca Borgo for pointing me to this source.

81. Giovanni Paolo Lomazzo, *Trattato dell'arte della pittura, scoltura, et architettura* (Milan: Paolo Gottardo Pontio, 1585), f. 198: "per il che si adopera

l'asp[h]alto per dar il lucido à i capelli biondi, e castanei [. . .]. Le quali cose tutte soleva usar molto Leonardo." Leonardo noted a recipe for dying hair blond in 1490. It is part of the so-called "Foglio Tema" (Windsor RCIN 912283), on which see Carlo Pedretti, *Studi di natura dalla Biblioteca Reale nel Castello di Windsor* (Florence: Giunti Barbera, 1982), 35.

82. Antonella Astorri, "Appunti sull'esercizio dello Speziale a Firenze nel Quattrocento," *Archivio storico italiano* 147, no. 1 (1989): 31–62, esp. 33.
83. "Vita quidem mundi omnibus infinita, propagatur evide[nter] in herbas et arbores, quasi pilos sui corporis atque capillos." Marsilio Ficino, *De vita* 1.8. The English translation is from Carol V. Kaske and John R. Clark, *Three Books on Life* (Binghamton, NY: Medieval & Renaissance Texts & Studies, 1989).

CHAPTER NINE

1. *De vita sana* was published in 1489 after almost a decade of drafts. Alessandra Tarabochia Canavero, "Il 'De triplici vita' di Marsilio Ficino: Una strana vicenda ermeneutica," *Rivista di filosofia neo-scolastica* 69 (1977): 697–717.
2. Andrea Corsini, "Il 'De vita' di Marsilio Ficino," *Rivista di storia critica delle scienze mediche e naturali* 19 (1919): 5.
3. On medieval regulations, see Janet E. Burton, *The Cistercians in the Middle Ages* (Woodbridge, UK: Boydell Press, 2011), 114–16.
4. As mentioned in the previous chapter, Ficino was the son of a doctor, whose influence he openly acknowledges. Marsilio Ficino, *Three Books on Life*, ed. and tr. Carol V. Kaske and John R. Clark (Binghamton, NY: Medieval & Renaissance Texts & Studies, 1989), 104.
5. "Deinde remittes parumper mentis intentionem atque interim eburneo pectine diligenter et moderate pectes caput a fronte cervicem versus quadragies pectine ducto; tum cervicem panno asperirori perfrica." Ficino, *Three Books on Life*, 130.
6. *Regimen sanitatis* 2, in Paola Capone, *L'arte del vivere sano: Il "Regimen sanitatis salernitatum" e l'età moderna* (Milan: Guerini e associati, 2005), 130–31. On the popularity of this treatise, see pp. 215–27.
7. Georges Vigarello, *Concepts of Cleanliness: Changing Attitudes in France since the Middle Ages* (Cambridge, UK: Cambridge University Press, 1988), 17.
8. Ficino, *Three Books on Life*, 132 and 158–60.
9. On ivory as a cold material, Peter Damian, *Opera omnia*, ed. Constanti-

nus Cajetanus, Patrologia Latina 144, 2 vols. (Paris: Migne, 1853), vol. 1, 737: "Ebur enim et mirabilis candore relucet, et multa paeeminet fortitudine, frigiorisque naturae sortitur auspicium." The point is repeated in Albertus Magnus, *Enarrationes in Matthaeum* 28.7–8: "ebur candens et infrigidans, refrigerium est."

10. "And I think that life itself is represented by the number forty, because the number ten, in which is the perfection of our happiness [. . .], is made known in time to the world, because the world is divided by four winds, made up of four elements, and goes through the changes of four seasons annually." Augustine of Hippo, *Letters*, tr. Wilfrid Parsons, 3 vols. (Washington: Catholic University of America Press, 1951), vol. 1, 284.

11. Marsilio Ficino, *Consilio contro la pestilentia* 5, in Teodoro Katinis, *Medicina e filosofia in Marsilio Ficino: Il "Consilio contro la pestilentia"* (Rome: Edizioni di storia e letteratura, 2007), p. 168: "pettinati bene et expurga ogni superfluità et tieni tutta la persona bene lavata."

12. Ficino, *Consilio contro la pestilentia* 5: "Nel tempo della peste, ti debbi astenere dalle cose che infiammano e aprono molto, perché fanno presto pigliare il veleno." Generally, see Vivian Nutton, "The Seeds of Disease: An Explanation of Contagion and Infection from the Greeks to the Renaissance," *Medical History* 27 (1983): 1–37. There was no agreement on how the plague spread: while some believed in the existence of toxic air particles, others spoke of plague-bearing seeds that entered the ground and the skin. Combing was presented as a preventive measure against plague also in the *Regimen sanitatis* 2.

13. Giulia Calvi, *Histories of a Plague Year: The Social and the Imaginary in Baroque Florence* (Berkeley: University of California Press, 1989), 66–67. Anger was often associated with women. Bernardino da Siena, *Le prediche volgari dette nella piazza del campo l'anno 1427*, ed. Luciano Bianchi, 3 vols. (Siena, Italy: Tipografia arciv. San Bernardino, 1880–88), vol. 1, 373: "Io ci vedo di magre, che mi pare che ci sia alcuna che talvolta fa a' capegli!" ("I see [in the audience] some women who are so dried up [heated by anger] that I believe they could tear their girlfriends' hair!")

14. Michel Foucault, *The Hermeneutics of the Subject: Lectures at the Collège de France, 1981–1982* (New York: Palgrave Macmillan, 2005), 56–57; Giorgio Agamben, *The Use of Bodies* (Stanford, CA: Stanford University Press, 2015), 31–37.

15. Jen Cruse, *The Comb: Its History and Development* (London: Robert Hale, 2007), 62.

16. As we saw in chapter 7, the comparison of hair to pastries comes from Bernardino da Siena, *Prediche volgari sul campo di Siena 1427*, ed. Carlo DelCorno, 2 vols. (Milan: Rusconi, 1989), vol. 2, 1093.
17. "Sit etiam virgo simplex et verecunda . . . oblivi facit virgo ornamenti sui: debet est verecunda ornari ut omnia ornate et ordinate siant in ea." Gilbert of Tournai, *Sermones ad omnes status* (Lyon: 1511), f. 147v. The first edition of this manual for preachers was published in Lyon in 1475. The text, part of the second book of Gilbert's *Rudimentum doctrinae,* had been a staple of Franciscan education since the thirteenth century, when it was composed. A copy was kept in the "armarium" of Florence's Santa Croce library (the manuscript is now Florence: Biblioteca Medicea Laurenziana, Plut. 36. dex.6). Charles T. Davis, "The Early Collection of Books of S. Croce in Florence," *Proceedings of the American Philosophical Society* 107, no. 5 (1963): 399–414, esp. 407n41.
18. "Quale stolto dubiterà che la donna la quale non si diletti d'essere veduta netta e pulita non ne' panni solo e membra, ma in ogni atto ancora e parole, costei non sarà da riputarla ben costumata?" Leon Battista Alberti, *I libri della famiglia*, ed. Ruggiero Romano (Turin: Einaudi, 1972), 272–73. On self-constraint as civilization, Norbert Elias, *Power & Civility* (New York: Pantheon, 1982), 229–47.
19. "Piacerammi vedervi con i capegli ne' suoi luoghi assettati: nulla tinte in parte alcuna, ma ben monde e pulite; e forse alcuna volta qualche negligenza nel comporre de' capegli o simile cosa rende le bellezze vostre più chiare et più aperte." Carlo Alberti, "Amiria," in *Tutti gli scritti,* ed. Alberto Martelli (Florence: Polistampa, 2015), 177. Carlo Alberti's casual approach clashes with that of his brother Leon Battista, who was critical of those who did not maintain their buildings impeccably. Pierluigi Panza, *Leon Battista Alberti: Filosofia e teoria dell'arte* (Milan: Guerini, 1994), 213.
20. Apuleius, *Metamorphoses* 2.8.
21. Florentines called those veils "frenelli" because they restrained like horse bits (*freni*, in Italian). Rosita Levi Pisetzky, *Storia del costume in Italia*, 5 vols. (Milan: Istituto editoriale italiano, 1964–75), vol. 2, 127–28. The term is documented since c. 1320—that is, since Francesco da Barberino, *Reggimento e costumi di donna*, ed. Giuseppe E. Sansone (Turin: Loescher, 1957), 234.
22. Francesco da Barberino, *Reggimento*, 92: "Domandato perché dunque pettinava ella i suoi capelli: perch'ella volea mostrare che femina era, di cui è cosa di natura d'acconciarsi."

23. Carole Collier Frick, *Dressing Renaissance Florence: Families, Fortunes, and Fine Clothing* (Baltimore: Johns Hopkins University Press, 2002), 304–5.
24. Michele Bacci, *The Many Faces of Christ: Portraying the Holy in the East and West, 300 to 1300* (London: Reaktion, 2014), 169–218. For Tuscans, Christ's likeness could be seen in Lucca's *Volto santo*, a monumental crucifix that was thought to be an authentic reproduction of Christ on the cross: Christ has a beard and his hair is parted. The accuracy of the sculpture was confirmed by the so-called "Letter of Publius Lentulus," a description of Christ's appearance that was included in the famous *Meditations on Christ's Life*, published in 1483. Cora E. Lutz, "The Letter of Lentulus Describing Christ," *Yale University Library Gazette* 50, no. 2 (1975): 91–97.
25. Joseph Ziegler, "Physiognomy, Science, and Proto-Racism 1200–1500," in *The Origins of Racism in the West*, ed. Miriam Eliav-Feldon, Benjamin Isaac, and Joseph Ziegler (Cambridge, UK: Cambridge University Press, 2009), 183–84. Ziegler quotes from Michele Savonarola's unpublished *Speculum physonomie*, which is Paris: Bibliothèque Nationale de France, Lat. 7357, f. 54r-b.
26. Michele Bacci, "L'invenzione della memoria del volto di Cristo: Osservazioni sulle interazioni fra iconografia e letteratura prosopografica primae dopo l'iconoclastia," in *Medioevo: Immagine e memoria*, ed. Arturo C. Quintavalle (Milan: Electa, 2009), 93–108.
27. The chronicler Giovanni Villani criticizes Florentine knights for their vanity, as exemplified by their care for hair and depilation. Giovanni Villani, *Cronica*, ed. Giovanni Aquilecchia (Turin: Einaudi, 1979), 496: "si lisciavano, come donne, e pettinavansi le zazzere." Boccaccio gives a *zazzera* to Biondello, the pedantic prankster of his *Decameron* 9.8, described as "piccoletto della persona, leggiadro molto e più pulito che una mosca [. . .] con una zazzerina bionda e per punto senza un capel torto avervi." See also Matteo Palmieri, *Vita civile*, ed. Gino Belloni (Florence: Sansoni 1983), 36: "Fuggasi sempre ogni femminile ornamento, però che none le pettinate zazzere, none i crespi capelli, né l'artificiali dirizature si richiegono a chi è nato atto a virtù." On the money spent to straighten hair, Lorenzo de' Medici, "Nencia da Barberino," in *Tutte le opere*, ed. Paolo Orvieto, 2 vols. (Rome: Salerno, 1992), vol. 2, 698 ("et non mi fo far sazzera col ferro, / perch'al barbier non do più d'un soldino"). Clerics were prohibited from sporting a *zazzera*, as discussed in note 93 of chapter 5.

28. In his treatise on chess, published in Florence in 1493, Jacopo da Cessole recalls a story of how a king was afraid of letting his daughters shave him with scissors (in case they killed him), and asked to be shaved with hot walnut shells and acorns. Jacopo da Cessole, *Volgarizzamento del libro de' costumi e degli offizii de' nobili sopra il giuoco degli scacchi* (Milan: 1829), 74.
29. The idea that any practice of control is a form of governmentality comes from Michel Foucault, "Governmentality," in The Foucault Effect: Studies in Governmentality, ed. Graham Burchell, Colin Gordon, and Peter Miller. (Chicago: University of Chicago Press, 1991), 87–104.
30. Francesco da Barberino, Reggimento, 106: "Che quando [the wife] il fa lavar suo testa, e altre alcune simile bisogne, faccia, se può, ch'apresso gli sia: divisi e dica quel che mestier vede."
31. Sandra Cavallo, "Health, Beauty and Hygiene," in *At Home in Renaissance Italy*, ed. Marta Ajmar-Wollheim and Flora Dennis (London: Victoria & Albert Museum, 2006): 178.
32. Romana Guarnieri, "Pinzochere," in *Dizionario degli istituti di perfezione*, ed. Guerrino Pelliccia and Giancarlo Rocca, 10 vols. (Milan: Paoline, 1962–2003), vol. 7, 1721–49. The services of *pinzochere* are listed in a carnival song, "Canzone delle pinzochere andate a Roma," in *Trionfi e canti carnascialeschi toscani del Rinascimento*, ed. Riccardo Bruscagli, 2 vols. (Rome: Salerno, 1986), vol. 2, 432–34, esp. vv. 50–67.
33. "Puossi male una acconciare / da sé, ch'esser voglio due: stia giú l'una e lasci fare / bella a noi le trecce sue." *Trionfi e canti carnascialeschi*, 2.446. *Mazzocchiaie* also sewed pearls onto headgear and knitted nets, as discussed in Collier Frick, *Dressing Renaissance Florence*, 46–48.
34. "Ché non ben lava chi non è ben netta." Francesco da Barberino, *Reggimento*, 107.
35. Christiane Klapisch-Zuber, *Women, Family, and Ritual in Renaissance Italy* (Chicago: University of Chicago Press, 1985), 213–46.
36. On this typology of mirror portraits, see John Pope-Hennessy, *Catalogue of Italian Renaissance Sculpture in the Victoria and Albert Museum*, 3 vols. (London: Her Majesty's Stationery Office, 1964), vol. 1, 270–71.
37. The British Museum sheet is not the only two-sided drawing to reproduce this process. Another is Raphael's bust of young lady. Florence: Gallerie degli Uffizi, Gabinetto dei Disegni e delle Stampe 57E r-v.
38. "El nono comandamento sì è che ttu g'ingegni di mantenere la tua persona frescha, bella, adorna et netta, in ghiusa et modo che sia honesta, sança alchuno caro o disonesto o brutto adornamento. Imperciò che

quando il tuo marito ti vedesse disonestamente ornare oltre al suo piacere, leggiermente t'arebbe et potrebbe avere a sospecto; et tenendoti honestamente adorna, te n'amerà et terractene più chara." Anonymous, *Ammaestramenti matrimoniali*, in Rossella Mosti, "Come de' Dire la Madre alla Figliuola quando la manda a marito," in *Briciole di discorsi amorosi*, ed. Marco and Paolo Castellano (Pisa, Italy: Campano, 2018), 185.

39. "Virgo [. . .] non incessu: non gestu: non vultu non affatu: non habitu arguenda. [. . .] Quid de crinibus qui dati sunt tibi in signum erubescentie et pudoris; non est furis de patibulo vel signo suspendii superbire debes caput tuum secundum apostolum [that is, Saint Paul in 1 Corinthians 11:7] operire." Gilbert of Tournai, *Sermones*, f. 147v. See also Carla Casagrande, *Prediche alla donne del secolo XIII* (Milan: Bompiani, 1978), 83–84.

40. Da Barberino, *Reggimento*, 235: "non mi sarà cotanto faticoso intender ciò che Temperanza dice degli ornamenti ch'alle donne insegna."

41. "Una donna fiorentina avea una sua figliuola, che molto volentieri portava il cappuccio, e sforzvasi molto di avere belli capelli, ma ancora vi mettea degli altrui [that is, hair extensions]. Disse la madre, per divezzarla di queste due cose: Il portare il capo coverto annera i capelli; e'l gran peso delle trecce rompe e fa cadere i capelli; il tenerli allo scoverto, e spezialmente al lume della luna, fa biondi i capelli. E perché questa sua figliuola tal fiata si lavava troppo rado, e tal fiata troppo spesso, dissele: Lo troppo rado lavare a chi ha grassa la testa fa cadere i capelli; e'l troppo spesso a chi l'à magra fa rompere i capelli." Da Barberino, *Reggimento*, 234.

42. Bonaventura da Bagnoregio, *Commentaria in quatuor libros sententiarum* 4.16, art. 3, q. 1, in *Opera omnia*, 10 vols. (Florence: Quaracchi, 1882–1902), vol. 4, 409: "Primo ergo quaeritur utrum veniale peccatum possit fieri mortale. Et quod sic per complacentiam specialiter [. . .] Item placitum est quietata vountas; sed quiescens in creatura fruitur illa, et ita peccat mortaliter: ergo veniale fit per complacentiam mortale."

43. "Virtue is not in the hair, but in the heart." *The Florentine Fior di Virtù of 1491*, tr. Nicholas Fersin (Philadelphia: E. Stern, 1953), 89. This example is featured in chapter 33, about temperance, which the manual defines as "a firm and sure mastery over the covetousness of one's soul." Ibid. p. 86. On the manual's audience, see Francesco Botana, *Learning through Images in the Italian Renaissance: Illustrated Manuscripts and Education in Quattrocento Florence* (Cambridge, UK: Cambridge University Press, 2020), 5–6. Leonardo da Vinci read the *Fior*

di virtù. Gerolamo Calvi, "Il manoscritto H di Leonardo da Vinci e il 'Fiore di virtù' e l' 'Acerba' di Cecco d'Ascoli," *Archivio storico lombardo* 25 (1898): 73–116, esp. 77–86.

44. The passage is worth quoting in full: "Et nota che in pulirsi o acconciarsi o vero lisciarsi in quactro modi puo essere peccato mortale. El primo si e quando sacconcia overo liscia per provocare altri a disonestade o inamoramento disonesto o acto carnale fuori de matrimonio. El secundo modo quando fa per superbia o vanagloria la quale sia peccato mortale come e dichiarato quivi el suo fine ponendo. El terzo sie quando fa questo con tanta vanita posto che non intenda di inducere altri a disonesta o a luxuria che se credessi o sapessi del certo che per suo lisciare o pulirsi o per altri suoi hornamenti superflui alcuni ne pigliassi scandalo cioe ruina di peccato mortale nondimeno elle vuole pur fallo lisciare o vano hornare questo e peccato mortale. El quarto si e in istato religioso o quasi religioso come e monache o pizochere. In questo le piu volte & quasi sempre e peccato mortale pero che e in tucto contrario allo stato loro. Ne gli altri casi quando bene non fussi peccato mortale rade volte e pero che non sia grande e grosso veniale." Antoninus Florentinus, *Omnis mortalium cura* (Milan: C. Valdarfer, 1470), f. 26v. Pierozzi may state that the emotions (which he calls "modi") are four; the last item on his list is not one of them, but a special warning for religious people.

45. Francesco da Barberino, *Reggimento*, 92: "Perché dunque pettinava ella i suoi capelli? Perch'ella volea mostrare, che femina era, di cui è cosa di natura è d'acconciarsi. [. . .] Donna addornata: cerbio alla fontana." Catherine Harding, "Speaking in Pictures: Reading, Memory and Interpretation in Francesco da Barberino's Advice to Women in his Reggimento e costumi di donna," *Revue d'art canadienne / Canadian Art Review* 36, no. 1 (2011): 29–40, esp. 31.

46. "Quemadmodum desiderat cervus ad fontes aquarum, ita desiderat anima mea ad te, Deus," Psalm 42. On its interpretations, see Germana Strola, "I Sal. 42–43 nella storia dell'esegesi," *Gregorianum* 82 no. 4 (2001): 637–88, esp. 666–74.

47. "Cervio [. . .] tira a ssé [. . .] grandi serpenti e mangiali, e lo loro veneno bolle molto in del suo corpo. E allora viene con grande volontà a la fonte dell'acqua ed [ri]empiesene molto di quella acqua lo suo ventre, e cusì vince lo veneno effassi giovano e gitta le corna. Cusì dovemo fare noi quando è i[n] noi luxuria [. . .] sì dovemo correre ala fonte viva, cioè a Cristo." *Libro della natura degli animali: Bestiario Toscano del secolo XIII*,

ed. Davide Checchi (Florence: SISMEL, 2020), 298–99. This bestiary is known through fifteen manuscripts, eight of which are in Florence.

48. Michele Tomasi, "L'età gotica," in *Collezioni del Museo Civico d'Arte Antica di Torino: Avori medievali*, ed. Simonetta Castronovo, Fabrizio Crivello, and Michele Tomasi (Savigliano, Italy: L'artistica editrice, 2016), 118–21.

49. Both options are considered in Michele Tomasi, "Note su due avori gotici del Museo Civico d'Arte Antica," *Palazzo Madama: Studi e notizie* 3, no. 2 (2012–13): 16–27, esp. 21.

50. Florentines also returned to the use of combs routinely and for long periods of time, rediscovering the images carved on them in ever new lights. On the duration of combing, see Giovanni Dominici, *Regola del governo di cura familiare*, ed. Donato Salvi (Florence: Garinei, 1860), 149–50: "Quanto tempo si perde in pettinargli spesso, tener biondi i capelli se son femine, e forse ancora fargli ricciuti!"

51. Luigi Mallé, *Smalti, avori del Museo d'Arte Antica* (Turin: Impronta, 1969), 316. The giving of an ivory comb as a gift is dramatized in Boccaccio's story of Calandrino and Niccolosa (*Decameron* 9.5). In particular, see Giovanni Boccaccio, *Decameron*, ed. Vittore Branca, 2 vols. (Florence: Le Monnier, 1960), vol. 2, 481.

52. Diane Wolfthal, "The Sexuality of the Medieval Comb," in *Thresholds of Medieval Visual Culture: Liminal Spaces*, ed. Elina Gertsman and Jill Stevenson (Woodbridge, UK: Boydell Press, 2012), 176–94. On ivory objects in romances, see Michele Tomasi, "'Les fais des preudommes ausi com s'il fussent present': Gli avori cavallereschi tra romanzi e immagini," in *Le Stanze di Artù: Gli affreschi di Frugarolo e l'immaginario cavalleresco nell'autunno del Medioevo*, ed. Enrico Castelnuovo (Milan: Electa, 1999), 128–37.

53. On combs as invitations to moderation, Julia Saviello, "Instrumente Der Ordnung-Objekte der Verführung: Elfenbeinkämme als Bildträger im 14. und 15. Jahrhundert," in *Werkzeuge und Instrumente*, ed. Philippe Cordez and Matthias Kruger (Berlin: De Gruyter, 2012), 49–65.

54. Cristoforo Landino defines Paris as "libidinous" in *Comento sopra la Comedia*, ed. Paolo Procaccioli, 4 vols. (Rome: Salerno, 2001), vol. 1, 298. A comb depicting the judgment of Paris is Paris: Louvre, OA 143. Paul Williamson and Glyn Davies, *Medieval Ivory Carvings 1200–1550* (London: V&A, 2014), n218.

55. The story of Bathsheba is represented on an ivory comb in Limerick's Hunt Museum (inv. 150). Like most combs, this one was carved in France,

and it is a French text that offers an interpretation. The *Livre du Chevalier de la Tour Landry pour l'enseignement de ses filles*, started by Geoffroy IV de la Tour Landry in 1371, describes Bathsheba as thoughtless, and warns readers "that every woman ought religiously to conceal herself when dressing and washing. And neither out of vanity, nor yet to attract attention show either her hair, or her neck, or her breast, or any part which ought to be covered." Geoffrey de la Tour Landry, *The Book of the Knight of the Tower*, tr. A. Vance (Dublin: 1868), 67. On this didactic text, see Anne-Marie De Gendt, *L'Art d'éduquer les nobles damoiselles: Le Livre du Chevalier de la Tour Landry* (Paris: Honoré Champion, 2003), 9–36. On the circulation of Bathsheba's iconography outside religious texts, see Clare L. Costley, "David, Bathsheba, and the Penitential Psalms," *Renaissance Quarterly* 57, no. 4 (2004): 1235–77, esp. 1246–53. On combs representing Bathsheba, see Saviello, "Instrumente der Ordnung," 54–61.

56. Giovanni da Capistrano, *Trattato degli ornamenti, specie delle donne*, ed. Aniceto Chiappini (Siena, Italy: Cantagalli, 1956), 132–33: "Le donne quindi si dovrebbero astenere assolutamente dall'abbigliamento o almeno usarne con molta parsimonia e timore, affinché nascendo scandalo per loro colpa non si abbia a ripetere: Guai a loro! Devono pure per quanto possono guadarsi da ogni aspetto degli uomini, e assicurarsi che non siano spiate da qualche finestra, onde non abbia a ripetersi di loro il caso di Bersabea."
57. "L'ornamento è regolarmente proibito e solo può renderlo lecito una vera ad imminente necessità. [. . .] Ester pregava così (14.16): 'Signore, tu conosci la mia necessità, e che io abbomino il segno della gloria e della superbia, imposto sul mio capo.'" Giovanni da Capistrano, *Trattato degli ornamenti*, 138.
58. Margaret T. Gibson, *The Liverpool Ivories: Late Antique and Medieval Ivory and Bone Carving in Liverpool Museum and the Walker Art Gallery* (London: Her Majesty's Stationary Office, 1994), n43.
59. André Chastel, *Art et Humanisme à Florence au temps de Laurent le Magnifique: Etudes sur la Renaissance et l'Humanisme Platonicien* (Paris: Presses universitaires de France, 1959), 50–54.
60. Villani, *Cronica*, 974–75.
61. Ancient sources took hairstyle as an expression of mores. Anthony Corbeill, *Controlling Laughter: Political Humor in the Late Roman Republic* (Princeton, NJ: Princeton University Press, 1996), 151–68. On hairstyling as revelatory of weakness (*mollitia*), see Catharine Edwards, *The Politics of*

Immorality in Ancient Rome (Cambridge, UK: Cambridge University Press, 1993), 90–92.

62. Giovanni da Capistrano, *Trattato*, 146. It is a reference from Ecclesiastes 19:1.

63. Giovanni Boccaccio, *Corbaccio*, ed. Pier Giorgio Ricci (Turin: Einaudi, 1977), 51: "Oh, s'io ti dicessi di quante maniere ranni il suo auricome capo si lavava e di quante ceneri fatto, e alcuni più fresco e alcuno meno, tu ti maraviglieresti: e vie più, se io ti disegnassi quante e quali solennità si servavano nello andare alle stufe e come spesso: dalle quali io creda lei lavata dovere tornare, ed ella più unta ne venìa che non v'era ita. Erano sommo suo desiderio e ricreazione grandissima certe feminette, delle quali per la nostra città sono assai, che vanno facendo gli scorticatoi alle femmine e pelando le ciglia e le fronti e col vetro sottile radendo le gote e del collo assotigliando le buccia e certi peluzzi levandone; né era mai che due o tre con lei non se ne fossero a stretto consiglio trovate, come che altri trattati spesse volte tenessero, sì come quelle che, oltre a quella loro arte, sotto titolo della quale baldanzose l'altrui case visitano." Some passages return in Alberti, "Amiria," 177: "perché tutte così credo desideriate aver capegli biondissimi, in copia e lunghissimi, cosa trovai niuna a farli ben lustri quanto lissia fatta con cenere di vite o di cavoli."

64. Boccaccio, *Corbaccio* (ed. Ricci), 55: "Io molte volte m'accorsi, a qualunque giovane, o qualunque altro che punto d'aspetto avesse piacevole, che dinanzi alla casa passasse, o dov'ella fosse, non altrimenti il falcone tratto di cappello si rifà tutto e sopra se torna, che faceva ella, sommamente desiderosa d'esser guardata; e così si turbava in sé medesima se altro passato fosse che non l'avesse guatata, come se una grave ingiuria avesse ricevuta." The similes and turns in this passage play on famous literary sources, on which see Giovanni Boccaccio, *The Corbaccio*, tr. Anthony K. Cassell (Urbana: University of Illinois Press, 1975), 129.

65. It is the most detailed description of hairstyling I know. It is more detailed than the list of hair accessories in Luigi Pulci, *Frottole*, ed. G. Volpi (Florence: 1912), verses 134–66. It is even more detailed than the six-stage description of hairstyling by the Augustinian friar Gottschalk Hollen (d. 1481), on which see Serena Franzon, "I gioielli da capo nelle raffigurazioni quattrocentesche della Vergine Maria," *OADI: Rivista dell'osservatorio per le arti decorative in Italia* 3 (2011): 43–60, esp. 43–44.

66. Boccaccio, *Corbaccio* (ed. Ricci), 52: "Era da ridere l'averla veduta, quando s'acconciava la testa, con quanta arte, con quanta diligenza, con quanta

cautela ciò si facesse: in quello per certo pendevano le leggi e' profeti." The translation is by Anthony Cassell in Boccaccio, *The Corbaccio*, 43. Some readers did take the book ironically. One of them was the Florentine book collector Francesco di Matteo Castellani, a friend of Luigi Pulci and Antonino Pierozzi. Francesco di Matteo Castellani, *Ricordanze*, ed. Giovanni Ciappelli, 2 vols. (Florence: L. S. Olschki, 1992–95), vol. 2, 52. Boccaccio's book was also taken literally, especially in the sixteenth century. Brian Richardson, "The *Corbaccio* and Boccaccio's Standing in Early Modern Europe," *Heliotropia* 14 (2017): 47–65.

67. Boccaccio, *Corbaccio* (ed. Ricci), 35: "Tutti i pensieri delle femmine, tutto lo studio, tutte l'opere a nunna altra cosa tirano, se non a rubare, a signoreggiare e ad ingannare gli uomini, perché leggermente credono sopra loro d'ogni cosa, che non sanno, simili trattati tenersi." The other references are at pp. 32 (beasts) and 33 (insatiability). The translation of the passage is by Anthony Cassell in Boccaccio, *The Corbaccio*, 28–29 (see note 64).

68. Boccaccio, *Corbaccio* (ed. Ricci), 94–95: "Ti guarda di non venire alle mani delle malvagie femine; e massimamente di colei che ogni demonio di malvagità trapassa." The translation, once again, is by Anthony Cassell, in Boccaccio, *The Corbaccio*, 77. On the invective as a genre, see Pier Giorgio Ricci, "La tradizione dell'invettiva tra il Medioevo e l'Umanesimo," *Lettere Italiane* 26, no. 4 (1974): 405–14. On Boccacio's *Corbaccio* as a caricature, see Gilbert Highet, *The Anatomy of Satire* (Princeton, NJ: Princeton University Press, 1962), 224–26; Robert Hollander, *Boccaccio's Last Fiction: "Il Corbaccio"* (Philadelphia: University of Pennsylvania Press, 1988), 42–43. Despite its misogyny, Boccaccio's *Corbaccio* was read by women. Elena Lombardi, *Imagining the Woman Reader in the Age of Dante* (Oxford, UK: Oxford University Press, 2018), 189.

69. Bernardino da Siena, *Le prediche volgari inedite: Firenze, 1424, 1425, Siena 1425*, ed. Dionisio Pacetti (Siena, Italy: Cantagalli, 1935), 354. Bernardino told the story also in Assisi and Siena. Dionisio Pacetti, "La predicazione di S. Bernardino da Siena a Perugia e ad Assisi nel 1425," *Collectanea Franciscana* 10 (1940): 5–28 and 161–88, esp. 24. On the old woman (*comare*) of Lucca, see Franco Mormando, *The Preacher's Demons: Bernardino of Siena and the Social Underworld of Renaissance Italy* (Chicago: University of Chicago Press, 1999), 77–80.

70. "Capudque suum atque capillos extra omnem ordinem posuit." In Ugolino Nicolini, "La stregoneria a Perugia e in Umbria nel Medioevo: Con i

testi di sette processi a Perugia e uno a Bologna," *Bollettino della Deputazione di storia patria per l'Umbria* 84 (1987): 5–87, esp. 53. On Matteuccia da Todi, tried in 1428 after Bernardino preached in her hometown, see Marina Montesano, *Classical Culture and Witchcraft in Medieval and Renaissance Italy* (London: Palgrave Macmillan, 2018), 174–79. On Filippa da Città della Pieve, tried in 1455, see Dinora Corsi, "Mulieres religiosae e mulieres maleficae nell'ultimo Medioevo," in *Non lasciar vivere la malefica: Le streghe nei trattati e nei processi*, ed. Corsi and Matteo Duni (Florence: Firenze University Press, 2008), 37–38.

71. *The Complete Odes and Satires of Horace*, tr. Sidney Alexander (Princeton, NJ: Princeton University Press, 1999), 231–32. On the reading of Horace in the Middle Ages, see Robert R. Bolgar, *The Classical Heritage and Its Beneficiaries* (Cambridge, UK: Cambridge University Press, 1954), 221. The first printed edition of Horace's *Satires* came out around 1470. Michael von Albrecht, *A History of Roman Literature*, 2 vols. (Leiden: Brill, 1997), vol. 1, 738. It was then published in Milan in 1474, in Caen in 1480, and in Padua in 1481. None of these editions was good enough for Cristoforo Landino, who in 1482 published a new edition in Florence, which was then reprinted in 1490 and 1492. Gaetano Curcio, *Q. Orazio Flacco studiato in Italia dal secolo XIII al XVIII* (Catania, Italy: F. Battiato, 1913), 75 and 85. More specifically on Landino, see Giuseppina M. S. Galbiati, "Per una teoria della satira tra Quattro e Cinquecento," *Italianistca* 16, no. 1 (1987): 9–37. On Horace's satires as source for witchcraft imagery, see Margaret A. Sullivan, "The Witches of Dürer and Hans Baldung Grien," *Renaissance Quarterly* 53, no. 2 (2000): 333–401, esp. 346–47.

72. On the recurrence of this classical trope in sermons and stories, see Marina Montesano, *Caccia alle streghe* (Rome: Salerno, 2012), 95–99.

73. "Ne era la mia cara donna, anzi tua, anzi del diavolo, contenta d'aver carne assai solamente, ma le volea lucenti, e chiara [. . .] la qual cosa cciocché avvenisse [. . .] a trovare sangue di diversi animali, ed erbe, e simili cose, s'intendeva se senza che la casa mia era piena di fornlli e di labicchi e di pentolini, e d'ampolle." Boccaccio, *Corbaccio* (ed. Ricci), 50.

74. "La quinta cosa si è che ti levi da studio de' libri disonesti, come il Corbaccio, et altri libri fatti da messer Giovan Boccacci, che [. . .] ne fe' parecchi che fusse il meglio se ne fusse taciuto. [. . .] E forse in vecchiezza se ne penté." Bernardino da Siena, *Le prediche volgari inedite*, 197–98.

75. On Bernardino, reader of Corbaccio, see Nicolò Maldina, "Retoriche e

modelli della predicazione medievale nel Corbaccio," *Studi sul Boccaccio* 39 (2011): 154–87, esp. 168–70. Maldina also shows that Boccaccio drew from the misogynistic sermons of his time.

76. *The Hammer of Witches: A Complete Translation of the Malleus Maleficarum*, tr. Christopher S. Mackay (Cambridge, UK: Cambridge University Press, 2009), 552.

77. The massacre took place in 1485 and is described in *The Hammer of Witches*, 554. On its chronicler, the inquisitor Lorenzo Soleri da Sant'Agata, see Michael Tavuzzi, *Renaissance Inquisitors: Dominican Inquisitors and Inquisitorial Districts in Northern Italy, 1474–1527* (Leiden, Netherlands: Brill, 2007), 168–70. Wormersbad was annexed to Napoleon's Cisalpine Republic in 1797. Horst Dippel, *Constitutional Documents of Italy and Malta 1787–1850* (Berlin: K. G. Saur, 2010), 209.

78. Guillaume d'Auvergne, *De universo creaturarum* 2.3.25, in id., *Opera omnia*, 2 vols. (Paris: 1674), vol. 1, col. 1072bE. See also *The Hammer of Witches*, tr. Mackay, 417, where the authors wonder if devils "seem to harass women and girls with beautiful hair more because such women pay more attention to caring for or grooming their hair or because it is their wish or habit to inflame men with their hair or because they vainly glory in it." On hair as devil's "weapons" (*arma*, in the plural, since the Latin *capilli* is also plural), Antoninus Florentinus, *Summa maior* (Lyon, France: 1506), 2.4.5.

79. "Mustrarà la misera ch'aia gran trecce avolte, la sua testa adornànnonse co' fossen trecce accolte? Oi de tomento fracedo oi so' pizzole molte cusì le gente stolte enganna con lor fraudate. Per temporale avèneise che l'om la veia esciolta, vide que fa la demona colla sua capovolta: le trecce altrui compónesse, non so con que girvolta; faràttece un'accolta che pago en capo nate." Iacopone da Todi, *Laude*, ed. Franco Mancini (Bari, Italy: Laterza, 1974), 126–29. The poems by the friar Jacopo da Todi, a contemporary of Dante, peaked in popularity in the fifteenth century. Angelo E. Mecca, "La tradizione manoscritta delle Laude di Iacopone da Todi," *Nuova rivista di letteratura italiana* 19, no. 2 (2016): 9–103, esp. 10. The first edition of Jacopo's poems dates from 1490. It was published in Florence by the priest Francesco Bonaccorsi. The poem I have just quoted, "O femene, guardate," is number 8 in that edition. The second song to which I refer is Boccaccio's popular "Canzone del nicchio," which he included at the end of the fifth day of the *Decameron*. Botticelli knew this song. See Stéphane Toussaint, "Botticelli, Politien et Boccace," in *Accademia* 21 (2019): 7–29, esp. 23–24.

80. Leon Battista Alberti, *L'architettura (De re aedificatoria)*, ed. Giovanni Orlandi, 2 vols. (Milan: Il Polifilo, 1966), vol. 2, p. 983.
81. Girolamo Savonarola, *Prediche sopra Ezechiel*, ed. Roberto Ridolfi, 2 vols. (Rome: Belardetti, 1955), vol. 1, 372 ("Poi germina il pelo, cioè le cogitazioni dei tuoi peccati").
82. "Come dire loro dell'orco essere in inferno peloso e cornuto per pigliare i tristi." The Florentine Matteo Palmieri advised women to tell their children this fable, to teach them how to live honorably. Matteo Palmieri, *Della vita civile* (Milan: 1825), 18.
83. Mina Gregori, Antonio Paolucci, and Cristina Acidini Luchinat, eds., *Maestri e botteghe: Pittura a Firenze alla fine del Quattrocento* (Milan: Silvana, 1992), 192–93. The image of the Virgin Mary protecting a child from the devil was popular in Tuscany. Kathleen G. Arthur, "The *Maria del Sochorso* Altarpiece: A Cretan Icon Transformed in Counter-Reformation Italy," *SCAC Review* 16 (2013): 151–70, 152; Everett P. Fahy, "Some Notes on the Stratonice Master," *Paragone* 197 (July 1966): 17–28, esp. 25.
84. See Girolamo Savonarola, *Predica dell'arte del bene morire* (Florence: Bartolomeo de' Libri, 1496), f. 12r.
85. "Cogita capillos tuos capistrum tuum esse dyavolicum quo traheris ad infernum." Gilbert of Tournai, *Sermones*, f. 147v.
86. Theologians had railed against the commerce in wigs at least since Jerome's so-called "Letter to Demetriade." Jerome, *Opera omnia*, Patrologia Latina 22 (Paris: Migne, 1845), 1113: "Polire faciem purpurisso, et cerussa ora depingere; ornare crinem, et alienis capillis turritum verticem struere." In fifteenth-century Florence this letter circulated in two translations. One, authored by the Dominican friar Zanobi, is in four manuscripts (Florence: Biblioteca Nazionale, Palat. 5, ff. 1r–28v; Palat. 19, ff. 75r–105r; Palat. 35, ff. 86r–121v; and Palat. 36, ff. 58r–76r). The second, by the notary Niccolò di Berto Martini, is in two exemplars (Florence: Biblioteca Medicea Laurenziana, Ms Ashb. 477, which was transcribed by Niccolò's son, Francesco, in 1466; and Florence: Biblioteca Riccardiana, Ms 1681).
87. Angelo Poliziano, *Lamia: Text, Translation, and Introductory Studies*, ed. and tr. Christopher S. Celenza (Leiden, Netherlands: Brill, 2010), 197: "Some of them [witches] even use teeth that are equally removable, which they store away at night like a toga, just like some of your little wives do with their wigs with the hair that hangs down in little curls."
88. "Et mirum est, quod cum mulieres sint multum timidae, quomodo non

expavescunt portare capillos mortuarum. Sed vanitas, vel potius diabolus assecurat eas, sed valde debent metuere ne sicut Absalon capillis suis, quos nutriebat ad magnam vanitatem, suspensus remansit ad arborem, unde et mortuus est, sic ipsae suspendantur in inferno." Antoninus Florentinus, *Summa maior* 2.6.6.

89. Sixtus IV, "Etsi dominici gregis" [1479], in Baptista de Salis, *Summa casuum conscientiae* (Nuremberg, Germany: Anton Koberger, 1488), 277v–b and 279v–b.

90. "O donna che porti tante cose non tue, se [. . .] i capelli che tu porti, tornassero a coloro che so' morti, di cui furono, e' crini che tu adopari." *Prediche volgari di S. Bernardino da Siena per la prima volta messe in luce* (Siena, Italy: Landi e Alessandri, 1853), 251–52. Bernardino devoted a sermon to fake hair. It is Bernardino da Siena, "Contra se fardantes et capillos adulterinos portantes, atque contra feminas caudatas," in *Quadragesimale de christiana religione, Opera omnia* (Florence: Quaracchi, 1950), vol. 2, 86–99.

91. *The Hammer of Witches,* 185–86. Cf. Matteo Duni, "Doubting Witchcraft: Theologians, Jurists, Inquisitors during the Fifteenth and Sixteenth Centuries," *Studies in Church History* 52 (2016): 203–31.

92. Guillaume d'Auvergne, *De universo creaturarum* 2.3.13. The passage draws from Daniel 14:36, which describes how an angel carried the prophet Habakkuk by his hair from Judea to Babylon. The episode was also recounted by Giordano da Pisa. *Racconti esemplari di predicatori del Due e Trecento,* ed. Giorgio Varanini and guido Baldassarri, 3 vols. (Rome: Salerno, 1993), vol. 2, 338–39.

93. *The Hammer of Witches*, 178.

94. On the demonic dimension of medieval love, see also Giorgio Agamben, *Stanzas: Word and Phantasm in Western Culture* (Minneapolis: University of Minnesota Press, 1993), 102–18.

95. Cardini and Montesano argue that the juridical and institutional apparatuses of witchcraft were built between the twelfth and fourteenth centuries. Franco Cardini and Marina Montesano, *La lunga storia dell' Inquisizione: Luci e ombre della "leggenda nera"* (Rome: Città nuova, 2005), 103–7. On the many treatises that preceded the *Malleus*, see Jeffrey B. Russell, *Witchcraft in the Middle Ages* (Ithaca, NY: Cornell University Press, 1972), 346–50. Among them, I highlight the one composed by the Florentine friar Francesco Micheli. Riccardo Pratesi, *Francesco Micheli del Padovano, di Firenze, teologo ed umanista francescano del secolo XV* (Florence: Quaracchi, 1955), 104–30.

96. Walter Stephens, *Demon Lovers: Witchcraft, Sex, and the Crisis of Belief* (Chicago: University of Chicago Press, 2002), 32–57. On the "late" sixteenth-century success of the *Malleus*, see Edward Peters, *The Magician, the Witch, and the Law* (Philadelphia: University of Pennsylvania Press, 1978), 173–74. And yet the *Malleus* went through eight editions before 1500.
97. Marina Warner, *Alone of All Her Sex: The Myth and the Cult of the Virgin Mary* (New York: Knopf, 1976), 58–61.
98. Sixtus IV, "Etsi dominici gregis," 278v–b and 279r–ab.
99. Romeo de Maio, *Donna e Rinascimento: L'inizio della Rivoluzione* (Naples: Edizioni scientifiche italiane, 1995), 37.
100. Liliana Poli, "Contributi sopra Bartolomeo de' Libri," *La Bibliofilía* 51, no. 1 (1949): 9–27, esp. 10. Bartolomeo signed his earliest publications as "clericus florentinus." This designation is not in *The Labyrinth of Love*, but can be found in a letter published by Bartolomeo in the same year (1487). On Bartolomeo's work organization, see Gustavo Bertoli, "Documenti su Bartolomeo de Libri e i suoi primi discendenti," *Rara volumina* 1–2 (2001), 19–56.
101. Henry C. Lea, *A History of Auricular Confession and Indulgences in the Latin Church*, 3 vols. (Philadelphia: Lea Brothers, 1896), vol. 1, 324–26. The bull *Etsi dominici gregis* dates December 30, 1479; see Battista Trovamala de Salis, *Summa casuum conscientiae* (Novi Ligure, Italy: Nicola Girardenghi, 1484).
102. On hair as social control, see Christopher R. Hallpike, "Social Hair," *Man* 4 (1969): 256–64.
103. "Munditiis capimur: non sint sine lege capilli." Ovid, *Ars Amatoria* 3.133.

CHAPTER TEN

1. On the reinstallation of Donatello's sculpture and relative documents, see Francesco Caglioti, *Donatello e i Medici: Storia del David e della Giuditta* (Florence: L. S. Olschki, 2000), 291–310.
2. Nicolai Rubinstein, *Il governo di Firenze sotto i Medici (1434–1494)*, ed. Giovanni Ciappelli (Florence: La Nuova Italia, 1999), 305–13; Ingeborg Walter, *Lorenzo il Magnifico e il suo tempo* (Rome: Donzelli, 2005), 214–27; Alison Brown, *Piero di Lorenzo de' Medici and the Crisis of Renaissance Italy* (Cambridge, UK: Cambridge University Press, 2020), 214–27.
3. Artur Rosenauer, *Donatello* (Milan: Electa, 1993), 246–49 and 286–87.

4. "EXEMPLUM SAL. PUB. CIVES. POS. MCCCCXCV."
5. On the previous inscription, see Horst W. Janson, *The Sculpture of Donatello*, 2 vols. (Princeton, NJ: Princeton University Press, 1979), vol. 2, 198 and 200. On the statue's dating, around 1457, see Antonio Natali, "Exemplum salutis publicae," in *Donatello e il restauro della Giuditta*, ed. Loretta Dolcini (Florence: Centro Di, 1988): 22–23.
6. The gesture is described in Judith 13:7.
7. Girolamo Manfredi, *Liber de homine / Libro del perché* (Bologna: 1474), f. 27v: "Perche gli uomini pilosi sono molto lussuriosi e quanto sono più piloti sono più lussuriosi: e similmente gli uccelli quanto hanno più penne tanto più sono inclinati al coito."
8. Proverbs 20:1: "Luxuriosa res est vinum." The passage was commented by Antonino Pierozzi in the sermon that he gave on the second Sunday of Lent in 1427. Florence: Biblioteca Nazionale Centrale, Ms Conventi Soppressi A.8.1750, 18r.
9. Isidore of Seville defines the luxurious person as one who strives after a life that is not necessary but is loaded with goods. Isidore of Seville, *Etymologies* 2.29.5, tr. Stephen A. Barney and others (Cambridge, UK: Cambridge University Press, 2006). On fur as a symbol of luxury, see Patricia Lurati, "'To dust the pelisse': The Erotic Side of Fur in Italian Renaissance Art," *Renaissance Studies* 31, no. 2 (2017): 240–60, esp. 254–57.
10. On Savonarola's sermons on the Apocalypse, which he gave from January 1491, and his rise to fame, see Donald Weinstein, *Savonarola: The Rise and Fall of a Renaissance Prophet* (New Haven, CT: Yale University Press, 2011), 75–78.
11. Volker Reinhardt, "Tyranny or Golden Age? Florence in Botticelli's Day," in *Botticelli: Likeness, Myth, Devotion*, ed. Andreas Schumacher and Cristina Acidini Luchinat (Ostfildern, Germany: Hatje Cantz, 2009): 126; Weinstein, *Savonarola*, 132–34.
12. Girolamo Savonarola, *Il quaresimale del 1491*, ed. Armando F. Verde and Elettra Giaconi, (Florence: SISMEL, 2001), 238: "Et discurre per omnes vanitates mulierum incipiendo a capillis."
13. "Firenze mia fa' penitenzia [. . .] El ti fu detto leva via e' capelli e le zazzere dei fanciulli e insieme tutte le vanità; et offensione delli occhi." Girolamo Savonarola, *Prediche sopra Ezechiel*, ed. Roberto Ridolfi, 2 vols. (Rome: Belardetti, 1955), vol. 2, 262.
14. "La viridità del giardino sono i vostri figlioli: mentre che eglino sono piccoli in virginità, l'erica comincia loro a mangiare il verde, quando voi con

vostre scarselline e con farli andare tanto ornati l'inducete alla lussuria. [. . .] E però ti ho detto piú volte [. . .] tagli loro i capelli." Girolamo Savonarola, *Prediche e scritti*, ed. Pasquale Villari (Florence: Sansoni, 1898), 165.

15. Savonarola, *Prediche sopra Ezechiele*, 2.277: "Figliuoli [. . .] non vogliate andare drieto alli comandamenti de' vostri cattivi padri. [. . .] Quando vi dicono: non andare alla predica, non ti tagliare e' capelli, ma voglionovi vedere lascivi, allora non gli ubbidire."
16. "Vi ricordo la riforma delle donne; che tutte le fanciulle vadino velate che non si vegghino e' capelli. Se voi non lo fate, sapete che è già uno anno che io vi dissi; una gran guerra farà porre giù le pompe e una gran morìa farà porre giù le vanità." Girolamo Savonarola, *Prediche sopra i salmi*, ed. Vincenzo Romano, 2 vols. (Rome: Belardetti, 1969–74), vol. 1, 156–57. This sermon was given on May 1, 1495.
17. Romeo de Maio, *Donna e Rinascimento: L'inizio della Rivoluzione* (Naples: Edizioni scientifiche italiane, 1995), 64. For de Maio, the moralists who came to Florence before Bernardino da Siena, such as Giovanni Dominici or Antonino Pierozzi, were moderate in their attacks against luxury.
18. "Non vi gloriate donne di bellezza. Voi siate brutte tutte quante." Savonarola, *Prediche sopra Ezechiele*, 1.376.
19. "Vanno vestite pulite e terse con veli o fazoleti tirati e crespai, non molto coperte dinanzi, cogli occhi levati senza vergogna." Savonarola, *Prediche e scritti*, 65.
20. "Verranno i barbieri che raderanno l'Italia insino alle ossa. Tu hai paura d'uno solo, ma credi a me che non sia solo, e saranno più di due che raderanno, e in tal modo che non lasceranno pelo nelle barbe." Savonarola, *Prediche e scritti*, 201–2.
21. "Decalvati Italia! Altro è tagliare e tosarsi, altro è decalvarsi. E però dice l'uno e l'altro, perché saranno alcuni che saranno decalcati e stirpati insano alle radici. E vi saranno sbarbati i capelli e sarete decalvati. [. . .] Voi non attendete se non a meretrici e a delizie. [. . .] La vita vostra è una vita da porci. [. . .] Dilata il calvizie tuo, Italia! L'aquila quando invecchia gli cascono le penne, così a te saranno cavate le penne, e saranti stracciati i capelli del capo." Savonarola, *Prediche e scritti*, 253.
22. "Tagliati li tuoi capelli e gettali via." Girolamo Savonarola, *Espositione sopra il Psalmo Miserere mei Deus con molte altre suo opere* (Venice: 1535), f. 91v. I cite from the Italian translation of *Expositio in Psalmum L (Miserere mei deus)*, one of the successful sermons Savonarola composed in jail

and released on May 8, 1498, less than three weeks before his execution. Francesco Santi, "La profezia nel tempo dei 'Martiri Novelli': Osservazioni sulla Expositio ac meditatio in psalmum 'Miserere' di Gerolamo Savonaola," in *Savonarola e la mistica*, ed. Gian Carlo Garfagnini (Florence: SISMEL, 1999), 51–62.

23. "O voi che avete le case vostre piene di vanità e di figure e cose disoneste e libri scellerati e el Morgante e altri versi contra la fede, portateli a me questi, per farne fuoco e uno sacrificio a Dio. E voi, madre che adornate le vostre figliuole con tante vanità e superfluità a capellature, portatele tutte qua a noi per mandarle al fuoco, acciò che, quando verrà l'ira di Dio, non trovi queste cose nelle case vostre." Girolamo Savonarola, *Prediche sopra Aggeo, con il Trattato circa il reggimento e il governo della città di Firenze* (1494), ed. Luigi Firpo (Rome: Belardetti, 1965), 19–20.

24. Bernardino da Siena's bonfire took place in 1434. Thomas M. Izbicki, "Pyres of Vanities: Mendicant Preaching on the Vanity of Women and Its Audience," in *"De ore Domini": Preacher and Word in the Middle Ages*, ed. Thomas L. Amos, Eugene A. Green, Beverly Mayne Kienzle (Kalamazoo, MI: Medieval Institute Publications, 1989): 211–34. In the early 1480s, the humanist Vespasiano da Bisticci described the event, which he attended when he was thirteen years old: "Venendo a Firenze, [Bernardino da Siena] la trovò molto corrotta ne' vizi. [. . .] Dannando ogni vizio nella sua natura, condusse in modo questa città, ch'egli la mutò, e fella, si può dire, rinascere. E per levare via i capegli alle donne, che li portano che non sono loro, e giuochi e vanità, fece fare uno capannuccio in su la piazza di Sancta Croce, e disse a ognuno che aveva di quelle vanità, che ve le portassi, e così feciono; misevi fuoco, e arse ogni cosa; che fu cosa mirabile a vedere di mutare gli animi di chi s'era volto in tutto alle pompe e fasti del mondo." Vespasiano da Bisticci, *Vite di uomini illustri*, ed. Paolo d'Ancona and Erhard Aeschlimann (Milan: Hoepli, 1951), 137. For the definition of "cappannuccio" as "sheaf," *Vocabolario della Crusca*, ed. Adriano Politi (Rome: Mascardi, 1614), 147. See also Bernardino da Siena, *Le prediche volgari*, ed. C. Cannarozzi, 2 vols. (Pistoia, Italy: Pacinotti, 1934), vol. 2, 87.

25. "Frate Bernardino da Feltro [. . .] publicamente arse molti capelli et libri disutili a leggere reputatisi." Piero di Marco Parenti, *Storia fiorentina*, ed. Andrea Matucci, 2 vols. (Florence: L. S. Olschki, 1994), vol. 1, 55. Piero was the son of Marco Parenti, the wealthy silk merchant we have already encountered in chapter 5, who spent a fortune on a garland (see note 2). Piero refers to the bonfires of 1493, but Bernardino da Feltre

also organized some in Perugia in 1486, on which see Maria Giuseppina Muzzarelli, *Penitenze nel medioevo: Uomini e modelli a confronto* (Bologna: Pàtron, 1994), 127 and 199; Muzzarelli, *Gli inganni delle apparenze: Disciplina di vesti e ornamenti alla fine del Medioevo* (Turin: Scriptorium, 1996), 194–97. See also Michel Plaisance, *Florence in the Time of the Medici: Public Celebrations, Politics, and Literature in the Fifteenth and Sixteenth Centuries* (Toronto: Centre for Reformation and Renaissance Studies, 2008), 67–69.

26. Weinstein, *Savonarola*, 183–89.
27. "E quali prima qual'è fussino e quanto immersi in ogni vizio, e tutti li uomini il sanno di essa città, quanto al vestir superbi e quanto alli altri ornamenti sfacciati, in modo che alla portatura de' capelli parevono non sol fanciulle immo pubbliche meretrice. [. . .] Li quali alle predicazioni del detto Padre mirabilmente si mutoron immo deposono ogni superfluità di vestimenti, di capelli, di scarselle e di altre vanità, emendoronsi da e vizii sopradetti e diventarono in tal modo ferventi che erono esempio a tutta Firenze." Placido Cinozzi, "Epistola," in *Scelta di prediche e scritti di Fra Girolamo Savonarola*, ed. Pasquale Villari and Eugenio Casanova (Florence: Sansoni, 1898), 7. The original is Florence: Biblioteca Riccardiana, Ms 2053, ff. 108–18.
28. The first bonfire took place on Shrove Tuesday (February 7), 1497. Plaisance, *Florence in the Time of the Medici*, 67–69; Stefano dall'Aglio, "Girolamo Savonarola e la sua riforma tra arte, denaro e rogo delle vanità," in Ludovica Sebregondi and Tim Parks, eds., *Denaro e bellezza: I banchieri, Botticelli e il rogo delle vanità* (Florence: GAM Giunti, 2011), 93–101; Weinstein, *Savonarola*, 217–19.
29. A second bonfire took place on Shrove Tuesday (February 27), 1498. Weinstein, *Savonarola*, 251–53.
30. Cinozzi, "Epistola," 7.
31. Richard A. Goldthwaite, "The Building of the Strozzi Palace: The Construction Industry in Renaissance Florence," *Studies in Medieval and Renaissance History* 10 (1973): 178–79; Marcia B. Hall, "Savonarola's Preaching and the Patronage of Art," in *Christianity and the Renaissance: Image and Religious Imagination in the Quattrocento*, ed. Timothy Verdon and John Henderson (Syracuse, NY: Syracuse University Press, 1990), 507.
32. Antonio Paolucci, "Botticelli and the Medici: A Privileged Relationship," in *Botticelli: From Lorenzo the Magnificent to Savonarola*, ed. Daniel Arasse, Pierluigi De Vecchi, and Patrizia Nitti (Milan: Skira, 2003), 76; James

Hankins, "From the New Athens to the New Jerusalem: Florence between Lorenzo de' Medici and Savonarola," in *Botticelli's Witness: Changing Style in a Changing Florence*, ed. Laurence Kanter, Hilliard T. Goldfarb, and James Hankins (Boston: Isabella Stewart Gardner Museum, 1997), 19–20.

33. Kenneth Clark, *The Drawings by Sandro Botticelli for Dante's Divine Comedy* (New York: Harper & Row, 1976), 10. The first to insist on this point was Giorgio Vasari, *Le vite de' più eccellenti pittori scultori e architettori nelle redazioni del 1550 e 1568*, ed. Rosanna Bettarini, 6 vols. (Florence: Sansoni and SPES, 1966–87), vol. 3, 130.

34. Frank Zöllner, *Sandro Botticelli* (Munich, London, and New York: Prestel), 170–81.

35. Lorenzo Violi, a Florentine notary and scribe of many of Savonarola's sermons, records that Doffo Spiri, the judge who eventually condemned Savonarola to death, regularly visited Botticelli's studio. Lorenzo Violi, *Giornate*, ed. Gian Carlo Garfagnini (Florence: L. S. Olschki, 1986), 78. Violi also praised Botticelli's brother Simone, a Savonarola supporter, whose chronicle, now lost, was one of Violi's main sources. Ibid., 70–71, and 78.

36. Ran Hatfield, "Botticelli's Mystic Nativity, Savonarola and the Millennium," *Journal of the Warburg and Courtauld Institutes* 58 (1995): 89–114; Marco Versiero, "Efficacia retorica e politica delle metafore animalistiche nella predicazione di Savonarola: Il caso della Crocifssione mistica di Botticelli," *Cahiers d'études italiennes* 29 (2019), https://doi.org/10.4000/cei.6074. I am also thinking of a fresco Botticelli painted in the Church of Ognissanti for Giorgio Antonio Vespucci, whom Savonarola convinced to join the Dominican order in June 1497. The fresco is gone but, thanks to Vespucci's will, we know that it represented the life of Dionysius the Areopagite, the mystic whose writings appealed to Savonarola's supporters. Ronald Lightbown, *Sandro Botticelli: Life and Work*, 2 vols. (Berkeley and Los Angeles: University of California Press, 1978), vol. 1, 130.

37. Michael Baxandall, *Painting and Experience in Fifteenth-Century Italy: A Primer in the Social History of Pictorial Style* (Oxford, UK: Oxford University Press, 1972), 1–11; Michelle O'Malley, *The Business of Art: Contracts and the Commissioning Process in Renaissance Italy* (New Haven, CT: Yale University Press, 2005), 21–76.

38. "Credete voi che la Vergine Maria andasse vestita a questo modo come voi la dipingete? Io vi dico che ella andava vestita come una poverella, semplicemente e coperta che appena se gli vedeva il viso. . . . Voi [dipin-

tori] fate parete la Vergine Maria vestita come meretrice. Or sì che il culto di Dio è guasto." Girolamo Savonarola, *Prediche e scritti*, ed. Mario Ferrara (Milan: Hoepli, 1930), 387.

39. Cristina Acidini, "Sandro Botticelli pittore del Rinascimento, tra i Medici e il Savonarola," in *Botticelli nel suo tempo*, ed. Acidini (Milan: Electa, 2009), 29–30; Lightbown, *Botticelli*, vol. 1, 122–26. Cf. Zöllner, *Botticelli*, 144–59. Cf. Ana Debenedetti, *Botticelli: Artist and Designer* (London: Reaktion, 2021), 89–139.

40. "Sandro di Botticelli pictore excellentissimo in tavola et in muro. Le cose sue hano aria virile et sono cum optima ragione et integra proportione." The report can be dated to the second half of 1493, as argued by Jonathan Nelson, "Botticelli's 'Virile Air': Reconsidering the Milan Memo of 1493," in *Sandro Botticelli: Artist and Entrepreneur in Renaissance Florence*, ed. Gert J. van der Sman and Irene Mariani (Florence: Centro Di, 2015), 166–81. Nelson highlights that fifteenth-century Italians took the word "virile" in the sense that Dante expressed in his *Convivio* 1.1.16—that is, as a quality far from the fervent and passionate work of young people. Fifteenth-century humanists also knew Quintilian's advice (*Institutio Oratoria* 5.12.20 and 10.1.76–77) that to write in a virile manner meant to shun effeminate, rhetorical figures. The *editio princeps* of Dante's *Convivio* dates to 1490.

41. Judith 8:1–8. I chose to reproduce the Cincinnati Judith (figure 10.2a), because it is taken to be an earlier version of a similar painting in the Uffizi. See Zöllner, *Botticelli*, 188.

42. Domenico Buonvicini, a collaborator of Savonarola appointed to oversee the reformation of Florentine youths (on which see Weinstein, *Savonarola*, 183–86), ordered that the boys "mantenere e capelli a misura." Josef Schnitzer, *Savonarolas Erzieher und Savonarola als Erzieher* (Berlin: Protestantischer Schriftenvertrieb, 1913), 137. On Botticelli's two Judiths, see Nadia Righi, "Note storico-artistiche su *Il ritorno di Giuditta a Betulia* e *La scoperta del cadavere di Oloferne* di Sandro Botticelli," in *Sandro Botticelli: La Giuditta*, ed. Paolo Biscottini (Milan: Silvana, 2008), 17–23.

43. Yet Lucian's text was not Botticelli's direct source. Botticelli read of Lucian's description in Cristoforo Landino's *Comento sopra la Comedia*, where he also found most of the sources for the background reliefs and sculptures. Angela Dressen, "From Dante to Landino: Botticelli's *Calumny of Apelles* and Its Sources," *Mitteilungen des Kunsthistorischen Institutes in Florenz* 59 (2017): 325–339, esp. 326–27.

44. Ernst Gombrich, "Botticelli's Mythologies: A Study in the Neoplatonic Symbolism of His Circle," *Journal of the Warburg and Courtauld Institutes* 8 (1945): 7–60, esp. 10n1. Cf. Stéphane Toussaint, "'My Friend Ficino': Art History and Neoplatonism. From Intellectual to Material Beauty," *Mitteilungen des Kunsthistorischen Institutes in Florenz* 59 (2017): 147–73, esp. 153–58.
45. We discussed these opinions in chapter 7; see notes 63–65.
46. Girolamo Savonarola, *Sermoni e prediche* (Prato, Italy: Ranieri Guasti, 1846), 86. Savonarola's sermon is part of the cycle on the Epistle of Saint John which he gave in the cathedral of Florence between October 31, 1491, and January 9, 1492. Pier Scapecchi, "Savonarola: Una biografia in San Marco," in *Savonarola e le sue "reliquie" a San Marco: Itinerario per un percorso savonaroliano nel Museo*, ed. Magnolia Scudieri and Giovanna Rasario (Florence: Giunti, 1999), 36–51, esp. 38. The dating of Botticelli's *Calumny* (ranging from c. 1495 to 1497) rests on the assumption that Botticelli's source was a printed edition of Lucian. This could have been either the Venetian edition of 1494 (known as *Opera varia*) or the Florentine edition of 1496. Hans Körner, *Botticelli* (Cologne: Dumont, 2006), 346 (he opts for c. 1495); Michel Feuillet, *Botticelli et Savonarole: L'humanisme à l'épreuve du feu* (Paris: Cerf, 2010), 98 (he opts for 1497). Yet, as Angela Dressen has demonstrated ("From Dante to Landino," 327), Botticelli relied on the 1481 comment on Dante's *Comedy* by Cristoforo Landino. Thus, he could have painted the allegory of *Calumny* earlier.
47. Antoninus Florentinus, *Summa maior* (Lyon: 1506), 2.4.5: "Volo mulieres orare in ecclesia in habitu ornato cum verecundia, et sobrietate idest temperate ornantes se non intortis crinibus, aut auro vel Margaritis, aut veste praeciosa in excessiva sui status, sed quod decem mulieres promittentes pietatem per bona opera."
48. "Per la reverenza degli angeli e sacerdoti che sono nella chiesa, acciocché alcun non sia preso dalla bellezza di lei [. . .]. E però voi, madre, non vogliate menar le vostre figliole a questo modo in chiesa, perché provocate l'ira di Dio contra di voi." Savonarola, *Sermoni e prediche* (1846), 86. The idea that women should veil their heads in respect to the angels comes from Paul, 1 Corinthians 11:10. Giovanni da Capistrano learned from the gloss that Paul's angels should be interpreted as priests. Giovanni da Capistrano, *Trattato degli ornamenti, specie delle donne*, ed. Aniceto Chiappini (Siena, Italy: Cantagalli, 1956), 118. The gloss was Peter Lombard's *Collectanea*, the go-to commentary to Paul's epistles, which draws a par-

allel between angels and priests when commenting on a different passage (1 Corinthians 8:1–4). Peter Lombard, *Collectanea in omnes D. Pauli Apostoli Epistolas*, Patrologia Latina 161 (Paris: Migne, 1854), col. 1604.

49. Antonino Pierozzi, *Opera a ben vivere,* ed. Francesco Palermo (Florence: Cellini, 1858), 164–65: "Andate cogli occhi sì bassi, che altro che la terra dove avete a porre li piedi non vi curate di vedere."

50. The following advice comes from *Le ménagier de Paris*, a French treatise on female behavior from 1393: "When walking in public keep your head upright, eyes downcast and immobile. Gaze four *toises* [a distance that corresponds to roughly eight meters] straight ahead and toward the ground [. . .]. Once you arrive at the church, select as private and solitary a place as you can [. . .]; keep your eyes continuously on your book." *The Good Wife's Guide: Le Ménagier de Paris, a Medieval Household Book*, tr. Gina L. Greco and Christine M. Rose (Ithaca, NY: Cornell University Press, 2009), 59. On *Le ménagier* as a possible source for Pierozzi, see Carla Casagrande, *La donna custodita* (Bari, Italy: Laterza, 1990), 116. On the Parisian *toise*, documented since 1394, see Paul Guilhiermoz, "De l'équivalence des anciennes mesures: A propos d'une publication récente," *Bibliothèque de l'école des chartes* 74 (1913): 267–328, esp. 273.

51. "Dice, dunque, [Saint Paul] alle donne grande e a te, cittadina: non portare oro, né pietre preziose, né veste, né capelli arricciati, ma andate alla semplice." Savonarola, *Prediche*, ed. Romano, 1.92.

52. I am thinking of Jerry Lewis, *The Ladies Man* (1961).

53. Julie A. Willett, *Permanent Waves: The Making of the American Beauty Shop* (New York: New York University Press, 2000); R. Weitz, *Rapunzel's Daughters: What Women's Hair Tells Us about Women's Lives* (New York: Farrar, Straus and Giroux, 2004); Rebecca Herzig, *Plucked: A History of Hair Removal* (New York: New York University Press, 2015); Kristen Barber, *Styling Masculinity: Gender, Class, and Inequality in the Men's Grooming Industry* (New Brunswick, NJ: Rutgers University Press, 2016). And let's not forget the memoirs: Herta Muller, *The Land of Green Plums* (New York: Metropolitan Books, 1996); Emma Dabiri, *Don't Touch My Hair* (London: Allen Lane, 2020).

54. On the use of gum arabic to make hair straight in 1480s Milan, see Francesco Malaguzzi Valeri, *La corte di Lodovico il Moro*, 4 vols. (Milan: Hoepli, 1913–23), vol. 1, 416–18. Leonardo da Vinci criticized it in his *Treatise on Painting: Codex Urbinas Latinus 1270*, 2 vols. (Princeton, NJ: Princeton University Press, 1956), vol. 1, 163.

55. On "feathery" (*piumoso*), see Vasari, *Le vite*, vol. 3, 620; vol. 5, 321; and vol. 6, 28. Vasari had already employed the adjective in his 1549 letter to Benedetto Varchi. See also Ann-Sophie Lehmann, "Hair," in *Textile Terms: A Glossary*, ed. Anika Reineke and Mateusz Kapustka (Berlin: Imorde, 2017), 138.
56. Cosmo Agnelli, *Amorevole aviso circa gli abusi delle donne vane* (Bologna: Rossi, 1592), 4–5; Giuseppe Passi, *I donneschi difetti* (Venice: Giacomo Antonio Somasco, 1599), 171–74.
57. Bruno Latour, *We Have Never Been Modern* (Cambridge, MA: Harvard University Press, 1993), 97–109.
58. Luciano Formisano, *Letters from a New World: Amerigo Vespucci's Discovery of America* (New York: Marsilio, 1992), 39. Amerigo claimed to have made his trip in May 1497, but all of his letters were published in 1504. David Abulafia, *The Discovery of Mankind: Atlantic Encounters in the Age of Columbus* (New Haven, CT: Yale University Press, 2009), 244–45. On the visual culture that shaped such a description, see Jill Burke, "Nakedness and Other Peoples: Rethinking the Italian Renaissance Nude," *Art History* 36, no. 4 (2013): 714–39.
59. *Italian Reports on America 1493–1522: Letters, Dispatches, and Papal Bulls*, ed. Geoffrey Symcox and Luciano Formisano, Repertorium Columbianum 10 (Turnhout, Belgium: Brepols, 2001), 43n13.
60. Formisano, *Letters*, 63.
61. Leon Battista Alberti, "Ecatonfilea," in *Opere Volgari*, ed. Cecil Grayson, 3 vols. (Bari, Italy: Laterza, 1973), vol. 2, 213: "Spesso mi tremavano tutti e' crini, impallidiva, e cadeva in palese dolore e tristezza." Gian Paolo Lomazzo, *Trattato dell'arte della pittura, scultura ed architettura*, 3 vols. (Rome: Saverio del Monte, 1844), vol. 1, 305–7; Charles Darwin, *The Expression of the Emotions in Man and Animals* (London: John Murray, 1872), 67 and 294–97.
62. Cesare Lombroso and Guglielmo Ferrero, *La donna delinquente, la prostituta e la donna normale* (Turin and Rome: Roux, 1893), 319–20. Cf. Joseph Deniker, *Les races et les peuples de la terre* (Paris: Masson, 1926), 52–69.
63. Giovanni Morelli, *Italian Painters: Critical Studies of Their Works*, 2 vols. (London: J. Murray, 1892–93), vol. 1, 107, 155, 181, 193, and 230.
64. Carlo Pedretti, *The Literary Works of Leonardo da Vinci*, 2 vols. (London: Phaidon, 1977) vol. 1, 285; David A. Brown, *Leonardo da Vinci: Origins of a Genius* (New Haven, CT, and London: Yale University Press, 1998), 86–88. Brown attributes the Uffizi *Annunciation* to Leonardo because of

the similarities between Gabriel's curls and one of Leonardo's drawings of water. See also the recent attribution of *Salvator Mundi* to Leonardo because its hair looks like "a living, moving substance." Ben Lewis, *The Last Leonardo: The Secret Lives of the World's Most Expensive Painting* (New York: Ballantine Books, 2019), 159.

65. Johann J. Winckelmann, *The History of Ancient Art*, 4 vols. (Boston: J. R. Osgood and Co., 1880), vol. 1, 326, 333–36, and 399–401.
66. Georg W. F. Hegel, *Aesthetics: Lectures on Fine Art*, 2 vols. (Oxford, UK: Clarendon Press, 1975), vol. 2, 737.
67. Tacitus, *Agricola* 11.
68. Seneca, *Epistulae Morales at Luciulum* 95.24. For a commentary on the expressive role of hair in Seneca's time, see John Pollini, "Slave-Boys for Sexual and Religious Service," in *Flavian Rome: Culture, Image, Text*, ed. Anthony Boyle and William J. Dominik (Leiden, Netherlands: Brill, 2003), 157–58.
69. Bernard Berenson, *The Drawings of Florentine Painters*, 2 vols. (London: J. Murray, 1903), vol. 1, 154; and vol. 2, 61.
70. Among art historians, an exception is Aby Warburg, "Sandro Botticelli's Birth of Venus and Spring," in *The Renewal of Pagan Antiquity*, tr. David Britt (Los Angeles: Getty Research Institute, 1999), 117–21.
71. Claude Levi-Strauss, *Tristes Tropiques* (Paris: Plon, 1955), 296–311; Edmund Leach, "Magical Hair," *Journal of the Royal Anthropological Institute of Great Britain and Ireland* 88, no. 2 (1958): 147–64; Emma Calderini and Eva Tea, *Acconciature antiche e moderne* (Milan: Sperling & Kupfer, 1962); Christopher R. Hallpike, "Social Hair," *Man* 4 (1969): 256–64; Mary Douglas, *Natural Symbols: Explorations in Cosmology* (New York: Routledge, 1996, 1st ed. 1973), 81; Pier Paolo Pasolini, "7 gennaio 1973: Il 'Discorso' dei capelli," in id., *Scritti corsari* (Milan: Garzanti, 2008, 1st ed. 1975), 5–11; Anthony Synnott, "Shame and Glory: A Sociology of Hair," *British Journal of Sociology* 38, no. 3 (1987): 381–413.
72. When I started my research in 2006, my interest was first sparked by Françoise Viatte, "Verrocchio et Leonardo da Vinci: À propos des 'têtes idéales,'" in *Florentine Drawing at the Time of Lorenzo the Magnificent*, ed. Elizabeth Cropper (Bologna: Nuova Alfa, 1992): 45–53; and Katherine L. Jansen's superb *The Making of the Magdalen: Preaching and Popular Devotion in the Later Middle Ages* (Princeton, NJ: Princeton University Press: 2000). Since then, many scholars have published studies that deal with or touch upon fifteenth-century hair. I have cited them throughout this

book, but I want to highlight Evelyn Welch, "Art on the Edge: Hair and Hands in Renaissance Italy," *Renaissance Studies* 23, no. 3 (2009): 241–68; Elisabetta Gnignera, *I soperchi ornamenti: Copricapi e acconciature femminili nell'Italia del Quattrocento* (Siena, Italy: Protagon, 2010); Sandra Cavallo and Tessa Storey, *Healthy Living in Late Renaissance Italy* (Oxford, UK: Oxford University Press, 2013), 240–69; Sefy Hendler, "'Pelo sopra Pelo': Sculpting Hair and Beards as a Reflection of Artistic Excellence during the Renaissance," *Sculpture Journal* 24, no. 1 (2015): 7–22; Lorenzo Pericolo, "Donna Bella e Crudele: Michelangelo's Divine Heads in Light of the *Rime*," *Mitteilungen des Kunsthistorischen Institutes in Florenz* 59, no. 2 (2017): 202–33; Julia Saviello, *Verlockungen: Haare in der Kunst der Frühen Neuzeit* (Emsdetten, Germany: Imorde, 2017); Stefan Hanß, "Face-Work: Making Hair Matter in Sixteenth-Century Central Europe," *Gender & History* 33, no. 2 (2021): 314–45; Virtus Zallot, *Sulle teste nel medioevo: Storie e immagini di capelli* (Bologna: Il Mulino, 2021); and many posts of Jill Burke's blog, https://renresearch.wordpress.com. Fundamental also were Janet Stephens, "Ancient Roman Hairdressing:: On (Hair)Pins and Needles," *Journal of Roman Archaeology* 21 (2008): 110–32, which details the impressive craft behind many ancient coiffures; and Rajyashree Pandey, *Perfumed Sleeves and Tangled Hair: Body, Women, and Desire in Medieval Japanese Narratives* (Honolulu: University of Hawaii Press, 2016), in which eroticism is defined in relation not to bodies but to the status evinced from hairstyling. For hairstyling as expressions of morals, I am indebted to Maria Giuseppina Muzzarelli, with whom I studied in Bologna and whose *Gli inganni delle apparenze* was fundamental to me. Useful were also Chiara Frugoni, "La donna nelle immagini, la donna immaginata," in *Storia delle donne: Il Medioevo*, ed. Christiane Klapish-Zuber (Bari and Rome: Laterza, 1990), 424–57; Gabriela Signori, "Veil, Hat or Hair? Reflections on an Asymmetrical Relationship," *Medieval History Journal* 8 (2005): 25–47; and Roberta Milliken, *A Cultural History of Hair in the Middle Ages* (New York: Bloomsbury Academic, 2019).

73. The approach of focusing on specific elements one at a time necessarily shapes encyclopedic approaches, such as those in Roberta Milliken, *Ambiguous Locks: An Iconology of Hair in Medieval Art and Literature* (Jefferson, NC: McFarland, 2014); and *A Cultural History of Hair*, ed. Geraldine Biddle-Perry, 6 vols. (London: Bloomsbury, 2019).

74. *La vie Parisienne* 32 (January 1894): 20. Cited in Francesco Ventrella, "Befriending Botticelli: Psychology and Connoisseurship at the Fin de

Siècle," in *Botticelli Past and Present*, ed. Ana Debenedetti and Caroline Elam (London: UCL Press, 2019), 116–17. On the "rediscovery" of Botticelli, see Jeremy Melius, "Art History and the Invention of Botticelli" (PhD dissertation, University of California-Berkeley, 2010), 46–103.

75. On hair as denoting foreignness, Anthony Corbeill, *Controlling Laughter: Political Humor in the Late Roman Republic* (Princeton, NJ: Princeton University Press, 1996), 128–73. On the various categories that historians collapse into the falsely homogeneous bracket of masculinity, see Ben Griffin, "Hegemonic Masculinity as a Historical Problem," *Gender & History* 30, no. 2 (2018): 377–400.

76. On Leonardo's Roman trip, Giovanni Poggi, *Leonardo da Vinci: La vita di Giorgio Vasari nuovamente commentata* (Florence: Pampaloni, 1919), 41–43. Cf. Carlo Pedretti, *A Chronology of Leonardo da Vinci's Architectural Studies after 1510* (Geneva: Droz, 1962), 64, where he argues that the journey took place in 1505.

77. The interpretation of Moses as noble and perceptive comes from Gregory of Nyssa, *The Life of Moses*, ed. and tr. Abraham J. Malherbe and Everett Ferguson (New York: Paulist Press, 1978), 34. Nyssa's biography was a main source for the frescoes of the Sistine Chapel. See Charles L. Stinger, *The Renaissance in Rome* (Bloomington: Indiana University Press, 1998), 209–12.

78. Philo, "De vita Mosis," in *On Abraham. On Joseph. On Moses*, tr. F. H. Colson (Cambridge, MA: Harvard University Press, 1935): 302–5. Philo's account, one source for Gregory of Nyssa's biography (see previous note), was translated in 1480 by the Italian humanist Lilio Tifernate. Stinger, *The Renaissance in Rome*, 209–12.

79. Leonardo, *Codex Atlanticus*, f. 331r: "Sandro, tu non di' perché tali cose seconde paiano più basse che le terze." Lionello Venturi, *La critica e l'arte di Leonardo da Vinci* (Bologna: Zanichelli, 1919), 37; Edoardo Villata, *Leonardo da Vinci: I documenti e le testimonianze contemporanee* (Milan: Ente raccolta vinciana, 1999), 92n1. Leonardo's passage is dated around 1504.

80. Carlo Pedretti, *Leonardo da Vinci on Painting: A Lost Book (Libro A)* (Berkeley: University of California Press, 1964), 52–53.

81. Romano Nanni, "Gli studi di acconciature nei disegni di Leonardo: Studi per Leda?" in *Leda: Storia di un mito dalle origini a Leonardo*, ed. Nanni and Maria Chiara Monaco (Florence: Zeta Scorpii, 2007), 169–70. Leonardo developed two versions of Leda, one while he was in Florence and Rome (1501–6) and one while he was in France (1516–19). Paul Müller-

Walde, "Beiträge zur Kenntnis des Leonardo da Vinci: ii. Eine Skizze Leonardos zur stehenden Leda," in *Jahrbuch der Königlich Preussischen Kunstsammlungen* 18 (1897): 137–43.

82. Giovanni Boccaccio, "Amorosa Visione," in *Tutte le opere*, ed. Vittore Branca, 10 vols. (Milan: Mondadori, 1964–98), vol. 3, 191–92.

83. Leonardo took the hairline as the starting point of human proportion in two drawings. On the first (Windsor: RL 12601), see Leonardo da Vinci, *Corpus of the Anatomical Studies in the Collection of Her Majesty the Queen at Windsor Castle*, ed. Kenneth D. Keele and Carlo Pedretti (London: Johnson, 1978–80), n19. On the second, the so-called "Vitruvian Man" (Venice: Gallerie dell'Accademia, inv. 228), see Jean Paul Richter, *The Literary Works of Leonardo da Vinci*, 2 vols. (London: Oxford University Press, 1939), vol. 1, 182. Vitruvius (*De architectura* 3.1.2) also considered the hairline the upper limit of human proportions. His modular system started from "the roots of the hair" (*radices capilli*), whose distance from the chin bone corresponded to one-tenth of the whole body. Vitruvius, *De architectura*, ed. Paul Gros, 2 vols. (Turin: Einaudi, 1997), vol. 1, 238. On Leonardo as reader of Vitruvius, see Giovanna Nepi Sciré and Pietro C. Marani, eds., *Leonardo & Venezia* (Milan: Bompiani, 1992), 216–17. The hairline also marked the starting point of proportions for Leon Battista Alberti in his treatise on sculpture, which Leonardo knew. See J. A. Aiken, "Leon Battista Alberti's System of Human Proportions," in *Journal of the Warburg and Courtauld Institutes* 43 (1980): 68–96, esp. 81n49.

INDEX